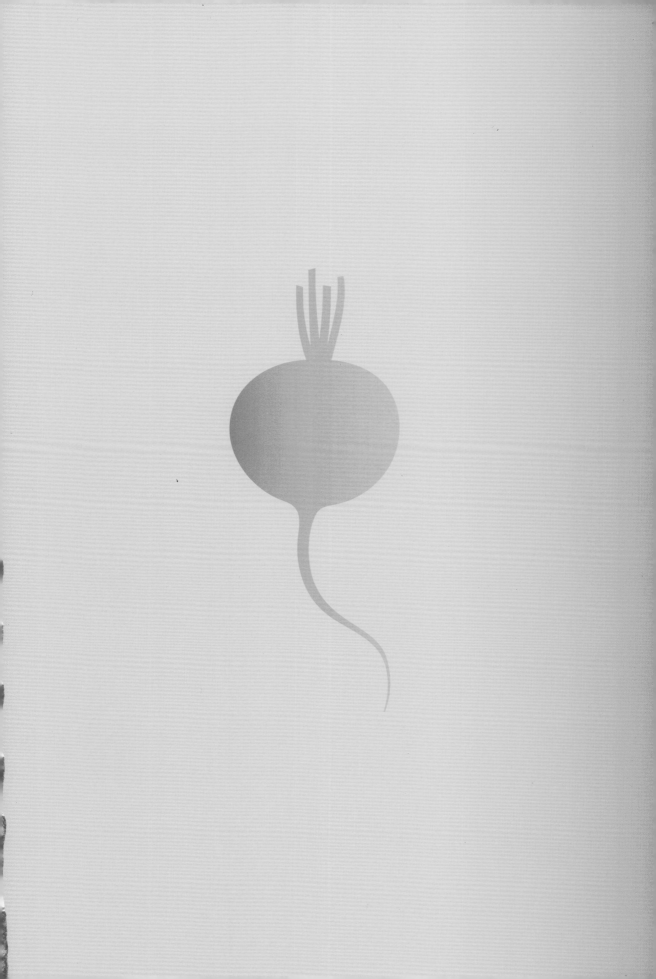

JEAN-CHRISTIAN JURY

VEGAN

THE COOKBOOK

INTRODUCTION

At the root of it, vegan food is just food: vibrant, flavorful, fresh—
making you feel good inside and out. The recipes in this book
are a celebration of plant vitality and variety. The possibilities are
seemingly endless and delicious.

I had my first professional kitchen experience at the age of fourteen,
spending my summer vacations as an apprentice in a five-star hotel
kitchen. My mom was a single parent who worked night shifts
as a head nurse, so I became the designated home cook, happy to
transition from pasta and potatoes, favorites in her repertoire.

Despite my love of cooking, I decided to study engineering,
graduating with a degree in electro-mechanics. After traveling to
North Africa, Spain, the Canary Islands, Ibiza, and Italy, working
mostly in kitchens, I searched for a job in the hospitality industry and
was hired by a Swiss firm. I spent the next twelve years developing
fusion food from Southeast Asia and India, as well as the wonderful
Japanese flavors that I still use today in my cooking.

In 2001, I went to London. I had always loved the buzz of the city
and now that I was running restaurants and kitchens, I was focused
on developing new concepts. My eating habits, like many chefs', were
erratic. Often, the food was anything but healthy.

After years of working sixteen-hour days, with no holidays, a poor
diet, and very little sleep, I had a heart attack. After I recovered and
got stronger, I developed a new concept based on raw food that
had bases in London, Munich, Stockholm, Dubai, and Paris. Seduced
by the idea, I decided to completely change my diet and lifestyle.
I devoted time to study raw food ideas and best practices and create
a new restaurant based on organic vegan and raw food and wine.
I settled in Berlin.

I opened La Mano Verde restaurant on World Vegan Day—
November 1, 2007. I created a new generation of dishes cooked
with only plants, and that appealed to a wider clientele. I wanted
to make my food visually stunning, using the same techniques as
my colleagues cooking non-vegan food: three- and four-course
menus, meticulously plated, with exceptional-quality ingredients,
outstanding service, and a great wine list. I used porcini, truffles,
seaweed, and house-made vegan cheeses. I explored new side
dishes, incorporated wild and black rice in addition to basmati and
jasmine, and, before too long, my new menu looked as exciting
as any high-end restaurant that served meat. I created a vegan
destination where people would travel just to eat at my restaurant.

For years, my goal was to surprise non-vegans with delicious vegan recipes, to show that meat wasn't necessary for a delicious and satisfying meal. When food is fresh and brimming with flavor, it will leave you feeling sated.

Plant-based food is vital for our well being. I encourage those of you who are considering becoming vegan, to do so carefully and thoughtfully, to balance the intake of nutrients the same way as with any other eating. You can use this book to supplement your regular eating habits or to increase plant-based food in your meals. Should you choose to become entirely vegan, I suggest procuring the best ingredients you can. If there is a farmers' market in your area, get to know the farmers and how they grow the food, and eat your way through the seasonal calendar.

With *Vegan: The Cookbook*, I share how plant-based food can be accessible and appealing to everyone, and show the world just how enjoyable and nourishing this food can be, from appetizers straight through to desserts. Most of these recipes have been created in my kitchen, and some are from cooks I have traveled with or people I have met throughout my journeys to more than 100 countries. As I travel across the globe, I continue to learn about new ingredients and techniques: like the Mexican huitlacoche mushroom, Peruvian black corn, Brazilian caja, or Cuban apple guavas. These recipes should excite and satisfy vegans, vegetarians, and omnivores and expand your home kitchen repertoire. Enjoy the cooking.

Jean-Christian Jury

THE
ESSENTIAL
VEGAN
PANTRY

FRESH FRUITS AND VEGETABLES

- **AVOCADOS**
- **BROCCOLI**
- **CABBAGE**
- **CARROTS**
- **CAULIFLOWER**
- **GARLIC**
- **HERBS**
- **KALE AND OTHER HEARTY GREENS**
- **LEMONS**
- **LIMES**
- **MUSHROOMS**
- **ONIONS**
- **POTATOES**
- **PUMPKIN**
- **SQUASH**
- **SWEET POTATOES**

GRAINS

- BARLEY
- BUCKWHEAT
- BULGUR
- COUSCOUS
- FARRO
- KAMUT
- MILLET
- OATS
- QUINOA
- RICE: BASMATI, BLACK, BROWN, JASMINE, RED, WHITE, WILD
- SPELT
- WHEATBERRIES

PASTA AND NOODLES

- BEAN THREAD NOODLES
- RICE NOODLES
- SOBA
- UDON
- VARIOUS DRY PASTAS

FLOURS

- ALL-PURPOSE (PLAIN) FLOUR
- ALMOND MEAL OR ALMOND FLOUR
- BROWN RICE FLOUR
- BUCKWHEAT FLOUR
- CHICKPEA FLOUR
- CORNMEAL
- KAMUT FLOUR
- OAT FLOUR
- SPELT FLOUR
- WHOLE WHEAT (WHOLE MEAL) PASTRY FLOUR

BEANS AND LEGUMES

- CHICKPEAS: CANNED, DRY
- LENTILS: BLACK BELUGA, GREEN, RED, YELLOW
- TEMPEH
- TOFU
- BEANS: BLACK BEANS, BLACK-EYED PEAS, NAVY BEANS, EDAMAME, RED KIDNEY BEANS, SPLIT PEAS

RAW NUTS AND SEEDS

- ALMONDS
- CASHEWS
- MACADAMIA
- PECANS
- SEEDS: CHIA, HEMP, PUMPKIN, SUNFLOWER, WHOLE FLAX
- WALNUTS

DRIED FRUIT AND VEGETABLES

- APRICOTS
- CHERRIES
- CRANBERRIES
- DATES
- MANGOS
- MUSHROOMS
- PRUNES
- RAISINS

VINEGARS

- BALSAMIC VINEGAR
- RAW APPLE CIDER VINEGAR
- RED WINE VINEGAR
- RICE VINEGAR

SWEETENERS

- MEDJOOL DATES
- MOLASSES
- PURE MAPLE SYRUP
- RAW AGAVE SYRUP
- RAW COCONUT SUGAR
- SUCANAT SUGAR
- UNREFINED CANE SUGAR
- UNREFINED DARK BROWN SUGAR

CHOCOLATE

- DARK CHOCOLATE: SWEETENED, UNSWEETENED

SUNDRIES AND CONDIMENTS

- ALMOND MILK
- BREAD, PITA, NAAN, TORTILLAS
- CANNED BEANS
- CANNED TOMATOES
- CAPERS
- COCOA BUTTER
- COCONUT MILK: FULL-FAT, LIGHT
- HARISSA
- KETCHUP
- MUSTARD
- NUT AND SEED BUTTERS: RAW ALMOND BUTTER, ROASTED NATURAL PEANUT BUTTER
- NUTRITIONAL YEAST
- OLIVES
- PICKLES
- PRESERVED LEMONS
- SAMBAL OELEK
- SOY MILK
- SOY SAUCE
- SRIRACHA
- TAHINI
- TAMARI
- TOMATO PASTE
- VEGAN MAYONNAISE
- VEGETABLE BROTH
- UNSWEETENED APPLESAUCE

SPICES

- ALLSPICE
- ANISE SEED
- BAY LEAVES
- CARAWAY
- CAYENNE
- CELERY SEED
- CHILI POWDER
- CHINESE FIVE-SPICE BLEND
- CINNAMON
- CREAM OF TARTAR
- CUMIN
- CURRY
- DRY MUSTARD
- GARAM MASALA
- GARLIC POWDER
- GROUND CARDAMOM
- GROUND CLOVES
- GROUND CORIANDER SEED
- GROUND GINGER
- GROUND TURMERIC
- MUSTARD SEED: BLACK, YELLOW
- NUTMEG
- OREGANO
- PAPRIKA: HOT, SMOKED, SWEET
- PEPPERCORNS: BLACK, PINK, WHITE
- RED PEPPER FLAKES
- SALT: COARSE SEA, FINE SEA, FLAKY, KOSHER
- STAR ANISE

STARTERS

HUMMUS

Preparation time: 15 minutes, plus
   1 hour chilling
Cooking time: none

Serves 4

- 2 cups (350 g) canned chickpeas
- 1 teaspoon baking soda
   (bicarbonate of soda)
- juice of 1 lemon
- juice of 1 orange
- 4 tablespoons tahini
- 2 cloves garlic, crushed
- 2 teaspoons ground cumin
- salt and freshly ground black pepper
- 1 tablespoon olive oil
- warmed naan, to serve

Put the chickpeas with their canning water into a large bowl, mix in the baking soda, and stir well. Set aside overnight, covered with a clean kitchen towel. The next day, drain the chickpeas, reserving the water.

Using a food processor or high-speed blender, process the chickpeas until smooth. Add the citrus juices and tahini and process for another 2 minutes, until very smooth.

Transfer to a bowl, add the garlic and cumin, stir well, then season to taste with salt and freshly ground black pepper. Top with the olive oil. Chill in the refrigerator for 1 hour before serving with warm naan.

BEET HUMMUS

Preparation time: 15 minutes, plus
   1 hour chilling
Cooking time: none

Serves 4

- 1 lb (450 g) canned chickpeas
- 1 teaspoon baking soda
   (bicarbonate of soda)
- 4 beets (beetroot), peeled and boiled
   until tender, roughly chopped
- 4 cloves garlic, crushed
- juice of 1 lemon
- 6 tablespoons olive oil
- 2 tablespoons tahini
- 1 teaspoon ground cumin
- salt and freshly ground black pepper

Put the chickpeas with their canning water into a bowl and mix in the baking soda. Stir well and set aside overnight, covered with a clean kitchen towel. The next day, drain the chickpeas.

Using a food processor or high-speed blender, combine the chickpeas with the beets, garlic, lemon juice, 5 tablespoons of the olive oil, the tahini, and the cumin until the mixture is very smooth. Adjust the texture by blending in water if necessary.

Season to taste with salt and freshly ground black pepper. Transfer to a serving bowl, drizzle over the remaining olive oil. Chill in the refrigerator for 1 hour before serving.

BAKED HUMMUS WITH MUSHROOMS

Preheat the oven to 350°F/180°C/Gas Mark 4.

Put the hummus into an ovenproof baking dish. Mix in the cumin and both types of paprika, half the olive oil, and the pine nuts. Drizzle with 2 tablespoons olive oil and cover with aluminum foil. Bake for about 15 minutes or until slightly browned on top. Turn off the heat and leave the dish in the oven until needed.

Heat the remaining olive oil in a skillet (frying pan) and gently fry the onion over medium heat for about 4–5 minutes, until golden brown. Add the garlic and halved mushrooms and cook for 15 minutes or until the mushrooms are tender.

Remove the hummus from the oven. Add the mushroom mix to the hummus and season to taste with salt and freshly ground black pepper. Garnish with parsley and serve with warm pita or naan.

Preparation time: 20 minutes
Cooking time: 35 minutes

Serves 4

- 2¼ cups (450 g) Hummus (page 20) or store-bought
- 1 teaspoon ground cumin
- 1 teaspoon hot paprika
- 1 teaspoon sweet paprika
- 5 tablespoons olive oil
- 1 tablespoon toasted pine nuts
- 1 onion, sliced
- 1 clove garlic, finely chopped
- 1 lb (450 g) shiitake mushrooms, trimmed and halved
- salt and freshly ground black pepper
- 1 tablespoon chopped parsley, to garnish
- warmed pita or naan, to serve

JALAPEÑO HUMMUS

Using a food processor or blender, blend the chickpeas, jalapeño, tahini, 2 tablespoons of the olive oil, the lemon juice, garlic, baking soda, and tomato purée on a high-speed setting for 3–4 minutes, until very smooth. Season to taste with salt and freshly ground black pepper.

To serve, put the hummus into a bowl, make a well in the center, and fill the hole with the remaining olive oil. Sprinkle with the sweet paprika and garnish with the chopped cilantro. Serve at room temperature with crackers or pita.

Preparation time: 10 minutes
Cooking time: none

Serves 4

- 2 cups (350 g) canned chickpeas, drained
- 1 large jalapeño pepper, seeded and finely chopped
- 2 tablespoons tahini
- 4 tablespoons olive oil
- 1 tablespoon fresh lemon juice
- 2 cloves garlic
- 1 teaspoon baking soda (bicarbonate of soda)
- 2 tablespoons tomato purée (passata)
- salt and freshly ground black pepper
- 1 teaspoon sweet paprika, to garnish
- 1 tablespoon chopped cilantro (coriander), to garnish
- crackers or pita, to serve

CREAMY HUMMUS WITH CARROTS AND GINGER

Preparation time: 20 minutes, plus
  overnight soaking
Cooking time: 45 minutes

Serves 4

- 1 lb (450 g) dried chickpeas
- 2 teaspoons baking soda (bicarbonate
  of soda)
- 4 cloves garlic, unpeeled
- 5 tablespoons fresh lemon juice
- 1 tablespoon grated fresh ginger
- 1 cup (65 g) carrots, sliced and cooked
- ½ cup (125 g) tahini
- 1 tablespoon nutritional yeast
- 1 teaspoon ground cumin
- salt and freshly ground black pepper
- 2 tablespoons olive oil, to garnish
- warmed pita or naan, to serve

Put the chickpeas and 1 teaspoon baking soda into a medium bowl and add enough cold water to cover completely. Soak overnight at room temperature. The next day, rinse the chickpeas and drain.

Combine the soaked chickpeas and remaining baking soda in a large saucepan and add enough cold water to cover completely. Bring to a boil, then reduce the heat to low and simmer for 45 minutes. Drain the chickpeas and set aside to cool.

Using a food processor or high-speed blender, blend the garlic and lemon juice until smooth, then add the ginger and carrots and process until very smooth. Add the tahini and pulse until well blended. Add the chickpeas, along with the nutritional yeast and cumin, and process until smooth, blending in water to reach desired consistency.

Season to taste with salt and freshly ground black pepper. Transfer to a serving bowl, top with the olive oil, and chill in the refrigerator for 1 hour before serving with warm pita or naan.

ROASTED RED PEPPER HUMMUS

Preparation time: 20 minutes, plus
  overnight soaking
Cooking time: 30 minutes, plus 1½ hours
  chilling

Serves 4

- 1½ cups (265 g) canned chickpeas,
  drained (liquid reserved)
- 1 teaspoon baking soda (bicarbonate
  of soda)
- 2 red bell peppers
- 2 cloves garlic
- ⅔ cup (150 g) tahini
- ½ cup (120 ml/4 fl oz) fresh lemon juice
- 1 tablespoon nutritional yeast
- 2 tablespoons chopped cilantro (coriander),
- salt and freshly ground black pepper
- 1 tablespoon olive oil
- naan or chapati, to serve

Put the chickpea canning water into a bowl and mix in the baking soda until completely dissolved. Stir in the chickpeas. Cover and refrigerate overnight.

The next day, preheat the oven to 400°F/200°C/Gas Mark 6.

Arrange the peppers on a baking sheet and roast for 20 minutes, until dark brown. Using tongs, flip over the peppers and roast for another 10 minutes. Transfer to a bowl, cover with plastic wrap (clingfilm), and let cool for 20 minutes. Remove and discard the skin and seeds.

Drain the chickpeas, reserving the canning water. Using a food processor or high-speed blender, blend all the ingredients except the olive oil until very smooth. If the mixture is too thick, add some of the reserved chickpea water.

Transfer the mixture to a bowl, top with the olive oil, and refrigerate for 1 hour before serving with naan or chapati.

EGGPLANT DIP

Char the eggplants on the flame of your stove (you can also char them under a broiler). Once they are soft and burnt, set aside the eggplants until just cool enough to handle, then peel off the skins.

Put the peanut butter into a bowl, pour in the lemon juice and whisk together. Add the eggplant to the mixture and mash with a fork. Add the pepper, onion, chilies, garlic, cumin, and vinegar, and stir well to blend, then season to taste with salt and freshly ground black pepper. Serve at room temperature with rice or breads.

Preparation time: 10 minutes
Cooking time: 15 minutes

Serves 4

- 4 eggplants (aubergines)
- 3 tablespoons smooth or crunchy
  peanut butter
- juice of 5 lemons
- 1 green bell pepper, seeded and chopped
- 1 onion, chopped
- 2 chilies, finely chopped
- 3 cloves garlic, minced
- 1 teaspoon ground cumin
- 1 teaspoon balsamic vinegar
- salt and freshly ground black pepper
- cooked long-grain rice or fresh bread,
  to serve

EGGPLANT AND YOGURT DIP

Preheat the oven to 400°F/200°C/Gas Mark 6.

Arrange the eggplant on a baking sheet and bake for 40–45 minutes or until soft. Set aside to cool for 20 minutes.

Remove and discard the eggplant skin and put the flesh into a large bowl. Mash the flesh with a fork. Mix in the cucumber, yogurt, garlic, mint, and olive oil and season to taste with salt and freshly ground black pepper. Transfer to a serving bowl and garnish with the walnuts and parsley. Serve with crackers or warm naan.

Preparation time: 30 minutes
Cooking time: 45 minutes,
  plus 20 minutes chilling

Serves 4

- 4 eggplants (aubergines),
  cut into large chunks
- 1 cucumber, peeled and julienned
- 1 cup (225 g) unsweetened vegan yogurt
- 4 cloves garlic, minced
- 2 tablespoons chopped mint
- 1 tablespoon olive oil
- salt and freshly ground black pepper
- 2 tablespoons walnuts, crushed, to garnish
- 2 tablespoons chopped parsley, to garnish
- crackers or warmed garlic naan, to serve

EGGPLANT AND RED BELL PEPPER DIP

Preparation time: 20 minutes
Cooking time: 30 minutes

Serves 4

- 2¼ pounds (1 kg) red bell peppers
- 3 eggplants (aubergines)
- juice of 1 lemon
- 2 cloves garlic, crushed
- 1 teaspoon smoked paprika
- 1 teaspoon cayenne pepper
- 4 tablespoons extra-virgin olive oil
- salt and freshly ground black pepper
- bread or warmed naan, to serve

Preheat the oven to 425°F/220°C/Gas Mark 7. Line a baking sheet with parchment paper.

Arrange the red bell peppers and eggplants on the prepared baking sheet. Roast for 30 minutes, until they are tender and the skins are dark brown.

Transfer the peppers and eggplants to a large bowl, cover with plastic wrap (clingfilm), and set aside to cool. Remove and discard the eggplant skins and also the red bell peppers skins and seeds.

Using a food processor or high-speed blender, blend the eggplant and bell peppers until smooth. Using a low-speed setting, slowly add the lemon juice, then blend in the garlic, smoked paprika, cayenne pepper, and olive oil. Process until well combined. Season to taste with salt and freshly ground black pepper, then transfer to a bowl and serve with fresh bread or warm naan.

EGGPLANT AND RED BELL PEPPER DIP

EGGPLANT AND TAHINI MEZA

Preparation time: 25 minutes
Cooking time: 20 minutes

Serves 4

- 2 eggplants (aubergines), cut into thick
  slices
- ⅓ cup (75 g) tahini
- 3 tablespoons fresh lemon juice
- 2 tablespoons olive oil, plus extra to serve
- 2 cloves garlic, crushed
- salt and freshly ground black pepper
- 2 tablespoons chopped parsley, to garnish
- naan or crackers, to serve

Preheat the oven to 400°F/200°C/Gas Mark 6.

Place the eggplant in a baking pan and bake for 1 hour, until very soft. Let cool for 20 minutes, then discard the skins.

Transfer the eggplant flesh to a large bowl and mash with a fork. Add the tahini, lemon juice, olive oil, and garlic. Season to taste with salt and freshly ground black pepper, and mash the mixture with a fork (alternatively, blend using a food processor).

Transfer to a bowl, garnish with chopped parsley, drizzle with olive oil, and serve with naan or crackers.

EGGPLANT AND TAHINI MEZA

FIVE-LAYER HUMMUS VERRINES

Preparation time: 20 minutes
Cooking time: 5 minutes, plus
  30 minutes chilling

Serves 4

- 1 clove garlic, finely grated
- 3 tablespoons fresh lemon juice
- 3 tablespoons olive oil
- 2 tablespoons finely chopped dill
- 1 cup (25 g) mint, finely chopped
- ½ cup (120 g) plain unsweetened vegan Greek yogurt
- salt and freshly ground black pepper
- 1 cup (150 g) bulgur or couscous
- ½ cup (120 ml/4 fl oz) hot vegetable stock (broth)
- 1 plum tomato, finely diced
- 1 cucumber, peeled and finely diced
- 1 cup (25 g) parsley, chopped
- 4 radishes, finely sliced on a mandoline
- ½ cup (80 g) pomegranate seeds
- 1 cup (225 g) Hummus (page 20)
- 1 tablespoon harissa
- 2 tablespoons carrot juice
- 1 tablespoon finely grated fresh ginger
- warmed pita or garlic naan, to serve

Mix the garlic in a bowl with 1 tablespoon of lemon juice, 1 tablespoon of olive oil, 1 tablespoon of dill, half the mint, and the yogurt. Season to taste, cover, and refrigerate.

Put the bulgur or couscous into a medium bowl and pour over the vegetable broth. Cover with a clean kitchen towel and set aside for 15 minutes. Fluff the grains with a fork, then transfer to a large bowl and add the tomato, cucumber, parsley, and the remaining lemon juice, olive oil, and mint. Mix well and season to taste with salt and freshly ground black pepper. Cover and refrigerate.

Put the radish slices into a bowl with the pomegranate seeds.

Mix half of the hummus with the harissa in a bowl until well blended, then season to taste with salt and freshly ground black pepper. Set aside. Mix the remaining hummus in a bowl with the carrot juice and grated ginger. Set aside.

Using large, clear, thick glasses or *verrines*, make layers with the harissa-hummus mixture, the bulgur or couscous tabbouleh, the carrot-ginger hummus, and the yogurt mixture. Top with the radish-pomegranate mixture. Refrigerate for 30 minutes, then garnish with the remaining chopped dill just before serving. Serve with warm pita or garlic naan.

RED BELL PEPPER AND WALNUT DIP

Preheat the oven to 425°F/220°C/Gas Mark 7.

Arrange the red bell peppers on a large baking sheet and roast for 30 minutes.

Transfer the peppers to a large bowl, cover with plastic wrap (clingfilm), and set aside to cool for 30 minutes. Remove and discard the skin and seeds. Using a food processor or high-speed blender, process the bell pepper flesh with the olive oil and garlic until smooth and creamy. Set aside.

Soak the bread slices in the stock for 20 minutes. Using your hands, squeeze out the stock. Add the softened bread along with the remaining ingredients to the pepper mixture in the food processor and pulse to a purée. Season to taste with salt and freshly ground black pepper. Serve with warm naan or chapati.

Preparation time: 1 hour 10 minutes
Cooking time: 30 minutes

Serves 4

- 2¼ lb (1 kg) red bell peppers
- 2 tablespoons olive oil
- 1 clove garlic, finely chopped
- 3 slices bread
- 1 cup (240 ml/8 fl oz) vegetable stock (broth)
- ½ cup (80 g) walnuts, crushed
- 3 tablespoons gochujang (fermented chili paste)
- 2 tablespoons tomato purée (passata)
- 1 tablespoon pomegranate molasses
- 2 tablespoons chopped mint
- 1 teaspoon ground cumin
- 1 teaspoon ground coriander
- 1 teaspoon red chili flakes
- salt and freshly ground black pepper
- warmed naan or chapati, to serve

ASPARAGUS AND AVOCADO TOSTADAS

Cut the cooked asparagus into 1½ inch (4 cm) slices. Combine these in a bowl with the tamari or soy sauce, jalapeño, onion, and scallions and refrigerate.

Preheat the broiler (grill).

Arrange the tortillas on a large baking sheet, leaving space between them. Brush them with vegetable margarine, then cover each tortilla with a layer of tomato slices. Divide the asparagus mixture equally among the tortillas, then cover with a layer of avocado slices. Sprinkle a little salt on top, then cover with the vegan cheddar. Place the sheet in the broiler and broil until the cheese is melted and starts to turn golden brown. Transfer the tortillas to serving plates.

Mix the vegannaise, sesame oil, mustard, and sriracha in a bowl and sprinkle the mixture over the cheese just before serving. Scatter over the cilantro and serve immediately.

Preparation time: 20 minutes
Cooking time: 10 minutes

Serves 4

- 1 lb 2 oz (500 g) white asparagus, trimmed and cooked
- 3 tablespoons tamari or soy sauce
- ½ jalapeño pepper, seeded and minced
- ½ onion, sliced
- 4 scallions (spring onions), sliced
- 4 soft corn tortillas
- vegetable margarine, for brushing
- 2 plum tomatoes, sliced
- 1 avocado, sliced
- salt
- 4 slices vegan cheddar cheese
- 2 tablespoons vegannaise (page 52) or store-bought
- 2 teaspoons toasted sesame oil
- 1 teaspoon Dijon mustard
- 1 teaspoon sriracha
- 3 tablespoons roughly chopped cilantro (coriander)

RED PEPPER, EGGPLANT, AND PINE NUT TERRINE

Preparation time: 25 minutes, plus overnight chilling
Cooking time: 40 minutes

Serves 4

- 8 red bell peppers
- grated zest and juice of 1 lemon
- 1 lb 2 oz (500 g) eggplant (aubergine), cut into slices ½ inch (1 cm) thick
- 2 tablespoons olive oil
- 1 tablespoon dried oregano
- salt
- 9 oz (250 g) smoked vegan mozzarella, thinly sliced
- 2 tablespoons pine nuts
- salad, to serve

Preheat the oven to 400°F/200°C/Gas Mark 6.

Place the red bell peppers on a baking sheet and bake for about 10 minutes, until dark brown. Transfer to a bowl, cover with plastic wrap (clingfilm), and let cool. Then remove and discard the skin and seeds and cut the flesh into long strips. Put the bell pepper back into the bowl, sprinkle with the lemon juice and zest, and set aside.

Arrange the eggplant slices on the baking sheet and bake for 10–20 minutes, until soft. Remove from the oven, sprinkle over the olive oil, oregano, and a little salt, and set aside.

Line a terrine mold that has a capacity of 17 fl oz (500 ml) with plastic wrap (clingfilm), ensuring there is plenty of plastic wrap overhanging the edges of the mold. Arrange a layer of half the red pepper strips to cover the bottom of the mold, followed by a layer of the smoked vegan mozzarella slices, then a layer of the eggplant slices. Arrange the remaining red pepper slices over the top in a final layer. Sprinkle over the pine nuts. Fold the plastic wrap tightly over the terrine. Refrigerate overnight.

When ready to serve, preheat the oven to 225°F/110°C/Gas Mark ¼. Transfer the terrine from the mold to a baking sheet, remove the plastic wrap, and bake for 10–12 minutes, until the mozzarella starts to melt. Serve immediately with a salad.

VEGAN CREAM CHEESE

Preparation time: 15 minutes, 1 hour chilling
Cooking time: none

Serves 4

- 1 cup (125 g) cashews, soaked in water overnight and drained
- 2 tablespoons fresh lemon juice
- 1 tablespoon nutritional yeast
- 1 tablespoon agave syrup
- 1 cup (240 g) silken tofu, crumbled
- 1 tablespoon garlic powder
- salt and freshly ground black pepper
- 1 tablespoon chopped chives, to garnish
- crackers, to serve

Using a food processor or high-speed blender, blend the cashews, lemon juice, nutritional yeast, and agave syrup with 3 tablespoons water for 3–4 minutes, until the mixture is very smooth. Add the silken tofu and garlic powder and process again until very smooth. Season to taste with salt and freshly ground black pepper.

Transfer the mixture to a bowl and chill in the refrigerator for 1 hour before serving. Garnish with the chives and serve with crackers.

SHIITAKE AND TOASTED HAZELNUT PÂTÉ

Preheat the oven to 225°F/110°C/Gas Mark ¼. Grease a 5–6-inch (13–15 cm) square ovenproof dish with vegetable margarine.

Remove the stems from the shiitake mushrooms. Chop the stems finely and set aside. Slice the shiitake mushroom caps.

Melt the vegetable margarine in a skillet (frying pan) over medium heat and add the garlic. Stir fry for 2 minutes, then add the mushroom stems and caps and sauté for 5–6 minutes. Stir in the thyme and season to taste with salt and freshly ground black pepper.

Using a food processor, pulse the parsley and hazelnuts to break down the nuts to a breadcrumb texture. Transfer the mixture to a bowl and set aside.

Now put the vegan mozzarella cheese into the food processor and pulse briefly two or three times, then return the hazelnut crumbs to the food processor, add the sherry or white port, nutritional yeast, and the shiitake mixture, and pulse a couple of times until well mixed.

Press the mixture into the prepared ovenproof dish and bake for 20 minutes, until the mozzarella has melted completely. Let cool for 20 minutes, then refrigerate for 1 hour before serving with bread or crackers.

Preparation time: 15 minutes
Cooking time: 30 minutes, plus 1 hour chilling

Serves 4

- ½ pound (225 g) shiitake mushrooms
- 3 tablespoons vegetable margarine, plus extra for greasing
- 1 clove garlic, chopped
- 1 tablespoon thyme, chopped
- salt and freshly ground black pepper
- 1 tablespoon fresh parsley, chopped
- ½ cup (60 g) toasted hazelnuts, crushed
- ½ cup (120 g) vegan mozzarella (or moxarella)
- 1 tablespoon dry white sherry or white port
- 1 tablespoon nutritional yeast
- bread or crackers, to serve

GREEN LENTIL PÂTÉ

Cook the lentils in the stock according to the packet instructions until tender. Drain and let cool for 20 minutes.

Using a food processor or high-speed blender, pulse the garlic and half the lentils until the mixture forms a smooth mass, then add the beets, sherry, cognac or brandy, coconut oil, and sage and process until smooth.

Transfer the mixture to a large bowl, add the remaining lentils, mix well, and set aside.

Heat the olive oil in a large saucepan and stir fry the mushrooms for 5–6 minutes, stirring frequently. Season to taste wth salt and freshly ground black pepper. Set aside for 20 minutes to cool.

Add the cooled mushrooms to the lentil mixture and stir until well blended. Transfer the mixture to a square glass or metal form, press down the surface, then sprinkle over the crushed roasted hazelnuts. Press the nut crumbs into the pâté, cover, and refrigerate overnight. Serve with French bread.

Preparation time: 20 minutes
Cooking time: 5 minutes, plus 40 minutes chilling

Serves 4

- 1 cup (240 g) Puy lentils
- 3 cups (720 ml/24 fl oz) hot vegetable stock (broth)
- 3 cloves garlic, finely chopped
- 1 beet (beetroot), cooked and diced
- 2 tablespoons dry sherry
- 1 tablespoon cognac or brandy
- 2 tablespoons coconut oil
- 1 pinch of ground dried sage
- 2 tablespoons olive oil
- 2 cups (250 g) porcini mushrooms, chopped
- salt and freshly ground black pepper
- ¼ cup (60 g) crushed roasted hazelnuts
- French bread, to serve

CHICKPEA AND CURRANT PATÉ

Preparation time: 20 minutes

Cooking time: around 55 minutes, plus
  overnight chilling

Serves 4

- 1 cup (150 g) dried currants
- 4 tablespoons olive oil
- 6 onions, diced
- 1 teaspoon ground cinnamon, plus extra
  for sprinkling
- 1 teaspoon ground allspice
- ½ cup (60 g) toasted pine nuts
- 2 cups (400 g) canned chickpeas, drained
  (liquid reserved)
- 3 tablespoons tahini
- 2 tablespoons fresh lemon juice
- 2 sweet potatoes, peeled and diced
- salt and freshly ground black pepper
- bread, to serve

Put the currants into a medium bowl, cover completely with hot water, and let stand for 30 minutes. Drain and reserve the soaking liquid.

Heat the oil in a large skillet (frying pan) over medium-low heat and gently cook the onions for 7 minutes, until golden brown. Reduce the heat to low and continue to cook for another 20 minutes, until caramelized. Periodically, add some of the reserved soaking liquid, 1 tablespoon at a time.

Add the currants and another 2–3 tablespoons of their soaking liquid and cook for 5 minutes, stirring frequently. Add the cinnamon and allspice, stir well, and cook for another 2 minutes. Remove the skillet from the heat and let the mixture cool to room temperature. Stir in the pine nuts.

Using a food processor or high-speed blender, purée the chickpeas in 2 batches with the tahini, lemon juice, and 4–5 tablespoons of the reserved chickpea liquid until very smooth. Transfer the mixture to a large bowl.

Bring a saucepan of water to a boil and cook the sweet potatoes until tender, about 15–20 minutes. Using a fork or potato masher, mash the potatoes to a smooth purée. Transfer the purée to the skillet and combine it with the onions and currants. Season to taste with salt and freshly ground black pepper.

Line an 8-inch (20 cm) square baking pan with plastic wrap (clingfilm), leaving a 4-inch (10 cm) overhang on all sides. Spread half the chickpea mixture evenly on the bottom. Spread the onion mixture evenly on top. Spread the remaining chickpea mixture on the top. Fold the overhanging plastic wrap to cover the pâté completely. Place a weight, such as a can of beans, on top and refrigerate overnight.

To serve, bring the pâté back to room temperature. Flip it onto a serving plate and remove the plastic wrap. Sprinkle the top with ground cinnamon and serve with bread.

SQUASH AND CORN CASSEROLE

Put the mung beans into a bowl and cover with cold water. Let soak overnight. The next day, drain the mung beans.

Bring 8½ cups (2 liters/70 fl oz) water to a boil in a large saucepan. Add the mung beans and cook for 15 minutes, until softened. Drain and set aside.

Heat the olive oil in a large skillet (frying pan) over medium heat. Add the onion and garlic and sauté for 8 minutes, stirring, until golden brown.

Add the stock, pumpkin, and corn to the skillet. Raise the heat to high and bring to a boil, then immediately reduce the heat to medium and cook, stirring occasionally, for 20 minutes, until the squash is tender and the stock has reduced by half.

Add the mung beans, stir well, and season to taste with salt and freshly ground black pepper. Remove from the heat and serve with rice.

Preparation time: 15 minutes
Cooking time: 35 minutes

Serves 4

- 9 oz (250 g) dried mung beans
- 3 tablespoons olive oil
- 2 onions, diced
- 4 cloves garlic, finely chopped
- 4 cups (960 ml/32 fl oz) vegetable stock (broth)
- 2¼ lb (1 kg) pumpkin or butternut squash, peeled and diced
- 1 lb 2 oz (500 g) fresh or frozen corn
- salt and freshly ground black pepper
- cooked long-grain rice, to serve

BAKED POTATO NEST

Cook the whole potatoes in boiling water for about 15 minutes, until tender but still firm. Drain and let cool for 15 minutes, then chill in the refrigerator.

Mix the cucumbers, tomatoes, olive oil, sriracha, oregano, and cheese in a large bowl and season to taste with salt and freshly ground black pepper. Refrigerate until ready to serve.

Preheat the oven to 400°F/200°C/Gas Mark 6. Grease a 6-hole muffin pan with the vegetable margarine.

Peel the cooked potatoes and coarsely grate them into a bowl. Gently season with salt and freshly ground black pepper. Place 2 tablespoons of the potato mixture in each hole of the muffin pan. Press the mixture to the bottom and up the sides of each recess to form a "nest." Bake for 20 minutes, or until golden and crisp. Allow the potato nests to cool completely in the pan.

Carefully remove the nests from the muffin pan and transfer them to a serving platter. Divide the cucumber-tomato mixture equally among the nests and garnish with the chopped cilantro. Serve immediately.

Preparation time: 15 minutes, plus 30 minutes chilling
Cooking time: 35 minutes

Serves 4

- 3 large potatoes
- 2 cucumbers, diced
- 3 plum tomatoes, diced
- 1 tablespoon olive oil
- 1 tablespoon sriracha
- 1 teaspoon ground oregano
- 9 oz (250 g) vegan mozzarella, diced
- salt and freshly ground black pepper
- 1 tablespoon vegetable margarine
- 2 tablespoons chopped cilantro (coriander), to garnish

COLCANNON

Preparation time: 20 minutes
Cooking time: around 50 minutes

Serves 4

- 1¾ lb (800 g) russet potatoes or similar, cut into medium-size chunks
- ¼ cup (60 g) vegetable margarine, plus extra for brushing
- ½ cup (120 ml) soy cream
- salt and freshly ground black pepper
- 1 cup (240 g) kale or curly kale, cut into strips
- 1 clove garlic, finely chopped
- green salad, to serve
- French dressing, to serve

Preheat oven to 350°F/180°C/Gas Mark 4. Grease a deep ovenproof dish with vegetable margarine.

Meanwhile, put the potato chunks into a saucepan of salted water and bring to a boil. Boil the potatoes for about 15 minutes, until very tender. Drain the potatoes, return them to the pan, and add half the vegetable margarine on top. Leave to melt, then mix well and mash the potatoes with a fork. Stir in the soy cream and season to taste with salt and freshly ground black pepper. Set aside.

Bring a saucepan of water to a boil, add the kale, and blanch over high heat for 3 minutes. Drain in a strainer (sieve).

Heat the remaining vegetable margarine in a skillet (frying pan), add the garlic, and stir fry gently over medium heat for about 2–3 minutes, until it starts to brown. Add the kale and toss carefully.

Arrange alternating layers of mashed potato and kale in the prepared ovenproof dish, starting with kale and finishing with mashed potato. Transfer to the oven and bake for 30 minutes, until lightly browned on top. Garnish with a pinch each of salt and pepper. Serve with a lightly dressed salad.

COLCANNON

EGGPLANT AND CHILI CASSEROLE

Preparation time: 20 minutes
Cooking time: 35 minutes

Serves 4

- 2¼ lb (1 kg) eggplant (aubergine), halved lengthwise
- 2 cups (350 g) plum tomatoes, chopped
- 2 onions, chopped
- 3 cloves garlic, finely chopped
- 1 teaspoon superfine (caster) sugar
- 1 teaspoon salt
- 2 teaspoons ground red chilies
- freshly ground black pepper
- 2 tablespoons olive oil
- 1 tablespoon chopped basil, to garnish

Preheat the oven to 400°F/200°C/Gas Mark 6.

Cut each eggplant half into half-moon slices and place in a baking pan. Bake for 25 minutes, until soft but not mushy.

Using a food processor or high-speed blender, pulse the tomatoes, onions, garlic, sugar, salt, and ground chili with ¼ cup (60 ml) water until the mixture forms a paste. Season to taste with pepper.

Heat the olive oil in a skillet (frying pan) and cook the tomato paste for 8–10 minutes, until the liquid has thickened.

Arrange the eggplant in the middle of a serving plate and cover with the tomato paste. Garnish with the chopped basil leaves and serve immediately.

EGGPLANT GRATIN

Preparation time: 20 minutes
Cooking time: 50 minutes

Serves 4

- 2 tablespoons vegetable oil, plus extra for greasing
- 2 onions, chopped
- 8 squares of shredded wheat breakfast cereal, crushed
- salt
- 2¼ lb (1 kg) eggplant (aubergine), halved lengthwise
- 1 cup (240 g) plum tomatoes
- 2 tablespoons tomato purée (passata)
- ⅓ oz (10 g) fresh basil
- Cooked basmati rice or other long-grain rice, to serve

Preheat the oven to 400°F/200°C/Gas Mark 6.

Heat 2 tablespoons of the vegetable oil in a skillet (frying pan) and sauté the onions over medium heat for about 3–4 minutes, until golden brown. Add the crushed cereal and stir fry gently for about 3–4 minutes, until golden. Season with salt.

Slice each eggplant half into half-moons. Cover the base of a greased baking pan with a layer of eggplant slices and sprinkle over some of the shredded wheat–onion mixture. Add a second layer of eggplant and sprinkle over more cereal-onion mixture. Repeat until all the ingredients are used.

Using a food processor or high-speed blender, blend the plum tomatoes, tomato purée, and basil leaves. Pour the mixture over the contents of the baking pan.

Bake for 45 minutes, until the eggplant is tender. Serve with rice.

EDAMAME WONTONS

Put the edamame into a bowl and mash with a fork. Add the breadcrumbs, tamari, sriracha, sesame oil, and scallions (spring onions) and mix well to blend. Season to taste with salt and freshly ground black pepper.

Lay a wrapper flat on your work surface. Place 1 teaspoon of the filling in the center of the wrapper. Dip a finger in water and moisten around the edges of the wrapper, all around your filling. Fold the wrapper in half, diagonally, creating a triangle. Press the edges together. Now fold each of the triangle corners in toward the center of the wrapper. Press them onto the body of the wonton to seal completely. Repeat with the remaining wrappers and filling.

Heat the margarine in a skillet (frying pan) over medium heat. Cook the wontons for about 4 minutes on 1 side, until golden brown. Flip, add more margarine if needed, and fry the other side gently for another 4 minutes. Transfer to a serving platter. Serve with your favorite dipping sauce or tamari.

Preparation time: 15 minutes
Cooking time: 15 minutes

Serves 4

- 1½ cup (240 g) cooked edamame, drained
- 1 tablespoon breadcrumbs
- 1 tablespoon tamari or soy sauce
- 1 teaspoon sriracha sauce
- 1 teaspoon toasted sesame oil
- 2 scallions (spring onions), chopped
- salt and freshly ground black pepper
- 16–20 square or round wonton wrappers
- 2 tablespoons vegetable margarine, plus extra as needed for frying
- your favorite dipping sauce or tamari, to serve

EGGPLANT AND PINEAPPLE YAKITORI

Preheat the broiler (grill). Soak 8 bamboo skewers in water.

Put the pineapple pieces into a large bowl and add the eggplant and yakitori sauce. Mix to coat the pineapple and eggplant in the sauce. Marinate at room temperature for 20 minutes.

Thread 2 chunks of pineapple onto a bamboo skewer, followed by 2 slices of eggplant. Continue alternating the pineapple and eggplant until the skewer is full. Repeat with the remaining skewers until all skewers are prepared. Spray the skewers with the cooking spray and place on a baking sheet. Broil at mid-height for 4–5 minutes on each side, until the pineapple caramelizes.

Transfer the skewers to a serving platter. Sprinkle over the black and white sesame seeds, followed by the chopped scallions. Serve immediately.

Preparation time: 15 minutes, plus 20 minutes marinating
Cooking time: around 10 minutes

Serves 4

- 1 super-sweet pineapple, peeled, cored, and cut into 1-inch (2.5 cm) pieces
- 4 eggplants (aubergines), cut into 1-inch (2.5 cm) pieces
- 4 tablespoons yakitori or teriyaki sauce
- cooking spray
- 2 tablespoons black and white sesame seeds, to garnish
- 2 tablespoons chopped scallions (spring onions), to garnish

CABBAGE DOLMAS

Preparation time: 40 minutes
Cooking time: around 50 minutes

Serves 4

- 1 lb 2 oz (500 g) basmati rice or other long-grain rice
- 2 onions, finely chopped
- 2 cups (480 g) plum tomatoes, thinly sliced
- 2 tablespoons chopped mint
- 5 tablespoons extra-virgin olive oil
- 2 tablespoons balsamic vinegar
- juice of 3 lemons
- salt and freshly ground black pepper
- 2 heads of savoy cabbage

Mix the rice, onion, tomatoes, mint, olive oil, balsamic vinegar, and lemon juice a large bowl and season to taste with salt and freshly ground black pepper. Set aside.

Bring a large saucepan of water to a boil. Separate the cabbage leaves. Remove the ribs but keep the leaves intact. Select the largest cabbage leaves (reserve the smaller leaves for other dishes). Once the water is boiling, blanch the larger leaves for 1 minute, then drain and let cool.

To assemble the dolmas, spread out a cooked cabbage leaf on a work surface. Arrange 1 tablespoon of the rice mixture in a line, positioning it at one side of the leaf. Roll up the leaf tightly around the filling to form a cigar shape. Repeat with the remaining cabbage leaves and rice mixture.

Arrange the dolmas in a large, wide saucepan with a lid. Make two or three layers, depending to the size of the pan. Cover the dolmas with water and bring to a boil, then immediately reduce the heat to medium-low and simmer gently for 45 minutes, until the water has almost completely evaporated. Remove the pan from the stove. Fold up two or three paper towels and position these inside the saucepan on the top of the dolmas. Put the lid on and leave to stand for 20 minutes before serving. Serve at room temperature.

CHOW MEIN

Preparation time: 10 minutes
Cooking time: around 10 minutes

Serves 4

- 1 tablespoon olive oil
- ½ onion, sliced
- 2 cloves garlic, finely chopped
- 1 red chili, seeded and finely chopped
- 1 cup (75 g) button mushrooms, sliced
- ½ cup (85 g) snow peas (mange-tout), halved
- 1½ cups (120 g) green beans, trimmed
- salt
- 1½ cups (120 g) rice noodles
- 1 tablespoon vegetable oil
- 2 tablespoons agave syrup
- 4 tablespoons mirin or rice vinegar
- 3 tablespoons tamari or soy sauce
- 2 tablespoons toasted peanuts, crushed, to garnish

Heat the olive oil in a large wok over medium heat, add the onion, garlic, and chili, and stir fry gently for 3–4 minutes. Add the remaining vegetables, cover, and cook for 5 minutes, stirring regularly, until the vegetables have softened. Remove from the heat and set aside.

Bring a large saucepan of salted water to a boil and cook the noodles according to the packet instructions. Drain, cool under cold running water, drain again, then transfer to a bowl and mix in the vegetable oil. Add the oiled noodles to the vegetables in the wok.

Whisk the agave syrup, mirin or rice vinegar, and tamari or soy sauce in a small bowl until smooth. Sprinkle the mixture over the vegetables and noodles and toss to mix well.

Transfer the mixture to large serving bowls, garnish with the crushed peanuts, and serve immediately.

CARAMELIZED ONION AND
SPINACH QUESADILLAS

Heat a slick of olive oil in a large skillet (frying pan) over medium heat. Add the onions and stir fry gently for about 3–4 minutes, until golden brown. Add the salt, then reduce the heat to low and cook for 20 minutes, stirring frequently, until caramelized, adding a little extra olive oil if the pan becomes dry. Transfer the onions to a bowl and set aside.

Heat a little more olive oil in the same skillet, then add the baby spinach and sauté for 3–4 minutes, until wilted. Transfer spinach to a bowl and set aside.

Clean the skillet and return it to the stove. Add a little olive oil and heat it over low heat. Lay 1 tortilla flat inside the pan. Evenly scatter a quarter of the cheese on the top, then top with a quarter of the caramelized onions. Arrange a quarter of the baby spinach over the onion layer, then raise the heat to medium-low and cook until the cheese has melted and the tortilla is crispy. Add a quarter of the sliced avocado and some salt to taste, then fold the tortilla in half, lay it on a plate, cover it with a clean kitchen towel to keep it warm, and set aside while you repeat with the remaining quesadilla ingredients. Serve with your favorite sauce or salsa.

Preparation time: 15 minutes
Cooking time: around 30 minutes

Serves 4

- olive oil
- 2 onions, sliced
- a pinch of salt, plus more as needed
- 8 oz (225 g) baby spinach
- 4 large flour tortillas
- 1 lb (450 g) vegan cheddar cheese, grated
- 2 ripe avocados, sliced
- your favorite sauce or salsa, to serve

CAULIFLOWER FRITTERS

Using a food processor or high-speed blender, pulse the cauliflower and scallions until well chopped. Transfer the mixture to a bowl. Stir in the flour, spices, and baking soda. Set aside for 30 minutes.

Begin to heat enough oil to deep-fry the fritters in a deep saucepan or deep-fat fryer. Dust a plate or tray with flour. Line another plate with paper towels.

Meanwhile, take 1 tablespoon of the cauliflower mixture and form a patty, compressing the mixture well in your hands. Place it on the flour-dusted plate and repeat until you have used all the remaining mixture. When the oil is hot, carefully drop the patties into it. Cook for 4–5 minutes, until the edges start to turn golden brown, then flip the patties to fry the other sides for about 3–4 minutes, until golden brown. Drain the patties and transfer to the paper towel–lined plate to absorbthe excess oil. Serve warm with chili-tomato-garlic sauce or your favorite dipping sauce.

Preparation time: 20 minutes
Cooking time: around 15 minutes

Serves 4

- 1 cauliflower, cut into small pieces, stems trimmed
- 4 scallions (spring onions), chopped
- 1 cup (125 g) all-purpose (plain) flour, plus extra for dusting
- 1 teaspoon ground cumin
- 1 teaspoon curry powder
- 1 teaspoon baking soda (bicarbonate of soda)
- vegetable oil, for deep-frying
- chili-tomato-garlic sauce or your favorite dipping sauce, to serve

CHICKPEA PATTIES

Preparation time: 30 minutes, plus
  1 hour chilling
Cooking time: 15 minutes

Serves 4

- 2 cups (350 g) cooked chickpeas, drained
- 1 onion, finely chopped
- 2 tablespoons chopped parsley
- 2 tablespoons chopped mint
- 1 tablespoon breadcrumbs
- 1 slice of bread, soaked in soy milk
- ½ cup (60 g) all-purpose (plain) flour, plus
  extra for rolling
- salt and freshly ground black pepper
- vegetable oil, for deep-frying
- your favorite dipping sauce, to serve

Using a food processor or high-speed blender, pulse the chickpeas, onion, parsley, mint, breadcrumbs, bread, flour, and salt and freshly ground black pepper to taste until well mixed. Transfer to a bowl and refrigerate for 1 hour.

Begin to heat enough oil to deep-fry the patties in a deep saucepan or deep-fat fryer. Dust a plate or tray with flour. Line another plate with paper towels.

Using your hands, form the mixture into small patties. Roll these in the flour. When the oil is hot, carefully slide the patties into it and fry for 7–8 minutes, until golden brown on both sides. Drain with a slotted spoon and transfer to the paper towel–lined plate to absorb excess oil. Serve with your favorite dipping sauce.

CHICKPEA PATTIES

DAIKON ROLLS WITH AVOCADO AND MICRO GREENS

Preparation time: 35 minutes
Cooking time: none

Serves 4

- 1 tablespoon tamari or soy sauce
- 1 tablespoon rice vinegar
- 1 tablespoon grated galangal
- juice of 1 lemon
- 1 large daikon radish, sliced thinly into 12 long strips
- 12 shiso leaves
- 1 ripe avocado, finely diced
- 1 cucumber, finely diced
- 1 tablespoon snow pea shoots, minced
- 1 tablespoon chopped mint leaves
- 1 tablespoon radish sprouts
- 2 tablespoons yuzu juice
- black sesame seeds, to garnish

In a bowl, whisk together the tamari, rice vinegar, galangal, and lemon juice and set aside.

Lay out the daikon sheets on a tray or work surface. Place 1 shiso leaf on each daikon sheet.

Mix the avocado, cucumber, snow pea shoots, and mint together in a bowl. Stir in the lemon dressing. Divide the mixture equally among the daikon sheets, positioning the mixture at one end of each length. Roll up each daikon sheet tightly, pushing the roll away from you. Transfer the rolls to a serving plate, garnish with the sprouts, and use a tablespoon to sprinkle the yuzu juice over the top.

DAIKON ROLLS WITH AVOCADO AND MICRO GREENS

FRIED LEEK PATTIES

Preparation time: 45 minutes
Cooking time: around 30 minutes

Serves 4

- 2 cups (250 g) all-purpose (plain) flour, plus extra for dusting
- 1 teaspoon salt, plus extra to season
- 1 tablespoon olive oil
- 2 large leeks
- ½ cup (120 g) silken tofu
- ¼ teaspoon hot chili powder
- freshly ground black pepper
- 1 tablespoon vegetable oil, plus extra for deep-frying
- your favorite dipping sauce, to serve

Sift the flour and salt into a bowl. Make a well in the center of the flour and add ²/₃ cup (150 ml/5 fl oz) cold water. Mix to form a firm dough, then add the olive oil and knead for 5 minutes, until the dough is soft and elastic, dusting with more flour if necessary. Wrap in plastic wrap (clingfilm) and let rest for 30 minutes in a warm place.

Cut most of the dark green tops from the leeks, halve the leeks lengthwise, and slice them ¼ inch (5 mm) thick. Transfer the slices to a bowl, add the tofu and chili powder, season to taste with salt and freshly ground black pepper, and stir in the vegetable oil.

Roll out the dough into a large rectangle and, using a 3¼–4-inch (8–10 cm) round metal cutter, cut out circles.

Place 2 teaspoons of the leek filling in the center of a dough round. Using your finger, wet the edges of the dough and fold the dough over the filling, pressing the edges together to seal well. Using a fork, crimp the edge to seal the semicircle tightly. Repeat with the remaining dough circles and filling.

Heat the oil for deep-frying in a large saucepan over low heat. Line a plate with paper towels.

Carefully drop batches of 4–5 of the patties into the hot oil and deep-fry gently for 4–5 minutes, until golden. Drain on the paper towel–lined plate and serve hot or warm with your favorite dipping sauce.

GREEN SUSHI ROLLS WITH PEANUT SAUCE

Preparation time: 40 minutes
Cooking time: none

Serves 4

- 1 tablespoon smooth peanut butter
- 1 tablespoon soy sauce, plus extra to serve
- 1 tablespoon tahini
- 1 clove garlic, minced
- 8 sheets of nori
- 2 avocados, diced
- 8 oz (225 g) baby spinach
- 8 oz (225 g) mixed sprouts or micro greens
- wasabi, to serve

Using a food processor or high-speed blender, pulse the peanut butter, soy sauce, tahini, garlic, and 2 tablespoons water until the mixture is well blended. Transfer to a bowl and set aside.

Lay out the nori sheets. Place 1 teaspoon each of the avocado, baby spinach, and sprouts or micro greens across one end of each sheet. Sprinkle over the peanut sauce, then roll up each sheet of nori tightly around the filling. Serve with soy sauce and wasabi on the side.

FRIED VEGETABLES
WITH COCONUT

Bring a saucepan of water to a boil.

Wash the bean sprouts, removing any brown tails. Put the sprouts into a heatproof bowl. Pour the boiling water over the sprouts, then rinse under the cold running water. Drain and set aside.

Bring a saucepan of salted water to a boil, add the green beans, and boil for about 4–5 minutes, until the beans are tender but al dente. Drain and set aside.

Bring another saucepan of salted water to a boil, add the carrot slices, and boil until tender. Drain and set aside.

Bring a third saucepan of salted water to a boil. Add the cabbage and blanch for 2 minutes. Drain the leaves in a colander, then hold under cold running water and drain to cool.

Put the shredded coconut into a large bowl with the scallions, sriracha, lime juice, and tamari or soy sauce and mix well until blended.

Combine the bean sprouts, green beans, carrots, cabbage, and bamboo shoot slices in a steamer basket. Sprinkle the coconut mixture over the vegetables, reserving some to garnish the dish. Transfer the vegetables to a steamer and steam for 8 minutes. Season with salt and freshly ground black pepper to taste.

Arrange the steamed vegetables on a serving plate and sprinkle with the reserved coconut mixture. Serve with bread or rice.

Preparation time: 20 minutes
Cooking time: around 15 minutes

Serves 4

- 2 cups (220 g) bean sprouts
- salt
- 2 cups (180 g) green beans, halved
- 4 carrots, sliced
- ½ Napa cabbage, trimmed and shredded
- 1 cup (240 g) chopped coconut pulp
- 1 scallion (spring onion), chopped
- 1 teaspoon sriracha
- 2 tablespoons fresh lime juice
- 1 tablespoon tamari or soy sauce
- ½ cup (35 g) drained bamboo shoots, sliced to a size similar to the beans
- freshly ground black pepper
- bread or cooked plain rice, to serve

GARDEN SPRING ROLLS

Preparation time: around 45 minutes
Cooking time: none

Serves 4

- ½ pound (225 g) rice vermicelli
- 1 cup (125 g) mung bean sprouts
- ½ cup (120 g) grated carrot
- ½ cup (120 g) grated daikon radish
- 1 clove garlic, minced
- 1 tablespoon tamari or soy sauce
- 4 tablespoons roasted unsalted peanuts, crushed
- ¼ cup (30 g) mint, chopped
- ¼ cup (30 g) cilantro (coriander), chopped, plus a few sprigs to garnish
- 1 tablespoon fresh lime juice
- 12 sheets of rice paper
- 1 tablespoon sriracha

Soak the rice vermicelli in hot water for 5 minutes, until soft. Drain, immerse in cold water, then drain again. Cut the noodles into 2-inch (5 cm) lengths and set aside.

Put the sprouts, carrot, daikon, garlic, and tamari or soy sauce into a large bowl and mix well. Add the vermicelli, then add half of the crushed peanuts, the mint, and the cilantro, and sprinkle with the lime juice. Toss together until combined.

Put some warm water into a large, shallow bowl. Immerse 1 sheet of rice paper in the water, quickly remove it, and lay the wrapper on a plate. Place about 2 tablespoons of the noodle mixture toward one end of the wrapper. Fold that end up over the mixture and roll it tightly to form a tube. Place the roll on a tray and cover with a clean, damp kitchen towel. Repeat with the remaining rice paper sheets and filling mixture.

Mix the sriracha with the remaining crushed peanuts and serve alongside the rolls.

GARDEN SPRING ROLLS

GREEN PEA PATTIES

Preparation time: 20 minutes
Cooking time: around 30 minutes

Serves 4

- salt
- 9 oz (250 g) fresh or frozen green peas
- ½ cup (125 g) all-purpose (plain) flour
- 2 tablespoons soy cream
- 1 cup (100 g) vegan parmesan cheese
- vegan substitute for 1 egg
- 1 teaspoon baking powder
- freshly ground black pepper
- 2 tablespoons olive oil
- your favorite dipping sauce, to serve

Bring a large saucepan of lightly salted water to a boil. Cook the peas in the boiling water for 5 minutes, stirring occasionally, until tender. Drain the peas and transfer them to a bowl. Mash with a fork.

Put about two-thirds of both the flour and the soy cream into a bowl, add the cheese, egg replacer, baking powder, salt and freshly ground black pepper to taste, and mashed peas, and mix well, adding just enough additional soy cream or flour to make the mixture firm. Using your hands, mold the mixture into patty shapes about 2-inches (4–5 cm) thick.

Heat the olive oil in a skillet (frying pan) over medium heat. Fry the patties for about 4–5 minutes on each side, until golden brown.

Serve with your favorite dipping sauce, or use the patties to make burgers.

GRILLED PORTOBELLO MUSHROOM TOSTADAS

Preparation time: 30 minutes
Cooking time: around 10 minutes

Serves 4

For the basil pesto:
- 4 cups (100 g) basil
- 1 tablespoon fresh lemon juice
- 2 cloves garlic, finely chopped
- 2 tablespoons olive oil
- ¼ cup (30 g) walnuts
- salt and freshly ground black pepper

For the tostadas:
- 4 large portobello mushrooms
- 2 teaspoons extra-virgin olive oil
- salt and freshly ground black pepper
- burger buns, split, or sandwich breads, to serve
- handful of baby spinach leaves
- your favorite burger sauce, to serve

Preheat the broiler (grill).

To make the basil pesto, use a food processor or high-speed blender to pulse the basil, lemon juice, garlic, olive oil, and walnuts until blended and smooth. Transfer to a bowl and season to taste with salt and freshly ground black pepper. Set aside.

To make the tostadas, brush the portobello mushrooms with the olive oil, season to taste with salt and freshly ground black pepper, then place the mushrooms on a baking sheet. Broil (grill) at mid-height for 3–4 minutes, then flip over the mushrooms and broil for another 3–4 minutes, until they have begun to turn golden brown.

Place a grilled mushroom, with gill side facing up, on the bottom half of each burger bun, then add 1 tablespoon of the basil pesto in the center. Top with a few baby spinach leaves, then cover with the top half of the burger bun. Serve with your favorite burger sauce.

STIR-FRIED CHINESE SPINACH

Heat the oil in a wok or skillet (frying pan) over medium heat. Add the onion, garlic, and ginger and stir fry for 3–4 minutes, until the onion and garlic start to turn golden brown. Add the Chinese spinach, chili, 2 tablespoons water, and the soy sauce. Stir fry for another 2 minutes. Serve immediately, garnished with white sesame seeds and chopped basil, with steamed rice on the side.

Preparation time: 20 minutes
Cooking time: 5 minutes

Serves 4

- 1 tablespoon sesame oil
- 1 onion, chopped
- 4 cloves garlic, minced
- 1 tablespoon minced fresh ginger
- 2¼ lb (1 kg) Chinese spinach, trimmed
- 1 red chili, seeded and finely chopped
- 1 tablespoon soy sauce
- 1 tablespoon white sesame seeds, to garnish
- 1 tablespoon chopped basil, to garnish
- steamed rice, to serve

MANGO-AVOCADO ROLLS

Combine the diced avocado, lime juice, and lime zest in a medium bowl. Stir in the bell pepper, cream cheese, scallions, cilantro, and sriracha. Add the mango, alfalfa sprouts, and mung sprouts and set aside.

Fill a large bowl with warm water. Soak 1 rice paper wrapper in the warm water for 10 seconds. Drain the wrapper, lay it out on a work surface, and leave to rest for 30 seconds. Arrange 4 tablespoons of the avocado-mango mixture across the width of the wrapper, just below center, leaving a 1-inch (2.5 cm) space on either side. Fold the bottom of the rice paper wrapper up over the filling, then fold the top down over it, and roll up completely. Set aside. Repeat with the remaining wrappers and filling. Serve with a sweet and sour sauce or soy sauce.

Preparation time: 30 minutes
Cooking time: none

Serves 4

- 1 cup (225 g) diced avocado
- 2 tablespoons fresh lime juice
- 2 teaspoons finely grated lime zest
- ½ cup (75 g) diced red bell pepper
- ½ cup (120 g) Vegan Cream Cheese (page 30) or store-bought, softened
- 4 scallions (spring onions), finely chopped
- ¼ cup (30 g) cilantro (coriander), chopped
- 1 tablespoon sriracha
- 1½ cups (360 g) diced mango
- ½ cup (30 g) alfalfa sprouts
- 1 cup (120 g) mung bean sprouts
- 8 Vietnamese rice paper wrappers
- sweet and sour sauce or soy sauce, to serve

KIMCHI-FRIED RICE

Preparation time: 20 minutes
Cooking time: around 10 minutes

Serves 4

- 2 cups (300 g) vegan kimchi
- 1 tablespoon vegetable oil
- 1 tablespoon toasted sesame oil
- 1 tablespoon Korean gochujang
  (fermented chili paste)
- 4 tablespoons coconut cream
- 4 cups (920 g) cooked jasmine or short-
  grain rice
- 3 scallions (spring onions), finely sliced
- 1 tablespoon tamari or soy sauce
- 1 tablespoon toasted sesame seeds,
  to garnish
- 4 sheets of nori, toasted and crumbled,
  to garnish

Drain the vegan kimchi in a colander set over a bowl, pressing to get as much juice out as possible. Reserve the juice. Chop the kimchi and set aside.

Heat the oils in a wok or skillet (frying pan), add the kimchi, and stir fry gently for about 4–5 minutes over medium heat, until fragrant. Add the gochujang and coconut cream and toss for about 1 minute, until well blended. Add the rice, reserved kimchi juice, scallions, and tamari or soy sauce, mix well, and continue to stir fry for 3–4 minutes over medium heat, allowing the rice to lightly toast. Transfer to a serving plate and sprinkle with sesame seeds and nori crumbles. Serve immediately.

KIMCHI-FRIED RICE

LEMONGRASS AND JACKFRUIT BOATS

Preparation time: 15 minutes
Cooking time: 20 minutes

Serves 4

For the boats:
- 1 large carrot, sliced into 2-inch
  (5 cm) sticks
- ½ cup (120 ml/4 fl oz) white vinegar
- ⅓ cup (90 g) superfine (caster) sugar
- 1 lemongrass stalk
- 1 tablespoon olive oil
- 1 teaspoon minced garlic
- 1 lb (450 g) canned young green jackfruit,
  cut into small pieces
- 2 cucumbers
- 1 large red chili, seeded and sliced
- 2 scallions (spring onions), sliced
- ¼ cup (30 g) cilantro (coriander)
- a pinch of salt
- 4 tablespoons tamari or soy sauce
- 1 crusty French baguette, to serve

For the vegannaise:
- ¾ cup (180 g) silken tofu
- 4 tablespoons vegetable oil
- juice of 1 lemon
- 1 teaspoon onion powder
- 1 tablespoon white vinegar
- 1 teaspoon Dijon mustard

Put the carrot sticks into a glass jar with a lid.

Pour the white vinegar into a saucepan, set the pan over medium heat, and dissolve the sugar in the vinegar. Set the marinade aside until cool, then add to the carrots in the jar. Close the lid, shake the jar, and refrigerate.

Remove the first 2–3 leaves from the lemongrass stalk and mince the heart.

Heat the olive oil in a large skillet (frying pan) or wok and add the garlic, lemongrass, and jackfruit. Cook over medium heat for 4–5 minutes, then add the half of the tamari or soy sauce. Cook, stirring occasionally, for another 10 minutes, until the jackfruit pieces start to turn golden brown. Set aside to cool.

To make the vegannaise, use a food processor or blender to combine all the ingredients, processing for 2–3 minutes. Set aside in refrigerator.

Cut the cucumber in half lengthwise and spoon out the seeds and pulp to make 4 "boats". Reserve the pulp and seeds.

Drain the carrot sticks. Mix the vegannaise with the jackfruit, carrot sticks, chili, scallion, reserved cucumber pulp and seeds, cilantro, salt, and tamari or soy sauce. Divide the mixture into four equal portions and use these to fill the cucumber boats. Serve with a crusty baguette.

JAPANESE PANCAKES

To make the sauce, in a bowl whisk together the ketchup, Worcestershire sauce, mustard, garlic powder, and pepper. Cover and refrigerate until needed.

To make the pancakes, put the flour, almond milk, apple cider vinegar, and baking soda into a large bowl and mix until very smooth. Season to taste with salt.

Heat a little oil in a skillet (frying pan) over medium heat. Pour half the pancake batter into the pan. Add half the spinach or Napa cabbage, sprinkle over half the scallions, and cook for 3–4 minutes until the pancake is golden brown. Flip the pancake and cook the other side until golden brown. For a crispier pancake, flip it again and cook until it is to your liking. Repeat with the remaining ingredients.

Transfer the pancakes to a serving plate, drizzle with the sauce, and serve immediately.

Preparation time: 30 minutes
Cooking time: 30 minutes

Serves 4

For the sauce:
- 4 tablespoons ketchup
- 3 teaspoons Worcestershire sauce
- 2 teaspoons powdered mustard
- 2 teaspoons garlic powder
- 1 teaspoon black pepper

For the pancakes:
- 1 cup (125 g) all-purpose (plain) flour
- ¾ cup (180 ml) almond milk
- 1 tablespoon apple cider vinegar
- 1 teaspoon baking soda (bicarbonate of soda)
- salt
- vegetable oil
- 1 cup (30 g) spinach or shredded Napa cabbage
- ½ cup (50 g) chopped scallions (spring onions)

POTATO AND HORSERADISH CREAM

Toss the shallot rings in the flour, then transfer them to a strainer (sieve) and tap off the excess flour. Line a plate with paper towels.

Heat 2 tablespoons of the olive oil in a small saucepan over high heat. Reduce the heat to medium and fry the shallots for 4–5 minutes at medium heat, until golden brown. Transfer to the paper towel–lined plate to absorb excess oil, sprinkle over a little salt, and set aside.

Mix the soy yogurt, horseradish, bread pieces, red onion, dill pickle, and chives in a large bowl and season to taste with salt and freshly ground black pepper. Set aside.

Heat the remaining olive oil in a skillet (frying pan) over medium heat and gently stir fry the potato slices for 5–6 minutes on each side, until golden brown. Transfer to a serving plate, top with the yogurt mixture, garnish with the fried shallots, and serve immediately.

Preparation time: 25 minutes
Cooking time: 20 minutes

Serves 4

- 3 shallots, sliced into rings
- ¼ cup (30 g) all-purpose (plain) flour
- 3 tablespoons olive oil
- salt and freshly ground black pepper
- ¼ cup (60 ml) unsweetened soy yogurt
- 2 teaspoons grated horseradish
- 2 slices brown rye bread, torn into small pieces
- 1 red onion, sliced
- 1 large dill pickle, finely diced
- 2 tablespoons finely chopped chives
- 4 russet potatoes, boiled until tender, peeled, and thinly sliced

MARINATED MUSHROOMS

Preparation time: 20 minutes
Cooking time: 10 minutes, plus
  1 hour chilling

Serves 4

- 2 tablespoons olive oil
- 1 lb 6 oz (625 g) shiitake mushrooms,
  stems removed, caps sliced
- 2 tablespoons rice vinegar
- 2 tablespoons tamari or soy sauce
- 1 tablespoon chili powder
- 1 tablespoon soy cream
- ¼ cup (30 g) green shiso, chopped
- 1 daikon radish, grated
- 2 carrots, grated
- salt
- 2 tablespoons red shiso leaves, to garnish
- soba noodles or sticky rice, to serve

Heat the olive oil in a wok or skillet (frying pan) over high heat, then add the mushrooms. Stir fry for about 5–6 minutes, until the mushrooms are cooked and their juices have evaporated.

Remove the pan from the heat, then add the rice vinegar, tamari or soy sauce, chili powder, soy cream, shiso, daikon, and carrots. Stir to combine, then season to taste with salt. Return the pan to the heat and cook for 2 minutes. Remove the pan from the stove and set aside to cool. Transfer mushroom mixture to a bowl and refrigerate for 1 hour.

To serve, garnish with red shiso leaves. Serve with soba noodles or sticky rice.

MUSHROOMS À LA GRECQUE

Preparation time: 15 minutes
Cooking time: 15 minutes, plus
  30 minutes standing

Serves 4

- 3 tablespoons olive oil
- 3 cloves garlic, crushed
- 1 lb 2 oz (500 g) button mushrooms, sliced
- 2 tablespoons kalamata olives, pitted
  (stoned) and sliced
- 4 tablespoons red wine vinegar
- 2 tablespoons herbes de Provence
- 3 tablespoons tomato purée (passata)
- 2 tablespoons fresh lemon juice
- 2 tablespoons chopped parsley, to garnish

Heat the olive oil in a skillet (frying pan), add the garlic and mushrooms, and stir fry over medium heat for 5–6 minutes. Add the olives, 5 tablespoons water, the vinegar, herbes de Provence, and tomato purée and bring to a simmer. Cook for 10 minutes over medium heat at a low simmer.

Remove the skillet from the heat, add the lemon juice, stir well, and let cool for about 30 minutes.

Serve at room temperature, garnished with the parsley.

MUSHROOM CAPS STUFFED WITH FRESH HERBS

Preheat the oven to 350°F/180°C/Gas Mark 4.

Remove the stems from the mushrooms and finely chop the stems. Arrange the mushroom caps on a baking sheet.

Heat the vegetable margarine in a saucepan, add the scallions, and stir fry gently for 3–4 minutes. Add the mushroom stems and cook for another 3–4 minutes, then add the parsley, garlic, and herbes de Provence and season to taste with salt and freshly ground black pepper. Add the breadcrumbs and olive oil and mix well.

Fill the mushroom caps with the stuffing. Bake for 15 minutes or until the breadcrumbs are golden brown and crisp. Serve immediately.

Preparation time: 30 minutes
Cooking time: 25 minutes

Serves 4

- 1 lb 2 oz (500 g) large button mushrooms
- 1 tablespoon vegetable margarine
- 2 tablespoons scallions (spring onions), finely chopped
- 2 tablespoons chopped parsley
- 1 clove garlic, finely chopped
- 1 tablespoon herbes de Provence
- salt and freshly ground black pepper
- 3 tablespoons breadcrumbs
- 1 tablespoon olive oil

MUSHROOM FRITTERS

Preheat the oven to 400°F/200°C/Gas Mark 6. Grease an ovenproof dish with the vegetable margarine.

Mix the flour, nutritional yeast, salt, paprika, garlic powder, black pepper, and curry powder in a bowl until well blended.

Using a food processor or high-speed blender, blend the tofu and soy cream until very smooth. Slowly add the dry ingredients until the mixture is well blended and has no lumps.

Add the button mushrooms and toss until well coated. Transfer them in a single layer to the prepared dish and bake for 12–15 minutes, until the mushrooms are golden brown.

Serve immediately with sriracha or a spicy sauce of your choosing.

Preparation time: 20 minutes
Cooking time: 15 minutes

Serves 4

- 2 tablespoons vegetable margarine
- ½ cup (63 g) all-purpose (plain) flour
- 1 tablespoon nutritional yeast
- 3 teaspoons salt
- 2½ teaspoons sweet paprika
- 2 teaspoons garlic powder
- 1 teaspoon freshly ground black pepper
- ½ teaspoon curry powder
- 1 cup (240 g) silken tofu
- 4 tablespoons soy cream
- 1 lb 2 oz (500 g) small button mushrooms
- sriracha or other spicy dipping sauce, to serve

MUSHROOM DUMPLINGS

Preparation time: 30 minutes, plus
 2 hours resting
Cooking time: around 30 minutes

Serves 4

- 1 lb 2 oz (500 g) all-purpose (plain) flour,
  plus extra for dusting
- 1 teaspoon salt, plus extra to season
- 2 cups (460 g) sticky or glutinous rice
- 1 tablespoon vegetable oil, plus extra
  for brushing
- 1 lb 2 oz (500 g) shiitake mushrooms,
  stems removed, caps quartered
- 2 shallots, chopped
- 2 scallions (spring onions), chopped
- 1 tablespoon rice wine or dry sherry
- 2 teaspoons tamari or soy sauce
- 1 teaspoon mushroom soy sauce or
  soy sauce
- 1 teaspoon five-spice powder
- 1 teaspoon toasted sesame oil
- 1 cup (150 g) frozen peas
- freshly ground black pepper
- your favorite dipping sauce, to serve

Mix the flour and salt with ¾ cup (175 ml/6 fl oz) water in a large bowl and knead until the mixture forms a smooth dough. (Alternatively, use a stand mixer fitted with a dough hook attachment.) Cover the bowl with a clean, damp kitchen towel and let the dough rest for 2 hours.

Cook the sticky rice according to the packet instructions. (Alternatively, use a rice cooker.)

Heat the oil in a wok over medium heat, then add the mushrooms and shallots and stir fry for 3–4 minutes, until the shallots are translucent. Add the scallions, rice wine or sherry, soy sauces, five-spice powder, sesame oil, and ¼ cup (60 ml) warm water. Stir well, and cook for 2 minutes. Stir in the cooked rice and peas and remove the wok from the heat. Season to taste with salt and freshly ground black pepper.

Divide the dough into 4 equal pieces. Roll 1 piece with your hands into a long rope and cut it into small pieces about the size of a small walnut. Repeat with the remaining dough portions.

Prepare a steamer pan, lining it with a layer of damp cheesecloth (muslin), or brush the steamer basket with oil to prevent sticking.

Dust a clean work surface with flour and roll out each piece of dough into a 4-inch (10 cm) diameter circle. Place 1 teaspoon of the sticky rice mixture in the center of each circle, then bring up the sides of the wrapper tightly around the filling and press the dough together to seal it, to form a dumpling.

Transfer the dumplings to the steamer basket, arranging them so that they sit about 1 inch (2.5 cm) apart. Steam the dumplings for about 5 minutes. Serve immediately with your favorite dipping sauce.

ROASTED FENNEL AND WHITE PEACH

Preheat the oven to 350°F/180°C/Gas Mark 4.

Remove the stalks and fronds from the fennel bulbs and cut each bulb into 6 pieces. Put the pieces into on ovenproof dish.

Peel and pit (stone) the peaches. Cut each peach into 6 slices. Add these to the fennel in the ovenproof dish along with the garlic cloves. Drizzle over the olive oil and bake for about 20 minutes. Peel the garlic cloves and place the cloves in a mortar. Transfer the peaches and fennel to a serving plate and set aside to cool.

Press the garlic to a pulp. Add the lemon juice and, using a fork, purée the mixture until smooth.

Drizzle the garlic-lemon mixture over the fennel and peach slices. Season to taste with salt and freshly ground black pepper, then sprinkle over the capers. Serve at room temperature.

Preparation time: 30 minutes
Cooking time: 20 minutes

Serves 4

- 2 fennel bulbs
- 3 ripe but firm white peaches
- 1 garlic head, cloves separated, unpeeled
- 6 tablespoons olive oil
- 4 tablespoons fresh lemon juice
- salt and freshly ground black pepper
- 1 tablespoon capers, to garnish

ROASTED EGGPLANT, TOMATO, AND RED BELL PEPPER

Preheat the oven to 400°F/200°C/Gas Mark 6. Line two rimmed baking sheets with aluminum foil.

Toss the eggplant pieces in a large bowl with 2 tablespoons of the olive oil.

Arrange the bell peppers and jalapeño on one prepared baking sheet and the eggplant pieces on the other. Roast the vegetables for 12 minutes. Using tongs, flip the bell peppers and eggplants and roast for another 4 minutes, until the eggplants are tender.

Put the eggplant and jalapeño in one bowl, and the bell peppers in another bowl. Cover the bowl with the bell peppers with plastic wrap (clingfilm) and let cool for 15 minutes.

Remove and discard the skin and seeds of the cooled bell peppers. Transfer the flesh to a saucepan, add the tomatoes, garlic, tomato purée, and crushed red chili flakes, and season to taste with salt. Bring to a simmer and cook over low heat for 35 minutes. Add the eggplant cubes and jalapeño and cook over low heat for another 10 minutes, until the mixture is thick. Remove the pan from the heat, sprinkle in the sugar, mix well, and season to taste with salt and freshly ground black pepper. If you like it spicier, add more crushed red chili flakes.

To serve, mix the remaining olive oil with the sweet paprika and smoked paprika in a small jar (jug). Sprinkle over the vegetables.

Preparation time: 30 minutes
Cooking time: 1 hour, plus 15 minutes chilling

Serves 4

- 2¼ lb (1 kg) eggplant (aubergine), cut into 1½-inch (4 cm) dice
- 5 tablespoons olive oil
- 2 red bell peppers
- 1 jalapeño pepper, seeded and chopped
- 1 lb 10½ oz (750 g) plum tomatoes, diced
- 1 clove garlic, finely chopped
- 2 tablespoons tomato purée (passata)
- 1 teaspoon crushed red chili flakes, plus more to taste
- salt and freshly ground black pepper
- 1 tablespoon superfine (caster) sugar
- 2½ teaspoons sweet paprika
- 1 teaspoon smoked paprika

OKRA STUFFED WITH COCONUT

Preparation time: 25 minutes
Cooking time: 30 minutes

Serves 4

- 1 lb 2 oz (500 g) okra (ladies' fingers)
- 1 tablespoon sesame seeds
- 1 tablespoon coconut oil
- 1 cup (240 g) coconut strips, chopped
- 3 tablespoons raw peanuts
- 1 teaspoon ground turmeric
- 1 teaspoon ground coriander
- 1 teaspoon ground cumin
- 1 teaspoon ground allspice
- ½ teaspoon salt
- 2 tablespoons olive oil, plus more as needed
- 8 curry leaves
- 1 green chili, seeded and chopped
- 1 teaspoon mustard seeds
- 1 teaspoon asafoetida
- 2 tablespoons fresh lemon juice
- cooked wild or basmati rice, to serve

Wash and drain the okra and set aside to dry on paper towels.

Toast the sesame seeds in a dry skillet (frying pan) set over low heat for 2–3 minutes. Using a mortar and pestle, crush the seeds and set aside.

Heat the coconut oil in the same skillet over medium heat. Add the coconut meat and toast for 3–4 minutes, until golden brown. Set aside.

Toast the peanuts in a dry skillet for 5–6 minutes, stirring constantly. Let cool.

Using a food processor or high-speed blender, pulse the peanuts. Add the crushed sesame seeds, turmeric, coriander, cumin, allspice, coconut meat, and salt and pulse again to mix well. Set aside.

Trim the okra at both ends. Using a small knife, carefully cut a full-length slit along one side of each piece. Stuff the coconut-peanut-spice mixture into the okra. Reserve the remaining stuffing.

Heat 1 tablespoon of the olive oil in a large skillet over medium heat. Add the curry leaves, green chili, mustard seeds, and asafetida and gently fry for about 2 minutes, until the mustard seeds start to pop. Immediately add a layer of the stuffed okra to the skillet and sprinkle over half of the remaining stuffing. Cook for 10–12 minutes over low heat—if the mixture becomes too dry, sprinkle with 1 more tablespoon olive oil. Transfer to a serving plate. Cook the second batch of stuffed okra the same way. Transfer to the serving plate and sprinkle over the lemon juice. Serve hot, with rice on the side.

OKRA STUFFED WITH COCONUT

PALAWAN SPRING ROLLS

Preparation time: 30 minutes
Cooking time: around 50 minutes

Serves 4

For the dipping sauce:
- 1 small red onion, finely chopped
- 3 cloves garlic, minced
- 1 cup (240 ml/8 fl oz) white wine vinegar
- 4 tablespoons soy sauce
- ½ cup (120 ml) ketchup
- a pinch of crushed red chili flakes
- salt

For the spring rolls:
- 2 tablespoons olive oil
- 1 onion, chopped
- 4 cloves garlic, finely chopped
- 1 lb 2 oz (500 g) sweet potato, peeled and diced
- 1 lb 2 oz (500 g) carrots, diced
- ½ cup (120 ml/4 fl oz) vegetable stock (broth)
- 9 oz (250 g) celery, chopped
- 4¼ oz (125 g) roasted peanuts
- 1 tablespoon soy sauce
- 9 oz (250 g) green beans, trimmed
- 1 cup (100 g) shredded green cabbage
- 20 spring roll or rice wrappers
- vegetable oil, for deep-frying
- lettuce leaves, to serve

To make the dipping sauce, use a food processor or high-speed blender to combine the red onion, garlic, white wine vinegar, soy sauce, ketchup, and crushed red chili flakes until smooth and creamy. Season with salt and set aside.

To make the spring rolls, heat the olive oil in a skillet (frying pan) or wok over medium heat. Add the onion and garlic and sauté for about 4–5 minutes, until just softened and translucent. Add the sweet potato, carrot, and stock and simmer for 6–7 minutes. Then add the celery and peanuts and continue to cook for about 10 minutes, until the sweet potato and carrot are just tender. Reduce the heat to very gently simmer the stock, then add the soy sauce, green beans, and shredded cabbage and cook for 5 minutes. Drain the vegetables in a colander, reserving the remaining stock, and set aside to dry and cool a little.

Lay a spring roll wrapper on a work surface and add 2 teaspoons of the vegetable mixture across the center of the wrapper, leaving space at each side. Fold the bottom of the wrapper over the filling, then fold the top of the wrapper over the filling and roll firmly to form a spring roll. Repeat with the remaining wrappers and filling.

Heat the vegetable oil in a deep-fat fryer or deep saucepan over high heat. Line a plate with paper towels.

When the oil is hot, cook the spring rolls in the oil, in batches of five, for about 4–5 minutes, turning frequently, until golden brown and crispy. Remove the spring rolls with a slotted spoon and transfer to the paper towel–lined plate to absorb excess oil.

Serve immediately, with lettuce leaves and the prepared dipping sauce on the side.

SWEET CARDAMOM CARROTS

Mix the almond milk, cardamom, lemon zest, and sugar in a saucepan. Bring to a boil, stirring constantly then reduce the heat to a low simmer. Put the carrot into a strainer (sieve) and set it on the saucepan above the almond milk, ensuring it does not touch the liquid. Cover the pan and steam for 15 minutes, stirring regularly. When tender, press the carrot to remove excess liquid. Reserve the almond milk.

Melt the vegetable margarine in a saucepan over medium heat. Slowly add the all-purpose flour, stirring constantly with a wooden spoon, until the mixture is well blended, without any lumps. Add the carrot, stir to coat completely, then remove the pan from the heat and leave to sit for 5 minutes. Pour the reserved almond milk over the carrot, put the pan back on the stove, mix well, and cook over low heat for about 5 minutes, stirring occasionally. Pour into individual ramekins and garnish with the pistachios and raisins.

Preparation time: 20 minutes
Cooking time: around 20 minutes, plus
    5 minutes standing

Serves 4

- 2 cups (475 ml/16 fl oz) almond milk
- 1 teaspoon ground cardamom
- 1 tablespoon grated lemon zest
- 1 cup (200 g) superfine (caster) sugar
- 1 lb 2 oz (500 g) carrots, grated
- 2 tablespoons vegetable margarine
- 2 tablespoons all-purpose (plain) flour
- 1 tablespoon ground pistachios,
    to garnish
- 1 tablespoon raisins, to garnish

SUKHOTHAI ROLLS

THAILAND

To make the dipping sauce, use a food processor or high-speed blender to blend the peanut butter, 3 tablespoons hot water, the lime juice, soy sauce, brown sugar, grated ginger, and garlic until the mixture is smooth and creamy. Transfer to a bowl and set aside in the refrigerator.

To make the rolls, cut the steamed beets into slices, then cut them again into sticks. Set aside in a bowl.

Put the carrots into a bowl, the cucumber into a second bowl, and the bell pepper into a third bowl.

Mix together the mint, cilantro, and basil, and set aside on a plate or bowl.

Fill a large bowl with hot water. Soak 1 rice paper wrapper in the hot water for 10 seconds, then remove it immediately and lay it on a clean work surface. Place 1 teaspoon of the herbs in the center of the wrapper, top with 1 tablespoon beets, 1 tablespoon carrots, and 1 tablespoon bell peppers, then fold the bottom and top of the wrapper toward the center, over the filling. Roll the wrapper around the filling into a tight tube. Repeat the process with the remaining ingredients. Serve with the dipping sauce on the side.

Preparation time: 35 minutes
Cooking time: none

Serves 4

For the dipping sauce:
- ⅓ cup (120 g) smooth or crunchy
    peanut butter
- 3 tablespoons fresh lime juice
- 2 tablespoons soy sauce
- 2 teaspoons brown sugar
- 1 tablespoon grated fresh ginger
- 1 clove garlic, chopped

For the rolls:
- 2 beets (beetroot), steamed
- 2 carrots, grated
- 1 cucumber, peeled, seeded, and cut
    into sticks
- 1 yellow bell pepper, seeded and
    thinly sliced
- ¼ cup (30 g) chopped mint
- ¼ cup (30 g) chopped cilantro (coriander)
- ¼ cup (30 g) chopped Thai basil
- 12 round rice paper wrappers

PORTOBELLO CARPACCIO WITH ORANGE TARTARE

Preparation time: 20 minutes
Cooking time: around 5 minutes

Serves 4

- 4 portobello mushrooms, stems and
  gills removed
- 2 tablespoons olive oil, plus extra
  for brushing
- salt and freshly ground black pepper
- 2 oranges
- ½ cup (120 g) black kalamata olives, pitted
  (stoned) and sliced
- 2 teaspoons capers, crushed
- 1 shallot, chopped
- 2 tablespoons cilantro (coriander), chopped,
  to garnish

Preheat the broiler (grill). Line a baking sheet with aluminum foil.

Using a pastry brush, grease the mushrooms caps with olive oil and season to taste with salt and freshly ground black pepper. Arrange the mushrooms on the prepared baking sheet with the open sides facing upward. Set aside.

Grate the orange zest and set aside. Peel the oranges and separate the segments. Using a small knife, remove and discard as much of the fibers as possible, then chop the pulp. Transfer the chopped pulp to a bowl and mix in 1 teaspoon of the reserved orange zest along with the olives, capers, shallots, and olive oil. Season to taste with salt and freshly ground black pepper. Fill the mushroom caps with the mixture.

Broil (grill) the mushrooms at mid-height for 4–5 minutes. Transfer to serving plates, garnish with chopped cilantro, and serve immediately.

PORTOBELLO CARPACCIO WITH ORANGE TARTARE

RAW NORI AND VEGETABLE ROLLS

Preparation time: 40 minutes
Cooking time: none

Serves 4

- 1 cup (150 g) sunflower seeds, soaked in water overnight
- 4 scallions (spring onions), chopped
- ¼ cup (20 g) cilantro (coriander)
- 4 tablespoons fresh lemon juice
- 2 cloves garlic, finely chopped
- 1 tablespoon tamari or soy sauce
- ½ cup (50 g) cauliflower florets
- 8 romaine (cos) lettuce leaves
- 8 sheets raw nori
- 1 carrot, peeled and julienned
- 1 avocado, halved, stoned, and thinly sliced
- 1 cucumber, peeled, seeded, and julienned
- 1 tablespoon black sesame seeds, to garnish
- ½ cup (40 g) microgreens or sprouts, to garnish
- soy sauce, to serve
- wasabi, to serve

Rinse and drain the soaked sunflower seeds.

Using a food processor or high-speed blender, blend the sunflower seeds with the scallions, cilantro, lemon juice, garlic, tamari or soy sauce, and 3 tablespoons water. Process until the mixture is very smooth. Transfer to a large bowl and set aside.

Now put the cauliflower florets into the bowl of the food processor or high-speed blender and pulse just until the cauliflower has the consistency of rice. Transfer to the bowl with the sunflower seed mixture and mix well.

Place 1 romaine lettuce leaf on a nori sheet, covering half the sheet. Spread 2 tablespoons of the sunflower seed–cauliflower mixture on the lettuce leaf. Divide the carrot, avocado, and cucumber strips into eight portions and arrange one portion over the sunflower seed–cauliflower mixture. Fold the nori sheet over the filling and roll the sheet away from you as tightly as possible. Using your finger, wet the end of the nori sheet, then close and seal the roll. Repeat with the remaining nori sheets, lettuce leaves, and filling.

Using a very sharp knife, cut each roll into 4 or 6 pieces. Arrange the rolls on a serving plate. Sprinkle with black sesame seeds and garnish with microgreens or sprouts. Serve with soy sauce and wasabi on the side.

RAW NORI AND VEGETABLE ROLLS

SCALLION PANCAKES

Preparation time: 35 minutes, plus
  12 hours soaking
Cooking time: 30 minutes

Serves 4

For the pancakes:
- 2 tablespoons glutinous or sticky rice
- 1 cup (240 g) mung beans
- 1 cup (240 g) mung bean sprouts
- 2 scallions (spring onions), thinly sliced
- ⅓ cup (80 g) chopped green bell pepper
- ⅓ cup (80 g) chopped onion
- 1 teaspoon baking soda (bicarbonate of soda)
- 2 teaspoons sesame oil
- 1 tablespoon black sesame seeds, toasted and crushed
- 2 teaspoons tamari or soy sauce
- salt and freshly ground black pepper
- ¾ cup (175 ml/6 fl oz) vegetable oil

For the sauce:
- 4 tablespoons light soy sauce
- 3 tablespoons mirin or rice vinegar
- 1 clove garlic, minced
- 1 tablespoon ketchup

To make the pancakes, wash and drain the rice. Place the rice and mung beans in separate bowls and cover each with 5 cups (1.2 liters/ 40 fl oz) water. Leave to soak for at least 12 hours.

Drain the rice and beans. Remove the skins from the beans by rubbing the beans between your hands. Rinse the beans under cold running water until almost all the skins are removed and drained away. Drain again.

Using a food processor or high-speed blender, blend the rice and beans until the mixture forms a thick paste. Gradually add ¾ cup (175 ml/ 6 fl oz) water to the paste as the motor is running, and blend until the mixture is very smooth. Transfer to a large bowl.

Bring a large saucepan of water to a boil, add the mung sprouts, and blanch for 2 minutes. Drain and add the sprouts to the mung bean–rice batter. Stir in the scallions, bell pepper, onion, baking soda, sesame oil, black sesame seeds, and tamari or soy sauce and mix well to blend all the ingredients. Season to taste with salt and freshly ground black pepper. Set aside for 30 minutes.

To make the sauce, put the light soy sauce, mirin or rice vinegar, ketchup, and garlic into a bowl and whisk until the mixture is smooth. Set aside until ready to serve.

Heat 1 teaspoon of the vegetable oil in a skillet (frying pan) over medium heat. Pour in about 5 tablespoons of the batter. Use a large wooden spoon to spread the batter in a spiral motion in the skillet until the pancake measures 6–7 inches (15–18 cm) across. Cook for 2–3 minutes, then flip the pancake and cook for another 2–3 minutes, until golden brown. Transfer to a plate and repeat the process with the remaining batter. Serve immediately with the sauce.

SPICY UDON

Bring a large saucepan of water to a boil. Add the noodles and cook for 8–10 minutes, until tender. Drain the noodles, then transfer them to a bowl and stir in the toasted sesame oil to prevent sticking. Set aside.

Meanwhile, put the 5 tablespoons of vegetable stock, ginger, and garlic into a large saucepan. Bring to a boil, then simmer over medium heat for 3 minutes. Add the scallions and mushrooms and cook for 3 minutes. Add the remaining broth, the soy sauce, and chili paste. Cover and bring to a boil. Add the tofu and bok choy and cook for 4 minutes. Turn off the heat. Season to taste with salt and freshly ground black pepper or tamari or soy sauce.

Serve the noodles in 4 deep bowls, topped with the tofu–bok choy mixture and garnished with the chopped cilantro.

Preparation time: 20 minutes
Cooking time: around 20 minutes

Serves 4

- 1 lb 2 oz (500 g) uncooked udon noodles
- 1 tablespoon toasted sesame oil
- 4 cups (960 ml) plus 5 tablespoons vegetable stock (broth)
- 1 tablespoon grated fresh ginger
- 2 cloves garlic, finely chopped
- 2 scallions (spring onions), finely chopped
- ½ lb (250 g) fresh mushrooms, such as white button or shiitake, sliced
- 4 tablespoons soy sauce
- 1 teaspoon chili paste
- 1 cup (240 g) smoked tofu, cut into cubes
- 1 cup (240 g) bok choy, sliced, stems removed
- salt and freshly ground black pepper or tamari or soy sauce
- 1 tablespoon cilantro (coriander), chopped

SPINACH WITH TOMATO AND PEANUT BUTTER SAUCE

Heat the olive oil in a skillet (frying pan) over medium heat, add the onion, and fry gently for 5–6 minutes, until golden brown. Add the chopped plum tomatoes, garlic, and herbs and simmer for 5–6 minutes. Season to taste with salt and freshly ground black pepper. Add the spinach or Swiss chard and cook over medium heat for 2–3 minutes, then stir in the peanut butter and mix to blend well. Add more chili powder to taste and serve immediately.

Preparation time: 15 minutes
Cooking time: 15 minutes

Serves 4

- 2 tablespoons olive oil
- 1 onion, chopped
- 6 plum tomatoes, chopped
- 2 cloves garlic, finely chopped
- 2 teaspoons mixed aromatic herbs
- salt and freshly ground black pepper
- 9 oz (250 g) spinach or Swiss chard
- 1 tablespoon peanut butter
- 1 teaspoon chili powder (or more to taste)

SPINACH ENCHILADAS WITH LENTILS

Preparation time: 20 minutes
Cooking time: around 30 minutes, plus
  10 minutes chilling

Serves 4

For the sauce:
- 4½ oz (125 g) canned tomatoes
- ½ cup (120 ml/4 fl oz) vegetable stock
  (broth)
- 2 red onions, chopped
- 2 cloves garlic, finely chopped
- 1 teaspoon chili powder
- 1 teaspoon ground cumin
- 1 teaspoon ground coriander
- 1 teaspoon dried oregano
- 1 teaspoon smoked paprika
- 1 teaspoon cayenne pepper
- 2 tablespoons cilantro (coriander)
- 2 tablespoons apple cider vinegar
- salt and freshly ground black pepper

For the enchiladas:
- olive oil, for greasing
- 2 cups (60 g) baby spinach
- ½ cup (120 g) canned black lentils, drained
- 1 red onion, chopped
- 5 tablespoons chopped cilantro (coriander)
- 1 tablespoon fresh lime juice
- salt and freshly ground black pepper
- 8 soft corn tortillas
- ½ onion, finely chopped, for topping
- ½ avocado, diced, for topping

Preheat the oven to 350°F/180°C/Gas Mark 4. Grease an ovenproof dish with the olive oil.

To make the sauce using a food processor or high-speed blender, blend all the ingredients, except the salt and pepper, until the mixture is smooth and creamy. Transfer the mixture to a saucepan, bring to a simmer, and cook over low heat for 10 minutes. Season to taste with salt and freshly ground black pepper. Set aside.

To make the enchiladas, combine the baby spinach, black lentils, onion, 3 tablespoons of the cilantro, and the lime juice in a bowl. Season to taste with salt and freshly ground black pepper and set aside.

Soak the tortillas in the tomato sauce for 2 minutes to soften them.

Pour ½ cup (120 ml/4 fl oz) of the sauce into the prepared ovenproof dish and spread it across the bottom.

Put a tortilla on a work surface. Place 1 heaped tablespoon of the filling in the center and spread the sauce along the tortilla. Roll up the tortilla gently and place it in the ovenproof dish. Repeat the process with the remaining tortillas, arranging them in the dish around one another. Cover the enchiladas with the remaining filling and sauce, then bake for 20 minutes. Let cool for 5 minutes, then top with finely chopped onion, diced avocado, and the remaining chopped cilantro before serving.

STEAMED TOFU ROLLS

Heat the vegetable oil in a skillet (fying pan) over medium heat. Add the garlic and ginger and fry gently for 2–3 minutes. Add the diced tofu and fry for 5 minutes, until golden brown on all sides. Let cool for 10 minutes.

Using a food processor, pulse the tofu mixture a couple of times to make a thick paste. Add the chopped scallion and tamari or soy sauce and pulse one more time. Season to taste with salt and freshly ground black pepper.

Put a wonton wrapper on a work surface and place 1 teaspoon of the tofu mixture in the center. Using your finger, moisten the edge of the wrapper and fold it to make a "purse," pressing the edges to seal firmly. Transfer to a bamboo steamer basket and repeat the filling and folding process with the remaining wrappers until all the filling is used up.

Bring a saucepan of water to a boil. Set the bamboo steamer on top and steam the rolls in batches for about 5 minutes, until cooked. Serve with soy sauce or your favorite dipping sauce.

Preparation time: 30 minutes
Cooking time: around 30 minutes, plus 10 minutes chilling

Serves 4

- 1 tablespoon vegetable oil
- 1 clove garlic, finely chopped
- 1 tablespoon grated fresh ginger
- 1 lb 3 oz (520 g) smoked tofu, diced
- 1 scallion (spring onion), finely chopped
- 1 tablespoon tamari or soy sauce
- salt and freshly ground black pepper
- 15–20 round or square wonton wrappers
- your favorite dipping sauce or soy sauce, to serve

STUFFED ZUCCHINI FLOWERS

Preheat the oven to 250°F/120°C/Gas Mark ½. Grease a rimmed baking sheet with the vegetable oil.

Cook the rice according to packet instructions, then let cool. Mix the cooked rice in a bowl with the onion, tomato, nutritional yeast, olive oil, and mint. Season to taste with salt and freshly ground black pepper.

Using a small teaspoon, carefully stuff the flowers with the rice mixture, closing up the flower petals around the filling. Arrange the stuffed flowers on the prepared baking sheet and bake for 20 minutes. Flip the flowers over and bake for another 10 minutes. Serve immediately, with soy sauce or sweet and sour chili sauce.

Preparation time: 20 minutes
Cooking time: 30 minutes

Serves 4

- 1 tablespoon vegetable oil
- 4½ oz (125 g) long-grain rice
- 1 onion, finely chopped
- 2 plum tomatoes, finely diced
- 1 tablespoon nutritional yeast
- 1 tablespoon olive oil
- 2 tablespoons chopped mint
- salt and freshly ground black pepper
- 20 marrow flowers or 10 zucchini (courgette) flowers, stems and pistils removed
- soy sauce or sweet and sour chili sauce, to serve

STUFFED ZUCCHINI WITH VEGETABLES AND CHEESE

Preparation time: 30 minutes
Cooking time: 30 minutes

Serves 4

- 4 zucchini (courgettes)
- 4 tablespoons olive oil
- 1 celery stalk, finely chopped
- ½ cup (120 g) sliced carrots
- 1 onion, chopped
- 2 plum tomatoes, diced
- salt and freshly ground black pepper
- 1 cup (240 g) tomato sauce
- 1 cup (260 g) crumbled vegan feta cheese
- chopped parsley, to garnish

Preheat the oven to 400°F/200°C/Gas Mark 6.

Slice the zucchini (courgettes) in half lengthwise and scoop out the white flesh, leaving the shells intact. Reserve the flesh.

Heat 2 tablespoons of the olive oil in a skillet (frying pan) over medium heat, add the zucchini flesh, celery, carrot, onion, and tomato and gently fry for 7–8 minutes. Season to taste with salt and freshly ground black pepper. Stuff the zucchini shells with the vegetable filling.

Pour the tomato sauce into an ovenproof dish. Arrange the zucchini boats in the dish. Top with the crumbled feta cheese and sprinkle over the remaining olive oil. Bake for 20 minutes. Garnish with chopped parsley to serve.

STUFFED ZUCCHINI WITH VEGETABLES AND CHEESE

SWEET AND SOUR TEMPEH BUNS

Preparation time: 30 minutes
Cooking time: 1 hour

Serves 4

For the sweet and sour sauce:
- 2 tablespoons ketchup
- 1 tablespoon tamari or soy sauce
- 1 tablespoon rice vinegar
- 1 teaspoon agave syrup

For the filling:
- ½ cup (120 g) smoked tempeh, diced
- 2 tablespoons sweet and sour sauce
- 1 teaspoon sriracha
- 1 teaspoon garlic powder
- salt and freshly ground black pepper
- ¼ cup (55 g) chopped celery

For the wrappers:
- ½ cup (75 g) rice flour, plus extra for dusting
- 2 tablespoons tapioca starch
- 1 teaspoon salt
- 1 teaspoon vegetable oil
- 2 tablespoons sesame oil, plus extra for brushing

- your favorite dipping sauce, to serve

To make the sweet and sour sauce, whisk together the ketchup, tamari or soy sauce, vinegar, and agave in a bowl. Set aside.

To make the filling, put the diced tempeh into a skillet (frying pan) and add 4 tablespoons water. Bring to a boil over medium heat, then simmer for 2 minutes. Add 2 tablespoons of the sweet and sour sauce, the sriracha, and the garlic powder and mix well. Reduce the heat to low and cook until almost all the liquid has evaporated. Season to taste with salt and freshly ground black pepper. Add the celery, stir well, and set aside.

To make the wrappers, whisk together the rice flour and tapioca starch in a large bowl, then whisk in the salt and vegetable oil. Add 6 tablespoons hot water, 1 tablespoon at a time, stirring well between each addition. Press the dough with your hands to dissolve any remaining lumps, and blend in a little extra hot water if necessary to achieve an elastic, springy dough. Cover with a clean, damp kitchen towel and set aside for 30 minutes at room temperature.

Divide the dough into 8 equal balls. Dust a work surface with a little rice flour and roll out the balls to 5-inch (13 cm) circles. Place 1 tablespoon of the tempeh mixture in the center of each circle, then bring up the sides of the dough circle and close the bun at the center of the top, above the filling. Press to seal. Brush the buns with sesame oil.

Heat the sesame oil in a skillet (frying pan). Carefully add the buns and fry gently over medium heat for 5–6 minutes on each side, until golden brown.

Transfer the buns to a serving dish and serve with the remaining sauce on the side.

TAMARIND POTATOES

Dissolve the tamarind paste in 4 tablespoons hot water and set aside for 30 minutes.

Bring a saucepan of salted water to a boil. Add the potatoes and boil for about 11–12 minutes, until tender but firm. Drain the potatoes and set aside until cool enough to handle, then peel and slice them.

Heat 1 tablespoon of the oil in a large, heavy skillet (frying pan) over medium heat. Add the onion and fry gently for 10 minutes until crisp and lightly browned, stirring frequently. Transfer to a bowl and set aside.

Put the potatoes and 1 tablespoon of the oil in the same skillet and fry gently for about 5–6 minutes on each side, until golden brown. Transfer to a bowl and set aside.

Heat the remaining oil in the same skillet. Add the ginger and garlic and fry gently over medium heat for 2–3 minutes. Add the crushed chili flakes and turmeric and stir well, then add 2 tablespoons of the stock along with the fried onion and cook for 2 minutes. Now add the potatoes, tamarind, and the remaining stock. Stir in the ground cardamom, fennel, and cinnamon, and season to taste with salt and freshly ground black pepper. Cover the skillet with a lid and simmer for 15 minutes, until the sauce has thickened slightly.

Preparation time: 20 minutes, plus
  30 minutes standing
Cooking time: 50 minutes

Serves 4

- 1 tablespoon tamarind paste
- salt
- 1 lb 10½ oz (750 g) firm potatoes, unpeeled
- 4 tablespoons vegetable oil
- 1 onion, sliced
- 1 tablespoon finely chopped fresh ginger
- 4 cloves garlic, finely chopped
- 1 teaspoon crushed red chili flakes
- 1 teaspoon ground turmeric
- 2 cups (475 ml/16 fl oz) vegetable stock (broth)
- 1 teaspoon ground cardamom
- 1 teaspoon ground fennel
- 1 teaspoon ground cinnamon
- 1 teaspoon freshly ground black pepper

SWEET AND SOUR RED CABBAGE WITH PORTOBELLOS

Preheat the oven to 325°F/160°C/Gas Mark 3. Grease a rimmed baking sheet with the olive oil.

Pour the wine, broth, and vinegar into a large saucepan. Add the brown sugar, cloves, and caraway seeds and bring to a boil over high heat, then immediately reduce the heat to medium and add the cabbage and apple. Cook, stirring occasionally, for 45 minutes.

Brush the tops of the mushroom caps with melted vegetable margarine, then sprinkle over the chopped garlic. Put the remaining melted vegetable margarine into a skillet (frying pan), add the mushrooms, and fry gently for 2–3 minutes on each side.

Transfer the mushrooms to the prepared baking sheet and bake for 15 minutes, until browned. Place 1 mushroom on each plate, season to taste with salt and freshly ground black pepper, and cover with the red cabbage mixture to serve.

Preparation time: 30 minutes
Cooking time: 1 hour

Serves 4

- 1 tablespoon olive oil
- 1 cup (240 ml/8 fl oz) red wine
- 1 cup (240 ml/8 fl oz) vegetable stock (broth)
- 3 tablespoons balsamic vinegar
- 2 tablespoons brown sugar
- 1 teaspoon ground cloves
- 1 teaspoon ground caraway seeds
- ½ head of red cabbage, cored and shredded
- 1 large green apple, peeled, cored, and sliced
- 4 large portobello mushrooms, stems removed
- 2 tablespoons vegetable margarine, melted
- 2 cloves garlic, finely chopped
- salt and freshly ground black pepper

VEGETABLE FRITTERS

Preparation time: 20 minutes
Cooking time: 30 minutes

Serves 4

- 1 cup (90 g) chickpea flour
- ½ cup (60 g) all-purpose (plain) flour
- 1 tablespoon nutritional yeast
- 1 teaspoon baking soda (bicarbonate of soda)
- 1 teaspoon cayenne pepper
- 1 teaspoon ground cumin
- 1 teaspoon ground coriander
- 1 teaspoon ground turmeric
- salt
- 2 tablespoons fresh lemon juice
- vegetable oil, for deep-frying
- 1 cup (240 g) sliced potatoes
- 1 cup (240 g) cauliflower florets
- ½ cup (120 g) chopped red bell pepper
- your favorite dipping sauce, to serve

Blend the flours, yeast, baking soda, and spices in a jar. Season to taste with salt. Gradually whisk in 4 tablespoons water and the lemon juice to make a smooth batter. Set aside.

Fill a deep-fat fryer or large saucepan with oil to a depth of 3–4 inches (7.5–10 cm) and heat the oil over high heat. Line a plate with paper towels. Insert a wooden spoon into the oil; when the oil is hot enough for frying, it will bubble around the spoon.

Dip the vegetables individually into the batter to coat them. Carefully slide vegetables, in batches, into the hot oil. Do not overcrowd. Cook for about 5 minutes, until golden brown, turning them regularly so that they cook evenly. Remove with a slotted spoon and transfer to the paper towel–lined plate. Cover to keep warm while you cook the remaining vegetables. Serve immediately, with your favorite dipping sauce.

SWEET POTATO AND OLIVE PASTRIES

Preparation time: 15 minutes
Cooking time: 20 minutes

Serves 4

- vegetable oil, for greasing
- 1 lb 2 oz (500 g) sweet potatoes, peeled and diced
- 2 shallots, finely chopped
- ¼ cup (60 g) black kalamata olives, pitted (stoned) and chopped
- 2 tablespoons capers
- 2 tablespoons chopped fresh parsley
- 1 tablespoon olive oil
- 1 teaspoon harissa
- ½ teaspoon ground cumin
- 1 packet of phyllo (filo) dough
- ½ cup (120 g) vegetable margarine, melted
- your favorite dipping sauce, to serve

Preheat the oven to 325°F/160°C/Gas Mark 3. Grease a rimmed baking sheet with vegetable oil and set aside.

Bring a saucepan of water to a boil, then boil the sweet potato for about 9–10 minutes, until tender. Drain and transfer to a large bowl. Mash the sweet potato with a fork until smooth. Mix in the shallots, olives, capers, parsley, olive oil, harissa, and cumin.

Lay out a sheet of phyllo dough and cut it into 3 rectangles of equal size. Brush with melted vegetable margarine, then fold each rectangle in half to make a square. Place 1 tablespoon of the filling in the center of each square and fold the pastry over the filling to form a triangle. Transfer the parcels to the prepared baking sheet and brush the tops with vegetable margarine. Repeat with the remaining dough and filling.

Bake for 12 minutes, until just golden brown. Serve immediately with your favorite dipping sauce.

VEGETABLE THAI TEMPURA

THAILAND

Mix the flours in a large bowl with the chili powder and season to taste with salt and freshly ground black pepper. Gradually whisk in just enough water to make a smooth batter.

Fill a deep-fat fryer or large saucepan with oil to a depth of 3–4 inches (7.5–10 cm) and heat the oil over high heat. Line a plate with paper towels. Insert a wooden spoon into the oil; when the oil is hot enough for frying, it will bubble around the spoon.

Put all the vegetables into the batter and stir well. Take 1 tablespoon of the mixture and carefully slide it into the hot oil, then repeat with the remaining batter, frying the fritters in batches, so as not to overcrowd. Fry for 4–5 minutes, turning frequently, until the fritters are golden brown and cooked through. Drain with a slotted spoon, then transfer to the paper towel–lined plate. Cover to keep warm while you cook the rest. Serve immediately, with sweet and sour sauce or green chutney.

Preparation time: 25 minutes
Cooking time: 35 minutes

Serves 4

- ½ cup (60 g) all-purpose (plain) flour
- ½ cup (45 g) chickpea flour
- 1 teaspoon chili powder
- salt and freshly ground black pepper
- vegetable oil, for deep-frying
- 1 red bell pepper, seeded and diced
- 1 sweet potato, peeled and diced
- 1 onion, chopped
- 1 plum tomato, diced
- 2 tablespoons fresh or frozen corn
- sweet and sour sauce (page 72) or green chutney to serve

ZUCCHINI FLOWERS STUFFED WITH NUTS AND HERBS

ITALY

Preheat the oven to 350°F/180°C/Gas Mark 4. Grease a large ovenproof dish with olive oil.

Heat the oil in a small saucepan over medium heat. Add the onion and sauté for about 4–5 minutes until golden brown. Add the dill and mint and mix well. Add the cumin, freshly ground black pepper, tomato sauce, walnuts, and 2 tablespoons water. Bring to a simmer and add the rice. Cook over low heat for 5 minutes. Mix in the breadcrumbs and nutritional yeast. Set aside to cool.

Using a teaspoon, carefully fill the center of each flower with the rice mixture, then close the petals over the filling. Arrange the stuffed flowers in the prepared baking dish, laying them side by side. Drizzle over some olive oil, season to taste with salt and freshly ground black pepper, and bake for about 20 minutes until the filling is cooked through. Serve immediately.

Preparation time: 30 minutes
Cooking time: 30 minutes

Serves 4

- 2 tablespoons olive oil, plus extra for greasing and drizzling
- 1 onion, finely diced
- 1 tablespoon chopped dill
- 1 tablespoon chopped mint
- 1 teaspoon ground cumin
- 1 teaspoon freshly ground black pepper, plus extra to season
- ½ cup (120 ml/4 fl oz) tomato sauce
- 2 tablespoons walnuts, crushed
- ¼ cup (65 g) cooked white rice
- ¼ cup (25 g) breadcrumbs
- 1 tablespoon nutritional yeast
- 20 zucchini (courgette) flowers, stems and pistils removed
- salt

SALADS

AVOCADO WITH RED RADISH
AND CARROT CARPACCIO

Preparation time: 25 minutes, plus
  overnight chilling
Cooking time: none

Serves 4

For the pickled onion:
- ⅓ cup (50 g) finely chopped red onion
- ¼ cup (60 ml) fresh lemon juice
- pinch of salt

For the sauce:
- 3 tablespoons finely chopped parsley
- 3 tablespoons olive oil
- 2 tablespoons fresh lemon juice
- 1 tablespoon chopped mint
- 1 tablespoon chopped tarragon
- 1 clove garlic, finely chopped
- salt and freshly ground black pepper

For the salad:
- 2 ripe avocados, thinly sliced
- 1 carrot, shaved into ribbons with
  a vegetable peeler
- 1 medium daikon radish, finely sliced
  on a mandoline
- 3 red radishes, finely sliced on a mandoline
- 1 tablespoon cilantro (coriander), chopped

To make the pickled onion, combine the ingredients in a small bowl. Cover the bowl with plastic wrap (clingfilm) and refrigerate overnight.

To make the sauce, combine all the ingredients in a small bowl and season to taste with salt and freshly ground black pepper. Set aside.

To make the salad, arrange the avocado slices along with the carrot, daikon, and radish ribbons on a serving plate. Spoon over the pickled onions, followed by the sauce, then garnish with the chopped cilantro.

NAPA CABBAGE
AND DAIKON KIMCHI

Preparation time: 8 days fermenting
Cooking time: none

Serves 4

- 1 cup (240 g) pickling salt
- 1 lb 10½ oz (750 g) Napa cabbage,
  quartered lengthwise
- 9 oz (250 g) daikon radish, finely diced
- 6 tablespoons gochugaru (Korean red
  chili powder)
- 8 cloves garlic, finely chopped
- 2 tablespoons grated fresh ginger
- 1 tablespoon superfine (caster) sugar
- 2 scallions (spring onions), julienned
- salt

Mix the pickling salt with enough water to cover the cabbage chunks in a large bowl. Soak the cabbage in the brine, ensuring all parts are submerged. Cover and refrigerate overnight.

Drain the cabbage, reserving the brine. Rinse the cabbage, then cut it into bite-size pieces, discarding the hard center stems. Set aside.

Mix the daikon, gochugaru, garlic, ginger, sugar, and scallions in a large bowl and season with salt. (If you choose to mix by hand, use clean kitchen gloves for hygiene, and since gochugaru is strong.) Add the cabbage and toss well.

Transfer the mixture to glass pickling jars. The mixture should be completely submerged in the jar. Should you need more liquid, add some of the reserved brine. Refrigerate for 8 days before using. The kimchi will keep, refrigerated, for up to 6 months.

AVOCADO CEVICHE

Combine all the ingredients in a large bowl. Mix well, then chill in the refrigerator for 30 minutes before serving with bread or tortilla chips.

Preparation time: 30 minutes
Cooking time: none, 30 minutes chilling

Serves 4

- 2 ripe but firm avocados, diced
- 2 cups (240 g) cauliflower florets, chopped
- 2 plum tomatoes, diced
- ⅓ cup (50 g) chopped red onion
- 1 tablespoon finely chopped jalapeño pepper
- 1 clove garlic, finely chopped
- 1 tablespoon chopped cilantro (coriander)
- 1 tablespoon fresh lime juice
- 2 tablespoons olive oil
- salt and freshly ground black pepper
- bread or tortilla chips, to serve

PINEAPPLE SALAD

Heat 1 tablespoon of the oil in a skillet (frying pan) over medium heat, add the cashews, and cook until light golden. Set aside.

Add the remaining oil to the same skillet and cook the coconut flakes over medium heat for 4–5 minutes, until light golden. Set aside to cool.

Pour the soy cream, agave, and rum into a large bowl and mix well. Add the pineapple and toss to coat. Add the cashews and coconut and stir to combine. Refrigerate for 30 minutes. Top the salad with the passionfruit pulp to serve.

Preparation time: 20 minutes
Cooking time: 10 minutes,
  plus 30 minutes chilling

Serves 4

- 2 tablespoons vegetable oil
- 1 cup (240 g) cashews
- ½ cup (60 g) coconut flakes
- 1 cup (240 ml/8 fl oz) soy cream
- 2 tablespoons agave syrup
- 2 tablespoons white rum
- 1 large, sweet pineapple, cored and diced
- 1 passionfruit

CHICKPEA AND CILANTRO SALAD

Preparation time: 20 minutes
Cooking time: 15 minutes

Serves 4

- 3 tablespoons olive oil
- 3 cloves garlic, finely chopped
- 1 red onion, finely chopped
- 1 tablespoon ground cumin
- 1 tablespoon finely chopped fresh ginger
- ½ teaspoon chopped piment d'espelette
- 2 tablespoons fresh lime juice
- 9 oz (250 g) plum tomatoes, quartered
- 1¼ cups (250 g) canned chickpeas, rinsed and drained
- salt and freshly ground black pepper
- 1 bunch of cilantro (coriander), chopped

Heat the oil in a wok or deep saucepan over medium heat. Add the garlic and onion and stir fry for 5–6 minutes, until golden brown. Add the cumin, mix to incorporate, and fry for another 2 minutes. Now add the ginger, chili, lime juice, tomatoes, and chickpeas, reduce the heat to low, and simmer for 7–8 minutes.

Season to taste with salt and freshly ground black pepper, then transfer to a large serving bowl. Sprinkle with the chopped cilantro and serve immediately.

CHICKPEA AND CILANTRO SALAD

CUCUMBER RELISH

Preparation time: 20 minutes
Cooking time: none, 30 minutes chilling

Serves 4

- 3 cucumbers, peeled and thinly sliced
  on a mandoline
- 4 cloves garlic, finely chopped
- 5 scallions (spring onions), white parts only,
  finely chopped
- 4 tablespoons tamari or soy sauce
- 4 tablespoons white vinegar
- 1 tablespoon sesame oil
- 1 teaspoon gochugaru (Korean red
  chili powder)
- steamed jasmine or basmati rice, to serve

Put the cucumber ribbons into a large bowl. Add the garlic and scallions. Set aside.

Pour the tamari or soy sauce, white vinegar, and sesame oil into a small jar. Add the gochugaru, and whisk well. Dress the vegetables, refrigerate for 30 minutes, and serve with rice.

CUCUMBER RELISH

EGGPLANT WITH YOGURT SAUCE

Preparation time: 30 minutes
Cooking time: 35 minutes

Serves 4

- 4 eggplants (aubergines), peeled and sliced ½-inch (1 cm) thick
- salt and freshly ground black pepper
- approximately 4 tablespoons olive oil
- 2 onions, chopped
- 4 plum tomatoes, sliced
- 1 green bell pepper, seeded and sliced
- naan or garlic bread, to serve

For the sauce:
- 2 cups (480 g) unsweetened vegan yogurt
- 2 cloves garlic, finely chopped
- 1 teaspoon chili powder
- naan or garlic bread, to serve

Arrange the eggplant slices on a tray and sprinkle liberally with salt. Leave to stand for 1 hour. Using paper towels, remove the excess salt and pat the eggplant slices dry.

Select a large skillet (frying pan) that has a lid, and pour in enough olive oil to cover the base well (about 3 tablespoons). Heat the oil over medium heat, then add the eggplant slices in batches and fry for about 5 minutes on each side, until lightly browned. Set aside on a large plate, allowing the excess oil to drip onto the plate. Pour the excess oil from the plate with the eggplants back into the skillet.

Add the onion to the skillet and stir fry over medium heat for about 5–6 minutes, until golden brown. Set aside.

Put a layer of eggplant slices into the same skillet, then cover this with a layer of tomato and bell pepper slices. Sprinkle over some fried onions. Make a second layer of eggplant and repeat the process until all the eggplant, tomato, and bell pepper slices are used. Add 4 tablespoons water to the skillet, reduce the heat to low, cover the skillet, and simmer for 15 minutes.

To make the sauce, put the ingredients into a small bowl and mix well.

Once the cooking time has elapsed, pour the sauce over the contents of the skillet, then drizzle over 1 tablespoon olive oil. Cook gently for 2 minutes, season to taste with salt and freshly ground black pepper, then serve with naan or garlic bread.

EGGPLANT WITH GARLIC
AND WALNUT SAUCE

Arrange the eggplant slices on a tray and sprinkle with the salt. Leave to stand for 1 hour. Using paper towels, remove the excess salt and pat the eggplant slices dry.

Select a large skillet (frying pan) that has a lid. Heat 2 tablespoons of the olive oil in the skillet over medium-low heat. Put the eggplant slices into the skillet, cover with the lid, and fry for 5 minutes, until the slices are soft and the bottoms are lightly browned. Remove the lid, flip the slices over, add another tablespoon of oil, and cover with the lid. Fry for another 3–4 minutes, until lightly browned on the other side. Line a plate with paper towels and transfer the fried eggplant to the plate to absorb excess oil.

Using a food processor or high-speed blender, pulse the nuts and garlic to make a paste. Add the vinegar and vegetable stock and pulse to blend well. Sprinkle the nut-garlic paste lightly onto the eggplant slices in the skillet and leave to stand for 15 minutes.

Transfer the eggplant to a large bowl, season to taste with salt and freshly ground black pepper, and garnish with chopped parsley. Serve at room temperature, with crackers or pita bread.

Preparation time: 30 minutes, plus 1 hour standing
Cooking time: 10 minutes, plus 15 minutes standing

Serves 4

- 2 large eggplants (aubergines), halved, then cut into ½-inch (1 cm) thick slices
- 1 tablespoon salt
- 3 tablespoons olive oil
- 1 cup (240 g) walnuts, crushed
- 3 cloves garlic, finely chopped
- 2 tablespoons balsamic vinegar
- 3 tablespoons hot vegetable stock (broth)
- salt and freshly ground black pepper
- 1 tablespoon parsley, chopped, to garnish
- crackers or pita bread, to serve

YOGURT, TOMATO, CUCUMBER,
AND NAAN

Put the yogurt into a bowl, season to taste with salt and freshly ground black pepper, and whisk. Set aside, stirring regularly.

Heat the oil in a skillet (frying pan) over medium heat, add the onion and sauté for 8 minutes, until golden brown.

Put the pieces of naan into a large bowl. Top with the yogurt. Mix in the onion with the hot cooking oil. Top with the scallions, cucumber, tomatoes, and cilantro.

Season to taste with salt and freshly ground black pepper. Serve immediately, with sliced bread.

Preparation time: 15 minutes
Cooking time: 10 minutes

Serves 4

- 3 cups (700 g) unsweetened vegan Greek yogurt
- salt and freshly ground black pepper
- 2 tablespoons vegetable oil
- 2 onions, chopped
- 4 oz (120 g) naan, torn into small pieces
- 2 scallions (spring onions), thinly sliced
- 1 cucumber, peeled and diced
- 3 tomatoes, diced
- ½ bunch of cilantro (coriander), chopped
- sliced bread, to serve

LENTIL SALAD

Preparation time: 20 minutes
Cooking time: 25 minutes, plus
 30 minutes chilling

Serves 4

- 9 oz (250 g) green lentils
- ½ cup (120 g) shallots, chopped
- ¼ cup (60 g) canned green chilies, chopped
- 3 red chilies, seeded and finely chopped
- 3 tablespoons white vinegar
- 3 tablespoons olive oil
- 1 tablespoon chopped basil
- salt and freshly ground black pepper
- 1 plum tomato, finely diced, to garnish

Cook the green lentils following the packet instructions, ensuring they are cooked only until al dente. Drain and transfer to a large bowl.

Add the shallots, both kinds of chilies, vinegar, olive oil, and basil and toss to combine. Season to taste with salt and freshly ground black pepper. Refrigerate, stirring occasionally, for 1 hour.

To serve, transfer the green lentil mixture to serving bowls and garnish with the diced tomato.

MANGO SALAD

Preparation time: 20 minutes
Cooking time: none

Serves 4

- ½ pineapple, cored and diced
- 2 ripe mangos, diced
- ½ cup (120 ml/4 fl oz) fresh lemon juice
- 1 cup (240 ml/8 fl oz) fresh orange juice
- 2 tablespoons balsamic vinegar
- 2 tablespoons olive oil
- 1 tablespoon grated fresh ginger
- salt and freshly ground black pepper
- 1 head Romaine lettuce, leaves separated
- ½ cup (100 g) sliced strawberries,
 to garnish

Mix the pineapple and mangos in a large bowl.

Combine the citrus juices, vinegar, olive oil, and ginger in a jar, season to taste with salt and freshly ground black pepper, and whisk. Pour the dressing over the salad and stir to combine.

Arrange the lettuce leaves in 4 bowls to form a cup in each bowl. Divide the salad evenly among the lettuce cups. Garnish with the strawberry slices and serve.

MUSHROOM SALAD

Heat the olive oil in a saucepan over medium heat, add the mushrooms and cook for 6–7 minutes, stirring frequently.

Stir in the lime juice, tamari or soy sauce, and sugar, mix well, and cook for 2 minutes over medium heat. Reduce the heat to low, add the chili powder, ground rice, and lemongrass, and cook for another minute. Remove the pan from the heat, add the shallots, stir, and set aside for 20 minutes.

Add the scallions, cilantro, and mint to the saucepan and stir well. Transfer the salad to bowls, garnish with crushed toasted peanuts, and serve.

Preparation time: 25 minutes
Cooking time: 10 minutes, plus
   20 minutes chilling

Serves 4

- 2 tablespoons olive oil
- 9 oz (250 g) white button mushrooms, sliced
- juice of 1 lime
- 2 tablespoons tamari or soy sauce
- 1 teaspoon superfine (caster) sugar
- 1 teaspoon chili powder
- 2 tablespoons toasted and ground rice
- 1 lemongrass stalk, finely chopped
- 2 shallots, finely chopped
- 2–3 scallions (spring onions), finely chopped
- 2 tablespoons chopped cilantro (coriander)
- 2 tablespoons chopped mint
- 1 tablespoon crushed toasted peanuts, to garnish

PASTA SALAD

To make the salad, combine the pasta, pineapple, green beans, mushrooms, corn, bell pepper, red onion, apple, and olives in a large bowl.

To make the dressing, use a food processor or high speed blender to blend the vegannaise, ketchup, and orange juice until the mixture is very smooth and creamy. Season to taste with the garlic powder and salt and pepper.

Pour the dressing over the salad and toss to coat. Garnish with the mint sprigs and serve.

Preparation time: 20 minutes
Cooking time: none

Serves 4

For the salad:
- 9 oz (250 g) penne, cooked until al dente
- 9 oz (250 g) sweet pineapple, cored and diced
- 10 oz (120 g) green beans, trimmed
- 12 button mushrooms, sliced
- 1 cup (240 g) canned corn, drained
- 1 small red bell pepper, seeded and cut lengthwise into strips
- 1 red onion, cut into thin rings
- 1 red apple, cored and finely diced
- ½ cup (70 g) kalamata olives, pitted (stoned) and sliced
- 3–4 mint sprigs, to garnish

For the dressing:
- ½ cup (120 g) vegannaise (page 52) or store-bought
- 2 tablespoons ketchup
- 4 tablespoons fresh orange juice
- garlic powder
- salt and freshly ground black pepper

CHILI-MANGO BOWL

Preparation time: 20 minutes
Cooking time: none, 30 minutes chilling

Serves 4

- 3 ripe mangos, peeled and sliced
- 1 green apple, peeled, cored, and diced
- 1 fennel bulb, trimmed and finely chopped
- 2 tablespoons minced mint
- 1 red onion, finely chopped
- 1 tablespoon grated fresh ginger
- juice of 2 limes
- 1 tablespoon agave syrup
- 1 jalapeño pepper, seeded and finely chopped
- salt and freshly ground black pepper

Put the mangos, apple, fennel, mint, onion, and ginger into a large bowl. Sprinkle over the lime juice, add the agave syrup, and stir well to combine. Now sprinkle over the jalapeños and season to taste with salt and freshly ground black pepper. Refrigerate for 30 minutes before serving.

CHILI-MANGO BOWL

PEACH AND CHERRY TOMATO SALAD

Preparation time: 35 minutes
Cooking time: 5 minutes

Serves 4

- 2 shallots, thinly sliced
- 3 tablespoons red wine vinegar
- salt and freshly ground black pepper
- 1 teaspoon granulated sugar
- 1 lb 10½ oz (750 g) cherry tomatoes, halved
- 1 clove garlic, sliced
- 6 tablespoons olive oil
- 13 oz (375 g) bread, cut into bite-size cubes
- 1 lb 10½ oz (750 g) ripe white peaches, each cut into 6 wedges
- ¼ cup (6 g) basil, chopped

Preheat a broiler (grill) to medium heat.

Combine shallots and 2 tablespoons of the vinegar in a bowl, add a pinch of salt and the sugar, stir well to combine, and set aside.

Put the tomatoes, garlic, and 3 tablespoons of the oil into a large bowl and season to taste with salt. Toss to combine, then set aside.

Brush the bread on both sides with 1 tablespoon of the oil, transfer to a broiling rack, and broil (grill) for 2–3 minutes on each side. Remove from heat and set aside.

Brush the peach wedges with 1 tablespoon of the remaining oil, season to taste with salt, transfer to the broiling rack and broil for about 2 minutes, until just charred but still firm. Remove from the heat and set aside.

Put the bread cubes into a serving bowl. Add the shallots with their vinegar and toss to coat the bread. Just before serving, add the tomatoes and peaches to the bread mixture, season to taste with salt and freshly ground black pepper, and drizzle with the remaining olive oil and red wine vinegar. Mix all the ingredients well, gently stirring to coat. Garnish with basil and serve.

POTATO SALAD

Combine the chives, sour cream, vegannaise, onion powder, and turmeric in a jar and mix until smooth. Season to taste with salt and freshly ground black pepper. Cover the dressing and refrigerate.

Heat the olive oil in a skillet (frying pan) over medium heat. Add the potatoes and fry gently for about 6–7 minutes on each side, until golden brown.

To serve, divide the carrots, tomatoes, and potatoes among 4 large bowls, cover with the dressing, and garnish with the parsley.

Preparation time: 20 minutes
Cooking time: 10 minutes

Serves 4

- ¼ cup (30 g) chives, chopped
- ¼ cup (60 g) tofu sour cream
- ¼ cup (60 g) vegannaise
- 1 teaspoon onion powder
- 1 teaspoon ground turmeric
- salt and freshly ground black pepper
- 2 tablespoons olive oil
- 1 lb 2 oz (500 g) potatoes, diced and cooked
- ¼ cup (15 g) grated carrots
- 4 cherry tomatoes, halved
- 2 tablespoons chopped parsley, to garnish

QUINOA SALAD WITH MANGO DRESSING

To make the dressing, use a food processor or blender to blend the mango with the lemon juice, soy cream, and ginger until smooth.

Transfer to a bowl, stir in the lemon zest, and season to taste with salt and freshly ground black pepper. Refrigerate until ready to serve.

Cook the quinoa in salted boiling water, uncovered, for 12 minutes, until almost tender. Drain in a heatproof strainer (sieve). Add water to the same saucepan to a depth of 2 inches (5 cm) and bring to a simmer. Set the strainer over the pan above the simmering water, cover the quinoa with a clean kitchen towel and steam for 4–5 minutes, until tender. Transfer the quinoa to a large bowl and, using a fork, fluff the grains. Set aside to cool.

When the quinoa is cool, add the mixed vegetables, corn, and dressing and toss to combine. Garnish with the chopped mint and scallions.

Preparation time: 20 minutes
Cooking time: 20 minutes, plus 20 minutes chilling

Serves 4

For the dressing:
- 1 ripe mango, sliced
- 2 tablespoons fresh lemon juice
- 2 tablespoons soy cream
- 1 tablespoon finely grated fresh ginger
- 1 tablespoon finely grated lemon zest
- salt and freshly ground black pepper

For the salad:
- 2 cups (350 g) quinoa
- salt
- 2 cups (240 g) canned or frozen chopped mixed vegetables
- 1 cup (175 g) fresh or frozen corn kernels
- ½ cup (12 g) chopped mint, to garnish
- 4 scallions (spring onions), finely chopped, to garnish

RED BEAN SALAD

Preparation time: 20 minutes, plus
  overnight chilling
Cooking time: none

Serves 4

- ¼ cup (60 g) tomato purée (passata)
- juice of 1 lime
- 4 tablespoons olive oil
- 1 tablespoon white wine vinegar
- 1 tablespoon vegannaise (page 52) or
  store-bought
- 1 tablespoon Dijon mustard
- 1 teaspoon superfine (caster) sugar
- salt and freshly ground black pepper
- 1 lb 2 oz (500 g) canned red or kidney
  beans, drained
- 1 green bell pepper, seeded and finely
  diced
- 1 red bell pepper, seeded and finely diced
- 1 red onion, finely chopped
- 1 cup (170 g) cooked basmati or other
  long-grain rice rice
- 1 tablespoon chopped cilantro (coriander),
  to garnish

Put the tomato purée, lime juice, oil, vinegar, vegannaise, mustard, and sugar into a large bowl, season to taste with salt and freshly ground black pepper, and whisk until creamy. Add the red beans, bell peppers, and onion to the bowl and toss to mix. Refrigerate overnight.

To serve, stir in the rice, mix well, and garnish with chopped cilantro.

RED BEAN SALAD

ROASTED COUSCOUS SALAD WITH VEGETABLES

Preparation time: 20 minutes, plus
  30 minutes standing
Cooking time: 10 minutes

Serves 4

For the dressing:
- ½ cup (120 ml/4 fl oz) balsamic vinegar
- 1 teaspoon Dijon mustard
- 2 cloves garlic, finely chopped
- ½ cup (120 ml/4 fl oz) olive oil
- salt and freshly ground black pepper

For the salad:
- 1 red bell pepper, seeded and chopped
- 1 yellow bell pepper, seeded and chopped
- 2 zucchini (courgettes), quartered
  lengthwise and sliced
- 2 summer squash (courgettes), quartered
  lengthwise and sliced
- 6 asparagus spears, trimmed and chopped
- 4 tablespoons olive oil
- 1 lb 2 oz (500 g) medium-grain couscous
- 2 cups (475 ml/16 fl oz) vegetable stock
  (broth)
- 12 cherry tomatoes, halved
- 2 tablespoons chopped basil leaves,
  to garnish

To make the dressing, put the vinegar, mustard, and garlic into a large jar and whisk, then slowly whisk in the olive oil until combined. Season to taste with salt and freshly ground black pepper and set aside.

To make the salad, mix the bell peppers, zucchini, summer squash, and asparagus in a large bowl, pour over half the dressing, and toss to mix. Set aside for 30 minutes.

Heat 2 tablespoons of the olive oil in a skillet (frying pan), add the marinated vegetables, and cook over medium heat for 5–7 minutes, until tender. Transfer to a large bowl and set side.

Heat the remaining olive oil in a saucepan over medium heat, add the couscous, and toast for about 3–4 minutes until lightly golden brown. Cover the couscous with the stock and bring to a boil, then remove the pan from the stove. Set aside, covered, until the couscous is al dente and almost all the stock has been absorbed.

Fluff the grains of couscous with a fork, then transfer to the bowl containing the vegetables. Add the tomatoes and the remaining dressing and mix well. Serve at room temperature, garnished with the chopped basil.

ROASTED COUSCOUS SALAD WITH VEGETABLES

INDONESIAN SALAD

Preparation time: 30 minutes
Cooking time: 20 minutes

Serves 4

For the dressing:
- 2 tablespoons olive oil
- 1 onion, chopped
- 1 clove garlic, finely chopped
- ¼ cup (60 g) coconut powder
- 1 tablespoon peanut oil
- ½ cup (120 g) smooth peanut butter
- 1 teaspoon sugar
- 1 teaspoon chili powder
- 1 teaspoon ground ginger

For the salad:
- 1 cup (150 g) mung bean sprouts
- 1 head of Napa cabbage, shredded
- 2 tablespoons vegetable oil
- 4½ oz (125 g) tofu, diced
- ½ cup (120 g) sliced potatoes, cooked
- ½ cup (120 g) green beans, cooked
- ½ cup (120 g) diced carrots, cooked
- 1 cucumber, diced
- 2 tablespoons toasted peanuts, crushed, to garnish

To make the dressing, heat the olive oil in a saucepan over medium heat, add the onion and garlic, and fry gently for about 5–6 minutes, until golden brown. Add all the remaining ingredients along with 1 cup (240 ml/8 fl oz) hot water and heat for 2–3 minutes.

Using a food processor or high-speed blender, process the mixture for 2 minutes, until smooth and creamy. Refrigerate until ready to serve.

To make the salad, bring a saucepan of water to a boil. Put the mung bean sprouts and shredded cabbage into a large bowl and pour over the boiling water to cover. Leave to soak for 3–4 minutes, then drain and set aside.

Heat the vegetable oil in a skillet (frying pan) over medium heat. Add the tofu and cook for 5–6 minutes, turning the tofu pieces gently, until light brown. Remove with a slotted spoon and drain on paper towels.

Put the potatoes into the same skillet and cook for 5 minutes on each side, until light brown. Set aside.

Arrange the bean sprouts, cabbage, tofu, potatoes, and the remaining ingredients, except the garnish, in a serving bowl. Pour over the dressing. Garnish with the crushed toasted peanuts and serve immediately.

RADISH-TOMATO-MINT SALAD

Put the olive oil, lemon juice, and mustard into a large bowl, season to taste with salt and freshly ground black pepper, and mix until creamy. Stir in the radishes, cherry tomatoes, mint, and scallions. Refrigerate for 30 minutes. Garnish with the walnuts before serving.

Preparation time: 20 minutes, plus
   30 minutes chilling
Cooking time: none

Serves 4

- 4 tablespoons olive oil
- 3 teaspoons fresh lemon juice
- 1 tablespoon Dijon mustard
- salt and freshly ground black pepper
- 9 oz (250 g) radishes, sliced
- 9 oz (250 g) cherry tomatoes, halved
- 4½ oz (125 g) mint, chopped
- 4 scallions (spring onions), finely chopped
- 1 tablespoon walnuts, crushed, to garnish

CUCUMBER AND OLIVE SALAD

To make the dressing, pour the oil, soy cream, vinegar, and mustard into a jar and whisk until creamy. Season to taste with salt and freshly ground black pepper. Set aside.

To make the salad, in a large bowl, combine the cucumbers, olives, peppers, and mint and carefully stir to mix.

Pour the dressing over the salad and toss to coat. Garnish with the cilantro and serve at room temperature.

Preparation time: 30 minutes
Cooking time: none

Serves 4

For the dressing:
- 5 tablespoons olive oil
- 4 tablespoons soy cream
- 2 tablespoons red wine vinegar
- 1 tablespoon Dijon mustard
- salt and freshly ground black pepper

For the salad:
- 5 cucumbers, peeled, halved, seeded, and thinly sliced
- 1 cup (240 g) green and black olives, pitted (stoned) and sliced
- 4 pickled red peppers, sliced
- 1 tablespoon mint, chopped
- 2 tablespoons chopped cilantro (coriander), to garnish

SPINACH-SHIITAKE SALAD
WITH YUZU-WASABI DRESSING

Preparation time: 25 minutes
Cooking time: none

Serves 4

For the dressing:
- 4 tablespoons yuzu juice
- 1 tablespoon soy sauce
- 1 teaspoon wasabi purée
- 4 tablespoons vegetable oil
- 1 teaspoon whole-grain Dijon mustard
- salt and freshly ground black pepper

For the salad:
- 1 lb 2 oz (500 g) fresh shiitake mushrooms, stems removed, sliced
- 1 lb 2 oz (500 g) baby spinach
- 4½ oz (125 g) baby asparagus
- 4 radishes, thinly sliced
- ½ cup (120 g) cherry tomatoes, halved

To make the dressing, using a food processor or high-speed blender, blend the yuzu juice, soy sauce, wasabi purée, vegetable oil, and mustard until smooth. Season to taste with salt and freshly ground pepper.

To make the salad, transfer the dressing to a large bowl, add the salad ingredients, and mix gently to coat with the dressing. Serve immediately.

HOT LENTIL SALAD

Preparation time: 20 minutes
Cooking time: 35 minutes, plus
   5 minutes chilling

Serves 4

For the salad:
- 2½ cups (600 ml/20 fl oz) vegetable stock (broth)
- 2 cups (400 g) brown lentils, washed and drained
- 2 tablespoons chopped cilantro (coriander), to garnish

For the dressing:
- 3 tablespoons red wine vinegar
- 2 tablespoons vegetable oil
- 1 teaspoon salt, plus extra to season
- 2 hot red chilies, seeded and minced
- freshly ground black pepper

To make the salad, heat the stock in a large saucepan, add the lentils, and bring to a boil. Reduce the heat to medium and simmer for 30–35 minutes, until the lentils are tender. Drain the lentils and transfer to a serving bowl.

To make the dressing, whisk the vinegar, oil, 1 teaspoon salt, and chilies in a small bowl until combined. Season to taste with salt and pepper.

Mix the dressing into the lentils and leave to sit for 5 minutes. Sprinkle with the chopped cilantro and serve.

PEACH GUACAMOLE

Put the peach dice into a large bowl. Add the avocados, mint, and ginger and mix to combine.

Heat the sliced vegan bacon in a skillet (frying pan) for 3–4 minutes over medium heat, until golden brown.

Transfer the bacon to the bowl with the peaches and avocado. Add the onion, season to taste with salt and freshly ground black pepper, and mix well. Serve with tortilla chips.

Preparation time: 20 minutes
Cooking time: 5 minutes

Serves 4

- 3 ripe peaches, peeled and diced
- 2 ripe avocados, peeled and mashed
- 1 bunch of mint, chopped
- 1 tablespoon finely chopped fresh ginger
- 4 strips of vegan bacon, sliced
- 1 red onion, finely chopped
- salt and freshly ground black pepper
- tortilla chips, to serve

SEASONED SPINACH SALAD

To make the salad, bring a large saucepan of water to a boil. Put the spinach or kale into a steamer basket or heatproof strainer (sieve) and steam for 5 minutes until bright green. Strain and squeeze out as much water as possible. Chop the spinach or kale removing, any hard stems.

To make the dressing, combine the soy sauce, sesame oil, black sesame seeds, garlic, galangal, sugar, white wine vinegar, and gochugaru and stir well. Season to taste with salt and pepper.

Put the chopped spinach or kale into a large bowl. Stir in the grated daikon and the dressing, mix well, and serve immediately.

Preparation time: 30 minutes
Cooking time: 5 minutes

Serves 4

For the salad:
- 1 lb 2 oz (500 g) spinach or kale
- 1 daikon radish, grated

For the dressing:
- 3 tablespoons soy sauce
- 2 tablespoons sesame oil
- 1 tablespoon black sesame seeds
- 2 cloves garlic, minced
- 1 tablespoon grated galangal
- 1 teaspoon superfine (caster) sugar
- 1 tablespoon white wine vinegar
- 1 teaspoon gochugaru (Korean red chili powder)
- salt and freshly ground black pepper

SOUPS

BEAN AND COCONUT SOUP

Preparation time: 30 minutes
Cooking time: 20 minutes

Serves 4

- 1 tablespoon vegetable oil
- ½ cup (75 g) chopped onion
- 1 cup (200 g) chopped tomatoes
- ½ cup (90 g) chopped green bell pepper
- 1 tablespoon curry powder
- 3 tablespoons vegetable margarine
- salt and freshly ground black pepper
- 2 cups (480 g) canned kidney beans
- 2 cups (475 ml/16 fl oz) coconut milk
- 1 cup (250 g) cooked basmati or
  jasmine rice
- 4 tablespoons shredded fresh coconut

Heat the oil in a stockpot, add the onion, and sauté over medium heat for about 5–6 minutes, until softened. Add the tomatoes, bell peppers, curry powder, and margarine and season to taste with salt and freshly ground black pepper. Simmer for 3–4 minutes. Add the beans with their canning liquid along with the coconut milk. Simmer gently over low heat for 10 minutes.

Stir in the rice and heat for about 2 minutes. Ladle the soup into bowls. Top each bowl with 1 tablespoon shredded fresh coconut and serve.

BUTTERNUT SQUASH AND APPLE SOUP

Preparation time: 20 minutes
Cooking time: 35 minutes

Serves 4

- 2 cups (475 ml/16 fl oz) vegetable stock
  (broth)
- 1 cup (240 ml/8 fl oz) coconut milk
- 3 cups (720 g) peeled and chopped
  butternut squash
- 4 green apples, peeled, cored, and chopped
- 1 teaspoon ground nutmeg
- 1 teaspoon ground allspice
- 1 tablespoon coconut oil
- 1 cup (125 g) pecans, chopped

Heat the stock and coconut milk in a stockpot over medium heat until simmering. Add the squash and apple, raise the heat to medium-high, bring to a boil, and cook for 2 minutes. Decrease the heat to low and cook at a low simmer for 30 minutes, until the squash is tender.

Add the nutmeg and allspice to the soup, then remove the pot from the heat and set aside to cool.

Heat the coconut oil in a saucepan over medium heat, add the pecans, and cook for 2–3 minutes, until golden brown. Set aside.

In a food processor or high-speed blender, purée the soup in batches until smooth. Return the soup to the pot and bring to a boil. Immediately remove from the heat and ladle into bowls. Garnish with the toasted pecans and serve.

BROCCOLI SOUP WITH GINGER AND LIME

Preheat the oven to 400°F/200°C/Gas Mark 6.

Put the broccoli florets into an ovenproof dish, add 1 tablespoon of the olive oil, and toss to coat. Bake for 20 minutes, until tender. Remove from the oven and set aside.

Heat the remaining olive oil in a saucepan over medium heat, add the shallot, and stir fry for 4 minutes, until the shallot has softened. Add the ginger and cook for another 2 minutes. Add the broccoli stems, broth, and lemon zest and juice. Season to taste with salt and freshly ground black pepper, then bring to a simmer and cook for about 10 minutes, until the broccoli stems are tender.

Add the broccoli florets and bring to a boil, then remove the pan from the heat and set aside to cool for 20 minutes.

In a food processor or high-speed blender, purée the soup in batches until smooth. Return the soup to the saucepan, add the coconut milk, and bring to a boil, stirring frequently. Then immediately remove the saucepan from the heat.

Ladle the soup into bowls, garnish with the scallions and white sesame seeds, and serve.

Preparation time: 25 minutes
Cooking time: 35 minutes, plus
 20 minutes chilling

Serves 4

- 2 heads of broccoli, trimmed and separated into florets, stems reserved
- 2 tablespoons olive oil
- 1 shallot, finely chopped
- 1 tablespoon finely grated fresh ginger
- 3 cups (750 ml/25 fl oz) vegetable stock (broth)
- 1 teaspoon finely grated lemon zest
- 2 tablespoons fresh lemon juice
- salt and freshly ground black pepper
- ½ cup (120 ml/4 fl oz) coconut milk
- 2 scallions (spring onions), finely chopped, to garnish
- 1 tablespoon white sesame seeds, to garnish

CABBAGE AND GINGER SOUP

Heat the olive oil in a stockpot over medium heat. Add the scallions, ginger, and garlic and stir fry for 3–4 minutes, until fragrant. Add the tamari or soy sauce and miso and cook for another 2 minutes, stirring constantly. Add the stock and bring to a boil. Immediately reduce the heat to low and simmer, then add the ramen noodles. Cook for 4 minutes, then add the shredded cabbage. Cook for another 5 minutes until the ramen and cabbage are tender.

Ladle the soup into bowls, garnish with the tofu, sesame oil, crushed chili flakes, and sesame seeds, and serve.

Preparation time: 25 minutes
Cooking time: 15 minutes

Serves 4

- 1 tablespoon olive oil
- 2 scallions (spring onions), finely chopped
- 2 tablespoons grated fresh ginger
- 1 clove garlic, finely chopped
- 2 tablespoons tamari or soy sauce
- 1 tablespoon clear miso
- 4 cups (960 ml/32 fl oz) vegetable stock (broth)
- 1 lb 2 oz (500 g) ramen noodles
- 2 cups (200 g) shredded Napa cabbage
- 4 tablespoons silken tofu, to garnish
- 4 teaspoons toasted sesame oil, to garnish
- 1 teaspoon crushed red chili flakes, to garnish
- 1 tablespoon white sesame seeds, to garnish

BLACK BEAN AND MANGO SOUP

Preparation time: 20 minutes
Cooking time: 25 minutes

Serves 4

- 1 tablespoon vegetable oil
- 1 large onion, chopped
- 2 cloves garlic, minced
- 2 medium sweet potatoes, peeled and diced
- 1 large red bell pepper, seeded and diced
- ½ cup (110 g) canned plum tomatoes
- 1 small hot green chili, chopped
- 1½ cups (350 ml/12 fl oz) vegetable stock (broth)
- 1 cup (220 g) canned black beans, drained
- salt and freshly ground black pepper
- 1 ripe mango, diced
- ¼ cup (12 g) chopped cilantro (coriander), to garnish

Heat the oil in a large saucepan over medium heat. Add the onion and cook, stirring often, for about 5 minutes, until softened. Stir in the garlic and cook, stirring, for 3–4 minutes, until the onion and garlic are golden. Stir in the sweet potatoes, bell peppers, the tomatoes with their juice, the chili, and the stock. Bring to a boil, then reduce the heat to low, cover the pan, and simmer for 15 minutes, until the sweet potatoes are tender.

Stir in the beans and simmer gently, uncovered, until they are heated through. Season to taste with salt and freshly ground black pepper. Stir in the mangos and cook until they are heated through, about 1 minute.

Ladle the soup into bowls, garnish with cilantro, and serve.

BLACK BEAN AND MANGO SOUP

CILANTRO SOUP

Preparation time: 20 minutes
Cooking time: 40 minutes, plus
  15 minutes chilling

Serves 4

- 2 tablespoons olive oil
- 2 onions, finely chopped
- 2 cloves garlic, finely chopped
- 2 tomatoes, finely chopped
- 3 potatoes, peeled diced
- 1 teaspoon sweet paprika
- 3 cups (750 ml/25 fl oz) vegetable stock
  (broth)
- 1 green bell pepper, halved and seeded
- 1 bunch of cilantro (coriander), stems tied
  together with kitchen string
- 1 cup (225 g) long-grain rice
- salt and freshly ground black pepper

Heat 1 tablespoon of the olive oil in a stockpot over medium heat. Add the onion and stir fry gently for 5–6 minutes, until the onion is translucent. Add the garlic, tomatoes, and potatoes and continue to cook for 4–5 minutes, until the potatoes are tender but firm.

Sprinkle the paprika over the mixture, stir well, then add the stock, green bell pepper, and cilantro and bring to a boil. Immediately reduce the heat to low and simmer for 15 minutes. Add the rice and cook for another 15 minutes, until the rice is tender. Take the pan off the heat. Remove and reserve the cilantro and green pepper. Cover the pan with a lid and leave the soup to cool for 15 minutes.

Meanwhile, separate the cilantro stems from the leaves and discard the stems. Using a food processor or high-speed blender, blend the green pepper and cilantro leaves until smooth. Add the remaining olive oil and season to taste with salt and freshly ground black pepper. Blend again for 1 minute to combine.

Ladle the soup into large bowls, top with the cilantro–green bell pepper coulis, and serve.

CILANTRO SOUP

COLD CUCUMBER AND SESAME SOUP

Preparation time: 20 minutes, plus 1½ hours
  standing and chilling
Cooking time: none

Serves 4

- 1 lb 10½ oz (750 g) cucumbers, thinly sliced
  on a mandoline
- 2 teaspoons salt
- 2 tablespoons toasted white sesame seeds
- 3 tablespoons clear miso
- 2 teaspoons agave or maple syrup
- 2½ cups (550 ml/18½ fl oz) vegetable
  stock (broth)
- 3 cups (750 g) hot cooked short-grain rice
- 2 teaspoons *shichimi togarashi* (Japanese
  spice blend)
- 2¼ oz (60 g) shiso or mint, finely chopped,
  to garnish
- tamari or soy sauce

Put the cucumbers into a bowl and sprinkle over the salt. Mix well, then set aside for 30 minutes.

Using your hands, squeeze out excess water from the cucumbers and set aside.

Using a mortar and pestle or high-speed blender, grind the sesame seeds into a paste. Add the miso and agave or maple syrup and blend until smooth. Pour the sesame-miso sauce over the cucumbers and add the stock. Stir to combine, then refrigerate for 1 hour.

To serve, fill a serving bowl with the rice, add the soup, and top with *shichimi togarashi*. Garnish with shiso or mint, and season to taste with tamari or soy sauce before serving.

PUMPKIN SOUP

Preparation time: 25 minutes
Cooking time: 1 hour 10 minutes, plus
  20 minutes chilling

Serves 4

- 2 tablespoons vegetable margarine
- 1 onion, chopped
- 1 clove garlic, crushed
- 2 cups (440 g) peeled and chopped
  pumpkin
- ½ cup (120 ml/4 fl oz) fresh orange juice
- 2 tablespoons finely grated orange zest
- 1 teaspoon ground nutmeg
- 3 cups (750 ml/25 fl oz) vegetable stock
  (broth)
- salt and freshly ground black pepper
- 2 teaspoons black sesame seeds,
  to garnish

Heat the margarine in a large stockpot over medium heat. Add the onion and garlic and sauté for about 5–6 minutes until soft. Add the pumpkin and cook over low heat, stirring frequently, for about 12 minutes, until tender. Stir in the orange juice, zest, and nutmeg, then add the stock and bring to a boil. Reduce the heat to medium and simmer for 30 minutes.

Once the cooking time has elapsed, season to taste with salt and pepper, then remove the pan from the heat and set aside for 20 minutes to cool. Transfer the mixture to a food processor or high-speed blender and purée in batches, until smooth. Return the soup to the pot and bring to a boil, reduce the heat to a low simmer, and cook for about 20 minutes, until the soup has reduced in volume by half.

Ladle the soup into bowls and sprinkle 1 teaspoon black sesame seeds over each serving to garnish.

VEGETABLE SOUP

SOUTH AFRICA

Heat the vegetable margarine in a stockpot over low heat. Add the carrots, potato, and onion and cook for about 15 minutes, until soft. Add the sugar and tomatoes and cook for another 5 minutes. Stir in the stock and bring to a boil. Reduce the heat to medium and simmer for 30 minutes, until the vegetables are cooked through.

Remove the pot from the heat and set aside for 20 minutes to cool. Transfer the mixture to a food processor or high-speed blender and purée, in batches, until smooth. Return the soup to the pot, put it back on the stove over medium heat, and stir in the sherry. Bring to a boil, then reduce the heat to medium and simmer for about 20 minutes, until the soup has reduced in volume by half. Take the pot off the heat, and season to taste with salt and pepper.

Ladle the soup into bowls and sprinkle 1 teaspoon black sesame seeds over each serving to garnish.

Preparation time: 25 minutes
Cooking time: 1 hour 10 minutes, plus
  20 minutes chilling

Serves 4

- 2 tablespoons vegetable margarine
- 3 large carrots, chopped
- 1 potato, chopped
- 1 onion, chopped
- 1 teaspoon granulated sugar
- 6 tomatoes, chopped
- 3 cups (750 ml/25 fl oz) vegetable stock (broth)
- 2 tablespoons dry sherry
- salt and freshly ground black pepper
- 2 teaspoons black sesame seeds, to garnish

ROOT VEGETABLE AND CABBAGE SOUP

NORWAY

Heat a slick of olive oil in a large stockpot over medium heat. Add the onion, garlic, celery, leeks, and a pinch of salt and sauté for 5 minutes, until the vegetables are translucent. Stir in the barley, then add the stock, bay leaves, and thyme, stir well, and bring to a boil. Add all the root vegetables and the cabbage and bring back to a boil, then immediately reduce the heat to a low simmer, and cook for 30 minutes until all the vegetables are tender.

Add the kale or Swiss chard and nutmeg to the pot, season to taste with salt and freshly ground pepper, and simmer for another 5–6 minutes.

Ladle the soup into bowls, garnish with parsley, and serve with lemon wedges and bread on the side.

Preparation time: 25 minutes
Cooking time: 40 minutes

Serves 4

- olive oil
- 1 onion, chopped
- 3 cloves garlic, finely chopped
- 1 celery stalk, diced
- 1 leek, white part only, thinly sliced
- salt and freshly ground black pepper
- 1 cup (200 g) barley, soaked overnight in cold water, drained
- 6¼ cups (1.5 liters/50 fl oz) vegetable stock (broth)
- 2 bay leaves
- handful of thyme sprigs
- 2 carrots, diced
- 2 parsnips, diced
- 1 small celery root (celeriac), diced
- ½ small rutabaga (swede), diced
- 1 turnip, diced
- 1 beet (beetroot), diced
- ½ head of small red cabbage, shredded
- 1 cup (225 g) kale or Swiss chard, chopped
- a pinch freshly ground nutmeg
- 1 tablespoon chopped parsley, to garnish
- 4 lemon wedges, to garnish
- sliced bread, to serve

MATZO BALL SOUP

Preparation time: 25 minutes
Cooking time: 45 minutes

Serves 4

For the matzo balls:
- 1 lb 2 oz (500 g) silken tofu
- 4 tablespoons olive oil
- 9 oz (250 g) matzo meal
- 2 tablespoons nutritional yeast
- 1 teaspoon baking powder
- 1 teaspoon onion powder
- 1 teaspoon garlic powder
- 1 teaspoon celery seeds
- salt and freshly ground black pepper

For the soup:
- 2 tablespoons olive oil
- 1 onion, chopped
- 2 carrots, sliced
- 2 celery stalks, chopped
- 2 tablespoons chopped dill
- 6¼ cups (1.5 liters/50 fl oz) vegetable stock (broth)
- salt and freshly ground black pepper
- 2 tablespoons fresh lemon juice
- 2 tablespoons chopped parsley, to garnish

To make the matzo ball dough using a food processor or high-speed blender, blend the tofu and olive oil. Transfer the mixture to a large bowl and stir in the matzo meal, nutritional yeast, baking powder, onion powder, garlic powder, and celery seeds. Season to taste with salt and freshly ground black pepper and stir well. Put the dough into an airtight container and refrigerate overnight.

Heat the olive oil in a large stockpot over medium heat. Add the onion, carrots, and celery and sauté for 5–6 minutes, until the onion is soft. Add the dill and stock, bring to a boil, then immediately reduce the heat to low and maintain a simmer.

Using your hands or a soup spoon, shape the dough into 2-inch (5 cm) balls. Carefully drop the dumplings into the soup, trying to not break them. Cover the pot and cook the soup at a low simmer for 40 minutes. Remove the pot from the heat, season the soup to taste with salt and freshly ground black pepper, and stir in the lemon juice. Garnish with the parsley and serve immediately.

MATZO BALL SOUP

JUNIPER BERRY SOUP

Preparation time: 30 minutes
Cooking time: 35 minutes

Serves 4

- 2¼ lb (1 kg) black juniper berries,
  stems removed
- strips of zest of 1 lemon
- 1 green apple, cored and thinly sliced
- 1 cup (220 g) Agen prunes, pitted (stoned)
  and chopped
- 2 tablespoons tapioca
- 4 tablespoons fresh lemon juice
- ¾ cup (175 ml/6 fl oz) agave
  or maple syrup

Put 3 cups (710 ml/24 fl oz) water into a saucepan. Add the juniper berries and lemon zest and bring to a boil, then reduce the heat to medium and simmer for about 20 minutes.

Strain out the cooked berries through a strainer (sieve) and discard. Return the liquid to the saucepan and bring back to a boil. Add the apples and prunes and stir well.

Put the tapioca into a small bowl, add 2 tablespoons of the soup, and whisk until completely dissolved. Slowly add the slurry to the boiling soup, reduce the heat to medium-low, and simmer for 15 minutes, until thickened.

Remove the saucepan from the heat, stir in the lemon juice and agave or maple syrup, and ladle into bowls.

MISO, LENTIL, AND PUMPKIN SOUP

Preparation time: 15 minutes
Cooking time: 10 minutes, plus
  20 minutes chilling

Serves 4

- 3 tablespoons olive oil
- 1 onion, chopped
- 1 clove garlic, finely chopped
- 1½ teaspoons cumin seeds
- 1 tablespoon grated fresh ginger
- 1 chili, finely chopped
- 2 carrots, coarsely chopped
- 3¼ lb (1.5 kg) pumpkin, chopped
- ½ cup (100 g) brown lentils
- 2 cups (475 ml/16 fl oz) vegetable stock
  (broth)
- 1 (3-inch/7½ cm) cinnamon stick
- 3 tablespoons *shiromiso* (white miso paste)
- 2 tablespoons micro greens, to garnish

Heat the oil in a stockpot over low heat, add the onion and garlic, and cook for 3–4 minutes, until golden brown. Add the cumin, ginger, and chili and cook for 3–4 minutes, until fragrant. Add the carrots, pumpkin, and lentils and stir well to coat them in the onion mixture. Pour in the stock and add the cinnamon. Bring to a boil, then reduce the heat to medium-low and cook for 30–35 minutes, until the lentils are cooked.

Remove from the heat and discard the cinnamon stick. Set aside for 20 minutes to cool.

Transfer the soup to a food processor or high-speed blender, add 1 cup (240 ml/8 fl oz) of water and process until smooth. Transfer the soup back to the stockpot, and heat, over medium heat, until simmering. Remove from the heat and slowly stir in the *shiromiso*. Ladle the soup into bowls, top with the micro greens, and serve.

VEGETABLE GAZPACHO

Using a food processor or high-speed blender, purée the tomatoes, celery, green bell pepper, cucumber, red onion, and balsamic vinegar for 3 minutes, until smooth. Transfer to a large bowl and season to taste with salt and freshly ground black pepper. Cover and refrigerate.

Heat 2 tablespoons of the olive oil in a stockpot over medium heat, add the onion and garlic, and stir fry gently for 4–5 minutes, until golden brown. Add the carrots and cook for 3 minutes, stirring frequently, then add the green peas and cook for another 3 minutes. Pour in the stock, bring to a simmer, and cook over low heat for 8 minutes, until the vegetables are tender. Remove from the heat and set aside to cool for 20 minutes.

Add the carrot-pea mixture and breadcrumbs to the chilled soup, stir to combine, and refrigerate for 1 hour.

Season to taste with salt and freshly ground black pepper. Ladle the soup into bowls, drizzle the remaining olive oil, and serve garnished with the herbs.

Preparation time: 20 minutes
Cooking time: 20 minutes, plus
   20 minutes chilling

Serves 4

- 3 tomatoes, chopped
- 2 celery stalks, finely chopped
- 1 green bell pepper, seeded and chopped
- 2 cucumbers, diced
- ¼ cup (40 g) finely chopped red onion
- 4 tablespoons balsamic vinegar
- salt and freshly ground black pepper
- 5 tablespoons olive oil
- 2 onions, chopped
- 3 cloves garlic, finely chopped
- ½ cup (75 g) sliced carrots
- ½ cup (75 g) green peas
- 3 cups (710 ml/24 fl oz) vegetable stock (broth)
- ½ cup (45 g) breadcrumbs
- 1 cup (30 g) baby spinach leaves, to garnish
- 1 tablespoon fresh basil, chopped, to garnish
- 1 tablespoon fresh oregano, chopped, to garnish

SPICY MUSHROOM SOUP

Pour the stock into a large stockpot and bring to a boil over high heat. Stir in the sriracha, reduce the heat to medium, and add the lemongrass, kaffir lime leaves, sugar, lemon juice, mushrooms, and chilies. Simmer for 10–12 minutes, stirring frequently, until the mushrooms are cooked. Mix in tamari or soy sauce to taste.

Ladle the soup into bowls, garnish with the cilantro, and serve.

Preparation time: 20 minutes
Cooking time: 15 minutes

Serves 4

- 3 cups (710 ml/24 fl oz) vegetable stock (broth)
- 2 teaspoons sriracha or similar sauce
- 2 lemongrass stalks, finely sliced into rings
- 4 kaffir lime leaves
- 1 teaspoon palm sugar
- 2 tablespoons fresh lemon juice
- 1 lb 2 oz (500 g) oyster mushrooms, chopped
- 9 oz (250 g) shiitake mushrooms, stems removed, quartered
- 2 green chilies, seeded and finely chopped
- tamari or soy sauce
- ⅛ cup (15 g) cilantro (coriander), to garnish

PEANUT BUTTER AND CELERY CREAM SOUP

Preparation time: 25 minutes
Cooking time: 30 minutes

Serves 4

- 2 cups (475 ml/16 fl oz) vegetable stock (broth)
- 2 celery roots (celeriac), chopped
- 2 tablespoons vegetable margarine
- 1 onion, finely chopped
- 4 celery stalks, finely chopped
- 2 tablespoons all-purpose (plain) flour
- 3 tablespoons crunchy peanut butter
- 2 cups (475 ml/16 fl oz) soy cream
- salt and freshly ground black pepper
- 1 teaspoon sweet paprika

Pour the stock into a large stockpot and bring to a boil. Add the celery root and cook over high heat for 20 minutes, until tender. Strain out and discard the celery root, reserving the stock.

Heat the vegetable margarine in a large saucepan over medium heat, add the onion, and sauté for 3–4 minutes, until golden brown. Add the celery and cook over medium heat for another 3 minutes, then stir in the flour until incorporated. Add the peanut butter and mix well, then mix in the soy cream and reserved stock. Bring to a boil, then immediately reduce the heat to medium and simmer for 3–4 minutes. Season to taste with salt and freshly ground black pepper.

Ladle the soup into bowls, sprinkle with paprika, and serve.

POTATO AND HORSERADISH CREAM SOUP

Preparation time: 20 minutes
Cooking time: 35 minutes,

Serves 4

- 2 tablespoons olive oil
- 9 oz (250 g) smoked tofu, diced
- 2 tablespoons vegetable margarine
- 9 oz (250 g) celery root (celeriac), chopped
- 1 lb (450 g) potatoes, diced
- 3 leeks, white and pale green parts only, chopped
- 2 onions, chopped
- 2 bay leaves
- 1 teaspoon thyme, finely chopped
- 6¼ cups (1.5 liters/50 fl oz) vegetable stock (broth)
- ½ cup (120 ml/4 fl oz) soy whipping cream
- ¼ cup (30 g) grated horseradish root
- salt and freshly ground black pepper
- 2 scallions (spring onions), sliced, to garnish

Heat the olive oil in a large stockpot over medium heat. Add the tofu and sauté for 4–5 minutes, until golden brown on all sides. Drain the tofu on paper towels and set aside.

Melt the margarine in the olive oil that remains in the pot, add the celery root, potatoes, leeks, onion, bay leaves, and thyme, and sauté over medium heat for about 5 minutes, until the vegetables are softened. Add the stock, stir, and bring to a boil. Reduce the heat to low, cover, and simmer the soup for 25 minutes, stirring occasionally, until the potatoes are tender. Remove from the heat and let the soup cool in the pot for 20 minutes.

Discard the bay leaves. Transfer the soup to a food processor or high-speed blender and purée until smooth. Return the soup to the pot, stir in the soy cream, horseradish, and tofu, and bring to a boil. Immediately reduce the heat to low and simmer for 4 minutes, until slightly thickened.

Season to taste with salt and pepper, ladle into bowls, garnish with the sliced scallions, and serve.

PUMPKIN SOUP WITH SWEET BASIL

Heat the oil in a medium stockpot over medium heat, add the garlic, and gently stir fry for 4–5 minutes, until golden brown. Add the pumpkin and stock and bring to a boil. Reduce the heat to low, cover the pot with a lid, and simmer for 25 minutes, until the pumpkin is tender.

Add tamari or soy sauce to taste, then remove the pot from the heat and let cool for 15 minutes. Transfer the soup to a food processor or high-speed blender and purée until smooth.

Ladle the soup into bowls and garnish with the sesame oil and basil.

Preparation time: 20 minutes
Cooking time: 30 minutes, plus 15 minutes chilling

Serves 4

- 2 tablespoons peanut oil
- 3 cloves garlic, finely chopped
- 3 pounds (1.4 kg) kabocha or another winter squash, peeled and diced
- 4 cups (960 ml/32 fl oz) vegetable stock (broth)
- tamari or soy sauce
- 1 tablespoon toasted sesame oil, to garnish
- ½ cup (12 g) sweet basil, finely chopped, to garnish

ROASTED CAULIFLOWER SOUP

Preheat the oven to 425°F/220°C/Gas Mark 7.

Arrange the cauliflower in a single layer on a baking sheet. Drizzle 2 tablespoons of the olive oil over the florets, toss to coat, and roast for 30 minutes, stirring halfway through the cooking time, until the cauliflower is caramelized.

Meanwhile, heat the remaining olive oil in a medium stockpot over medium heat. Add the onion and stir fry gently for 5 minutes, until fragrant and translucent. Add the garlic and thyme and cook for another 2 minutes. Pour in the stock and bring to a boil, then reduce the heat to low and simmer until the cauliflower has finished roasting.

Reserve a few smaller cauliflower florets for garnish. Transfer the remaining florets and the soup mixture to a food processor or high-speed blender and purée until smooth. Return the soup to the pot, bring to a boil over medium-high heat, then reduce the heat to low. Stir in the soy cream, if using, and simmer for another 5 minutes. Season to taste with salt and freshly ground black pepper.

Meanwhile, toast the slices of bread in a toaster until golden brown. Rub the cut sides of the garlic clove halves across the toast, then return the bread to the toaster and toast for 1 minute. Chop the bread slices into cubes.

Ladle the soup into bowls, garnish with cubes of toasted garlic bread, and serve.

Preparation time: 25 minutes
Cooking time: 45 minutes

Serves 4

- 3 cups (240 g) cauliflower florets
- 3 tablespoons olive oil
- 1 yellow onion, finely chopped
- 2 cloves garlic, finely chopped, plus 1 clove halved lengthwise for toasted bread
- 1 teaspoon thyme leaves
- 3 cups (710 ml/24 fl oz) vegetable stock (broth)
- ½ cup (120 ml/4 fl oz) soy cream (optional)
- salt and freshly ground black pepper
- 4 slices of bread

ROASTED PUMPKIN AND RED LENTIL SOUP

Preparation time: 35 minutes
Cooking time: 1 hour

Serves 4

- 3 cups (710 ml/24 fl oz) vegetable stock (broth)
- 1 cup (240 g) red lentils, soaked in water overnight and drained
- 2 teaspoons ground turmeric
- 1¼ teaspoons ground cumin
- 1 tablespoon grated fresh ginger
- 1 teaspoon freshly ground black pepper, plus more as needed
- 1 teaspoon salt, plus more as needed
- 6 tablespoons olive oil
- 2¼ lb (1 kg) Hokkaido pumpkin, peeled and diced
- 1 onion, quartered
- 1 head of garlic, unpeeled
- 1 lemon, cut into 6 wedges
- 3 sprigs sage, halved
- ¼ cup (6 g) finely chopped parsley
- 1 teaspoon sweet paprika, to garnish

Preheat the oven to 440°F/230°C/Gas Mark 7½. Line a rimmed baking sheet with parchment paper.

Pour the stock into a large saucepan, add the lentils, and bring to a boil, then reduce the heat to medium and simmer for 30 minutes, until the lentils are tender.

Combine the turmeric, 1 teaspoon of the cumin, the ginger, 1 teaspoon freshly ground black pepper, salt, and 2 tablespoons of the olive oil in a large mixing bowl. Add the pumpkin and onion chunks and mix well xto coat the vegetables in the spices. Transfer the pumpkin and onion to the prepared baking sheet and tuck the head of garlic and the lemon wedges in between the pumpkin and onion pieces. Arrange the sage around the pumpkin cubes. Bake for about 15 minutes, then remove the garlic and set aside. Return the other vegetables to the oven and bake for another 15 minutes.

Discard the sage and peel the baked garlic. Scrape the pulp from the lemon wedges, removing the seeds. Reserve the peel. Using a food processor or high-speed blender, blend the garlic, lemon pulp, pumpkin, and onion in batches until smooth. Season to taste with salt and freshly ground black pepper.

Finely chop the reserved roasted lemon peel. Heat the remaining olive oil in a small saucepan over medium heat. Stir in the parsley, lemon peel, paprika, and the remaining cumin. As the spices release their aroma, remove the pan from the heat.

Ladle the soup into bowls, garnish with the spiced parsley and lemon peel, and serve.

ROASTED PUMPKIN AND RED LENTIL SOUP

WILD MUSHROOM AND POTATO SOUP

Preparation time: 30 minutes
Cooking time: 35 minutes

Serves 4

- 2 tablespoons olive oil
- 2 tablespoons vegetable margarine
- 1 lb 10½ oz (750 g) wild mushrooms, roughly chopped
- 4 tablespoons dry white wine
- 6 russet potatoes, diced
- 4 cups (960 ml/32 fl oz) vegetable stock (broth)
- 2 tablespoons vegetable oil
- 1 onion, finely chopped
- 1 cup (240 g) smoked tofu, diced
- 1 cup (240 ml) soy cream
- 1 teaspoon sweet Hungarian paprika
- salt and freshly ground black pepper
- 4 tablespoons unsweetened vegan Greek yogurt, to garnish
- 2–3 dill sprigs, fronds chopped, to garnish

Heat the olive oil and margarine in a stockpot over medium heat. Add the mushrooms and sauté for 5–6 minutes, stirring frequently. Add the white wine, stir to combine, then add the potatoes and stock and bring to a boil. Immediately reduce the heat to medium and simmer for about 15–20 minutes, until the potatoes are cooked. Using a slotted spoon, transfer three-quarters of the potatoes to a food processor or high-speed blender and purée until smooth. Return the puréed potatoes to the pot.

While the potatoes are cooking, heat the vegetable oil in a saucepan over medium heat. Add the onion and tofu and stir fry gently for 7–8 minutes, until the tofu is golden brown on all sides. Add the onion-tofu mixture, soy cream, and paprika to the soup and stir to combine. Season to taste with salt and freshly ground black pepper. Ladle the soup into bowls, garnish with yogurt and dill, and serve.

WILD MUSHROOM AND POTATO SOUP

TOFU AND RICE NOODLE SOUP

Preparation time: 20 minutes
Cooking time: 10 minutes

Serves 4

- 1 lb 2 oz (500 g) rice noodles
- 3 cups (710 ml/24 fl oz) vegetable stock (broth)
- 1 tablespoon grated fresh ginger
- 2 tablespoons canola (rapeseed) oil
- 3 cloves garlic, finely chopped
- 9 oz (250 g) smoked tofu, diced
- 1 lb 2 oz (500 g) baby bok choy, trimmed
- 2 teaspoons toasted sesame oil, to garnish
- 1 cup (35 g) bean sprouts, to garnish

Cook the rice noodles according to the packet instructions. Rinse under cold water, drain, and set aside.

Pour the stock into a large pot, add the ginger, and bring to a boil. Reduce the heat to low and simmer for 5 minutes. Set aside.

Heat the canola oil in a skillet (frying pan) over medium heat, add the garlic, and stir fry gently for 2 minutes, until light golden. Remove the skillet from the heat and set aside.

Return the stock to a boil over medium heat. Add the smoked tofu and baby bok choy and cook for 2–3 minutes. Add the noodles and bring to a boil.

Ladle the soup into bowls, garnish with sesame oil, fried garlic, and sprouts, and serve.

TOFU AND RICE NOODLE SOUP

TOMATO GAZPACHO

Preparation time: 25 minutes, plus
  1 hour chilling
Cooking time: none

Serves 4

- 2¼ lb (1 kg) plum tomatoes, coarsely
  chopped
- ½ cup (120 ml/4 fl oz) olive oil, plus extra
  to garnish
- 1 teaspoon unrefined sugar
- ½ baguette, crust removed, cut into
  small pieces
- salt
- 2 cucumbers, roughly chopped
- 1 red bell pepper, seeded and roughly
  chopped
- 4 cloves garlic, roughly chopped
- 4 tablespoons white balsamic vinegar
- a handful of basil leaves, to garnish

Using a food processor or high-speed blender, blend the tomatoes until smooth. Transfer the tomatoes to a bowl, add the olive oil, sugar, and bread, season to taste with salt, and set aside at room temperature for 1 hour.

Return the mixture to the food processor or high-speed blender, add the cucumber, bell peppers, garlic, and vinegar, and process for 2–3 minutes until smooth. Transfer the gazpacho to a large bowl, cover, and refrigerate for at least 1 hour or until completely chilled.

Ladle the soup into bowls, garnish with basil and a drizzle of olive oil, and serve.

TOMATO SOUP

Preparation time: 20 minutes
Cooking time: 30 minutes

Serves 4

- 2¼ lb (1 kg) Italian plum tomatoes, cut
  into eighths
- 3 cups (710 ml/24 fl oz) vegetable stock
  (broth)
- 1 onion, chopped
- 1 celery stalk, chopped
- 1 tablespoon nutritional yeast
- 1 tablespoon tomato purée (passata)
- 1 teaspoon dried basil
- salt and freshly ground black pepper
- 2 tablespoons soy cream or unsweetened
  soy yogurt, to garnish
- 2 tablespoons chopped parsley, to garnish

In a large stockpot set over medium-high heat, combine the tomatoes with the stock and bring to a boil. Add the onion, celery, nutritional yeast, tomato purée, and basil. Stir, reduce the heat to low, and simmer for 30 minutes, until the vegetables are soft.

Transfer the soup to a food processor or high-speed blender and process until completely smooth. Strain the soup to remove the tomato skin and seeds.

Season to taste with salt and freshly ground black pepper, then ladle into bowls and garnish with soy cream or yogurt and parsley.

SMOKED TEMPEH NOODLE SOUP

Pour the stock into a stockpot and bring to a boil over high heat. Add the rice noodles, stir well, remove from the heat, and set aside for 15 minutes. Drain the noodles, reserving the stock, and divide the noodles among 4 bowls.

Return the stock to the pot and bring to a boil over high heat. Add the tempeh, reduce the heat to low, and simmer for 10 minutes until the tempeh is cooked through. Remove the tempeh with a slotted spoon and divide it among the 4 soup bowls.

Combine the bean sprouts, cabbage, scallions, and cilantro in a large bowl, then divide them among the 4 soup bowls.

Bring the stock back to a boil, add tamari or soy sauce to taste, and ladle the soup in the bowls.

Garnish with the peanuts and chilies and serve with lime wedges alongside.

Preparation time: 25 minutes
Cooking time: 30 minutes

Serves 4

- 6 cups (1.4 liters/48 fl oz) vegetable stock (broth)
- 1 lb 2 oz (500 g) rice noodles
- 1½ cups (360 g) smoked tempeh, diced
- 3 cups (100 g) bean sprouts
- ½ cup (120 g) shredded Napa cabbage
- ½ cup (12 g) chopped scallions (spring onions)
- ½ cup (12 g) cilantro (coriander), coarsely chopped
- tamari or soy sauce
- 3 tablespoons toasted peanuts, crushed, to garnish
- 3 red or green chilies, seeded and finely sliced into rounds, to garnish
- 1 lime, cut into 4 wedges, to serve

ZUCCHINI-MANGO-WALNUT-BASIL GAZPACHO

Heat the oil in a large saucepan over medium-high heat. Add the shallots and fry gently, stirring occasionally, for about 5–6 minutes, until golden brown. Add the thyme and cook for another 2–3 minutes, until fragrant. Stir in the zucchini, reduce the heat to medium-low, and cook for 10 minutes, stirring occasionally, until the zucchini are soft. Add the stock and simmer for about 20 minutes.

Transfer the zucchini mixture and 1 cup (100 g) of walnuts in batches to a food processor or high-speed blender and purée for 2 minutes until smooth. Transfer the blended soup to a large bowl and set aside until it reaches room temperature, about 30 minutes. Cover and refrigerate for 1 hour, until fully chilled.

Use a food processor or high-speed blender to purée the mango and citrus juices until smooth. Set aside until ready to serve.

Ladle the soup into large bowls, top with the mango, citrus purée, and garnish with the remaining walnuts and basil.

Preparation time: 25 minutes
Cooking time: 35 minutes, plus 30 minutes chilling

Serves 4

- 2 tablespoons olive oil
- 4 shallots, thinly sliced
- 1 teaspoon thyme leaves, finely chopped
- 1 lb 2 oz (500 g) zucchini (courgettes), sliced
- 4 cups (960 ml/32 fl oz) vegetable stock (broth)
- 1 cup (100 g) plus 1 tablespoon toasted walnuts, crushed
- 1 ripe mango, peeled and sliced
- 1 tablespoon fresh lemon juice
- ½ cup (120 ml/4 fl oz) fresh orange juice
- 1 tablespoon chopped basil leaves, to garnish

MAIN COURSES

CARROT AND PEA CURRY

Preparation time: 20 minutes
Cooking time: 25 minutes

Serves 4

- 2 tablespoons olive oil
- 4 curry leaves
- 1 tablespoon crushed red chili flakes
- 1 teaspoon mustard seeds
- 1 tablespoon finely chopped fresh ginger
- 1 cup (240 g) sliced carrots
- 2 cups (280 g) frozen green peas
- 2 teaspoons yellow curry powder
- 1 teaspoon ground turmeric
- salt and freshly ground black pepper
- 2 cups (275 ml/16 fl oz) vegetable stock (broth)
- chopped cilantro (coriander), to garnish
- chopped green chilies, to garnish
- chapati or garlic naan, to serve

Heat the oil in a skillet (frying pan) over medium heat. Add the curry leaves, then the crushed red chili flakes, mustard seeds, and ginger and stir fry for 2 minutes. Add the carrots, peas, curry powder, and turmeric and cook for 3–4 minutes. Season to taste with salt and freshly ground black pepper.

Add the stock and simmer at medium heat for about 15 minutes, until the liquid has reduced by half. Garnish with cilantro and green chilies and serve with chapati or garlic naan.

CARROT AND PEA CURRY

AFRICAN CAULIFLOWER CURRY

Preparation time: 30 minutes

Cooking time: 45 minutes

Serves 4

- 1 tablespoon olive oil
- 2½ cups (240 g) diced red onion
- 2 cups (200 g) diced red bell pepper
- 4 cups (320 g) cauliflower florets
- 2 cloves garlic, finely chopped
- 1 tablespoon curry powder
- 2 teaspoons cumin seeds
- 2 teaspoons coriander seeds
- 2 teaspoons ground turmeric
- 1 teaspoon ground cinnamon
- 1 teaspoon smoked paprika
- ¼ teaspoon ground cloves
- 4 cups (960 ml/32 fl oz) vegetable stock (broth), plus more as needed
- 2 cups (300 g) canned chickpeas
- ½ cup (80 g) golden raisins
- salt
- cooked brown rice, quinoa, or red lentils, to serve

Heat the olive oil in a large skillet (frying pan), add the onions and bell peppers and cook over medium heat, stirring, for about 5 minutes, until the onions are soft. Add the cauliflower and continue to cook until it starts to turn golden brown, about 4–5 minutes. Add the garlic and cook, stirring, for 1 minute more.

Combine the curry powder, cumin, coriander, turmeric, cinnamon, paprika, and cloves in a mortar and pestle and grind the spices to a fine powder. Add the spice blend to the vegetables and cook for 2–3 minutes, stirring constantly with a wooden spoon.

Add the stock, chickpeas, and raisins, then bring to a boil. Reduce the heat to low and simmer for 25–30 minutes, stirring and tasting occasionally, until the sauce thickens. Add extra stock if needed.

Season to taste with salt. Serve with brown rice, quinoa, or red lentils on the side.

JACKFRUIT CURRY

Preparation time: 20 minutes, plus 4 hours soaking

Cooking time: 25 minutes

Serves 4

- 2¼ lb (1 kg) young jackfruit, peeled and cut into 2 x 2 x 1.5-inch (5 x 5 x 4-cm) slices
- 2 tablespoons vegetable oil
- 1 tablespoon coriander seeds
- 4 cloves garlic, crushed
- 10 small shallots, sliced
- 2 tablespoons raw cashews
- 4 cups (960 ml/32 fl oz) coconut milk
- 10 curry leaves
- 10 lime leaves
- 4 bay leaves
- 1 cup (240 ml/8 fl oz) coconut cream
- 1 teaspoon superfine (caster) sugar
- 2 tablespoons chopped cilantro (coriander)
- cooked basmati rice, to serve

Immerse the jackfruit slices in a large bowl of cold water and refrigerate for 4 hours.

Heat the vegetable oil in a large saucepan over medium heat. Add the coriander seeds, garlic, and shallots and stir fry gently for 3 minutes, until fragrant. Add the cashews and stir fry for another 3 minutes, then add the coconut milk and bring to a boil.

Drain the jackfruit and add it to the pan along with the curry leaves, lime leaves, and bay leaves. Stir the mixture, bring it to a simmer, and simmer for about 15 minutes, until the jackfruit is tender. Stir in the coconut cream and bring the mixture to a simmer, then add the sugar, stir well, and cook at a low simmer for 5 minutes. Garnish with the chopped cilantro and serve immediately with rice.

CHEESE AND POTATO CURRY

To make the curry, put the boiled potatoes into a bowl and mash them. Add the peas, carrots, vegan cheese, turmeric, chili powder, cumin, chilies, and salt to taste and mix well. Shape the mixture into small balls.

Combine the flours and spread the mixture across a plate. Add the potato balls and roll them around on the plate to coat them in the flour mixture.

Meanwhile, heat enough oil to deep-fry the balls in a wok, deep saucepan, or deep-fat fryer. Dust a plate with flour. Line another plate with paper towels. When the oil is hot, carefully drop the balls into it. Deep-fry the balls for about 6–7 minutes, until lightly golden. Drain the balls and transfer to the paper towel–lined plate to absorb excess oil. Set aside, covered with a clean kitchen towel to keep them warm.

To make the gravy, put the stock into a saucepan, bring to a boil, then add the chopped onions and tomatoes and boil for 5 minutes. Transfer the mixture to a bowl and chill in the refrigerator for 15 minutes. Then, using a food processor or high-speed blender, blend the mixture to a smooth paste. Season to taste with salt.

Heat the oil in a saucepan, add the garlic, and sauté over medium heat for 4–5 minutes, until light golden. Add the turmeric, five-spice powder, chili powder, and ground coriander and season to taste with salt and freshly ground white pepper. Stir fry for about 3–4 minutes, until the oil separates from the gravy and pools around the edges of the pan. Add the tomato-onion mixture and stir fry for 3–4 minutes. Add the vegetable balls and the soy cream and cook over low heat for 2–3 minutes, stirring carefully.

Remove the pan from the heat, garnish with the chopped cilantro or parsley, and serve with the mung bean sprouts on side.

Preparation time: 25 minutes
Cooking time: 50 minutes, plus
   15 minutes chilling

Serves 4

For the curry:
- 1 lb 2 oz (500 g) potatoes, boiled
- 1 cup (140 g) frozen green peas, defrosted
- 1 cup (140 g) diced carrots, cooked
- 1 cup (100 g) vegan grated cheese
- 1 teaspoon ground turmeric
- 1 teaspoon chili powder
- 1 teaspoon ground cumin
- 2 teaspoons chopped seeded green chilies
- salt
- ½ cup (65 g) cornstarch (cornflour)
- ½ cup (65 g) all-purpose (plain) flour
- vegetable oil, for deep-frying
- chopped cilantro (coriander) or parsley, to garnish
- ½ pound (250 g) mung bean sprouts, to serve

For the gravy:
- ½ cup (120 ml/4 fl oz) vegetable stock (broth)
- 2 onions, chopped
- 4 tomatoes, chopped
- 3 tablespoons vegetable oil
- 1 tablespoon grated garlic
- 1 teaspoon ground turmeric
- 1 teaspoon five-spice powder
- 1 teaspoon chili powder
- 1 tablespoon ground coriander
- salt and freshly ground white pepper
- 1 cup (240 ml/8 fl oz) soy cream

POTATO MASALA

Preparation time: 20 minutes
Cooking time: 25 minutes

Serves 4

- 2 tablespoons sunflower or corn oil
- 1 onion, diced
- 2 cloves garlic, finely chopped
- 1 tablespoon garam masala
- 1 lb 2 oz (500 g) potatoes, quartered
- about 3½ cups (870 ml/28 fl oz) coconut milk
- 1 lb (450 g) canned chickpeas, drained
- salt and freshly ground black pepper
- cooked basmati or jasmine rice, to serve

In a large skillet (frying pan) over medium heat, warm the oil, add the onion and garlic, and cook, stirring, until, for about 4–5 minutes, until golden brown.

Add the garam masala to the pan and stir to coat the onion and garlic with it. Immediately add the potatoes and enough coconut milk to cover the potatoes. Cook over medium heat for about 15 minutes, until the potatoes are tender. Add the chickpeas, reduce the heat to low, and simmer for 3–4 minutes.

Season to taste with salt and freshly ground black pepper and serve with basmati or jasmine rice.

POTATO MASALA

COCONUT TOFU CURRY

Preparation time: 20 minutes
Cooking time: 30 minutes

Serves 4

- 4 tablespoons olive oil
- 4 cloves garlic, crushed
- 1 onion, finely chopped
- 1 lb 2 oz (500 g) firm tofu, diced
- 2 cups (475 ml/16 fl oz) coconut milk
- 1 tablespoon ground cumin
- 1 tablespoon yellow curry powder
- 1½ teaspoons grated fresh ginger
- 1 teaspoon chopped seeded green chili
- 1 tablespoon red pepper paste or ground
  paprika
- salt and freshly ground black pepper
- 6 cups (1.4 liters/48 fl oz) tomato purée
  (passata)
- 1 cup (240 g) frozen green peas, defrosted
- 3 carrots, finely grated
- cooked basmati or other long-grain rice
  or garlic naan, to serve

Heat the olive oil in a large saucepan over medium heat. Stir in the garlic, onion, and tofu. Cover and cook, stirring occasionally, about 8 minutes, until the tofu and onion are golden.

Stir in the coconut milk, cumin, yellow curry powder, ginger, chili, and red pepper paste or paprika. Season to taste with salt and freshly ground black pepper. Bring to a simmer. Stir in the tomato purée, peas, and carrots. Simmer, covered, for about 30 minutes, stirring occasionally, until the sauce has reduced by a quarter.

Serve with rice or garlic naan.

CURRIED SPINACH WITH PEANUT BUTTER CREAM

Preparation time: 30 minutes
Cooking time: 25 minutes

Serves 4

- 1 cup (240 ml/8 fl oz) coconut milk
- 1 tablespoon peanut butter
- 4 tablespoons vegetable margarine
- 1 onion, chopped
- 1 large tomato, diced
- 2 teaspoons curry powder
- 2¼ lb (1 kg) spinach leaves, chopped
- salt and freshly ground black pepper
- cooked long-grain rice, to serve

Heat the coconut milk in a saucepan over low heat and bring it to a low simmer. Add the peanut butter and whisk until the mixture is combined. Set aside.

Using a large saucepan, heat the vegetable margarine over medium heat, add the onion, tomato, and curry powder and sauté for about 5 minutes, until the onion is soft. Add the spinach and continue to cook for about 10 minutes over low heat.

Stir in the peanut butter–coconut milk slurry. Simmer over low heat for about 5–8 minutes, stirring constantly, ensuring the mixture does not stick to the bottom of the pan. Season to taste with salt and freshly ground black pepper. Serve with rice on the side.

EGGPLANT AND YOGURT CURRY

Preheat the oven to 375°F/190°C/Gas Mark 5.

Wrap each eggplant in aluminum foil and bake for 10 minutes, until tender. Let cool, then peel and mash the eggplant. Set aside.

Heat the oil in a skillet (frying pan) over medium heat. Add the onion and fry for 5–6 minutes, then add the garlic and sauté for 4 minutes, until it starts to turn golden. Add the mashed eggplant, crushed red chili flakes, and ground cumin and season to taste with salt and freshly ground black pepper. Mix well and cook for 5 minutes over medium heat.

Add the lemon juice, green chilies, and cilantro. Stir in the yogurt and mix well. Serve immediately, with garlic naan.

Preparation time: 20 minutes
Cooking time: 25 minutes

Serves 4

- 2 large eggplants (aubergines)
- 2 tablespoons olive oil or vegetable oil
- 1 onion, chopped
- 1 tablespoon finely chopped garlic
- 1 teaspoon crushed red chili flakes
- 1 teaspoon ground cumin
- salt and freshly ground black pepper
- 2 tablespoons fresh lemon juice
- 2 green chilies, seeded and chopped
- ½ cup (30 g) chopped cilantro (coriander)
- 1 cup (240 g) unsweetened vegan yogurt
- garlic naan, to serve

EGGPLANT AND TOMATO CURRY

Add enough oil to a large saucepan to cover the bottom of the pan. Warm the oil over medium heat until shimmering. Add the onion, chilies, and cumin and cook, stirring, for about 4–5 minutes, until the onion turns golden.

Stir in the tomatoes, garlic, ginger, curry powder, chili powder or cayenne pepper, turmeric, and ground coriander, and season to taste with salt. Add the eggplant, cook for 2 minutes, stirring, then cover and cook for about 8 minutes, until the eggplant is soft.

Garnish with cilantro leaves and serve with rice on the side.

Preparation time: 20 minutes
Cooking time: 15 minutes

Serves 4

- vegetable oil, for cooking
- 2 cups (280 g) chopped onion
- 2 green chilies, seeded and finely chopped
- 1 teaspoon cumin seeds
- 2 cups (400 g) chopped tomatoes
- 2 cloves garlic, finely chopped
- 1 tablespoon grated fresh ginger
- 1 tablespoon yellow curry powder
- 1 teaspoon chili or cayenne powder
- 1 teaspoon ground turmeric
- ¼ teaspoon ground coriander
- salt and freshly ground black pepper
- 1 lb 2 oz (500 g) eggplant (aubergine), cubed
- ¼ cup (30 g) cilantro (coriander) leaves
- cooked basmati or jasmine rice, to serve

FRUIT CURRY WITH PEANUTS

Preparation time: 30 minutes
Cooking time: 20 minutes

Serves 4

- 2 tablespoons vegetable oil
- 2½ cups (350 g) peeled, cored, and
  chopped tart apples such as Granny Smith
- 1 cup (140 g) chopped yellow onion
- 2 teaspoons curry powder
- 1½ cups (120 g) raisins
- 1½ cups (120 g) chopped dried apricots
- ½ cup (60 g) roasted peanuts
- salt and freshly ground black pepper
- sticky, Arborio, or Carnaroli rice cooked
  in coconut milk, to serve

Heat the vegetable oil in a large skillet (frying pan) over medium heat. Add the apple and onion and sauté, stirring frequently, for 6–7 minutes, until the onion is translucent. Add the curry powder, 2 tablespoons water, the raisins, apricots, and peanuts, and season to taste with salt and freshly ground black pepper. Stir well to blend the ingredients together, then bring the mixture to a low simmer and cook for 12 minutes.

Serve warm or cold with sticky, Arborio, or Carnaroli rice cooked in coconut milk.

FRUIT CURRY WITH PEANUTS

KALE IN PANANG CURRY

Preparation time: 45 minutes
Cooking time: 1 hour 30 minutes

Serves 4

For the panang curry paste:
- 12 dried small red Thai chilies, trimmed and de-seeded
- 1 tablespoon coriander seeds
- 1 teaspoon cumin seeds
- 1 teaspoon freshly ground black pepper
- 3 lemongrass stalks, finely chopped
- ½ cup (30 g) coarsely chopped cilantro (coriander) leaves and stems
- ¼ cup (40 g) chopped shallots
- 2 cloves garlic, coarsely chopped
- 1 tablespoon coarsely chopped galangal
- 1 teaspoon finely grated lime zest
- 1 teaspoon salt

For the curry:
- 1 cup (240 ml/8 fl oz) unsweetened coconut milk or coconut cream
- 1 teaspoon tamari or light soy sauce
- 1 tablespoon brown sugar
- 1 teaspoon finely chopped fresh ginger
- 1 cup (240 ml/8 fl oz) vegetable stock (broth)
- ½ cup (65 g) bamboo shoots, sliced
- ¼ cup (75 g) water chestnuts
- ¼ cup (60 g) shiitake mushrooms, trimmed and quartered
- 2 fresh small red Thai chilies, minced
- ½ cup (70 g) frozen green peas
- 2 scallions (spring onions), trimmed and sliced
- 3 cups (210 g) kale, shredded
- 9 oz (250 g) firm tofu, diced
- ½ cup (60 g) salted dry-roasted peanuts, coarsely chopped
- ½ cup (30 g) cilantro (coriander) leaves, shredded, to garnish
- juice of ½ lime
- cooked jasmine or basmati rice, to serve

To make the panang curry paste, crush the dry red chilies into large pieces and put them into a bowl. Cover with warm water and set aside to soften for 30 minutes.

Set a small skillet (frying pan) over medium heat, add the coriander seeds, and toast them, stirring constantly, for 2–3 minutes, until they darken. Set aside in a bowl. Using the same skillet, toast the cumin seeds in the same way for 1–2 minutes. Combine the coriander and cumin seeds in a mortar and pestle (or use a food processor) and grind them together, then add the freshly ground black pepper, mix well, and set aside.

Drain the soaked chilies. Using a food processor or high-speed blender, process the chilies, coriander-cumin-pepper mixture, lemongrass, cilantro leaves and stems, shallots, garlic, galangal, lime zest, and salt to a purée. Add a little water if necessary to achieve a smooth consistency. Set aside.

To make the curry, stir the coconut milk or cream well. Transfer half of it to a wok or medium saucepan. Bring to a gentle boil over medium heat, then reduce the heat to a low simmer and cook for about 10 minutes, stirring occasionally, until the milk or cream thickens. Add the panang curry paste to taste—about 2 tablespoons—and simmer over medium heat for 3–4 minutes, whisking and stirring to blend.

Add the remaining coconut milk and bring to a simmer. Continue to simmer over medium heat for about 10 minutes, until the mixture begins to thicken. Then add the tamari or soy sauce, sugar, and ginger and stir well to combine. Stir in the stock and simmer for 7 minutes. Add the bamboo shoots and water chestnuts and simmer for 10 minutes. Stir in the shiitakes, Thai chilies, and peas and simmer for 5 minutes. Add the scallions and kale and simmer for 2–3 minutes, then reduce the heat to low. Carefully stir in the tofu and peanuts and simmer for another 2–3 minutes.

Remove the pan from the stove, add the cilantro leaves and lime juice, stir well, and serve immediately, with rice on the side.

KIDNEY BEAN AND COCONUT CURRY

Rinse and drain the soaked kidney beans. Fill a large saucepan with enough water to cover the kidney beans and bring to a boil. Add the beans, bring to a simmer, and cook over low heat for 1 hour, until the beans are tender. Drain and set aside.

Heat the vegetable oil in a large saucepan over medium heat. Add the onion and stir fry for 3–4 minutes, until the onion becomes golden brown. Add the tomatoes and cook for 4–5 minutes. Add the coconut milk, cardamom, garlic, curry powder, and chili and season to taste with salt. Mix well to blend the ingredients together and bring the mixture to a simmer. Cook over low heat for 20 minutes.

Transfer to a large serving bowl, garnish with the cilantro, and serve with rice.

Preparation time: 25 minutes
Cooking time: 1 hour 30 minutes

Serves 4

- 2 cups (400 g) dried kidney beans, soaked in water overnight
- 2 tablespoons vegetable oil
- 2 red onions, chopped
- 2 tomatoes, chopped
- 2 cups (475 ml/16 fl oz) coconut milk
- 1 teaspoon ground cardamom
- 2 cloves garlic, crushed
- 1 tablespoon yellow curry powder
- 1 green chili, seeded and finely chopped
- salt
- 2 tablespoons chopped cilantro (coriander), to garnish
- cooked basmati or jasmine rice, to serve

MUSHROOM AND CASHEW MASALA

Heat the oil in a saucepan over medium heat, add the onion, and fry for 4–5 minutes, until golden brown. Add the cashews and stir fry for 3–4 minutes, until they gain some color. Add the garam masala, stir well, and cook for another 2 minutes, then add the potatoes, ginger, garlic, and crushed red chili flakes and cook over medium heat for 5 minutes. Add the mushrooms, tomatoes, green chillies, salt and freshly ground black pepper to taste and cook for 3 minutes, stirring frequently.

Add the stock, cover the pan, and reduce the heat to low. Cook for 15 minutes, until the potatoes are tender.

Transfer to a serving plate, garnish with the cilantro, and serve with rice or naan.

Preparation time: 30 minutes
Cooking time: 35 minutes

Serves 4

- ½ cup (120 ml/4fl oz) olive oil
- 3 onions, chopped
- 1 cup (240 g) raw cashews
- 1 tablespoon garam masala
- 2 potatoes, chopped
- 2 teaspoon finely chopped fresh ginger
- 2 cloves garlic, finely chopped
- 1 teaspoon crushed red chili flakes
- 2 cups (150 g) sliced button or shiitake mushrooms
- 3 tomatoes, chopped
- 2 green chilies, seeded and chopped
- salt
- 1 teaspoon freshly ground black pepper
- ½ cup (120 ml/4 fl oz) vegetable stock (broth)
- 2 tablespoons chopped cilantro (coriander), to garnish
- cooked white rice or warmed naan, to serve

MIXED VEGETABLE POTLUCK CURRY

Preparation time: 25 minutes
Cooking time: 30 minutes

Serves 4

- 4 tablespoons olive oil
- 1 white cabbage, stem trimmed, chopped
- 2 potatoes, sliced
- 2 large carrots, sliced
- 1 onion, chopped
- 3 cloves garlic, finely chopped
- 1 teaspoon ground turmeric
- 1 teaspoon curry powder
- 1 cup (240 ml/8 fl oz) vegetable stock (broth)
- salt
- cooked long-grain rice or warm naan, to serve

Preheat the oven to 350°F/180°C/Gas Mark 4.

Heat 2 tablespoons of the oil in a large skillet (frying pan) over medium heat. Add the cabbage and cook for 4–5 minutes, until it wilts. Transfer to a large bowl and set aside.

Return the skillet to the stove and add the potato slices to the hot oil left in the pan. Cook the potatoes over medium heat for 10–12 minutes, stirring occasionally, until half-cooked but golden brown on the surfaces. Transfer to a bowl and set aside. Repeat this process with the carrot slices.

Heat the remaining olive oil in the same skillet over medium heat. Add the onion and garlic and stir fry for about 4–5 minutes, until golden brown. Add the turmeric, curry powder, and 4 tablespoons of the stock (to prevent the spices from burning). Bring the stock to a low simmer, add the cabbage, potatoes, and carrots, and cook for 6–7 minutes, until the vegetables are tender.

Transfer the contents of the skillet to an ovenproof dish. Add the remaining stock, season to taste with salt, and bake until the liquid has reduced by half and the vegetables are all soft. Serve with long-grain rice or warm naan.

GREEN PLANTAIN CURRY

Preparation time: 30 minutes
Cooking time: 40 minutes

Serves 4

- 2 tablespoons vegetable margarine
- 1 onion, chopped
- 2 cloves garlic, crushed
- 1 tablespoon grated fresh ginger
- 2 green chilies, seeded finely chopped
- 1 tablespoon curry powder
- 1 cup (240 ml/8 fl oz) coconut cream
- 1 cup (240 ml/8 fl oz) vegetable stock (broth)
- 2 green plantains
- ½ cup (120 ml/4 fl oz) fresh lemon or lime juice
- salt and freshly ground black pepper
- cooked basmati rice, to serve

Melt the vegetable margarine in a saucepan over low heat. Add the onion, garlic, and ginger and stir fry for 4–5 minutes, until the aromatics start to turn golden. Add the chilies and curry powder, raise the heat to medium, and cook for about 5 minutes, until the mixture takes on a golden brown color. Stir in the coconut cream and stock, bring to a boil, then reduce the heat to a low simmer.

Peel and slice the plantains and stir into the curry sauce. Continue to cook at a low simmer for about 30 minutes, stirring occasionally. Add the fresh lemon or lime juice and season to taste with salt and freshly ground black pepper. Serve with rice.

MUSHROOM CURRY

Heat the oil in a large skillet (frying pan) over medium heat. Stir in the chopped onions, tomatoes, garlic, ginger, curry powder, ground coriander, and turmeric, mix well, and cook for 8 minutes, until the onions are translucent. Add the mushrooms and stir fry for 4–5 minutes, until softened.

Stir in the stock and cook for another 5 minutes. Add the chili powder, crushed red chili flakes, and green chilies, stir well, then add the soy yogurt and stir until it is smoothly incorporated. Stir in the fresh lemon juice and cook for another 4 minutes. Transfer to a serving plate. Garnish with the chopped cilantro and serve with chapati, roti, pita, or garlic naan.

Preparation time: 30 minutes
Cooking time: 25 minutes

Serves 4

- 3 tablespoons olive oil
- 5 onions, chopped
- 3 tomatoes, chopped
- 3 cloves garlic, finely chopped
- 1 tablespoon finely chopped fresh ginger
- 1 teaspoon yellow curry powder
- 1 teaspoon ground coriander
- 1 teaspoon ground turmeric
- 2¼ lb (1 kg) white button or shiitake mushrooms, trimmed and sliced
- ½ cup (120 ml/4 fl oz) vegetable stock (broth)
- 1 teaspoon chili powder
- 1 teaspoon crushed red chili flakes
- 2 green chilies, seeded and chopped
- 1 cup (240 g) unsweetened soy yogurt
- juice of 2 lemons
- ¼ cup (15 g) cilantro (coriander), chopped
- chapati, roti, pita, or garlic naan, to serve

JALAPEÑO CURRY

Heat 2 tablespoons of the vegetable oil in a wok or deep saucepan over medium heat. Add the jalapeños and stir fry for 3–4 minutes, until the peppers start to soften. Set aside.

Using a food processor or high-speed blender, process the onion, garlic, and ginger to a smooth paste. Set aside in a bowl.

Using a food processor or high-speed blender, process the sesame seeds, roasted peanuts, red chili, and coconut powder to a smooth paste.

Heat the remaining oil in a saucepan over medium heat. Add the five-spice powder and stir fry for 1 minute, then add the curry leaves and the onion-ginger-garlic paste and sauté for about 4–5 minutes, until the onion mixture turns light golden brown. Add the turmeric and ground coriander, mix well, then add the sesame-peanut-coconut-chili paste, stir well, and cook for 2–3 minutes.

Stir in the stock and bring to a boil. Reduce the heat to medium and simmer for 10 minutes, until the sauce starts to thicken. Stir in the tamarind pulp and cooked jalapeños and season to taste with salt. Reduce the heat to low and cook at a very low simmer for a further 10 minutes, until well cooked.

Serve with rice or warm naan on the side.

Preparation time: 20 minutes
Cooking time: 25 minutes

Serves 4

- 4 tablespoons vegetable oil
- 4 large green jalapeño peppers, trimmed and halved lengthwise
- 1 large onion, chopped
- 4 cloves garlic, crushed
- 2 tablespoons chopped fresh ginger
- 2 tablespoons sesame seeds
- 1 cup (120 g) roasted peanuts
- 1 red chili, seeded and finely chopped
- 1 tablespoon coconut powder
- 1 teaspoon five-spice powder
- 8 curry leaves
- 1 teaspoon ground turmeric
- 1 teaspoon ground coriander
- 1½ cups (350 ml/12 fl oz) vegetable stock (broth)
- 2 tablespoons tamarind pulp
- salt
- cooked wild rice or warm naan, to serve

NORTH INDIAN EGGPLANT CURRY

Preparation time: 30 minutes
Cooking time: 1 hour 5 minutes

Serves 4

- 4 tablespoons olive oil
- 1 lb 2 oz (500 g) eggplant (aubergine), cut into large dice
- 2 onions, chopped
- 1 teaspoon finely chopped fresh ginger
- 2 cloves garlic, finely chopped
- 1 teaspoon ground cinnamon
- 250 g (9 oz) tomatoes, diced
- 6 tablespoons vegetable stock (broth)
- 1 cup (250 g) canned chickpeas, drained
- salt and freshly ground black pepper
- cooked basmati or other long-grain rice rice, to serve

Heat 2 tablespoons of the olive oil in a large nonstick saucepan over medium heat. Add the eggplant and sauté for 10–12 minutes, until lightly brown and crisp, yet tender. Remove the eggplant from the pan and set aside.

Heat the remaining olive oil in the same saucepan and increase the heat to medium-high. Add the onion and sauté for 6–8 minutes, until lightly brown. Stir in the ginger, garlic, and cinnamon, reduce the heat to medium, and cook for 4–5 minutes.

Add the sautéed eggplant along with the tomatoes, stock, and chickpeas and bring to a boil. Then reduce the heat to low, cover the pan, and simmer for 30 minutes. Remove the lid and cook for another 10 minutes, adding a little water if the mixture becomes too dry. Season to taste with salt and freshly ground black pepper.

Serve with rice on side.

OKRA CURRY

Preparation time: 1 hour 5 minutes
Cooking time: 20 minutes

Serves 4

- 2 cups (480 g) okra (ladies' fingers)
- 2 teaspoons ground turmeric
- 2 teaspoons chili powder
- 2 teaspoons salt, plus extra to season
- 3 tablespoons vegetable oil
- 3 onions, sliced
- 1 tablespoon yellow curry powder
- 1 teaspoon finely chopped garlic
- 1 teaspoon grated fresh ginger
- freshly ground black pepper
- juice of 1 lemon
- handful of cilantro (coriander) leaves, chopped, to garnish

Cut the okra crosswise into thin slices and transfer to a large bowl. Add the turmeric, chili powder, and salt and toss to coat the okra. Refrigerate for 1 hour.

Heat the oil in a skillet (frying pan) over medium heat. Add the onion and stir fry for 4–5 minutes, until golden brown. Add the okra and stir fry for 6–7 minutes, until the okra becomes golden brown and crispy. Add the curry powder, stir to coat, then add the garlic and ginger. Cook for another 5 minutes, stirring frequently, until the sauce starts to thicken. Season to taste with salt and freshly ground black pepper, then transfer the curry to a platter, drizzle with the fresh lemon juice, and garnish with cilantro.

POTATO AND CAULIFLOWER CURRY

Heat the vegetable oil in a large skillet (frying pan) over low heat. Add the onion and garlic and stir fry for 4–5 minutes, until golden brown. Add the potato slices, increase the heat to medium, and stir fry for 7–8 minutes, until they start to turn golden brown. Add the coconut milk and bring to a boil, reduce the heat to a simmer, and add the mustard seeds, turmeric, curry powder, tomatoes, and chili. Stir to combine, then simmer for 3–4 minutes. Add the cauliflower and cook over very low heat for 20 minutes, until the potatoes are tender.

Season to taste with salt and freshly ground white pepper. Sprinkle the coconut flakes to garnish and serve with wild or brown rice.

Preparation time: 30 minutes
Cooking time: 35 minutes

Serves 4

- 2 tablespoons vegetable oil
- 1 onion, chopped
- 2 cloves garlic, finely chopped
- 1 lb 2 oz (500 g) potato, sliced
- 1 cup (240 ml/8 fl oz) coconut milk
- 2 teaspoon ground mustard seeds
- 1 teaspoon ground turmeric
- 1 tablespoon yellow curry powder
- 2 tomatoes, quartered
- 1 green chili, seeded and finely chopped
- 1 lb 2 oz (500 g) cauliflower florets, stems trimmed
- salt and freshly ground white pepper
- ½ cup (125 g) sun-dried coconut flakes, to garnish
- cooked wild or brown rice, to serve

TOFU CURRY

Heat the vegetable oil in a heavy-bottomed skillet (frying pan) over medium-high heat. Add the tofu and stir fry for 6–7 minutes, until golden brown on all sides. Set aside in a large bowl, leaving the oil in the skillet.

Add the garlic and ginger to the skillet and fry for 7–8 minutes, until sizzling and golden. Add the onions and stir to coat with oil. Cover the skillet with a lid and cook on low heat for 8 minutes, until the onions are translucent. Add the curry powder and sauté for 5–6 minutes, until fragrant. Add the stock, carrots, potatoes, grated apple, chuno sauce or chutney, tomato purée, cocoa powder, and bay leaves. Bring to a boil over high heat, then immediately reduce the heat to a low simmer. Cover the skillet with a lid and simmer for 30 minutes, until the carrots and potatoes are tender. Remove the skillet from the stove.

Melt the vegetable margarine in a saucepan over medium-low heat. Sprinkle in the flour slowly, stirring constantly with a wooden spoon, and continue to stir for 5–6 minutes, until the flour is golden brown. Add the mixture to the vegetables in the skillet. Return the skillet to the stove, bring the mixture to a low simmer, and cook for 5 minutes, until the sauce thickens.

Serve with udon or soba noodles. peas, and season to taste with salt and pepper.

Preparation time: 25 minutes
Cooking time: 1 hour

Serves 4

- 1 tablespoon vegetable oil
- 1 lb 2 oz (500 g) tofu, diced
- 3 cloves garlic, grated
- 2 tablespoons grated fresh ginger
- 1 lb 2 oz (500 g) onions, sliced
- 2 tablespoons curry powder
- 3 cups (710 ml/24 fl oz) vegetable stock (broth)
- 1 lb 2 oz (500 g) carrots, sliced
- 1 lb 2 oz (500 g) potatoes, cut into large chunks
- 1 small apple, peeled, cored, and grated
- 2 tablespoons chuno sauce or sweet and sour chutney
- 1 tablespoon tomato purée (passata)
- 1 teaspoon cocoa powder
- 2 bay leaves
- 1 tablespoon vegetable margarine
- 1 tablespoon all-purpose (plain) flour
- udon or soba noodles, to serve
- 1 cup (140 g) shelled green peas
- salt and freshly ground black pepper

TOFU AND PANEER TIKKA MASALA

Preparation time: 20 minutes
Cooking time: 10 minutes

Serves 4

- 2 green chilies, seeded and chopped
- 9 oz (250 g) tomatoes, diced
- 2 tablespoons grated fresh ginger
- 2 shallots, chopped
- 4 cloves garlic, chopped
- 4 tablespoons fresh lime juice
- 1 teaspoon sweet paprika
- 9 oz (250 g) unsweetened vegan Greek yogurt
- 2 teaspoons ground cumin
- 1 teaspoon ground allspice
- 1 teaspoon chili powder
- 3 tablespoons vegetable margarine
- 8 oz (225 g) firm tofu, cubed
- 1 tablespoon tomato purée (passata)
- 1 lb 2 oz (500 g) silken tofu, whisked
- salt and freshly ground black pepper
- ¼ cup (30 g) cilantro (coriander), chopped
- cooked basmati rice or warmed naan, to serve

Using a food processor or high-speed blender, process the chilies, tomatoes, ginger, shallots, garlic, lime juice, and paprika at high speed until smooth and creamy. Transfer the mixture to a large bowl, add the yogurt, cumin, allspice, and chili powder, and stir until well blended. Set aside.

Heat the vegetable margarine in a saucepan over medium-low heat. Add the firm tofu and stir fry 4–5 minutes, until golden brown. Add the tomato purée and bring the mixture to a simmer.
Add the silken tofu to the saucepan and cook over medium heat for 3–4 minutes. Season to taste with salt and freshly ground black pepper.

Transfer the mixture to a large bowl, top with the yogurt mixture, garnish with the chopped cilantro, and serve with rice or warm naan.

VEGETABLE STEW IN TURMERIC CURRY

Preparation time: 30 minutes
Cooking time: 35 minutes

Serves 4

- 5 tablespoons vegetable oil
- 2 onions, chopped
- 2 teaspoons grated fresh ginger
- 1 clove garlic, finely chopped
- 2 tomatoes, chopped
- 2¼ lb (1 kg) butternut squash, peeled and cubed
- 1 teaspoon ground coriander
- 1 teaspoon crushed red chili flakes
- 1 tablespoon grated fresh turmeric
- 1 teaspoon fenugreek seeds
- 4½ oz (125 g) cilantro (coriander), chopped
- basmati or other long-grain rice, to serve

Heat the vegetable oil in a saucepan over medium heat. Add the onion and fry gently for 5–6 minutes, until golden brown. Add the ginger and garlic, and fry over medium heat for 3–4 minutes, until lightly golden. Stir in the tomato and bring the mixture to a simmer. Add the squash and ground coriander and continue to cook over medium heat for 10 minutes, until the squash is tender but still firm.

Add the crushed red chili flakes, turmeric, and fenugreek seeds to the saucepan and mix well. Bring the mixture to a low simmer and cook for 15 minutes.

Transfer to a bowl, garnish with the cilantro, and serve with rice.

TOFU AND MANDARIN
ORANGE CURRY

Melt the vegetable margarine in a large sauté pan over medium heat. Add the onion and stir fry for 5–6 minutes, until golden. Reduce the heat to low, add the garlic and ginger, and cook for 5 minutes, stirring constantly, until the garlic starts to become golden brown. Stir in the chili and tomato, cover the pan, and cook for 5 minutes over low heat, until the tomato softens. Add the orange juice and stir well, bring the mixture to a simmer, then add the stock. Bring the mixture to a low simmer and cook for 3–4 minutes. Add the orange segments, cover the pan, and cook for 3–4 minutes. Season to taste with salt and stir in the Szechuan pepper. Set aside.

Heat the vegetable oil in a saucepan over medium-high heat. Add the tofu and stir fry for about 5–6 minutes, until golden on all sides.

Transfer the tofu to a serving plate, cover with the sauce, and garnish with cilantro. Serve with basmati rice.

Preparation time: 25 minutes
Cooking time: 30 minutes

Serves 4

- 4 tablespoons vegetable margarine
- 2 yellow onions, sliced
- 6 cloves garlic, finely chopped
- 2 tablespoons grated fresh ginger
- 2 red chilies, seeded and finely chopped
- 1 large tomato, diced
- ½ cup (120 ml/4 fl oz) fresh orange juice
- 1 cup (240 ml/8 fl oz) vegetable stock (broth)
- 2 Mandarin oranges, peeled, segmented
- salt
- 1 teaspoon ground Szechuan pepper
- 2 tablespoons vegetable oil
- 2¼ lb (1 kg) firm tofu, diced
- 1 tablespoon chopped cilantro (coriander), to garnish
- cooked basmati rice, to serve

SWEET AND SOUR
YELLOW CURRY

Preheat the oven to 400°F/200°C/Gas Mark 6.

Heat the oil in a large saucepan over medium heat, then add the onion and cook for 5–6 minutes, until translucent. Add the curry powder and ginger, and season to taste with salt, freshly ground black pepper, and chili powder. Stir fry gently for 2–3 minutes. Add the lemon juice, jam or dried apricots, raisins, chutney, and nutritional yeast and simmer over low heat for 4–5 minutes, until blended. Mix in the soaked and crumbled bread and the vegetables.

Transfer the mixture to a large ovenproof dish, add the coconut milk, cover with aluminum foil, and bake for 30 minutes, until the vegetables are tender. Serve with rice.

Preparation time: 25 minutes
Cooking time: 40 minutes

Serves 4

- 1 tablespoon vegetable oil
- 1 onion, chopped
- 2 tablespoons yellow curry powder
- 1 tablespoon grated fresh ginger
- salt and freshly ground black pepper
- chili powder
- 2 tablespoons fresh lemon juice
- 1 tablespoon apricot jam or chopped dried apricots
- 2 tablespoons raisins
- 2 tablespoons pineapple chutney
- 1 tablespoon nutritional yeast
- 4 slices of white bread, soaked in vegetable stock (broth) or water and mashed
- 1 cup (225 g) sliced potatoes
- 1 cup (150 g) peeled and sliced turnips
- 1 cup (75 g) sliced carrots
- 1 cup (70 g) chopped kale
- 1 cup (140 g) green peas
- 2 cups (475 ml/16 fl oz) coconut milk
- cooked brown or white rice, to serve

VEGETABLE CASSEROLE

Preparation time: 25 minutes
Cooking time: 45 minutes

Serves 4

- 2 tablespoons olive oil
- 1 small onion, finely diced
- 1 cup (60 g) finely chopped parsley
- 6 cloves garlic, finely chopped
- 2½ teaspoons sweet paprika
  or smoked paprika
- 2 cups (475 ml/16 fl oz) vegetable stock
  (broth)
- 3 carrots, diced
- 1 cup (200 g) diced potatoes
- 1½ cups (190 g) peeled and diced zucchini
  (courgette)
- 3 cups (300 g) diced eggplant (aubergine)
- 2 cups (200 g) green beans, cut into 1-inch
  (2.5 cm) pieces
- 1 cup (240 g) fava (broad) beans in the
  pod, stringed and cut into 1-inch (2.5 cm)
  pieces
- salt and freshly ground black pepper
- cayenne pepper
- cooked medium-grain couscous, to serve
- harissa, to serve

Heat the olive oil in a large nonstick saucepan over medium heat. Add the onion and cook, stirring, for 5–6 minutes, until golden brown. Add three-quarters of the parsley, three-quarters of the garlic, the paprika, and 1 tablespoon water and stir to combine. Then add the stock, carrots, and potatoes. Cover the pan and cook for about 10 minutes, until the carrots are tender.

Add the zucchini, eggplant, green beans, and fava beans to the saucepan. Cover the pan and cook for 25–30 minutes, until all the vegetables are tender.

Season to taste with salt, freshly ground black pepper, and cayenne pepper. Sprinkle with the remaining parsley and garlic, and serve with couscous and harissa.

EGGPLANT STEW

Preparation time: 20 minutes
Cooking time: 15 minutes

Serves 4

- 4 tablespoons vegetable oil
- 1 lb (450 g) eggplant (aubergine), cut
  in half and sliced 1-inch (2.5 cm) thick
- 1 tablespoon finely chopped shallots
- 1 clove garlic, finely chopped
- 1 tablespoon tamari or sweet soy sauce
- 1 teaspoon white vinegar
- 1 teaspoon granulated sugar
- ½ teaspoon ground nutmeg
- ½ teaspoon salt
- ½ teaspoon freshly ground black pepper
- cooked basmati or jasmine rice, to serve

Warm the oil in a skillet (frying pan) set over medium heat until it shimmers. Add the eggplant and cook for about 2 minutes, until golden brown on both sides and softened. Using a slotted spoon, transfer the eggplant to a paper towel–lined plate and set aside.

Add the shallots and garlic to the remaining oil in the pan and cook over medium heat, stirring, for about 5–6 minutes, until light brown. dd the tamari or soy sauce, vinegar, sugar, nutmeg, salt, pepper, and ½ cup (120 ml/4 fl oz) water and cook, stirring gently, for 3–4 minutes.

Return the eggplant to the pan and cook for about 2 minutes, shaking the pan a few times to combine—do not use a spoon to mix so as not to mash the eggplant.

Serve hot or warm, with rice on the side.

APPLE AND WALNUT ROAST

To make the stuffing, melt the vegetable margarine in a saucepan over medium-low heat. Add the onion, garlic, walnuts, parsley, thyme, rosemary, and celery salt. Cook, stirring, for about 5 minutes, until the onion has softened. Put the bread and apple into a large bowl and add the cooked vegetables and herbs. Pour in the stock, stir well, and set aside.

To make the dough, pour enough water for steaming into a large saucepan, position a large steamer basket inside, and bring the water to a simmer over medium heat.

Using a food processor or high-speed blender, purée the beans with the stock. Transfer the mixture to a large bowl and stir in the tomato sauce, Worcestershire sauce, maple syrup, dried herbs, garlic, and salt. Add the flour and mix with a fork until the dough starts to come together. Mix well by hand until the dough becomes stringy.

Roll the dough into a ball and make a large dent in the middle. Fill it with the stuffing and close the dough around the stuffing to make a large log, pinching the dough tightly where you bring the edges together (this will prevent the stuffing from running out of the dough during cooking). Place the log onto a large piece of aluminum foil and roll it up tightly, then twist the ends together to encase the log firmly. Transfer to the steamer basket, cover the saucepan with a lid, and steam for about about 1 hour 10 minutes, until the roast is firm but springs back when pressed. Refrigerate the roast, wrapped in aluminum foil, until ready to bake.

Preheat the oven to 400°F/200°C/Gas Mark 6. Grease a rimmedbaking sheet with margarine.

To make the glaze, put the garlic, stock, herbs, maple syrup, tamari or soy sauce, and fresh lemon juice into a bowl and whisk together.

Remove the foil from the roast and place the roast onto the prepared baking sheet. Brush it with half the glaze, then bake for 20 minutes. Remove the roast from the oven, brush it with the remaining glaze, then bake for another 20 minutes, until light golden brown.

Serve with roasted vegetables and gravy on the side.

Preparation time: 50 minutes
Cooking time: 1 hour 50 minutes

Serves 4

For the stuffing:
- 1 tablespoon vegetable margarine, plus extra for greasing
- 1 small onion, finely chopped
- 1 clove garlic, finely chopped
- 1 cup (100 g) walnuts, finely chopped
- 1 tablespoon chopped parsley
- 1 teaspoon thyme leaves
- 1 teaspoon chopped rosemary
- 1 teaspoon celery salt
- 3 slices of bread, toasted and finely chopped
- 1 apple, peeled, cored, and finely chopped
- 5 tablespoons vegetable stock (broth)

For the dough:
- ½ cup (120 g) cooked lima (butter) beans
- 2 tablespoons vegetable stock (broth)
- ¼ cup (60 ml) tomato sauce
- 1 tablespoon Worcestershire sauce
- 1 tablespoon maple syrup
- 1 tablespoon dried mixed herbs
- 1 clove garlic, finely chopped
- a pinch of salt
- 2½ cups (315 g) all-purpose (plain) flour

For the glaze:
- 1 clove garlic, finely chopped
- 4 tablespoons vegetable stock (broth)
- 1 teaspoon dried mixed herbs
- ½ cup (120 ml/4 fl oz) maple syrup
- 1 tablespoon tamari or soy sauce
- 1 teaspoon fresh lemon juice

To serve:
- roasted vegetables
- vegetable or onion gravy

ARTICHOKES WITH ALMONDS AND FAVA BEANS

Preparation time: 45 minutes
Cooking time: 35 minutes

Serves 4

- 2 tablespoons fresh lemon juice, plus juice of 1 lemon
- 4 large artichokes
- 2 tablespoons olive oil
- 2 cups (480 g) fava (broad) beans, shelled and cooked
- 1 cup (140 g) toasted almonds
- ½ cup (30 g) chopped dill
- salt and freshly ground black pepper
- 1 (14 oz/400 g) can chopped tomatoes

Fill a large bowl with cold water and add 2 tablespoons of lemon juice. Trim the stalks off each artichoke, pull off all the leaves, and reserve the meatiest ones. Using a teaspoon, dig out the choke and cut out the bases to make a neat cup. Drop the cups into the acidulated water and set aside until ready to cook.

Drain the artichoke cups and transfer them to a medium sauté pan.

In a small bowl, combine the oil, remaining lemon juice, and 4 tablespoons of water and pour the mixture over the artichokes in the pan. Set the pan over medium heat, cover with a lid, and poach the artichokes for 20 minutes, until fork-tender but firm.

Add the fava beans and almonds to the pan, cover again with the lid, and cook for another 10 minutes. Add half of the dill and season to taste with salt and freshly ground black pepper. Transfer the mixture to a platter.

Put the tomatoes into the same sauté pan and bring to a simmer over medium heat. Return the artichokes, fava beans, and almonds to the pan, reduce the heat to low, and cook for 10 minutes. Season to taste with salt and freshly ground black pepper, if needed.

Meanwhile, bring a saucepan of salted water to a boil and cook the reserved artichoke leaves for about 12 minutes, until tender, then drain.

Transfer the artichoke mixture to a platter and garnish the plate by surrounding the artichoke mixture with the leaves, like a flower. Garnish with the remaining dill.

ARTICHOKES WITH ALMONDS AND FAVA BEANS

BAKED POLENTA WITH SHIITAKE MUSHROOMS

Preparation time: 45 minutes
Cooking time: 45 minutes

Serves 4

- 3 tablespoons vegetable margarine, plus extra for greasing
- 4 cups (960 ml/32 fl oz) vegetable stock (broth)
- 1 cup (240 g) yellow cornmeal
- 1 cup (240 g) grated vegan cheese, preferably cheddar
- 4 tablespoons olive oil
- 3 cloves garlic, finely chopped
- 1 lb 2 oz (500 g) fresh shiitake mushrooms

Grease an 8-inch (20 cm) pie dish with vegetable margarine.

Put the stock into a medium saucepan and bring to a boil over medium heat. Add and melt the vegetable margarine, reduce the heat to low, and whisk in the cornmeal, pouring it into the pan in a slow stream. Continue to whisk for about 15 minutes, until the polenta is very thick. Slowly whisk in half of the vegan cheese until combined, then pour the mixture into the prepared dish and set aside to cool for 20 minutes

Preheat the oven to 375°F/190°C/Gas Mark 5. Line a baking sheet with parchment paper.

Slice the cooled polenta into 8 wedges. Place these on the prepared baking sheet and sprinkle over the remaining cheese. Bake for 20 minutes, until the cheese is melted and golden. Set aside.

Warm the olive oil in a heavy skillet (frying pan) over medium heat until shimmering. Add the garlic and cook, stirring, for about 2 minutes, until lightly golden. Add the mushrooms and cook, stirring, for about 8–9 minutes, until the mushrooms are lightly browned. Serve the mushrooms over the baked polenta on a large platter, family-style.

BEAN AND BANANA STEW

Preparation time: 30 minutes
Cooking time: 1 hour

Serves 4

- 2 cups (480 g) dried kidney beans
- 2 tablespoons palm oil
- 1 onion, sliced
- 4 green bananas or plantains
- salt and freshly ground black pepper
- 4 cups (960 ml/32 fl oz) vegetable stock (broth)
- 1–2 red or green chilies, to serve

Put the beans into a large bowl, cover with water, and leave to soak overnight. The next morning, drain the beans and transfer to a medium saucepan. Add enough water to cover the beans by ½ inch (1 cm), set the pan over high heat, and bring to a boil. Reduce the heat to medium-low and cook for 45 minutes or until tender. Drain the beans and set aside.

Heat the palm oil in a large skillet (frying pan) over medium heat, then add the onion. Cook, stirring, for about 5–6 minutes, until the onion is golden brown. Meanwhile, peel and slice the bananas or plantains. Add them and the beans to the pan and season to taste with salt and freshly ground black pepper.

Add the stock and bring the stew to a simmer. Cook for about 10 minutes, until the liquid has reduced to about 1 cup (240 ml/8 fl oz). Ladle into bowls and serve with red or green chilies.

EGGPLANT TARTARE AND
TOASTED NUTS

Halve the eggplants, then cut 4 x 1-inch (2.5 cm) slices from each eggplant and set aside. Dice the remaining eggplant and soak in a large bowl filled with salted water for about 10 minutes.

Heat the olive oil in a nonstick saucepan over medium heat. Add the garlic and thyme and cook, stirring, for about 4–5 minutes, until the garlic begins to turn golden. Drain the diced eggplant thoroughly with a kitchen towel and add it to the pan along with the sugar. Cover the pan and cook for about 10 minutes, until light golden.

Meanwhile, preheat the oven to 375°F/190°C/Gas Mark 5.

Put the pecans or walnuts and almonds in an ovenproof dish, sprinkle with 2 tablespoons water, then season to taste with salt and freshly ground black pepper and dust with the curry powder. Transfer to the oven and toast for about 5 minutes, until the water has evaporated, ensuring the nuts do not burn. Transfer the nuts to a plate and set aside until ready to serve.

Season the eggplant mixture with more salt and freshly ground black pepper and stir in the vinegar and hot sauce. Transfer the mixture to a bowl and set aside, leaving the remaining oil in the pan.

Put the reserved eggplant slices into the same pan and cook over medium-low heat for about 6–7 minutes, until soft and starting to brown, then set aside to garnish.

Divide the eggplant mixture among 4 plates. Using a hand-held mixer, whip the soy whipping cream or cashew cheese with a dash of salt for about 2–3 minutes, until creamy. Divide the toasted nuts among the plates and drizzle some of the soy cream or cashew cheese over the eggplant. Top with the eggplant slices. Serve with toasted bread or tortilla chips.

Preparation time: 35 minutes
Cooking time: 30 minutes

Serves 4

- 2 medium eggplants (aubergines)
- salt and freshly ground black pepper
- 2 tablespoons olive oil
- 2 cloves garlic, finely chopped
- 3 sprigs lemon thyme
- 2 tablespoons granulated sugar
- 2¼ oz (60 g) pecans or walnuts
- 2¼ oz (60 g) blanched almonds
- 2 teaspoons yellow curry powder
- 3 tablespoons sherry vinegar
- 3 dashes hot sauce, such as Tabasco
- 4 tablespoons soy whipping cream or cashew cheese
- toasted bread or tortilla chips, to serve

BAKED TOFU WITH TOMATO RICE

Preparation time: 1 hour
Cooking time: 45 minutes

Serves 4

- 1 lb 2 oz (500 g) firm tofu, sliced 1 inch
  (2.5 cm) thick
- a generous 2 cups (500 ml/17 fl oz)
  tomato sauce
- 2 tablespoons fresh lime juice
- 1 tablespoon finely chopped onion
- 1 teaspoon dried oregano
- ½ teaspoon garlic powder
- salt and freshly ground black pepper
- vegetable oil or cooking spray, for greasing
- 2 tablespoons coconut powder
- fresh basil, to garnish
- cooked white basmati or other long-grain
  rice, to serve

Place the tofu in a strainer (sieve), place the strainer in a clean sink, then place a weight, such as a cast-iron saucepan, over them and leave for 1–2 hours to squeeze out the water and compress the tofu.

Meanwhile, combine the tomato sauce, lime juice, onion, oregano, and garlic powder in a bowl and season to taste with salt and freshly ground black pepper. Set aside.

Preheat the oven to 350°F/180°C/Gas Mark 4. Lightly oil a 7 x 11-inch (18 x 28-cm) baking pan, or spray pan with a nonstick cooking spray.

Spoon about a third of the sauce into the prepared pan. Place the tofu slices on top and pour over the remaining sauce. Sprinkle over the coconut powder. Bake for 45 minutes.

Garnish with the basil and serve with rice.

BAKED TOFU WITH TOMATO RICE

BANANA BLOSSOM IN COCONUT CREAM

Preparation time: 30 minutes
Cooking time. 15 minutes

Serves 4

- 2 banana blossoms (fresh or canned)
- 2 tablespoons salt, plus extra to season
- 2 tablespoons vegetable oil
- 2 cloves garlic, finely chopped
- 2 yellow onions, sliced
- 1 cup (200 g) sliced tomatoes
- 2 dried red chilies, crushed
- 2 tablespoons white vinegar mixed with
  4 tablespoons water
- freshly ground black pepper
- 1 cup (240 ml/8 fl oz) coconut milk
- cooked long-grain or wild rice, to serve

If using fresh banana blossoms, remove the first couple of leaves. Thinly slice the blossoms crosswise and place the slices in a bowl. Add 2 tablespoons salt, mix well, and refrigerate for 1 hour. Rinse under cold water and squeeze to dry. Set aside.

Heat the oil in a large skillet (frying pan) over medium heat. Add the garlic and cook, stirring, for about 2 minutes, until light brown. Add the onion and cook, stirring, for about 5–6 minutes, until translucent, then add the tomato slices and chili and cook for about 3 minutes, until soft.

Add the banana blossoms and vinegar-water mixture to the vegetables and, without stirring, bring to a vigorous simmer. Cook for about 3 minutes, season to taste with salt and freshly ground black pepper, and stir. Continue to cook until the banana blossoms are tender, about 5–6 minutes. Add the coconut milk and remove the skillet from the heat. Let the mixture stand for a few minutes to allow the flavors to develop.

Serve with long-grain or wild rice on the side.

BANANA BLOSSOM IN COCONUT CREAM

BEAN STEW WITH MUSHROOM AND SEITAN

Preparation time: 20 minutes
Cooking time: 15 minutes

Serves 4

- 2 tablespoons vegetable margarine or vegetable oil
- 1 onion, chopped
- 2 cloves garlic, finely chopped
- 2 teaspoons sweet paprika, plus more to garnish
- salt and freshly ground black pepper
- 2 cups (240 g) chopped white button or shiitake mushrooms
- 1 cup (240 g) diced seitan or smoked tofu
- 2 bay leaves
- 2 cups (400 g) cooked white beans
- 1 cup (240 ml/8 fl oz) vegetable stock (broth)
- 1 tablespoon cornstarch (cornflour)
- 2 tablespoons nutritional yeast
- chopped fresh parsley or cilantro (coriander), to garnish
- bread, to serve

Heat the vegetable margarine or oil in a large saucepan over medium heat. Add the onion, garlic, and paprika and season to taste with salt and freshly ground black pepper. Cook, stirring constantly, for 3–4 minutes, until slightly golden. Add the mushrooms, seitan, and bay leaves, mix well, and cook, stirring, for about 5 minutes, until the seitan is golden brown.

Add the beans to the saucepan, stir to combine, and cook for 2–3 minutes. Add three-quarters of the stock and bring the stew to a simmer. Reduce the heat to low, maintaining the simmer, and cook for about 5 minutes, stirring regularly, until the beans are warmed through.

Put the remaining stock into a bowl with the cornstarch and whisk well until the cornstarch has completely dissolved. Add the mixture to the saucepan along with the nutritional yeast, and season to taste with salt and freshly ground black pepper. Simmer for about 5 minutes, stirring occasionally.

Garnish with parsley or cilantro, sprinkle with paprika, and serve with bread.

BEETS IN CHERRY SAUCE

Preparation time: 30 minutes
Cooking time: 1 hour 30 minutes

Serves 4

- 2¼ lb/1 kg beets (beetroot) (about 8 beets), greens trimmed to 1-inch (2.5 cm) lengths
- 3 tablespoons olive oil
- 1½ cups (270 g) dried cherries or cranberries
- 1¼ cups (300 ml/10 fl oz) vegetable stock (broth)
- 2 tablespoons vegetable oil
- 2 onions, chopped
- ¼ cup (15 g) chopped cilantro (coriander) or dill
- ¼ cup (15 g) chopped parsley
- ¼ teaspoon salt
- naan, to serve

Preheat the oven to 375°F/190°C/Gas Mark 5.

Coat the beets with the olive oil and arrange in a single layer in a baking pan. Roast for about 1 hour, until tender. Let cool slightly, then trim, peel, and slice the beets.

Combine the cherries or cranberries and the stock in a small saucepan and bring to a boil. Reduce the heat to low and simmer, uncovered, for about 20 minutes, until very tender. Using a food processor or high-speed blender, purée the mixture and set aside.

Warm the vegetable oil in a large skillet (frying pan) over medium heat. Add the onion and sauté for 5–10 minutes, until soft and translucent. Stir the onion into the purée. Add the beet greens, cilantro or dill, parsley, and salt.

Arrange the sliced beets on a serving platter. Pour the sauce over the beets. Serve warm or at room temperature, with naan.

TOFU AND MUSHROOM CASEROLE

Preheat the oven to 350°F/180°C/Gas Mark 4.

Using a food processor or high-speed blender, process the tofu until creamy. Transfer to a bowl, stir in the soy cream, and set aside.

Soak the white bread in the soy milk and set aside.

Heat the coconut oil in a large skillet (frying pan). Add the onion, garlic, and yellow curry powder and stir fry over medium heat for 5–6 minutes, until the onion is translucent. Add the mushrooms and stir fry for another 2 minutes. Add the peas and lentils and stir fry for 2 minutes. Now add the white bread and soy milk mixture along with the chili powder, vinegar, lemon juice, brown sugar, and mixed herbs. Stir and cook for 2 minutes.

Transfer the mushroom mixture to an ovenproof dish. Stir in the tofu mixture, add the apricots and raisins, mix well, and arrange the bay leaves on top. Set the dish on a baking sheet and bake for about 30 minutes, until golden brown.

Serve with wild rice, sambal, and your favorite chutney.

Preparation time: 35 minutes
Cooking time: 45 minutes

Serves 4

- 1lb 2 oz (500g) firm tofu (about 2 blocks), diced
- 2 tablespoons soy cream
- 1 thick slice of white bread, crusts removed
- ½ cup (120 ml/4 fl oz) soy milk
- 1 tablespoon coconut oil
- 1 onion, chopped
- 1 clove garlic, crushed
- 1 tablespoon yellow curry powder
- 4 cups (480 g) diced white button mushrooms
- 1 cup (240 g) fresh or frozen green peas
- ½ cup (120 g) cooked brown or green lentils
- 1 tablespoon chili powder
- 4 tablespoons white vinegar
- 1 tablespoon fresh lemon juice
- 1 teaspoon brown sugar
- 2 tablespoons dried mixed herbs
- ¼ cup (60 g) dried apricots, sliced
- ¼ cup (60 g) raisins
- 4 bay leaves

To serve:
- cooked wild rice
- sambal sauce
- 2 tablespoons of your favorite chutney

BEET BORANI

Preparation time: 1 hour, plus 3 hours chilling
Cooking time: 40 minutes

Serves 4

- kosher salt and freshly ground black pepper
- about 1½ lb (750 g) beets (beetroot),
  peeled, greens reserved
- 3 cups (720 g) unsweetened vegan
  Greek yogurt
- ½ bunch dill, finely chopped
- 5 sprigs oregano, leaves chopped
- 2 cloves garlic, crushed
- 2 cups (240 g) toasted pecans
- naan, to serve

Fill a saucepan with salted water and bring to a boil over high heat. Add the beets, reduce the heat to medium, and cook the beets, uncovered, for about 30–35 minutes, until tender.

Meanwhile, chop the greens. Wash but do not dry them. Put the greens into a sauté pan and set over high heat. Cover with a lid and steam in the water that remains on the leaves for 2–3 minutes, until wilted. Drain both the greens and the beets and let cool for 20 minutes.

Stir together the yogurt, dill, oregano, and garlic and season to taste with salt and freshly ground black pepper.

Cut the beets into medium slices and add them to the greens. Arrange them in a large bowl, alongside the yogurt dressing. Season to taste with salt and freshly ground black pepper. Cover the bowl with plastic wrap (clingfilm) and refrigerate for at least 3 hours. Spinkle with the pecans, and serve with naan.

BEET BORANI

BRAISED BARLEY AND VEGETABLES

Preparation time: 30 minutes, plus
  overnight soaking
Cooking time: 40 minutes

Serves 4

- 1 cup (240 g) pearl barley
- 2 tablespoons olive oil
- 1 large onion, chopped
- 2 celery stalks, sliced
- 2 carrots, halved lengthwise and sliced
- 1½ cups (250 g) peeled and chopped rutabaga (swede)
- 1½ cups (250 g) peeled and chopped turnips
- 2 cups (475 ml/16 fl oz) vegetable stock (broth)
- salt and freshly ground black pepper
- bread, to serve

Soak the barley in plenty of water overnight. The next morning, drain away some of the water, leaving enough to cover the barley, and set aside.

Heat the oil in a large saucepan over medium heat. Add the onion and sauté for 5 minutes, until transparent and golden brown. Add the celery and carrot and cook for another 5 minutes, until both soften.

Add the barley with its water, rutabaga, turnips, and stock to the saucepan. Bring to a boil, then reduce heat the to a light simmer and cover the pan. Cook for 30–35 minutes, until the carrot, turnips, and rutabaga are soft.

Season to taste with salt and freshly ground black pepper. Ladle into bowls and serve with fresh bread.

BRAISED BEANS À LA PROVENÇALE

Preparation time: 15 minutes
Cooking time: 10 minutes

Serves 4

- 3 tablespoons olive oil
- 2 onions, sliced
- 3 cloves garlic, crushed
- 1½ cups (300 g) canned tomatoes with their juice
- 1½ cups (300 g) canned black or red beans, drained
- 1 tablespoon tomato purée (passata)
- 1 tablespoon herbes de Provence
- 1 sprig marjoram
- 1 red bell pepper, chopped
- salt and freshly ground black pepper
- 1 teaspoon cayenne pepper (optional)
- cooked long-grain rice, to serve

Heat the olive oil in a saucepan over medium heat. Add the onions and garlic and sauté until softened, about 5 minutes. Add the tomatoes with their juice and stir well. Bring to a boil, then reduce the heat to a simmer. Add the black or red beans, tomato purée, herbes de Provence, marjoram leaves, and bell pepper. Bring to a boil, then partially cover, reduce heat to low, and simmer for 8 minutes.

Season to taste with salt and freshly ground black pepper, and, if you like it spicy, add the cayenne pepper. Serve with rice.

BRAISED GREEN BEANS
WITH MINT

Heat the olive oil in a skillet (frying pan) over medium heat. Add the green beans and parsley to the pan with enough water to just cover. Stir in the potato slices, partially cover the pan, and simmer for 20 minutes, until the potatoes are fork-tender. Season to taste with salt and freshly ground black pepper, then add three-quarters of the chopped mint and mix well.

Remove the lid and cook over low heat for about 2 minutes. Add the tomato juice or sauce and, bring to a boil. Remove from the stove, stir well, and transfer to a large bowl. Top with the yogurt and garnish with the remaining mint.

Preparation time: 20 minutes
Cooking time: 25 minutes

Serves 4

- 3 tablespoons olive oil
- 1 lb 2 oz (500 g) green beans, trimmed and halved
- 1 tablespoon chopped parsley
- 2 potatoes, sliced
- salt and freshly ground black pepper
- 3 tablespoons chopped mint
- 1 cup (240 ml/8 fl oz) tomato juice or tomato sauce
- 2 tablespoons unsweetened vegan Greek yogurt, to garnish

BROCCOLI AND TOFU IN
PEANUT SAUCE

To make the peanut sauce, put the peanut butter into a small saucepan with ½ cup (120 ml/4 fl oz) boiling water and whisk until the mixture is well blended. Whisk in the vinegar, tamari, and tamarind paste and season with cayenne pepper, salt, and freshly ground white pepper. Transfer to a large heatproof bowl and set aside.

To make the broccoli and tofu, heat 2 tablespoons of the oil in a deep saucepan or wok over medium heat. Add half of both the ginger and garlic and stir fry for 4–5 minutes, until the garlic is slightly golden. Add the tofu and stir fry for 6–7 minutes. Transfer the mixture to the bowl containing the peanut sauce, mix well, and set aside.

Wipe the deep pan or wok, pour in the remaining oil, and warm it over medium heat. Add the remaining ginger and garlic and sauté for 4–5 minutes. Add onions and sauté for about 5 minutes, until the onion is translucent. Add the broccoli, cashews, and tamari and stir fry for about 15 minutes, until the broccoli is tender.

Add the peanut sauce and tofu mixture to the pan or wok, mix well to coat the broccoli evenly with the sauce, then season to taste with salt and white freshly ground pepper.

Transfer the mixture to a serving plate and top with the scallions. Serve alongside rice.

Preparation time: 25 minutes
Cooking time: 40 minutes

Serves 4

For the peanut sauce:
- ½ cup (120 g) smooth or crunchy peanut butter
- 4 tablespoons apple cider vinegar
- 2 tablespoons tamari
- 2 tablespoons tamarind paste, seeds removed
- cayenne pepper
- salt and freshly ground white pepper

For the broccoli and tofu:
- 4 tablespoons vegetable oil
- 2 teaspoons grated fresh ginger
- 4 cloves garlic, crushed
- 1 lb 2 oz (500 g) tofu, diced
- 2 onions, thinly sliced
- 1 lb 2 oz (500 g) broccoli, chopped
- ½ cup (120 g) raw cashews, chopped
- 2 tablespoons tamari
- salt and freshly ground white pepper
- 2 scallions (spring onions), finely chopped, to garnish
- cooked jasmine or basmati rice, to serve

BRAISED RED CABBAGE AND BEETS

Preparation time: 45 minutes
Cooking time: 1 hour 35 minutes

Serves 4

- 1 head of red cabbage, finely shredded
- 2 tablespoons olive oil
- 1 onion, thinly sliced
- 2 cloves garlic, crushed
- 3 quinces, peeled, cored, and cut into large slices
- 4 tablespoons red wine vinegar
- 1¼ cups (300 ml/10 fl oz) vegetable stock (broth), plus more as needed
- salt and freshly ground black pepper
- 3 beets (beetroot), peeled and grated
- boiled or baked potatoes, to serve

Put the shredded cabbage into a Dutch oven (casserole).

Heat the oil in a skillet (frying pan) over medium heat. Add the onion and garlic and sauté for 5–6 minutes, until golden brown. Add the quince, vinegar, and stock and season to taste with salt and freshly ground black pepper. Cook for 5 minutes over medium heat, until the quince is fork-tender.

Transfer the mixture to the Dutch oven, stir to combine with the cabbage, cover with a lid and place the pot into an unheated oven. Set the oven temperature to 375°F/190°C/Gas Mark 5 and cook for about 1 hour.

Stir in the beets. Add extra stock if the vegetables seem a bit dry. Cover the pot and cook for another 25 minutes.

Serve hot, with potatoes.

BRAISED RED CABBAGE AND BEETS

BRAISED SHIITAKE
MUSHROOMS IN GRAVY

Preparation time: 20 minutes
Cooking time: 25 minutes

Serves 4

- 2 tablespoons vegetable oil
- 2½ tablespoons finely chopped shallots
- 1 lb 2 oz (500 g) fresh shiitake mushrooms, trimmed and chopped
- ½ cup (120 g) diced smoked tofu
- 4 tablespoons red cooking wine or dry sherry
- 2 star anise
- 2 tablespoons brown sugar or sugarcane
- 1 teaspoon freshly ground white pepper
- 1 teaspoon five-spice powder
- 2 tablespoons light soy sauce
- 1 tablespoon dark soy sauce
- ½ cup (120 ml/4 fl oz) vegetable stock (broth)
- 12 oz (350 g) rice noodles
- 1 tablespoon sesame oil
- 2 scallions (spring onions), green parts only, chopped, to garnish

Heat the vegetable oil in a deep saucepan or wok over medium heat. Add the shallots and stir fry for 5–6 minutes, until golden brown. Add the mushrooms and stir fry for 3–4 minutes. Now add the tofu and red wine or dry sherry and cook, stirring constantly, for 3–4 minutes. Add the star anise, sugar, white pepper, five-spice powder, both soy sauces, and the stock. Bring to a low simmer and cook for about 15 minutes, until the liquid has reduced by half.

Meanwhile, cook the rice noodles according to the packet instructions. Drain the noodles, transfer to a large bowl, add the sesame oil, and toss to coat.

Transfer the noodles to a serving owl. Top the noodles with braised mushrooms, garnish with the scallions, and serve immediately.

BROCCOLI WITH TOFU
AND LEMON

Preparation time: 30 minutes,
  plus 2 hours draining
Cooking time: 15 minutes

Serves 4

- 9 oz (250 g) silken tofu
- 2¼ lb (1 kg) broccoli florets, trimmed
- 4 tablespoons white sesame seeds
- 4 tablespoons miso, preferably white
- 4 tablespoons rice vinegar
- finely grated zest and juice of 1 lemon
- salt and freshly ground black pepper
- white bread or toasted naan, to serve

Place the tofu into a strainer (sieve), transfer to a clean sink, then place a weight, such as a cast-iron saucepan, over it and leave for 1–2 hours to squeeze out the water and compress the tofu.

Bring a large saucepan of water to a boil. Place a medium bowl of cold water in the sink. Drop the broccoli into the boiling water and boil for 4 minutes. Then, using a strainer, transfer the broccoli immediately to the bowl of cold water to cool. Drain and set aside.

Put the sesame seeds into a dry skillet (frying pan) and toast them over medium-high heat for about 2 minutes, until fragrant and just starting to pop. Transfer them to a mortar and pestle and grind them to a fine powder.

Using a high-speed blender, blend the miso with the vinegar. Squeeze the tofu with your hands to remove any remaining water, then add the tofu and ground sesame seeds to the blender and process until the mixture is creamy.

Transfer the broccoli to a large serving bowl and stir in the dressing. Add the lemon juice and zest, season to taste with salt and freshly ground black pepper, and mix to combine. Serve with white bread or toasted naan.

SWEET POTATO MASH WITH ONION SAUCE

To make the mash, put the drained kidney beans, mung beans, and peanuts into a large saucepan and cover with water. Bring to a boil over medium heat and boil for about 15 minutes, until half cooked. Add the sweet potatoes, season to taste with salt and freshly ground black pepper, and simmer for 20 minutes, until the sweet potatoes and beans are cooked. Drain the vegetables and return them to the saucepan, then add the vegetable margarine and, using a fork, mash the vegetables together. Set aside.

To make the sauce, heat the oil in a saucepan over medium heat. Add the onions, tomatoes, and chili powder to taste, and stir fry for 5–6 minutes, until the onion is about to brown. Add the stock and gently simmer for 15 minutes, until the mixture starts to thicken. Stir in the flour until combined, then add the soy milk, stirring constantly, until mixed. Simmer for 10 minutes, until the mixture starts to thicken. Season to taste with salt and freshly ground black pepper.

Transfer the mash to a large serving dish and pour over the sauce. Serve with rice on the side.

Preparation time: 45 minutes
Cooking time: 1 hour 10 minutes

Serves 4

For the mash:
- ½ cup (100 g) dried kidney beans, soaked in water overnight
- ½ cup (100 g) mung beans
- 2 cups (240 g) raw peanuts
- 4 sweet potatoes, peeled and diced
- salt and freshly ground black pepper
- 1 tablespoon vegetable margarine
- cooked long-grain rice, to serve

For the sauce:
- 2 tablespoons vegetable oil
- 3 onions, sliced
- 6 tomatoes, peeled and sliced
- chili powder
- 1 cup (240 ml/8 fl oz) vegetable stock (broth)
- 1 teaspoon all-purpose (plain) flour
- 1 cup (240 ml/8 fl oz) soy milk
- salt and freshly ground black pepper

BELUGA LENTIL STEW

To make the sauce, mix the ingredients in a bowl and whisk until the cumin and oil are well blended. Set aside in a small saucepan.

To make the stew, heat the olive oil in a saucepan over medium heat. Add the garlic and ginger and stir fry for 2 minutes, until golden. Add the beluga lentils and chopped tomatoes and cook for 5–6 minutes, until the tomatoes are soft. Add the turmeric and chili powder. Season to taste with salt and freshly ground black pepper, and stir well. Add a generous ¾ cup (200 ml/7 fl oz) water or vegetable stock and cook for 6–7 minutes. Add the coconut meat or coconut powder, stir well, and cook for 4 minutes, then add the green chili. Cook for another 2 minutes.

Transfer the stew to a serving bowl and sprinkle over the garam masala. Bring the sauce to a boil, then pour it over the cooked rice. Serve immediately with the lentil stew.

Preparation time: 25 minutes
Cooking time: 20 minutes

Serves 4

For the sauce:
- 1 teaspoon ground cumin
- 3–4 curry leaves
- ½ cup (120 ml/4 fl oz) vegetable oil

For the stew:
- 2 tablespoons olive oil
- 1 clove garlic, crushed
- 1 teaspoon grated fresh ginger
- 1 lb 2 oz (500 g) canned beluga lentils, drained
- 3–4 tomatoes, chopped
- 1 teaspoon ground turmeric
- 1 teaspoon chili powder
- salt and freshly ground black pepper
- ½ cup (120 g) fresh young coconut meat or 1½ cups (120 g) coconut powder
- 2 green chilies, seeded and chopped
- 1 teaspoon garam masala
- cooked basmati or wild rice, to serve

BUDAPEST STEW

Preparation time: 30 minutes
Cooking time: 30 minutes

Serves 4

- 2 tablespoons vegetable oil
- 1 large yellow onion, chopped
- 1 lb 2 oz (500 g) basmati or other long-grain rice
- a pinch of salt, plus extra to season
- 3 tablespoons sweet or hot Hungarian paprika
- freshly ground black pepper
- 3 yellow bell peppers, chopped
- 3 sweet red Romano peppers, chopped
- 3 fresh tomatoes, diced, or ½ cup (115 g/4 oz) tomato purée (passata)
- chopped cilantro (coriander) or parsley, to garnish

Heat the oil in a saucepan over medium heat. Add the onion and cook for 5–6 minutes, until golden brown. Remove one-third of the onion from the pan, transfer it to a large saucepan, and mix it with the rice. Set aside the pan containing the remaining onion.

Set the saucepan with the rice–onion mixture over medium heat and sauté for 2 minutes, stirring constantly. Cover with water, add a pinch of salt, and bring to a boil. Reduce the heat to medium-low, cover the pan with a lid, and cook for about 12–14 minutes, until the rice is soft but still al dente.

Place the pan containing the remaining onions on the stove. Add the paprika and mix well until it is dissolved. Add ½ cup (120 ml/4 fl oz) cold water, season to taste with salt and freshly ground black pepper, then bring to a boil. Add the bell peppers and tomatoes or tomato purée. Pour in enough water to cover the peppers and bring to a boil. Reduce the heat to low and simmer for 5 minutes.

Transfer the cooked rice to a serving plate, cover with the bell pepper sauce, and garnish with chopped cilantro or parsley.

BUDAPEST STEW

CARAMELIZED PINEAPPLE AND TOFU

Preparation time: 25 minutes
Cooking time: 30 minutes

Serves 4

- 1½ cups (270 g) chopped pineapple
- 1 lb 2 oz (500 g) diced tofu, fried
- 1 clove garlic, finely chopped
- 2 tablespoons tamari or soy sauce
- 1 tablespoon superfine (caster) sugar
- 2 scallions (spring onions), sliced
- salt and freshly ground black pepper
- 2 tablespoons chopped cilantro (coriander), to garnish
- cooked basmati or other long-grain rice, to serve

Put the pineapple, tofu, garlic, tamari or soy sauce, and ½ cup (120 ml/4 fl oz) water into a Dutch oven (casserole). Add the sugar and scallions and season to taste with salt and freshly ground black pepper. Stir well. Set the Dutch oven over medium heat and cook for about 30 minutes, until the liquid has reduced by half.

Transfer the stew to a serving dish, garnish with the cilantro, and serve over rice.

CARAMELIZED PINEAPPLE AND TOFU

CARIBBEAN JERK CHILI

Preparation time: 20 minutes
Cooking time: 30 minutes

Serves 4

- 2 tablespoons olive oil
- 3 cloves garlic, finely chopped
- 2 celery stalks, diced
- 1 onion, diced
- 1 red bell pepper, diced
- 2 teaspoons Jamaican jerk seasoning
  or chili sauce
- 1 cup (240 ml/8 fl oz) coconut milk
- 3 tablespoons tomato purée (passata)
- 1 cup (240 g) canned red or kidney beans,
  drained
- 2 tablespoons fresh lime juice
- 1 mango, diced
- ½ cup (30 g) chopped cilantro (coriander)
- cooked basmati rice, to serve

Heat the olive oil in large saucepan over medium heat. Add the garlic, celery, onion, and bell pepper and sauté for 5–6 minutes, until the onion is translucent. Add the jerk seasoning or chili sauce and cook for 2–3 minutes. Stir in the coconut milk, tomato purée, beans, and fresh lime juice and season to taste with salt and freshly ground black pepper, if needed. Cover the saucepan with a lid, reduce the heat to low, and simmer for 20 minutes, stirring occasionally.

Stir in half of the mango and half of the cilantro, then cover the saucepan and simmer for another 10 minutes. Serve the chili over rice, garnished with the remaining mango and cilantro.

CARIBBEAN JERK CHILI

CARIBBEAN SHIITAKE MUSHROOMS

Preparation time: 25 minutes
Cooking time: 35 minutes

Serves 4

- 2 tablespoons soy sauce
- 1 teaspoon brown sugar
- 2 teaspoons white wine vinegar
- 2 teaspoons cayenne pepper
- 2 teaspoons cornstarch (cornflour)
- 2 tablespoons olive oil
- 1 cup (100 g) medium-slice scallions (spring onions), white parts only
- 4 cloves garlic, thinly sliced
- 1 lb 2 oz (500 g) fresh shiitake mushrooms, trimmed
- ½ cup (90 g) diced pineapple
- 1 red bell pepper, sliced
- 1 green banana or plantain, sliced
- 2 tablespoons chopped cilantro (coriander)
- salt and freshly ground black pepper
- cooked wild or long-grain rice, to serve

Combine the soy sauce, brown sugar, vinegar, cayenne pepper, ½ cup (120 ml/4 fl oz) cold water, and the cornstarch in a bowl. Mix well until blended and set aside.

Heat the olive oil in a deep saucepan or wok over medium heat. Add the scallions and garlic and sauté for 3–4 minutes, until golden brown. Add the shiitake caps and stir fry for 2 minutes. Stir in 2 tablespoons water and the pineapple, bell pepper, and banana or plantain. Cover the pan or wok and simmer for 5 minutes. Slowly add the cilantro and soy sauce mixture while stirring, then cook for 15 minutes, until the plantain is fork-tender. Reduce the heat to low and simmer for about 10 minutes, until the liquid has reduced by half. Season to taste with salt and freshly ground black pepper. Serve with rice.

CARROTS IN GINGER SAUCE

Preparation time: 25 minutes
Cooking time: 30 minutes

Serves 4

- 6 tablespoons vegetable margarine
- 3¼ lb (1.5 kg) carrots, thinly sliced
- 4 large shallots, finely chopped
- ½ cup (50 g) grated fresh ginger
- 2 cloves garlic, minced
- 1 tablespoon ground coriander
- 1 cup (240 ml/8 fl oz) fresh orange juice
- 3 tablespoons tamari or soy sauce
- salt and freshly ground black pepper
- chopped chives, to garnish
- cooked basmati or other long-grain rice, to serve

Heat the vegetable margarine in a large saucepan over medium-low heat until melted. Add the carrots and shallots and sauté for 5 minutes, until slightly golden. Add the ginger, garlic, and coriander, reduce the heat, and cook for 2 minutes, stirring frequently to prevent burning.

Add the orange juice and tamari or soy sauce to the pan. Cook for about 20 minutes, until the sauce has reduced to a glaze. Season to taste with salt and freshly ground black pepper.

Transfer the vegetables to a bowl, garnish with chives, and serve with rice.

CATALAN PORTOBELLO MUSHROOM CASSEROLE

To make the marinade, combine the ingredients in a large bowl and whisk until blended. Put the mushrooms in the bowl and stir to coat. Cover the bowl with plastic wrap (clingfilm) and refrigerate overnight.

To make the casserole, heat the olive oil in a large skillet (frying pan) set over medium heat. Remove the mushrooms from the marinade and transfer them to the skillet. Stir fry the marinated mushrooms for about 1–2 minutes on each side. Add the potatoes, stock, smoked paprika, and cumin, season to taste with salt, and simmer, uncovered, for 20 minutes, until the potatoes are fork-tender.

Ladle the mushrooms and potatoes into bowls. Raise the heat under the skillet to high and reduce the sauce for 4–5 minutes. Spoon the sauce over the mushrooms and potatoes. Garnish with parsley and serve.

Preparation time: 20 minutes
Cooking time: 25 minutes

Serves 4

For the mushroom marinade:
- 2 tablespoons smoked paprika
- 4 cloves garlic, minced
- 1 onion, chopped
- 3 tablespoons finely chopped parsley
- 4 tablespoons olive oil
- 2 teaspoons ground cumin
- 1 teaspoon dried oregano
- 2 bay leaves
- salt and freshly ground black pepper

For the casserole:
- 6 large portobello mushrooms
- 2 tablespoons olive oil
- 3¼ lb (1.5 kg) new potatoes, roughly quartered
- 4 cups (960 ml/32 fl oz) vegetable stock (broth)
- 1 teaspoon smoked paprika
- 1 teaspoon ground cumin
- salt
- 2 tablespoons chopped parsley, to garnish

CHICKPEA AND ONION STEW

Heat the oil in a Dutch oven (casserole) or large saucepan over medium heat. Add the onion and stir fry for 5–6 minutes, until golden brown.

Meanwhile, combine chickpeas and stock in another saucepan and bring to a boil. When the onions are ready, add the chickpea mixture to the Dutch oven, then stir in the remaining ingredients. Bring to a boil, then reduce the heat to low and simmer for 20 minutes, until the chickpeas are tender.

Remove from the Dutch oven from the heat, ladle the stew into bowls, and serve with bread.

Preparation time: 20 minutes
Cooking time: 30 minutes

Serves 4

- 5 tablespoons vegetable oil
- 2 large onions, chopped
- 1 lb 2 oz (500 g) cooked chickpeas
- 2½ cups (600 ml/20 fl oz) vegetable stock (broth)
- 2 large tomatoes, chopped
- 1 teaspoon crushed red chili flakes
- 1 teaspoon ground coriander
- 1 teaspoon saffron powder mixed with 1 tablespoon warm water
- ½ teaspoon ground cumin
- ½ teaspoon smoked paprika
- ¼ teaspoon ground cinnamon
- salt and freshly ground black pepper
- bread, to serve

CAULIFLOWER À LA NIÇOISE

Preparation time: 25 minutes
Cooking time: 35 minutes

Serves 4

- 3 tablespoons olive oil
- 1 yellow onion, chopped
- 1 red bell pepper, diced
- 1 green bell pepper, diced
- 1½ cups (300 g) canned tomatoes with their juice
- 6 cloves garlic, crushed
- 1 bunch marjoram, chopped
- 4 tablespoons dry white wine
- salt and freshly ground black pepper
- 1 head of cauliflower, trimmed and cut into florets
- 1½ cups (225 g) garlic-stuffed kalamata olives, to garnish

Heat the oil in a saucepan over medium heat. Add the onion and stir fry gently for 5–6 minutes, until golden brown. Add the red and green bell peppers, stir to coat in the oil, and stir fry for 4–5 minutes, until peppers start to turn golden. Add the tomatoes with their juice, the garlic, marjoram leaves, and white wine. Bring the mixture to a boil, then reduce heat to a low simmer and cook for 10–12 minutes.

Season to taste with salt and freshly ground black pepper, then add the cauliflower to the saucepan. Cook over medium heat for 8–10 minutes, until the cauliflower is tender but still al dente.

Remove the pan from the stove and transfer the mixture to a large serving bowl. Garnish with the olives and serve immediately.

MUSHROOMS IN TOMATO SAUCE

Preparation time: 30 minutes
Cooking time: 25 minutes

Serves 4

- ½ cup (120 ml/4 fl oz) vegetable oil
- 3 onions, chopped
- 4 potatoes, sliced
- 2 teaspoons grated fresh ginger
- 3 cloves garlic, finely chopped
- 1 teaspoon crushed red chili flakes
- 4 cups (480 g) white button mushrooms, sliced
- salt and freshly ground black pepper
- 3 large tomatoes, chopped
- 4 green chilies, seeded and finely chopped
- 1 tablespoon chopped cilantro (coriander)
- warmed naan or cooked long-grain rice, to serve

Heat the oil in a saucepan over medium heat. Add the onion and stir fry for 5–6 minutes, until light golden. Add the potato, ginger, garlic, and crushed red chili flakes and cook for 4–5 minutes. Add the mushrooms and season to taste with salt and freshly ground black pepper. Cover the pan and cook over low heat for 3 minutes. Add the tomatoes, green chili, and cilantro, mix well, and cook for about 10 minutes, until the tomato juice has reduced by half. Serve with naan or rice.

CAULIFLOWER IN LEMON AND TARRAGON SAUCE

To make the sauce, put the stock into a large saucepan and bring to a boil, then reduce the heat to medium to maintain at a low simmer.

Meanwhile, melt the vegetable margarine in a saucepan over low heat, then stir in the flour. Cook over medium heat for 5–6 minutes, stirring constantly with a wooden spoon, until the mixture turns pale golden brown. Remove the saucepan from the heat and gradually blend in the hot stock, stirring constantly.

Return the saucepan to the heat and bring to a boil, still stirring constantly. Continue to boil at medium-low heat, stirring, for about 5 minutes, until the sauce base thickens. Then reduce the heat to low and simmer, stirring occasionally, for about 5 minutes, until the liquid has reduced to three-quarters of its original volume. Skim the surface of the sauce base occasionally. Remove the pan from the stove and stir in the soy cream. Set aside.

Put half of the lemon juice into a saucepan set over medium heat. Add the shallots, wine, and half of the tarragon and bring to a simmer. Strain the liquid into a clean pan and return the mixture to the stove. Add the sauce base, stir to blend, then add the heavy soy cream, the remaining lemon juice, and the lemon zest, brandy or cognac, and the remaining tarragon. Bring to a simmer, and season to taste with salt and freshly ground black pepper, if needed.

To make the cauliflower, steam the florets over boiling water for 4–5 minutes, until tender.

Transfer the cauliflower to a serving plate, pour over the sauce, garnish with the chopped cilantro, and serve.

Preparation time: 30 minutes
Cooking time: 30 minutes

Serves 4

For the lemon and tarragon sauce:
- 2½ cups (600 ml/20 fl oz) vegetable stock (broth)
- 2 tablespoons vegetable margarine
- ¼ cup (30 g) all-purpose (plain) flour
- 2 tablespoons soy cream
- juice and finely grated zest of 1 lemon
- 1 shallot, finely chopped
- 4 tablespoons dry white wine
- 1 bunch tarragon, chopped
- 3 tablespoons heavy soy cream
- 2 tablespoons brandy or cognac
- salt and freshly ground black pepper

For the cauliflower:
- 1 head of cauliflower, trimmed and cut into florets
- 1 tablespoon cilantro (coriander), chopped, to garnish

VEGETABLE STEW

Preparation time: 30 minutes
Cooking time: 25 minutes

Serves 4

- 2 tablespoons vegetable oil
- 2 cloves garlic, finely chopped
- 1 large onion, chopped
- 1 tablespoon yellow curry powder
- 2 red chilies, seeded chopped
- 1 tablespoon grated fresh ginger
- 5 vine-ripened tomatoes, roughly chopped
- 1 green bell pepper, roughly chopped
- 1 red bell pepper, roughly chopped
- 2 large carrots, grated
- 1½ cups (360 g) canned red beans, drained
- salt and freshly ground black pepper
- 1 small bunch cilantro (coriander), chopped, to garnish
- baked potatoes or cooked long-grain rice, to serve

Heat the oil in a saucepan over medium heat. Add the garlic and onion and fry for 5–6 minutes, until light golden brown. Add the yellow curry powder and stir fry for 3–4 minutes, stirring constantly, until the onions are well coated in the curry powder. Add the chilies, ginger, and tomatoes andcook over medium heat for 10 minutes, until the tomatoes start to fall apart. Add the bell peppers and carrots and cook for another 10 minutes, until the carrots are fork-tender.

Add the beans to the saucepan and bring the mixture to a simmer. Season to taste with salt and freshly ground black pepper.

Transfer the stew to a serving bowl and garnish with cilantro. Serve with baked potatoes or rice.

VEGETABLE-RICE STEW

Preparation time: 30 minutes
Cooking time: 30 minutes

Serves 4

- 1½ cups (360 g) brown rice
- 6 cups (1.4 liters/48 fl oz) vegetable stock (broth)
- 1 medium onion, diced
- 4 cloves garlic, finely chopped
- ½ cup (30 g) fresh cilantro (coriander), chopped
- 1 green bell pepper, sliced
- 2 large carrots, sliced
- 5 cups (450 g) shredded white cabbage
- 2 cups (480 g) diced butternut squash
- 4 tablespoons tomato purée (passata)
- 1 cup (100 g) canned pinto or navy (haricot) beans
- salt and freshly ground black pepper
- 1 diced avocado, to garnish

Cook the brown rice according to the packet instructions. Set aside.

Place all the remaining ingredients, except the seasoning and avocado, into a large soup pot and bring to a boil. Cover the pan, reduce the heat to low, and simmer for 30 minutes, until the squash and carrots are tender. Remove the pan from the stove. Pour the cooked warm brown rice into the soup pot and stir to combine well.

Season to taste with salt and freshly ground black pepper. Ladle the stew into bowls, garnish with avocado, and serve.

COCONUT AND SPICED
SWEET POTATOES

Put all the ingredients, except the sweet potatoes, into a large saucepan. Bring to a boil, stirring, then reduce the heat to low and simmer for 5 minutes. Add the sweet potatoes, mix well, and simmer over low heat for 20 minutes, until the sweet potatoes are tender and the liquid has reduced by half. Season to taste with salt and freshly ground black pepper. Serve hot.

Preparation time: 30 minutes
Cooking time: 25 minutes

Serves 4

- 2 onions, chopped
- 3 cloves garlic, crushed
- 2 large red chilies, seeded and finely chopped
- 2 teaspoons ground turmeric
- 2 teaspoons grated fresh ginger
- 2 tablespoons tamari or soy sauce
- 1½ cups (350 ml/12 fl oz) coconut milk or coconut cream
- 2 cups (475 ml/16 fl oz) vegetable stock (broth)
- 2 tablespoons fresh lemon or lime juice
- 2¼ lb (1 kg) sweet potatoes, peeled and diced
- salt and freshly ground black pepper

COLLARD GREENS
IN PEANUT POWDER

Pour 1 cup (240 ml/8 fl oz) of the stock into a medium saucepan. Add the baking soda and stir until thoroughly dissolved. Set the pan over medium heat and bring to a simmer, then add the collard greens and tomato. Cook for 8 minutes. Add the peanuts, season to taste with salt and freshly ground white pepper, and pour in the remaining stock. Stir thoroughly and reduce the heat to low. Cover the pan and simmer for 20 minutes, stirring frequently to prevent burning on the bottom of the pan.

Serve immediately with rice and sriracha.

Preparation time: 25 minutes
Cooking time: 30 minutes

Serves 4

- 2 cups (475 ml/16 fl oz) vegetable stock (broth)
- 1 teaspoon baking soda (bicarbonate of soda)
- 1 lb 10 oz (750 g) chopped collard greens
- 1 large tomato, chopped
- 3 cups (360 g) toasted peanuts, crushed
- salt and freshly ground white pepper
- cooked wild rice, to serve
- sriracha, to serve

CHICKPEA TAGINE

Preparation time: 30 minutes
Cooking time: 25 minutes

Serves 4

- 4 tablespoons olive oil
- 1 teaspoon ground cumin
- 2 teaspoons ground ginger
- 1 teaspoon chili powder
- 1 teaspoon ground coriander
- 1 teaspoon ground cinnamon
- 1 cup (240 g) canned chickpeas, drained
- 1 cup (240 ml/8 fl oz) vegetable stock (broth)
- 8 tomatoes, chopped
- 1 bunch cilantro (coriander), finely chopped
- ½ bunch parsley, finely chopped
- salt and freshly ground black pepper
- couscous, to serve
- harissa, to serve

Heat the oil in a saucepan over medium heat. Add the cumin, ginger, chili powder, ground coriander, and cinnamon. Stir fry for about 1 minute, until fragrant. Add the chickpeas and stock, mix well, then add the tomatoes, cilantro, and parsley and bring to a boil. Reduce the heat to medium-low and simmer for about 20 minutes, until the chickpeas are tender.

Season to taste with salt and freshly ground black pepper. Serve with a large bowl of couscous and a small bowl of harissa on the side.

CHICKPEA WAT

Preparation time: 30 minutes
Cooking time: 45 minutes

Serves 4

- 2 tablespoons vegetable oil
- 1 large red onion, finely chopped
- 2 carrots, sliced
- 2 potatoes, diced
- 1 teaspoon cayenne pepper
- 1 teaspoon paprika
- 1 teaspoon ground ginger
- 1 teaspoon freshly ground black pepper
- 1 teaspoon ground cumin
- ½ teaspoon ground cardamom
- 1 tablespoon tomato purée (passata)
- salt
- 1 cup (200 g) canned chickpeas, drained
- 1½ cups (350 ml/12 fl oz) vegetable stock (broth)
- 2 cups (280 g) frozen green peas, defrosted
- naan or long-grain rice, to serve

Heat the oil in a large saucepan over medium heat. Add the onion and stir fry for about 5–6 minutes, until softened. Add the carrots and potatoes, cover the saucepan with a lid, and cook for 10 minutes. Stir in the cayenne pepper, paprika, ginger, black pepper, cumin, cardamom, and tomato purée, and season to taste with salt. Add the chickpeas and stock and bring to a boil. Reduce heat to low and simmer, covered, for about 20 minutes, until the vegetables are tender and the flavors have developed.

Add the peas and cook for another 10 minutes over low heat, adding a little water if the stew is a bit dry.

Adjust the seasoning and serve with naan or rice.

CHILI-CHEESE PIE

To make the batter, mix the cornstarch, flour, garlic, and tamari or soy sauce in a bowl and season to taste with salt and freshly ground black pepper. Add just enough water to allow you to blend the mixture to a smooth batter. Adjust the batter texture by adding more or less water, but do not make it too liquid. Stir in the cheese and mix well.

Heat the oil in a large skillet (frying pan) over medium heat. Pour in the batter and stir fry for 7–8 minutes, until golden. Transfer to a plate lined with paper towels to drain, leaving the remaining oil in the skillet. Set aside.

To make the gravy, put the tamari or soy sauce, chili sauces, and nutritional yeast into a bowl, mix well, and set a side.

Reheat the oil in the skillet over medium heat, add the garlic and green chilies, and sauté for 2–3 minutes, until fragrant. Now add the green bell pepper and onion, season to taste with salt and freshly ground black pepper, and stir fry for 3–4 minutes. Add the sugar, chili powder, vinegar, and ketchup and stir until well blended.

Transfer the chili-cheese pie to a serving plate, cover with the gravy, garnish with scallions, and serve with rice.

Preparation time: 40 minutes
Cooking time: 20 minutes

Serves 4

For the batter:
- ¾ cup (95 g) cornstarch (cornflour)
- ⅓ cup (80 g) all-purpose (plain) flour
- 2 cloves garlic, finely chopped
- 2 tablespoons tamari or soy sauce
- salt and freshly ground black pepper
- 1 lb 2 oz (500 g) grated vegan cheese
- ½ cup (120 ml/4 fl oz) vegetable oil, for frying

For the gravy:
- 2 tablespoons tamari or soy sauce
- 2 tablespoons green chili sauce
- 2 tablespoons red chili sauce
- 1 tablespoon nutritional yeast
- 3 cloves garlic, minced
- 2 green chilies, seeded and finely chopped
- 1 green bell pepper, diced
- 1 onion, diced
- salt and freshly ground black pepper
- 2 tablespoons superfine (caster) sugar
- 1 tablespoon chili powder
- 1 tablespoon apple cider vinegar
- ½ cup (85 g) ketchup
- ½ cup (50 g) finely chopped scallions (spring onions), to garnish
- cooked long-grain rice, to serve

COCONUT CREAM AND SWEET POTATOES

Preparation time: 30 minutes
Cooking time: 1 hour 25 minutes

Serves 4

- 4 sweet potatoes
- ½ cup (120 g) vegetable margarine, cut into pieces
- salt and freshly ground black pepper
- 1 cup (240 ml/8 fl oz) coconut cream
- 1 onion, finely chopped
- 2 cloves garlic, crushed
- 2 tablespoons grated fresh ginger
- 4 tablespoons fresh orange juice
- 1 cup (125 g) grated vegan cheese
- green salad, to serve

Preheat the oven to 400°F/200°C/Gas Mark 6.

Wrap each sweet potato in aluminum foil and arrange them on a baking sheet. Bake for 1 hour, turning the sweet potatoes over halfway through the cooking time. After 1 hour, insert the tip of a knife into each sweet potato to check that it is cooked through. If not, continue to bake until the sweet potatoes are fully cooked. Leave to cool for 15 minutes.

Preheat the broiler (grill). Line a baking sheet with parchment paper.

Arrange the sweet potatoes on the prepared sheet. Gently scoop out the flesh from each sweet potato with a spoon. Transfer the flesh to a bowl and reserve the skins on the baking sheet. Mash the vegetable margarine with the sweet potato until completely blended. Season to taste with salt and freshly ground black pepper. Using a fork, whisk the mixture to a smooth purée. Add the coconut cream, onion, garlic, ginger, and orange juice and mix well.

Fill the sweet potato skins with the mixture and top each potato with ¼ cup grated cheese, then broil (grill) for about 8–10 minutes, until the cheese has completely melted. Serve immediately with a green salad.

CURRIED PUMPKIN STEW

Preparation time: 20 minutes
Cooking time: 20 minutes

Serves 4

- 3 tablespoons vegetable margarine
- 1 teaspoon fenugreek seeds
- 1 teaspoon mustard seeds
- 1 teaspoon cumin seeds
- 3 dried red chilies, crushed
- 1 tablespoon finely chopped garlic
- 1 tablespoon finely chopped fresh ginger
- 1 teaspoon ground cumin
- 1 teaspoon ground turmeric
- 1 lb 10½ oz (750 g) pumpkin, diced
- 2 cups (475 ml/16 fl oz) vegetable stock (broth)
- salt and freshly ground black pepper
- 1 teaspoon freshly ground Szechuan pepper, to garnish
- cooked basmati or other long-grain white rice, to serve

Heat the vegetable margarine in a large skillet (frying pan) over low heat until completely melted, then add the fenugreek, mustard, and cumin seeds. Raise the heat to medium, and fry for 1 minute, until fragrant. Add the crushed chili and cook for 1 minute, then add the garlic, ginger, ground cumin, and turmeric, reduce the heat to low, and cook for another minute. Add the pumpkin and stir fry for 2 minutes.

Pour the stock into the skillet, bring to a boil, then immediately reduce the heat to medium-low and simmer for 15 minutes, until the pumpkin is tender but not overcooked and the liquid has reduced to a thicker sauce.

Season to taste with salt and freshly ground Szechuan pepper and serve with basmati or other long-grain white rice.

CURRIED RED LENTIL
AND KALE STEW

Heat the oil in a saucepan over medium heat. Add the onions and garlic and sauté for 5–6 minutes, until translucent. Add the carrots and celery and cook for 10–12 minutes over medium heat, until carrots are fork-tender but still firm. Add the bay leaves, turmeric, cumin, coriander, chili powder, and cayenne pepper and cook for 2–3 minutes, until fragrant. Stir in the canned tomatoes, stock, lentils, and tomato purée and bring to a boil. Reduce the heat to medium-low and simmer for 3–4 minutes, until the lentils are hot. Add the kale and simmer for 3–4 minutes, until the kale is cooked, adding more stock if needed. Season to taste with salt and freshly ground black pepper.

Discard the bay leaves and serve with rice.

Preparation time: 25 minutes
Cooking time: 30 minutes

Serves 4

- 2 tablespoons olive oil
- 1 onion, diced
- 2 cloves garlic, finely chopped
- 2 carrots, diced
- 2 celery stalks, diced
- 2 bay leaves
- 1 tablespoon ground turmeric
- 2 teaspoons ground cumin
- 1 teaspoon ground coriander
- 1 teaspoon chili powder
- 1 teaspoon cayenne pepper
- 1½ cups (360 g) canned chopped tomatoes
- 4 cups (960 ml/32 fl oz) vegetable stock (broth), plus more as needed
- 1 cup (200 g) canned red lentils, drained
- 2 tablespoons tomato purée (passata)
- 1 lb 10½ oz (750 g) kale, trimmed and roughly chopped
- salt and freshly ground black pepper
- cooked basmati or other long-grain rice, to serve

EGGPLANT, ZUCCHINI,
AND BELL PEPPER STEW

Heat the olive oil in a large skillet (frying pan) over medium heat. Add the zucchini, eggplant, green and red bell peppers, carrot, onion, garlic, and stock, cover, and cook for 45 minutes. Stir in tomatoes and their juice and cook for 25 minutes, until sauce has reduced by one-third.

Stir in the basil and season to taste with salt and freshly ground black pepper. Serve in bowls, with couscous or basmati rice.

Preparation time: 25 minutes
Cooking time: 1 hour 10 minutes

Serves 4

- 4 tablespoons olive oil
- 2 medium zucchini (courgettes), cut into large slices
- 2 eggplants (aubergines), peeled and diced
- 2 green bell peppers, chopped
- 1 red bell pepper, chopped
- 1 medium carrot, chopped
- 3 onions, chopped
- 1 clove garlic, crushed
- 2½ cups (600 ml/20 fl oz) vegetable stock (broth)
- 4 cups (800 g) canned tomatoes with their juice
- 1 tablespoon dried basil
- salt and freshly ground black pepper
- cooked couscous or basmati rice, to serve

EGGPLANT AND ONION STEW

Preparation time: 30 minutes, plus
  30 minutes soaking
Cooking time: 1 hour 5 minutes

Serves 4

- 3 eggplants (aubergines), peeled and
  sliced 1-inch (2.5 cm) thick
- salt
- 6 cups (1.4 liters/49 fl oz) vegetable stock
  (broth)
- 6 onions, quartered
- 3 cinnamon sticks
- 3 teaspoons ground cardamom
- 2 teaspoons ground coriander
- 3 teaspoons dried cilantro (coriander)
  leaves, crushed
- 1 teaspoon cloves, crushed
- cooked basmati or other long-grain rice,
  to serve

Soak the eggplant slices in a large bowl of salted water for 30 minutes, using a plate or bowl to weigh down the eggplant if it will not remain submerged. Rinse the eggplant in cold water and dice.

Place the eggplant in a large saucepan with the stock. Add the onion quarters and bring to a boil. Then reduce the heat to low, cover the pan, and simmer for 25 minutes, stirring occasionally.

Add the cinnamon, cardamom, ground coriander, dried cilantro leaves, and cloves and continue to simmer, uncovered, for 40 minutes.

Serve with white long grain rice.

EGGPLANT AND MUSHROOM STEW

Preparation time: 25 minutes
Cooking time: 30 minutes

Serves 4

- 3 tablespoons vegetable margarine
- 3 eggplant (aubergine), peeled and sliced
  into 3 x ¼-inch (7.5 cm x 5 mm) sticks
- 1 lb 10½ oz (750 g) shiitake or portobello
  mushrooms, sliced
- ½ cup (120 ml/4 fl oz) vegetable stock
  (broth)
- 4 tablespoons chopped sage
- salt and freshly ground black pepper
- 1 cup (240 g) unsweetened vegan
  Greek yogurt
- cooked large noodles or rice, to serve

Melt the vegetable margarine in a skillet (frying pan) over medium heat. Add the eggplant and mushrooms and cook for 10 minutes. Add the stock, bring to a boil, then reduce the heat to medium-low and simmer for 15 minutes.

Add the sage, season to taste with salt and freshly ground black pepper, and cook for 2 minutes, until the sage is fragrant. Remove the pan from the stove and let cool for 5 minutes.

Add the yogurt, stir well, and serve with noodles or rice.

EGGPLANT AND TOFU IN PLUM SAUCE

To make the eggplants, heat the vegetable oil in a large skillet (frying pan) over medium-high heat. Add the tofu and stir fry for 8–10 minutes, until golden brown on all sides. Transfer to a paper towel–lined plate, leaving the remaining oil in the skillet, and set aside.

Put the garlic and onion into the same skillet and sauté, stirring constantly, over medium heat, until softened. Add the celery, mix well, and cook for 7–8 minutes, until the celery softens. Add the eggplant and cook, for 6–7 minutes, stirring occasionally to bring the vegetables at the bottom of the skillet up to the top, until the eggplant is completely soft and slightly translucent. Set aside.

To make the plum sauce, mix the prunes, vegetable margarine, ginger, cayenne pepper, vinegar, and 1 cup (240 ml/8 fl oz) water in a saucepan. Bring to a boil, then reduce the heat immediately to medium-low and simmer, stirring frequently, for 10 minutes. Add tamari or soy sauce to taste. Cook for about 10 minutes, until the sauce has reduced by one-third.

Transfer tofu and vegetables to a platter and top with the plum sauce. Garnish with parsley or cilantro and serve with rice.

Preparation time: 25 minutes
Cooking time: 45 minutes

Serves 4

For the eggplant:
- 2 tablespoons vegetable oil
- 1 lb 2 oz (500 g) extra-firm tofu, cut into ½-inch (1 cm) dice
- 3 cloves garlic, finely chopped
- 1 onion, chopped
- 3 celery stalks, finely chopped
- 2 large eggplants (aubergines), sliced
- chopped parsley or cilantro (coriander), to garnish
- cooked rice, to serve

For the plum sauce:
- ⅓ cup (160 g) prunes, pitted (stoned) and chopped
- 2 tablespoons vegetable margarine
- 1 teaspoon grated fresh ginger
- ½ teaspoon cayenne pepper
- 2 tablespoons apple cider vinegar
- tamari or soy sauce

JAIPUR VEGETABLE STEW

Put the carrots, cauliflower, and chickpeas into a large saucepan with the stock and sugar and season to taste with salt. Bring to a boil, then boil for 12–14 minutes over medium heat, until the carrots are fork-tender but firm. Drain the vegetables, reserving the stock, and set aside.

To make the gravy, heat the oil in saucepan over medium heat. Add the cumin and onion and sauté for 5–6 minutes, until the onion has softened and turns golden. Add the tomato purée, cardamom, poppy seeds, turmeric, chili paste, red chili flakes, cinnamon stick, star anise, and 2 tablespoons of the reserved stock. Cover the pan and cook over medium-low heat for 15 minutes, then add 2 more tablespoons of the reserved stock and the tamarind pulp, stir well, and cook for 10 minutes, until all ingredients are well blended. Add the carrots, cauliflower, and chickpeas, and cook at low heat for another 5 minutes.

Transfer the stew to a serving bowl and serve immediately with basmati rice.

Preparation time: 30 minutes
Cooking time: 50 minutes

Serves 4

- 9 oz (250 g) carrots, sliced
- 9 oz (250 g) cauliflower
- 9 oz (250 g) canned chickpeas
- 1 cup (240 ml/8 fl oz) vegetable stock (broth)
- 1 teaspoon granulated sugar
- salt
- ½ cup (120 ml/4 fl oz) vegetable oil
- 1 teaspoon cumin seeds
- 1 onion, chopped
- 9 oz (250 g) tomato purée (passata)
- 1 teaspoon ground cardamom
- 4 tablespoons poppy seeds
- 1 teaspoon ground turmeric
- 1 tablespoon green chili paste or similar
- 1 teaspoon crushed red chili flakes
- 1 cinnamon stick
- 2 star anise
- 4 oz (120 g) tamarind pulp
- cooked basmati rice, to serve

FAJITAS WITH MIXED MUSHROOMS

Preparation time: 45 minutes

Cooking time: 25 minutes

Serves 4

- ½ cup (120 g) brown or white rice
- 2 tablespoons fresh lime juice
- 3 tablespoons olive oil
- 2 cloves garlic, finely chopped
- 1 teaspoon ground cumin
- 1 teaspoon dried oregano
- salt
- 1 cup (240 g) portobello mushrooms, trimmed and thinly sliced
- 1 cup (240 g) shiitake mushrooms, trimmed and thinly sliced
- 1 cup (240 g) chanterelle or oyster mushrooms, trimmed and thinly sliced
- 1 green or red bell pepper, chopped
- 4 scallions (spring onions), sliced
- 8 flour tortillas
- ½ cup (55 g) slivered almonds, toasted
- your favorite sauce, guacamole, or vegan sour cream, to serve
- chopped cilantro (coriander), to garnish

Cook the rice according to the packet instructions. Set aside.

Put the fresh lime juice, 1 tablespoon of the olive oil, garlic, cumin, oregano, and 4 tablespoons of water into a large bowl and season to taste with salt. Add the mushrooms, pepper, and scallions. Mix carefully to coat the vegetables. Set aside for 20 minutes.

Meanwhile, preheat the oven to 350°F/180°C/Gas Mark 4.

Wrap the tortillas in aluminum foil and heat in the oven for 10 minutes to warm and soften.

Drain mushroom and vegetable mixture. Heat the remaining oil in a saucepan over medium heat. Add the mushroom-vegetable mixture and stir fry for 8 minutes or until tender and nearly all the liquid has evaporated. Stir in the rice and almonds until heated through.

To serve, spoon mushroom-rice mixture onto the warmed tortillas, add your favorite sauce, guacamole, or vegan sour cream and roll into fajitas. Garnish with chopped cilantro and serve immediately.

JAPANESE RATATOUILLE

Preparation time: 30 minutes

Cooking time: 30 minutes

Serves 4

- 4 tablespoons extra-virgin olive oil
- 3 eggplant (aubergines), cut into ½-inch (1 cm) slices
- 1 cup (240 g) cherry tomatoes
- ½ cup (120 g) peeled and sliced pumpkin
- 1 red bell pepper, sliced
- 1 onion, sliced
- salt and freshly ground black pepper
- 4 tablespoons sake
- 3 tablespoons miso
- 1 tablespoon tomato purée (passata)
- 1 tablespoon granulated sugar
- 1 teaspoon grated fresh ginger
- 1 teaspoon toasted sesame oil
- cooked rice or pasta, to serve

Preheat the oven to 440°F/230°C/Gas Mark 7½.

Put the olive oil into a large bowl. Add the eggplant and toss the slices in the olive oil until well coated. Add the cherry tomatoes, pumpkin, peppers, and onions and toss to coat evenly with the oil. Season to taste with salt and freshly ground black pepper and toss again. Transfer the vegetables to a baking pan and roast for 15 minutes.

Remove the pan from the oven and stir the vegetables. Roast for another 10–12 minutes, until the vegetables are cooked through and starting to caramelize.

Pour the sake into a bowl, add the miso, tomato purée (passata), sugar, ginger, sesame oil, and 4 tablespoons water, and whisk well to combine. Then transfer the mixture to a large saucepan and bring to a simmer. Add the vegetables, stir to coat, put a lid on the pan, and simmer gently for 5 minutes over low heat, until the vegetables are cooked al dente.

Season to taste with salt and freshly ground black pepper. Serve with rice or pasta.

TOFU STEAK FAJITAS

Preheat the oven to 400°F/200°C/Gas Mark 6.

To make the marinaded tofu, put the tamari, agave syrup, and lime juice plus 4 tablespoons water into a large bowl and whisk well.

Carefully dip the tofu slices into the marinade and coat them completely, then transfer the slices to a baking pan. Reserve the remaining marinade in the bowl.

Bake the tofu for 15 minutes, then turn the slices over, brush with the remaining marinade, and cook for another 15 minutes, until golden brown. Set aside.

To make the red peppers, heat the olive oil in a large skillet (frying pan) over medium heat. Add the onion and bell peppers and sauté for 5–6 minutes, until light golden. Deglaze the pan with a little of the stock. Bring to a simmer, cook for 5 minutes, then add the remaining stock and cook for 10–12 minutes, until the sauce has reduced by half. Add the beans and cook for 4–5 minutes, until tender. Season to taste with salt and freshly ground black pepper.

Transfer the red pepper mixture to a serving plate and top with the tofu steaks. Serve with warm corn tortillas, guacamole, vegan sour cream, and salsa on the side.

Preparation time: 30 minutes
Cooking time: 1 hour 5 minutes

Serves 4

For the marinaded tofu:
- 4 tablespoons tamari
- 4 tablespoons agave syrup
- juice of ½ lime
  1 lb 2 oz (500 g) tofu or smoked tofu, sliced into 8 rectangles

For the red peppers:
- 2 tablespoons olive oil
- 1 large onion, sliced
- 4 red bell peppers, julienned
- 1 cup (240 ml/8 fl oz) vegetable stock (broth)
- 4 cups (800 g) canned black beans, drained
- salt and freshly ground black pepper

- warm corn tortillas, to serve
- guacamole, to serve
- vegan sour cream, to serve
- salsa, to serve

LANCASHIRE HOTPOT

Preheat the oven to 325°F/160°C/Gas Mark 3.

Heat 1 tablespoon of the oil in a saucepan over medium heat. Add the onion and fry for 5–6 minutes, until light golden. Add the lentils, carrots, sweet potatoes, turnips, and margarine and cook for 5–6 minutes over medium heat. Sprinkle over the cornstarch, stir well, then reduce the heat to low and cook for 3–4 minutes, until the carrots are fork-tender. Sprinkle over the Worcestershire sauce, add the stock, and bring to a boil. Immediately reduce the heat to medium and stir in the tomatoes, texturized vegetable protein, and bay leaves. Season to taste with salt and freshly ground black pepper. Stir well and remove the pan from the stove. Add the nutritional yeast and mix well to incorporate.

Transfer the mixture to an ovenproof dish, add the sliced potatoes on top, and drizzle with the remaining vegetable oil. Bake for 1½ hours, until the potatoes are tender.

Garnish with parsley and serve immediately.

Preparation time: 30 minutes
Cooking time: 1 hour 40 minutes

Serves 4

- 2 tablespoons vegetable oil
- 1 onion, chopped
- 1 cup (240 g) green lentils
- 1 large carrot, sliced
- 1 sweet potato, peeled and sliced
- 1 turnip, peeled and sliced
- 2 tablespoons vegetable margarine
- 1 tablespoon cornstarch (cornflour)
- 2 teaspoons Worcestershire sauce
- ½ cup (120 ml/4 fl oz) vegetable stock (broth)
- 4 large tomatoes, chopped
- ½ cup (120 g) texturized vegetable protein (soya mince)
- 2 bay leaves
- salt and freshly ground black pepper
- 2 tablespoons nutritional yeast
- 2–3 potatoes, sliced
- chopped parsley, to garnish

INCA STEW

Preparation time: 30 minutes
Cooking time: 2 hours 10 minutes

Serves 4

- 2 tablespoons olive oil
- 1 onion, chopped
- 4 cloves garlic, finely chopped
- 1 green bell pepper, sliced
- 9 oz (250 g) green cabbage, chopped
- 9 oz (250 g) russet potatoes, sliced
- 4½ oz (125 g) tomato purée (passata)
- 2 teaspoons superfine (caster) sugar
- 1 tablespoon chili powder
- 1 teaspoon ground cumin
- 8 oz (225 g) brown or wild rice
- 5 cups (1.2 liters/40 fl oz) vegetable stock (broth)
- 1 lb 2 oz (500 g) canned kidney beans, drained
- chopped cilantro (coriander), to garnish

Heat the olive oil in a large saucepan over medium heat. Add the onion and garlic and sauté for 5–6 minutes, until light golden brown. Add the bell pepper, cabbage, potatoes, tomato purée, sugar, chili powder, and cumin. Stir well to combine, then cook, stirring constantly, for 4–5 minutes. Add the rice, stock, and beans. Bring the mixture to a boil, then immediately reduce the heat to low and simmer for 2 hours, until the rice and beans are tender.

Divide the stew across 4 bowls and garnish with the chopped cilantro before serving.

WINTER STEW

Preparation time: 30 minutes
Cooking time: 50 minutes

Serves 4

- 1 tablespoon olive oil
- 10 pearl onions, sliced
- 1 large carrot, peeled and sliced medium-thick
- 1 tablespoon all-purpose (plain) flour
- ½ cup (120 g) 1-inch (2.5 cm) thick slices seitan
- 2 slices smoky tempeh bacon, cut ½ inch (1 cm) thick
- 1 clove garlic, finely chopped
- 1 teaspoon chopped thyme
- 1 cup (240 ml/8 fl oz) stout or other dark beer
- 1⅓ cups (325 ml/11 fl oz) vegetable stock (broth)
- 1 cup (240 g) butternut squash, cut into ½-inch (1 cm) dice
- ½ cup (120 g) diced russet potatoes
- salt and freshly ground black pepper
- 2 tablespoons chopped parsley, to garnish

Heat the oil in saucepan over medium heat. Add the onion and carrot and cook for 5 minutes, until lightly golden. Stir in the flour and cook for 2 minutes. Add the seitan, tempeh bacon, garlic, and thyme, and cook for 4 minutes, until the seitan begins to put on color.

Pour in the stout beer and bring the mixture to a boil. Boil for 3 minutes, stirring and scraping any bits that may become stuck to the bottom of the saucepan. Add the stock and butternut squash and bring the mixture to a simmer. Reduce heat to low and cook for 15 minutes, until the stock starts to reduce. Add the potatoes and cook for 20 minutes, until fork-tender. Season to taste with salt and freshly ground black pepper.

Transfer the stew to a serving bowl, garnish with the chopped parsley, and serve immediately.

BLACK BEAN STEW

Wash the beans, then put them into a large bowl, cover with plenty of water, and refrigerate overnight. In the morning, drain the beans.

Heat 2 tablespoons of the vegetable oil in a saucepan over medium heat. Add the mushrooms and smoked tofu or smoked tempeh and sauté for 6–7 minutes, until slightly golden Set aside.

Put the beans, cilantro, scallions, bay leaves, cachaça, quartered orange, stock, and 2 cups (475 ml/16 fl oz) water into a large saucepan. Bring to a boil over medium heat, then reduce the heat to low and simmer for about 1 hour and 45 minutes, until the beans are soft and easy to mash. Set aside.

Heat the remaining 2 tablespoons vegetable oil in a small saucepan over medium heat. Add the onion and garlic and sauté for 5–6 minutes, until fragrant. Add 2 generous tablespoons of the cooked beans, season to taste with salt and freshly ground black pepper, and mash the beans to make a thick paste. Transfer the bean paste to the pan with the black beans, add the mushrooms and smoked tofu or smoked tempeh, bring to a simmer over low heat, and cook for 20 minutes. Cover to keep warm, and set aside.

To make the kale sauce, stack leaves, roll into cigar shapes, and slice into thin strips. Heat the oil in a saucepan over medium heat. Add the garlic and sauté for 4–5 minutes, until fragrant. Add the kale and sauté for about 2 minutes, until wilted. Season to taste with salt and stir well. Set aside.

To make the cassava flour crumbles, melt the vegetable margarine in a skillet (frying pan) over medium heat. Add the onion and sauté for 5–6 minutes, until fragrant. Add the cassava flour and stir well to ensure it absorbs the margarine. Toast for 1–2 minutes. Season to taste with salt and freshly ground black pepper. Transfer the crumbles to a bowl and garnish with chopped scallions.

Serve the stew, known in Brazil as *feijoada*, with white rice, peeled and sliced oranges, the kale sauce, and cassava crumbles on the side.

Preparation time: 35 minutes
Cooking time: 2 hours 45 minutes

Serves 4

For the beans:
- 1 cup (200 g) dried black beans or pinto beans
- 4 tablespoons vegetable oil
- 2 cups (240 g) trimmed and sliced shiitake mushrooms
- 1 cup (120 g) roughly chopped oyster mushrooms
- ½ cup (120 g) finely diced smoked tofu or smoked tempeh
- ¼ cup (15 g) fresh cilantro (coriander), chopped
- 3 scallions (spring onions), trimmed and chopped
- 5 bay leaves
- ½ cup (120 ml/4 fl oz) cachaça
- 1 orange, unpeeled, quartered, plus peeled and sliced oranges, to serve
- 2 cups (475 ml/16 fl oz) vegetable stock (broth)
- 1 onion, roughly chopped
- 4 cloves garlic, crushed and roughly chopped
- salt and freshly ground black pepper
- steamed white rice, to serve

For the kale sauce:
- ½ cup (35 g) trimmed kale or baby spinach
- 2 tablespoons vegetable oil
- 4 cloves garlic, finely chopped
- salt

For the cassava flour crumbles:
- 4 tablespoons vegetable margarine
- 1 onion, finely chopped
- ½ cup (65 g) cassava flour
- salt and freshly ground black pepper
- ½ cup (50 g) scallions (spring onions), chopped, to garnish

FLAMBÉ POTATOES WITH OYSTER MUSHROOMS

Preparation time: 35 minutes
Cooking time: 1 hour 10 minutes

Serves 4

- 1 lb 2 oz (500 g) fingerlong potatoes, halved
- 2 tablespoons olive oil
- 2 teaspoons mixed dried herbs of your choice
- salt and freshly ground black pepper
- 1 onion, chopped
- 2 cloves garlic, finely chopped
- 2 bay leaves
- 9 oz (250 g) oyster mushrooms, sliced
- 1 cup (240 ml/8 fl oz) vegetable stock (broth)
- 2 tablespoons light rum
- chopped cilantro (coriander), to garnish

Preheat the oven to 400°F/200°C/Gas Mark 6.

Arrange the potato quarters on a rimmed baking sheet, brush with 1 tablespoon of the olive oil, sprinkle with mixed herbs, and season to taste with salt and freshly ground black pepper. Bake for 35–40 minutes, until soft. Transfer potatoes to a skillet (frying pan) and set aside.

Heat the remaining olive oil in a large skillet over medium heat. Add the onion and stir fry for 5–6 minutes, until soft and translucent. Add the garlic and bay leaves and stir fry for 3–4 minutes, until lightly golden. Add the oyster mushrooms and stir fry for 2–3 minutes. Pour in the stock, bring to a boil, then reduce the heat to low and simmer for 15 minutes, until the liquid has reduced by nearly half. Transfer the mixture to a large serving plate.

In a small saucepan over medium heat, bring the rum to a simmer, then pour it over the potatoes. Ignite the alcohol with a lighter and flambé for 2–3 minutes, until the flames die out.

Arrange the flambéed potatoes over the stew on the serving plate, garnish with chopped cilantro, and serve immediately.

FLAMBÉ POTATOES WITH OYSTER MUSHROOMS

GINGER AND TAMARIND EGGPLANT

Preparation time: 35 minutes, plus
  30 minutes soaking
Cooking time: 40 minutes

Serves 4

  For the tamarind sauce:
- 1 tablespoon tamarind paste
- 1 teaspoon cornstarch (cornflour)
- 1 tablespoon grated fresh ginger
- salt and freshly ground black pepper

  For the eggplant:
- 1 lb 10½ oz (750 g) eggplant (aubergine)
- 3 tablespoons vegetable oil
- 2 cloves garlic, finely chopped
- 2 teaspoons ground coriander
- 1 teaspoon ground cinnamon
- 1 teaspoon ground cloves
- 1 cup (100 g) coconut powder
- 2 teaspoons cayenne pepper
- 1 tablespoon tamarind paste
- 2 tablespoons brown sugar
- salt
- ½ teaspoon black mustard seeds

To make the tamarind sauce, put the paste into a small saucepan, pour over 4 tablespoons boiling water, and let soak for 30 minutes. Then mash the pulp with a fork to release as much juice as possible. Add the cornstarch, and grated fresh ginger and season to taste with salt and freshly ground black pepper. Stir well to combine and set aside.

To make the eggplant, cut the eggplants in half lengthwise and scoop out 2–3 tablespoons of the flesh from each half, ensuring you remove flesh only from the center of each one. Reserve the eggplant flesh in a bowl. Cover the eggplant halves with a clean, damp kitchen towel and set aside.

Heat 2 tablespoons of the oil in a large skillet (frying pan) over medium heat for 2 minutes. Add the garlic and fry for 1 minute, then add the cilantro, cinnamon, and cloves and fry for another minute, until fragrant. Stir in the coconut powder, cayenne pepper, and eggplant flesh and continue to fry for about 4 minutes, until the eggplant is lightly toasted. Turn off the heat, sprinkle over the tamarind paste and sugar, mix well, and season to taste with salt. Stuff the eggplant halves with the spicy coconut mixture. Arrange on a rimmed baking sheet and set aside.

Preheat the oven to 400°F/200°C/Gas Mark 6.

Pour the remaining oil into the same pan you used to cook the filling and heat it over medium heat. When hot, add the mustard seeds and cook for 2 minutes, until the seeds begin to pop. Pour the oil and mustard seed mixture over the eggplant filling. Bake the filled eggplants for 20 minutes, until golden brown.

Meanwhile, set the tamarind sauce over medium heat and bring to a simmer stirring constantly until the cornstarch is completely blended into the liquid. Simmer for about 10 minutes, until sauce has reduced by half. Season to taste with salt and freshly ground black pepper, then set aside.

Serve the baked eggplants in deep plates, drizzled with the tamarind sauce.

GRILLED SHIITAKES WITH MIXED VEGETABLES

Preheat the broiler (grill).

Heat the vegetable margarine and thyme in a small saucepan over medium heat for 2–3 minutes, until the vegetable margarine melts.

Mix the peppers, zucchini, and mushrooms in an ovenproof dish. Drizzle over the thyme margarine, then broil (grill) for 14–15 minutes, until the vegetables are tender and golden brown.

Season to taste with salt and freshly ground black pepper and serve with rice.

Preparation time: 30 minutes
Cooking time: 20 minutes

Serves 4

- ¼ cup (60 g) vegetable margarine
- 4 teaspoons chopped thyme
- 9 oz (250 g) red bell peppers, sliced
- 9 oz (250 g) yellow bell peppers, sliced
- 9 oz (250 g) zucchini (courgettes), sliced
- 1 lb 10½ oz (500 g) shiitake mushrooms, trimmed and quartered
- salt and freshly ground black pepper
- cooked brown or basmati rice, to serve

VEGETABLES IN PEANUT SAUCE

Bring 2 cups (475 ml/16 fl oz) water to a boil in a large saucepan, then add the peanut butter, tomatoes, and onion. Cook over medium heat for 5–6 minutes, stirring often. Add the pumpkin, reduce the heat to medium-low, and stir in the greens and mushrooms. Season to taste with salt and freshly ground black pepper. Cover the pan and cook for 30 minutes, until the greens and peanut butter have blended to form a thick sauce.

Add the cabbage and broccoli to the saucepan and cook for another 5 minutes, until they are tender.

Transfer to a serving bowl, garnish with the crushed peanuts, and serve immediately, with rice.

Preparation time: 30 minutes
Cooking time: 40 minutes

Serves 4

- 1 cup (260 g) smooth or crunchy peanut butter
- 2 tomatoes, chopped
- 1 onion, chopped
- 1 cup (240 g) diced pumpkin
- 3 cups (210 g) assorted greens (collard greens, kale, and spinach or baby spinach)
- 2 cups (240 g) sliced button mushroom
- salt and freshly ground black pepper
- ½ cup (120 g) cabbage, shredded
- 1½ cups (150 g) broccoli florets
- 1 cup (120 g) peanuts, crushed, to garnish
- cooked basmati or wild rice, to serve

LEEKS IN MUSTARD SAUCE

Preparation time: 20 minutes
Cooking time: 30 minutes

Serves 4

For the vinaigrette:
- 4 tablespoons olive oil
- 3 tablespoons red wine vinegar
- 2 tablespoon whole grain mustard
- 2 shallots, finely chopped

For the leeks:
- salt
- 6 leeks, white and pale green parts only
- 2 tablespoons chopped parsley, to garnish
- 3 tablespoons chopped toasted walnuts, to garnish
- freshly ground black pepper
- baked potatoes or boiled potatoes, to serve

To make the vinaigrette, put the olive oil, vinegar, mustard, and shallot into a bowl and whisk together.

To make the leeks, bring a large saucepan of salted water to a boil. Carefully drop in the leeks and simmer over medium heat for about 15 minutes, until tender and easily pierced with the tip of a knife. Drain the leeks and pat dry with paper towels. Slice the leeks in half lengthwise.

Arrange the leeks on a serving plate and pour over the vinaigrette. Garnish with parsley and walnuts and season to taste with salt and freshly ground black pepper. Serve with baked or boiled potatoes.

LEEKS IN MUSTARD SAUCE

LEEK AND LENTIL CASSEROLE

Preparation time: 25 minutes
Cooking time: 1 hour 15 minutes

Serves 4

- 1 cup (200 g) dried Puy lentils
  or green lentils
- 2 tablespoons olive oil
- 2 large leeks, cut into 1½-inch
  (4 cm) lengths
- 1 onion, diced
- 1 cup (120 g) diced mushrooms
- 1 cup (240 ml/8 fl oz) vegetable stock
  (broth)
- 2 tablespoons tomato purée (passata)
- 1 teaspoon sweet or smoked paprika
- 1 teaspoon dried oregano
- 1 teaspoon dried rosemary
- salt and freshly ground black pepper
- cooked long-grain or wild rice

Preheat the oven to 400°F/200°C/Gas Mark 6.

Wash and drain the lentils a couple of times under cold water. Pour 3 cups (720 ml/24 fl oz) water into a large saucepan, add the lentils and bring to a boil. Cook over medium heat for 20–25 minutes, until tender. Drain and set aside.

Heat 1 tablespoon of the olive oil in a deep saucepan over medium-high heat. Add the leeks and sauté for 5–10 minutes, until softened and beginning to take on a golden color. Transfer the leeks to an ovenproof dish.

Heat the remaining olive oil in a saucepan over medium heat, add the onion, and fry for 5–6 minutes, until softened. Add the mushrooms and cook for 7–8 minutes, until they are soft and beginning to release their juices. Add the stock, lentils, tomato purée, paprika, oregano, and rosemary, stir well, then season to taste with salt and freshly ground black pepper. Simmer over low heat for 3–4 minutes.

Pour the mixture over the leeks in the ovenproof dish. Bake for 30 minutes, until most of the juices have evaporated and the top of the leeks are golden brown. Serve with long-grain rice or wild rice.

LENTIL STEW

Preparation time: 30 minutes
Cooking time: 35 minutes

Serves 4

For the spice mix:
- 1 teaspoon ground cardamom
- 1 teaspoon ground coriander
- 1 teaspoon ground fenugreek
- 1 teaspoon ground nutmeg
- 1 teaspoon ground cloves
- 1 teaspoon ground allspice
- 1 teaspoon ground cinnamon
- 1 teaspoon sweet paprika
- 1 teaspoon ground turmeric
- 1 teaspoon cayenne pepper
- 1 teaspoon freshly ground black pepper
- 1 teaspoon salt

For the stew:
- 1½ cups (360 g) green or brown lentils
- 1 clove garlic, crushed
- 1 onion, chopped
- 1 cup (200 g) canned crushed tomatoes
- cooked wild rice, to serve

To make the spice mix, combine the ingredients in a bowl, mix well, and set aside.

To make the stew, in a saucepan, mix the lentils with 2¼ cups (550 ml/18 fl oz) water, the garlic, onion, and 2 tablespoons of the spice mix. Bring the mixture to a simmer and cook over medium-low heat for 20 minutes, until the lentils have softened, adding extra water during cooking as necessary if the stew seems dry.

Add the tomatoes to the saucepan and cook over medium heat for 15 minutes, until well cooked.

Season to taste with salt and freshly ground black pepper. Serve with rice.

AFRICAN STEW

Heat the oil in a large saucepan. Add the tofu and onions and sauté over high heat until light golden. Then reduce the heat and simmer for 6–7 minutes, until the tofu takes on a nice golden color. Add all remaining ingredients except the peanut butter, bring to a boil, then immediately reduce the heat to low and simmer for about 30 minutes, until the vegetables are tender.

Transfer the cooked vegetables to a large bowl and set aside. Add the peanut butter to the sauce in the pan and stir well until smooth. Season to taste with salt and freshly ground black pepper. Pour the sauce over the vegetables, and serve the over rice.

Preparation time: 20 minutes
Cooking time: 45 minutes

Serves 4

- 4 tablespoons vegetable oil
- 1 lb 2 oz (500 g) smoked tofu, diced
- 2 onions, finely chopped
- 2 tablespoons tomato purée (passata)
- 4 tomatoes, chopped
- 1 red chili, finely chopped
- 2¼ lb (1 kg) mixed vegetables, such as cabbage, carrot, eggplant (aubergine), sweet potato, squash, and turnip
- 3 cups (750 ml/25 fl oz) vegetable stock (broth)
- ½ cup (130 g) smooth or crunchy peanut butter
- salt and freshly ground black pepper
- cooked rice, to serve

MIXED VEGETABLE STEW

Bring 2 saucepans of water to a boil. Put the potatoes, carrots, and cauliflower into the first pan, and the beets into the second. Boil the vegetables for 5 minutes. Drain and set aside separately.

Melt the vegetable margarine in a sauté pan. Add the onion and garlic and sauté gently over medium heat for about 5 minutes, until the onion is translucent. Add the ginger, saffron, and ground coriander, stir, and sauté for 2–3 minutes, until fragrant. Add the vegetables and cook for 20 minutes, until tender. Add the fava beans, scallions, and fresh cilantro. Stir well to combine and cook for about 10 minutes, until the favas are thoroughly heated. Season to taste with salt and freshly ground black pepper. Remove the pan from the stove.

Stir in the parsley and fresh lemon juice, transfer to a bowl, and serve with rice.

Preparation time: 20 minutes
Cooking time: 40 minutes

Serves 4

- 3 large firm potatoes, sliced
- 2 carrots, sliced
- ½ head of cauliflower, trimmed and cut into florets
- 2 beets (beetroot), peeled and sliced
- 2 tablespoons vegetable margarine
- 1 onion, chopped
- 8 cloves garlic, crushed
- 1 teaspoon ground ginger
- 1 teaspoon ground saffron
- 1 teaspoon ground coriander
- 1 lb 2 oz (500 g) canned fava beans (broad beans)
- 6 scallions (spring onions), trimmed and chopped
- 1 tablespoon chopped cilantro (coriander)
- salt and freshly ground black pepper
- 1 tablespoon chopped parsley
- juice of 2 lemons
- cooked long-grain rice, to serve

TORTILLA CASSEROLE

Preparation time: 30 minutes
Cooking time: 35 minutes

Serves 4

- 1 tablespoon vegetable oil
- 1½ cups (270 g) chopped onions
- 2 cloves garlic, finely chopped
- 1 teaspoon ground cumin
- 2 teaspoons chili powder
- 1 cup (200 g) chopped tomatoes
- 1 cup (240 ml/8 fl oz) vegetable stock
  (broth)
- 4 tablespoons tomato purée (passata)
- ½ cup (90 g) corn kernels
- 1 cup (200 g) cooked kidney beans
- salt and freshly ground black pepper
- 4 flour tortillas
- 1 cup (240 g) grated vegan cheddar cheese
- salad, to serve
- spicy salsa, to serve

Heat the oil in a large skillet (frying pan) over medium heat. Add the onion, garlic, cumin, and chili powder and cook for about 4 minutes, until the onion starts to turn golden. Stir in the tomatoes along with the stock and tomato purée, add the corn and beans, and cook over medium heat for about 10 minutes. Season to taste with salt and freshly ground black pepper.

Place 1 tortilla in a baking pan. Spread one-quarter of the bean mixture evenly over the tortilla, then sprinkle one-quarter of the cheese evenly over the top. Repeat with the remaining flour tortillas, bean mixture, and cheese to make 3 more layers, ending with the last quarter of the bean mixture and the remaining cheese. Bake for about 20 minutes, until the cheese on the top is golden brown. Serve warm, with a salad and spicy salsa on the side.

MING ART MUSHROOMS WITH RICE

Preparation time: 20 minutes
Cooking time: 20 minutes

Serves 4

- 2 tablespoons vegetable margarine
- 1 lb 2 oz (500 g) mixed mushrooms, such
  as white button, shiitake, and oyster
- salt and freshly ground black pepper
- 2 tablespoons all-purpose (plain) flour
- 2 tablespoons soy sauce
- 1 teaspoon ground Szechuan pepper
- cooked basmati or other long-grain rice,
  to serve

Melt the vegetable margarine in a saucepan over medium heat. Add the mushrooms and sauté for 8–9 minutes, until they just begin to release their juice. Season to taste with salt and freshly ground black pepper, then cover the pan and simmer for 4–5 minutes. Sprinkle in the flour, stir well, then add the soy sauce and stir again. Cover with the lid and simmer for 4–5 minutes. Sprinkle in the Szechuan pepper, stir to combine, and serve immediately, with rice.

MUSHROOMS AND WHITE ASPARAGUS

Heat 2 tablespoons of the oil in a large saucepan, add the onion, shallot, and garlic, and stir fry over medium heat, until golden brown. Add the asparagus and cook over medium heat for 5 minutes, turning the spears halfway through the cooking time, until fork-tender. Add the stock, bring to a boil, then reduce the heat to low and simmer for 15 minutes, until the asparagus is tender. Remove the asparagus and set aside on a serving plate; strain the cooking liquid into a bowl.

Heat the remaining oil in a skillet (frying pan) and stir fry the mushrooms over medium heat for 4 minutes, until they start to turn golden. Remove the mushrooms from the skillet and set aside. Add the wine to the pan and bring to a boil, then reduce the heat to medium-low and simmer for about 12 minutes, until the liquid has reduced by half. Add the reserved cooking liquid and the orange juice. Season to taste with salt and freshly ground black pepper, stir well, and simmer for 20 minutes, until the sauce starts to thicken. Add the asparagus and mushrooms, cook for 2 minutes. Serve immediately, with a lightly dressed salad.

Preparation time: 20 minutes
Cooking time: 1 hour

Serves 4

- 4 tablespoons olive oil
- 1 onion, chopped
- 1 shallot, chopped
- 3 cloves garlic, crushed
- 1 lb 10½ oz (750 g) white asparagus, trimmed
- 1 cup (240 ml/8 fl oz) vegetable stock (broth)
- 1 lb 2 oz (500 g) oyster mushrooms, chopped
- 2 portobello mushrooms, trimmed and chopped
- ½ cup (120 ml/4 fl oz) white wine
- juice of 1 orange
- salt and freshly ground black pepper
- salad, to serve
- French or Italian dressing, to serve

NOODLE STEW

Bring a saucepan of salted water to a boil, add the penne, and cook according to packet instructions until al dente. Drain in a colander, rinse with cold water until chilled, and drain again. Set aside.

Heat the oil in a wok or large saucepan, add the onion, garlic, and ginger, and cook over medium heat for 5–6 minutes, until golden brown. Stir in the tomatoes and the texturized vegetable protein and cook over medium heat for about 5 minutes. Stir in the stock, tamari or soy sauce, and paprika, bring to a boil, then reduce the heat to medium-low and simmer for 10 minutes, until well cooked.

Stir in the penne and simmer for 2 minutes. Stir in the spinach and cook for about 1 minute, until the leaves are wilted.

Adjust the seasoning to taste by adding tamari or soy sauce. Serve immediately.

Preparation time: 20 minutes
Cooking time: 25 minutes

Serves 4

- salt
- 6 cups (480 g) penne
- 2 tablespoons canola (rapeseed) oil
- 2 onions, thinly sliced
- 4 cloves garlic, thinly sliced
- 1 tablespoon finely chopped fresh ginger
- 2 tomatoes, diced
- 1 cup (240 g) texturized vegetable protein (soy mince)
- 4 cups (960 ml/32 fl oz) vegetable stock (broth)
- 4 tablespoons tamari or soy sauce
- 2 teaspoons hot paprika
- 5 cups (150 g) packed baby spinach leaves

MISO-GLAZED EGGPLANT

Preparation time: 20 minutes
Cooking time: 30 minutes

Serves 4

For the glaze:
- 4 tablespoons yellow miso
- 4 tablespoons mirin
- 4 tablespoons sake
- 2 tablespoons superfine (caster) sugar

For the eggplant:
- 2 large eggplants (aubergines)
- 2 tablespoons vegetable oil
- ½ cup (120 ml/4 fl oz) sake
- ½ cup (120 ml/4 fl oz) vegetable stock (broth)
- 2 scallions (spring onions), finely chopped, to garnish
- 2 teaspoons grated fresh ginger, to garnish

To make the glaze, use a whisk to mash the ingredients together in a saucepan, ensuring there are no lumps of miso remaining. Bring the sauce to a boil over medium heat, then immediately reduce the heat to heat and simmer, stirring constantly, for 8–9 minutes, until thick. Remove the pan from the stove, cover to keep warm, and set aside.

To make the eggplant, halve the eggplants lengthwise, then cut a cross-hatch pattern into the surface of the exposed flesh, ensuring the knife cuts about three-quarters of the way through the eggplant but does not cut through to the skin. (These cuts will help the glaze penetrate the eggplant during cooking.)

Heat the oil in a large sauté pan over medium heat. Fry the eggplant halves with the cut surfaces facing down for 6–7 minutes, until golden brown. Flip the eggplant halves over, then add the sake and immediately cover the pan to capture the steam. Cook, covered, for about 10 minutes, until the sake is reduced completely. Flip the eggplant halves back over, then add the stock. Cover with the lid and steam for about 15 minutes, until the tip of a knife passes through the eggplant easily. If the eggplant is still too hard, add a little water and continue to steam. Remove the lid to allow any excess water to evaporate.

Transfer the eggplant to a plate and brush with the glaze. Garnish with the chopped scallions and ginger and serve immediately.

MISO-GLAZED EGGPLANT

MUSHROOM STEW

Preparation time: 30 minutes
Cooking time: 10 minutes

Serves 4

For the spice blend:
- 2 cloves garlic, finely chopped
- 4 shallots, finely chopped
- 2 teaspoons finely chopped fresh ginger
- 1 teaspoon finely chopped fresh turmeric
- 1 red chili pepper, seeded and chopped
- 1 teaspoon tamarind paste
- 4 tablespoons vegetable stock (broth)
- salt and freshly ground black pepper

For the stew:
- 3 tablespoons tamarind sauce
- 2 tablespoons fresh lime juice
- 2¼ lb (1 kg) mushroom, such as shiitake, button, or portobello, sliced
- 1 lemongrass stalk, finely chopped
- 4 bay leaves
- 2 tablespoons vegetable oil
- 2 tomatoes, chopped
- 4 scallions (spring onions), white parts only, sliced
- 1 teaspoon granulated sugar
- salt and freshly ground black pepper
- 4 tablespoons chopped sweet basil, to garnish
- cooked rice, to serve

To make the spice blend, use a high-speed blender to pulse all the ingredients until well blended. Transfer the blend to a bowl and set aside.

To make the stew, mix the tamarind sauce and lime juice in a large bowl. Add the sliced mushrooms and toss to coat. Add the spice blend, lemongrass, and bay leaves and stir to combine.

Heat the vegetable oil in a large saucepan over medium heat. Add the mushroom mixture, tomatoes, scallion, and sugar and and stir fry for 7–8 minutes, until well cooked. Season to taste with salt and freshly ground black pepper, transfer to a serving bowl, garnish with the chopped sweet basil, and serve with rice.

MUSHROOM STEW WITH BABY SPINACH

Preparation time: 20 minutes
Cooking time: 10 minutes

Serves 4

- 2 cups (180 g) oyster mushrooms, chopped
- 2 cups (180 g) trimmed and chopped shiitake mushrooms
- 2 cups (180 g) white button mushrooms
- 2 tablespoons tamari or soy sauce
- 2 cloves garlic, finely chopped
- 1 tablespoon fresh lemon juice
- 2 tablespoons olive oil
- 2 cups (300 g) baby spinach
- 2 small red chilies, finely chopped
- 1 tablespoon white sesame seeds
- 1 tablespoon vegetable margarine
- salt and freshly ground black pepper
- sautéed potatoes or cooked rice, to serve

Combine the mushrooms in a large bowl. Add the tamari or soy sauce, garlic, and lemon juice and toss coat the mushrooms.

Heat the olive oil in a large skillet (frying pan) over medium heat. Add the mushroom mixture and stir fry for 4–5 minutes, until light golden. Add the spinach, chilies, sesame seeds, and margarine and cook for 3–4 minutes, until the spinach leaves are nicely wilted.

Season to taste with salt and freshly ground black pepper. Serve immediately, with potatoes or rice.

MUSHROOM AND CELERY STEW

SOUTH AFRICA

Bring a large saucepan of salted water to a boil. Add the celery and cook over medium-low heat for 35–40 minutes, until fork-tender. Drain the celery and set aside.

Melt the margarine in a large saucepan over low heat. Add the mushrooms, increase the heat to medium, and stir fry for 4 minutes, stirring frequently, until slightly golden. Sprinkle over the flour and stir well. Cut the cooked celery into 1-inch cubes, add to the saucepan along with the soy milk, and nutritional yeast, and mix to combine. Season to taste with salt and freshly ground black pepper. Cook gently over low heat for 5 minutes, until well blended. Serve immediately, with potatoes or rice.

Preparation time: 30 minutes
Cooking time: 45 minutes

Serves 4

- salt and freshly ground black pepper
- 2 medium heads or 1 large head of celery, peeled and cut into 2-inch (5 cm) pieces
- 4 tablespoons vegetable margarine
- 2 cups (240 g) button or shiitake mushrooms, sliced
- 1 teaspoon all-purpose (plain) flour
- ⅔ cup (150 ml/5 fl oz) soy milk
- 1 tablespoon nutritional yeast
- fried potatoes or cooked rice, to serve

OKRA STEW

KUWAIT

Using a paring knife, trim off the stem end of the okra pods at the base, then pare away the tough greenish-brown ring at the top of the pod.

Whisk the vinegar with the tamari or soy sauce and lime or yuzu juice in a large bowl. Toss the okra in the mixture until the pods are well coated. Refrigerate for 1 hour.

Heat the oil in a large heavy-bottomed saucepan or Dutch oven (casserole) over medium heat. Add the onion and garlic and stir fry for 5–6 minutes, until golden brown. Add the tomato purée and cook for 2 minutes. Add the chopped tomatoes with their juice, the ground cumin, cinnamon, allspice, and crushed red chili flakes, stir to combine, then bring the mixture to a low simmer and cook, uncovered, for 20 minutes, stirring frequently.

Using a strainer, drain the okra and transfer to a tray; pat dry with paper towels. Cut each okra pod crosswise into 3 slices and add them to the saucepan. Pour in the stock, bring the mixture to a low simmer, cover the pan, and simmer for 20 minutes, until the okra is tender.

Season to taste with salt and freshly ground black pepper. Stir in the parsley and lemon juice and serve immediately, with rice.

Preparation time: 30 minutes, plus 1 hour chilling
Cooking time: 50 minutes

Serves 4

- 1 lb 10½ oz (750 g) fresh okra
- ½ cup (120 ml/4 fl oz) white vinegar
- 1 tablespoon tamari or soy sauce
- 1 tablespoon fresh lime juice or yuzu juice
- 4 tablespoons olive oil
- 1 yellow onion, chopped
- 3 cloves garlic, finely chopped
- 2 tablespoons tomato purée (passata)
- 1 cup (200 g) canned chopped tomatoes with their juices
- 1 teaspoon ground cumin
- 1 teaspoon ground cinnamon
- 1 teaspoon ground allspice
- 1 teaspoon crushed red chili flakes
- 5 tablespoons vegetable stock (broth)
- salt and freshly ground black pepper
- ½ bunch parsley, chopped
- 1 tablespoon fresh lemon juice
- cooked rice, to serve

PLANTAIN CASSEROLE

Preparation time: 35 minutes
Cooking time: 1 hour 5 minutes

Serves 4

- 8 plantains
- juice of 2 lemons
- 4 tablespoons vegetable oil
- 1 onion, chopped
- 4 tomatoes, chopped
- 1 green bell pepper, seeded and chopped
- 1 green chili, seeded and chopped
- 4 cloves garlic, crushed
- 1 lb 2 oz (500 g) smoked tofu, diced
- 2 cups (475 ml/16 fl oz) vegetable stock (broth)
- salt and freshly ground black pepper
- 1 bunch cilantro (coriander), chopped, to garnish
- cooked rice, to serve

Peel and dice the plantains, and put them into a bowl. Drizzle with lemon juice and set aside.

Heat the oil in a large saucepan. Add the onion, tomatoes, bell pepper, chili, and garlic and stir fry over medium heat for 6–7 minutes, until lightly golden. Add the smoked tofu cubes and stir fry for 9–10 minutes, until golden on all sides. Add the stock and bring to a boil. Then reduce the heat to bring the mixture to a simmer. Add the plantains, cover the pan, and simmer for about 45 minutes, until the plantains are tender.

Season to taste with salt and freshly ground black pepper. Transfer to a serving bowl and garnish with cilantro. Serve hot, with rice.

PLANTAINS IN COCONUT CREAM

Preparation time: 25 minutes
Cooking time: 30 minutes

Serves 4

- 3 large green plantains
- salt and freshly ground black pepper
- 4 tablespoons vegetable oil
- 4 cloves garlic, finely chopped
- 1 onion, finely chopped
- 2 red chilies, finely chopped
- 2 cups (475 ml/16 fl oz) unsweetened coconut milk
- 2 tablespoons tamari or soy sauce
- 2 cups (300 g) baby spinach
- cooked white rice or fried sweet potatoes, to serve

Peel and halve the plantains lengthwise; then slice the halves and rub them with salt.

Heat 3 tablespoons of the oil in a skillet (frying pan). Fry the plantain slices in batches over medium heat for 6–7 minutes, until they are golden brown. Drain on paper towels and set aside.

Heat of the remaining vegetable oil in the same pan. Add the garlic, onion, and chili and stir fry for 5–6 minutes over medium heat, until golden brown. Add the coconut milk and tamari or soy sauce and bring the mixture to a simmer over medium heat. Add the fried plantain and spinach and simmer for 15 minutes, until the sauce becomes thick.

Season to taste with salt and freshly ground black pepper. Serve with rice or sweet potatoes.

PAPAYA, TOFU, AND COCONUT STEW

Heat the olive oil in a large skillet (frying pan) over high heat. Add the tofu and cook for 7-8 minutes, until golden brown. Add the onion and cook for 5–6 minutes, until the onion is golden brown. Add the papaya and cook for 5 minutes. Remove the saucepan from the heat and add the coconut milk.

Season to taste with salt and freshly ground black pepper. Serve alongside mashed sweet potatoes or fried plantains.

Preparation time: 20 minutes
Cooking time: 20 minutes

Serves 4

- 2 tablespoons olive oil
- 1 lb 2 oz (500 g) firm tofu, diced
- 1 onion, chopped
- 1 firm papaya, peeled, seeded, and thinly sliced
- 1½ cups (350 ml/12 fl oz) coconut milk
- salt and freshly ground black pepper
- mashed sweet potatoes or fried plantains, to serve

PEANUT STEW

Heat the oil in a large skillet (frying pan) over medium heat. Add the onion, garlic, and ginger and sauté for 5–6 minutes, until lightly golden brown and fragrant. Stir in the cumin, mix well, then pour in the stock. Whisk in the peanut butter and, when it is completely blended with the mixture, add the chopped tomatoes. Stir in the kale, cover the pan, reduce the heat to low, and simmer for 45 minutes, stirring occasionally, until thick.

Season to taste with salt and freshly ground black pepper, then transfer to a serving bowl. Garnish with peanuts and serve with long-grain rice and sriracha on the side.

Preparation time: 20 minutes
Cooking time: 50 minutes

Serves 4

- 2 teaspoons vegetable oil
- 1 red onion, roughly chopped
- 4 cloves garlic, finely chopped
- 2 tablespoons finely chopped fresh ginger
- 1 teaspoon ground cumin
- 6 cups (1.4 liters/49 fl oz) vegetable stock (broth)
- 1 cup (240 g) smooth or crunchy peanut butter
- 1 cup (200 g) canned chopped tomatoes
- 3 cups (450 g) kale, trimmed and chopped
- salt and freshly ground black pepper
- ½ cup (60 g) roasted peanuts, to garnish
- cooked long-grain rice, to serve
- 2 tablespoons sriracha, to serve

PEANUT STEW WITH CUCUMBER SAUCE

Preparation time: 30 minutes
Cooking time: 45 minutes

Serves 4

For the cucumber sauce:
- 1 cup (120 g) roasted peanuts, crushed
- ½ cucumber, peeled, seeded, and thinly diced
- ¼ cup (30 g) cilantro (coriander), chopped
- 1 jalapeño pepper, trimmed, seeded, and finely chopped
- 2 tablespoons fresh lime juice
- 1 tablespoon grated fresh ginger
- salt and freshly ground black pepper

For the peanut stew:
- 2 tablespoons olive oil
- 2 onions, chopped
- 1 celery stalk, chopped
- 1 tablespoon grated fresh ginger
- 2 green chilies, seeded and finely chopped
- 2 cloves garlic, finely chopped
- 2 sweet potatoes, peeled and sliced
- 7 oz (400 g) tomatoes, diced
- 2 cups (475 ml/16 fl oz) vegetable stock (broth)
- salt and freshly ground black pepper
- 1 lb 2 oz (500 g) butternut squash, peeled and diced
- 9 oz (250 g) cauliflower florets
- ¼ cup (60 g) peanut butter
- cooked brown rice, to serve
- ½ cup (60 g) watercress, trimmed, to garnish

To make the cucumber sauce, toss all the ingredients in a bowl. Refrigerate until ready to serve.

To make the peanut stew, heat the oil in large skillet (frying pan) over medium heat. Add the onion and celery and cook for 5–6 minutes, stirring occasionally, until translucent. Stir in the ginger, green chili, and garlic and cook for 5 minutes, until lightly golden. Add the sweet potatoes and tomatoes, increase the heat to medium, and cook for 5 minutes, stirring occasionally, until the sauce has thickened.

Stir in the stock and season to taste with salt and freshly ground black pepper. Bring to a simmer, partially cover the saucepan, and simmer for 10 minutes. Add the squash and cauliflower, bring the mixture to a low simmer over medium-low heat, and cook for 15 minutes, until the vegetables are tender.

Whisk together the peanut butter and ½ cup (120 ml/4 fl oz) hot water in a bowl. Add this mixture to the stew and cook for 5 minutes, stirring frequently, until well blended.

Spoon the stew over rice and garnish with watercress. Serve with the cucumber sauce on the side.

PINEAPPLE AND BEAN CASSEROLE

Combine the pineapple, onion, garlic, and agave syrup or maple syrup in a large skillet (frying pan). Cook over medium heat, stirring frequently, for 15 minutes, until the mixture becomes dry and the onion begins to brown. Add the remaining ingredients and mix well. Reduce heat to low, cover, and cook for 30 minutes, stirring frequently.

Serve over basmati or other long-grain rice or rice.

Preparation time: 25 minutes
Cooking time: 45 minutes

Serves 4

- 3 cups (540 g) ripe fresh pineapple, cored and finely chopped
- 1 cup (240 g) chopped onion
- 4 cloves garlic, finely chopped
- 1 tablespoon agave syrup or maple syrup
- 4 tomatoes, peeled and chopped
- 2 tablespoons fresh lime juice
- 2 teaspoons dried oregano
- 1 teaspoon grated lime zest
- 1 teaspoon cayenne pepper
- 2 cups (400 g) canned kidney beans, drained
- cooked basmati or other long-grain rice, to serve

PIRI-PIRI TOFU WITH WHITE CABBAGE

Heat the oil in a wok or deep saucepan. Add the garlic and sauté for about 2 minutes, until lightly golden. Add the cayenne, chili, cumin, and ginger and stir fry over medium heat for 2–3 minutes. Add the tofu and stir fry for 8–10 minutes, until golden on all sides. Add the cabbage, reduce the heat to low, and cook for about 20 minutes, until the cabbage is tender.

Season to taste with salt and freshly ground black pepper. Serve hot, with sriracha on the side.

Preparation time: 20 minutes
Cooking time: 50 minutes

Serves 4

- 2 tablespoons olive oil
- 5 cloves garlic, crushed
- 1 teaspoon cayenne pepper
- 1 red chili, finely chopped
- 1 teaspoon ground cumin
- 1 teaspoon ground ginger
- 1 lb 2 oz (500 g) firm tofu, diced
- 1 head Napa cabbage (about 1½ lb/750 g), trimmed and shredded
- salt and freshly ground black pepper
- sriracha, to serve

PORTOBELLO MUSHROOM AND VEGETABLE STEW

Preparation time: 25 minutes
Cooking time: 40 minutes

Serves 4

- 1½ cups (350 ml/12 fl oz) vegetable stock (broth)
- 2 cups (300 g) kale, trimmed and chopped
- 2 tablespoons vegetable margarine
- 1 tablespoon cornstarch (cornflour)
- 1 onion, chopped
- 9 oz (250 g) okra (ladies' fingers), sliced into thirds
- 1 green bell pepper, seeded and chopped
- 4 celery stalks, chopped
- 1 lb 2 oz (500 g) portobello mushrooms, sliced
- salt and freshly ground black pepper
- cooked rice, to serve
- sriracha, to serve

Pour the vegetable stock into a large saucepan and bring it to a boil, then reduce the heat to medium to bring the stock to a simmer. Add the kale and simmer for 5–6 minutes, until tender. Remove the pan from the heat and set aside.

Heat the margarine in a large heavy skillet (frying pan) over medium-low heat until completely melted and starting to simmer. Sprinkle in the cornstarch and cook, stirring constantly with a wooden spoon, for about 5–6 minutes, until the cornstarch starts to turn caramel colored and smells toasty. Add the onion, okra, bell pepper, celery, and mushrooms and stir fry for 6–7 minutes, until the onion is golden brown. Add the kale and stock, bring to a simmer, and cook over low heat for 20 minutes.

Season to taste with salt and freshly ground black pepper. Serve with rice and sriracha on the side.

PUMPKIN AND ZUCCHINI STEW

Preparation time: 25 minutes
Cooking time: 35 minutes

Serves 4

- 3 tablespoons coconut oil
- 1 onion, finely chopped
- 2 cloves garlic, crushed
- 1 large russet potato, diced
- 1 cup (240 g) diced pumpkin
- 1 cup (240 ml/8 fl oz) ruby port
- 2 cups (475 ml/16 fl oz) vegetable stock (broth)
- 1 cup (130 g) diced zucchini (courgette)
- 1 cup (120 g) unsalted peanuts, roughly crushed
- 2 tomatoes, roughly chopped
- 2 teaspoons crushed red chili flakes
- salt
- 9 oz (250 g) spinach, chopped
- 2 tablespoons cornstarch (cornflour), dissolved in 2 tablespoons water
- 1 bunch cilantro (coriander), chopped, to garnish
- cooked basmati rice, to serve

Heat the coconut oil in a large saucepan. Add the onion and sauté over medium heat for 5–6 minutes, until golden brown. Add the potatoes, pumpkin, port, and stock and bring to a quick boil. Reduce the heat to medium-low and add the zucchini, peanuts, tomatoes, and crushed red chili flakes. Season to taste with salt, then simmer gently for 25 minutes, until the potatoes and pumpkin are tender.

Stir the spinach and dissolved cornstarch into the mixture in the saucepan, cover the pan, and cook for about 4–5 minutes, just until spinach has wilted.

Transfer to a serving bowl, garnish with the cilantro, and serve with rice.

POTATO AND PEA STEW

Heat the oil in a large sauté pan over medium heat. Add the onion, garlic, and jalapeño and sauté for 5–6 minutes, until everything softens and starts to turn golden brown. Add the cumin and stir well. Add the potatoes, stir to coat with the oil, and sauté for 6 minutes, stirring frequently.

Add the stock and bring to a boil, then reduce the heat to low, cover the pan, and simmer for 20 minutes. Stir in the peas, parsley, and tarragon, then simmer, uncovered, for 5 minutes. Season to taste with salt and freshly ground black pepper. Serve with bread.

Preparation time: 20 minutes
Cooking time: 35 minutes

Serves 4

- 4 tablespoons olive oil
- 1 onion, finely chopped
- 4 cloves garlic, crushed
- 1 jalapeño pepper, finely chopped
- 1 teaspoon ground cumin
- 2¼ lb (1 kg) potatoes, sliced
- 6 cups (1.4 liters/49 fl oz) vegetable stock (broth)
- 1 lb 2 oz (500 g) frozen peas
- 2 tablespoons chopped parsley
- 1 tablespoon chopped tarragon
- salt and freshly ground black pepper
- bread, to serve

POTATO AND EGGPLANT STEW

Heat the oil in a saucepan over medium heat. Add the peppercorns and bay leaves and cook for 5–6 minutes, until the bay leaves start to be fragrant. Add the garlic and onion and fry for 5–6 minutes, until translucent. Add the sugar, season to taste with salt and freshly ground black pepper, stir briefly to mix, then add the tamari or soy sauce and vinegar. Reduce the heat to medium, then add the potatoes and eggplant. Stir briefly, cover the pan, and simmer for 40 minutes, until the potatoes and eggplant are soft but not mushy. Add a little water if the stew starts to become dry. Serve over rice.

Preparation time: 30 minutes
Cooking time: 50 minutes

Serves 4

- 2 tablespoons vegetable oil
- 1 tablespoon fresh green peppercorns
- 2 bay leaves
- 3 cloves garlic, finely chopped
- 1 onion, chopped
- 1 teaspoon granulated sugar
- salt and freshly ground black pepper
- 4 tablespoons tamari or soy sauce
- 4 tablespoons apple cider vinegar
- 1 lb 2 oz (500 g) potatoes, diced
- 1 lb 2 oz (500 g) eggplant (aubergine), diced
- cooked white rice, to serve

POTATO AND KALAMATA OLIVE STEW

Preparation time: 30 minutes
Cooking time: 45 minutes

Serves 4

- 4 tablespoons olive oil
- 1½ lb (680 g) potatoes, cut into wedges
- 8 cloves garlic, finely chopped
- 2 cups (280 g) kalamata olives, pitted (stoned) and sliced
- 9 oz (250 g) sun-dried tomatoes, rehydrated and chopped
- ½ cup (120 ml/4 fl oz) dry white wine
- ½ cup (120 ml/4 fl oz) vegetable stock (broth)
- 1 tablespoon dried oregano
- 1 tablespoon dried basil
- 1 tablespoon dried thyme
- salt and freshly ground black pepper
- green salad, to serve

Heat the oil a large skillet (frying pan) over medium heat. Add the potatoes and toss to coat. Add the garlic and cook for 3–4 minutes, until the garlic begins to turn golden. Add the olives and sun-dried tomatoes and stir well, then pour in the white wine and stock. Cover, reduce the heat to a low simmer, and cook for 30 minutes, until the potatoes are tender. Add the oregano, basil, and thyme and season to taste with salt and freshly ground black pepper. Stir well and simmer for another 10 minutes. Serve with a salad.

POTATO AND KALAMATA OLIVE STEW

SHIITAKE SCALOPPINE

Preparation time: 30 minutes
Cooking time: 30 minutes

Serves 4

- 1 lb 2 oz (500 g) spaghetti
- 4 tablespoons olive oil
- 2 cloves garlic, finely chopped
- 2 shallots, finely chopped
- about 1 lb (450 g) shiitake mushrooms,
  trimmed and thinly sliced
- 1 teaspoon dried thyme
- ½ cup (120 ml/4 fl oz) white wine
- 2 cups (260 g) chopped canned
  artichoke hearts
- ½ cup (75 g) capers in brine
- vegan parmesan cheese, to garnish
- basil, to garnish

Cook the spaghetti according to packet instructions until it is 2 minutes shy of al dente. Drain and mix with 1 tablespoon of the olive oil until well coated. Set aside.

Heat the remaining olive oil in a heavy skillet (frying pan) over medium heat. Add the garlic and shallots and stir fry for 5–6 minutes, until they start to turn golden brown. Increase the heat to medium-high, add the mushrooms and thyme, and stir fry for about 4–5 minutes, until the mushrooms start to turn golden. Add the wine, bring to a simmer, and cook for 3 minutes over medium heat. Stir in the artichokes and capers and simmer for another 4 minutes. Add the spaghetti, stir well, and cook over very low heat for 2–3 minutes, until the spaghetti is warmed through.

Transfer to a serving bowl, garnish with cheese and basil, and serve.

SPICY CABBAGE

Preparation time: 25 minutes, plus
  45 minutes soaking
Cooking time: 30 minutes

Serves 4

- 2 heads of Napa cabbage, trimmed and
  shredded
- 1 tablespoon salt, plus extra to season
- 2 tablespoons olive oil
- 3 onions, chopped
- 2 jalapeño peppers, seeded and sliced
- 1 lb 2 oz (500 g) sliced button mushrooms
- 1 yellow bell pepper, sliced
- 1 orange bell pepper, sliced
- 1 teaspoon five-spice powder
- 1 teaspoon ground cumin
- 1 tablespoon cayenne pepper
- 1 cup (240 ml/8 fl oz) vegetable stock
  (broth)
- 1 tablespoon cornstarch (cornflour)
- 1 tablespoon tamari or mushroom
  soy sauce
- boiled potatoes or cooked white rice,
  to serve

Put the shredded cabbage into a large bowl, toss with 1 tablespoon salt, and leave to stand for 45 minutes; this will help the cabbage to lose its strong bitter taste.

Heat the oil in a wok. Add the onion and jalapeños and sauté over medium heat for 5–6 minutes, until the onion is transparent and starts to turn golden brown. Add the mushrooms and bell peppers. Sprinkle the five-spice powder, ground cumin, and cayenne pepper on the top and stir well. Sauté for 10 minutes, until the peppers have softened. Stir in the cabbage and sauté for 4–5 minutes over medium heat, until the cabbage has just wilted.

Whisk the stock in a small bowl with the cornstarch and tamari or mushroom soy sauce, then stir this mixture into contents of the wok. Cook for about 10 minutes, until the sauce thickens.

Season to taste with salt and serve with potatoes or rice.

RICE AND SPINACH STEW

To make the stew, melt the margarine in a large skillet. Add the turnip and daikon and sauté for 10 minutes over medium heat, until they become translucent. Add the rice and stir to coat the grains. Add the sake along with 1 cup (240 ml/8 fl oz) of the stock and start stirring. Cook over low heat, stirring, until the stock is absorbed and the rice mixture is very thick. Continue adding ½ cup (120 ml/4 fl oz) of the stock at a time, stirring constantly and allowing the liquid to be fully absorbed after each addition. Stop adding liquid when the rice is at your desired consistency. Season to taste with salt.

Meanwhile, to make the pesto, use a small food processor to purée the spinach or kale, nuts, and olive oil.

Serve the rice with the pesto on side.

Preparation time: 30 minutes
Cooking time: 25 minutes

Serves 4

For the stew:
- 1 tablespoon vegetable margarine
- 2 baby turnips, peeled and quartered
- 2 medium-size daikon radishes, peeled and diced
- 1 cup (200 g) short-grain rice, such as sushi, Arborio, or Carnaroli
- 1 tablespoon sake
- 3 cups (710 ml/24 fl oz) vegetable stock (broth)
- salt

For the pesto:
- 2 cups (300 g) baby spinach or kale
- 1½ cups (135 g) walnuts or pine nuts
- 4 tablespoons olive oil

SEARED PORCINI

Put the mushrooms in a bowl and rub them with the garlic cloves. Season to taste with salt and freshly ground black pepper.

Heat the olive oil and vegetable margarine in a large skillet (frying pan). Add the porcini in batches and stir fry for 5–6 minutes, turning them halfway through the cooking time, until golden brown on both sides. Transfer to a bowl and set aside.

Put the vegetable oil into the same skillet and warm it over medium heat. Add the red onion and shallot and gently fry for 5–6 minutes, until golden brown. Add the brandy or cognac and cook over medium heat for about 8–10 minutes, until completely evaporated. Add the soy cream and nutritional yeast and simmer, stirring constantly, for 3–4 minutes. Season to taste with salt and freshly ground black pepper.

Transfer to a serving bowl. Serve with noodles or rice, with a lightly dressed salad on the side.

Preparation time: 30 minutes
Cooking time: 35 minutes

Serves 4

- 3 cups (330 g) fresh porcini, cut into ¾–1-inch (1.5–2.5 cm) slices
- 3 cloves garlic, peeled
- salt and freshly ground black pepper
- 2 tablespoons olive oil
- 2 tablespoons vegetable margarine
- 2 tablespoons vegetable oil
- 1 red onion, finely chopped
- 1 shallot, finely chopped
- 3 tablespoons brandy or cognac
- 1 cup (240 ml/8 fl oz) soy cream
- 1 tablespoon nutritional yeast
- cooked noodles or white rice, to serve
- green salad with French dressing, to serve

SPICY CAULIFLOWER

Preparation time: 15 minutes
Cooking time: 25 minutes

Serves 4

- 2 tablespoons olive oil
- 3 cloves garlic, finely chopped
- 2 green chilies, chopped
- 2 shallots, finely chopped
- 3 tomatoes, peeled and diced
- 2 tablespoons tamari or soy sauce
- 1 large head cauliflower, trimmed and cut into florets
- 1 onion, sliced
- 1 cup (240 ml/8 fl oz) vegetable stock (broth)
- 1 tablespoon fresh lemon juice
- 1 teaspoon five-spice powder
- 2 scallions (spring onions), white parts only, sliced
- 2 tablespoons cilantro (coriander), chopped, to garnish
- steamed rice, to serve

Heat the olive oil in a large skillet (frying pan). Add the garlic, chilies, and shallots and stir fry for 5–6 minutes, until golden brown. Add the tomatoes and tamari or soy sauce and sauté over medium heat for 3–4 minutes. Mix in the cauliflower, onion, stock, lemon juice, five-spice powder, and scallions. Bring to a simmer, then reduce the heat to low and cook for about 12–15 minutes, until the cauliflower is tender.

Transfer the mixture to a serving plate, garnish with cilantro, and serve with rice.

SPICY ASIAN RATATOUILLE

Preparation time: 25 minutes
Cooking time: 30 minutes

Serves 4

- 2 teaspoons vegetable oil
- 1 teaspoon toasted sesame oil
- 1 onion, diced
- 6 cloves garlic, finely chopped
- 1 tablespoon grated fresh ginger
- 2 cups (260 g) sliced zucchini (courgette)
- 2 cups (240 g) shiitake mushrooms, trimmed and sliced
- 2 cups (200 g) diced eggplant (aubergine)
- 1 cup (240 ml/8 fl oz) vegetable stock (broth)
- ½ cup (120 ml/4 fl oz) tomato sauce
- 4 tablespoons mirin
- 2 tablespoons dark soy sauce
- 2 tablespoons hoisin sauce
- 2 tablespoons tamari
- 1 tablespoon rice vinegar
- 1 tablespoon sriracha
- 1 lb 2 oz (500 g) rice noodles, cooked according to packet instructions
- ¼ cup (15 g) cilantro (coriander), finely chopped, to garnish

Heat the vegetable and sesame oils in a large saucepan, add the onion, garlic, and ginger, and sauté over medium heat for 5–6 minutes, until lightly golden. Add the zucchini, shiitake mushrooms, and eggplant and sauté for 8–10 minutes, until the vegetables begin to soften. Stir in the stock, tomato sauce, mirin, soy sauce, hoisin sauce, tamari, rice vinegar, and sriracha and bring to a boil, then immediately reduce the heat to low and simmer for 15 minutes, until the sauce starts to thicken.

Stir the rice noodles into the wok, then remove the wok from the stove. Transfer the mixture to a serving plate, garnish with cilantro, and serve.

SWEET POTATO AND PINEAPPLE STEW

Preheat the oven to 400°F/200°C/Gas Mark 6. Generously grease an ovenproof dish with the margarine.

Put the soy cream, tofu, and nutritional yeast into a bowl, season to taste with salt and freshly ground black pepper, and whisk together. Set aside.

Start layering the ingredients into the prepared dish, with 1–2 tablespoons of the tofu–soy cream mixture spooned on between each layer. Begin with a layer of pineapple, followed by sweet potato, coconut, and scallions. Repeat until all the sweet potato and pineapple have been used. Garnish with plum tomatoes and place in the oven. Bake for 30 minutes, until the plum tomatoes are cooked through and golden brown. Serve with salad or slaw.

Preparation time: 40 minutes
Cooking time: 30 minutes

Serves 4

- 2 tablespoons vegetable margarine
- 1 cup (240 ml/8 fl oz) soy cream
- 1 cup (240 g) silken tofu
- ½ cup (65 g) nutritional yeast
- salt and freshly ground black pepper
- 1 pineapple, peeled, cored, and sliced
- 4 sweet potatoes, peeled and sliced
- 2 tablespoons grated unsweetened dried coconut
- 2 tablespoons chopped scallions (spring onions)
- 2 plum tomatoes, sliced
- green salad or slaw, to serve

TEMPEH IN PAPRIKASH

Preheat the oven to 400°F/200°C/Gas Mark 6.

Pour the stock into a large saucepan and bring to a simmer. Remove the pan from the stove and cover to keep warm.

Put half the oil, the vinegar, cider, paprika, salt, caraway, thyme, chili powder, and garlic into a large bowl and whisk to combine. Add the tempeh and toss to coat. Transfer the mixture to a baking pan and bake for 30 minutes, until all the liquid is reduced by half. Set aside.

Heat the remaining olive oil in a large skillet (frying pan). Add the onion and stir fry over medium heat for 5–6 minutes, until golden brown. Add the stock, tomato purée, and sugar, and season to taste with salt and freshly ground black pepper. Cover the skillet, reduce the heat to low, and simmer for 10 minutes, until the liquid starts to thickens. Stir in the dissolved cornstarch and bring the mixture to a simmer. Cook over medium-low heat for about 4 minutes, whisking frequently, until the liquid is reduced half.

Add this sauce to the tempeh in the baking pan, cover with aluminum foil, and bake for 30 minutes. Serve with rice.

Preparation time: 35 minutes
Cooking time: 1 hour 15 minutes

Serves 4

- 4 cups (960 ml/32 fl oz) vegetable stock (broth)
- 4 tablespoons olive oil
- 2 tablespoons apple cider vinegar
- 1 cup (240 ml/8 fl oz) dry hard apple cider
- 1 tablespoon smoked paprika
- 1 teaspoon salt, plus extra as needed
- 1 tablespoon caraway seeds
- 1 teaspoon dried thyme
- 1½ teaspoons chili powder
- 6 cloves garlic, finely chopped
- 1 lb 2 oz (500 g) tempeh, cut into 1-inch (2.5 cm) dice
- 3 Spanish onions, chopped
- 3 tablespoons tomato purée (passata)
- 1 teaspoon granulated sugar
- salt and freshly ground black pepper
- 2 tablespoons cornstarch (cornflour), dissolved in 4 tablespoons hot vegetable stock (broth)
- cooked white or wild rice, to serve

SPINACH AND MUSHROOM STEW

Preparation time: 30 minutes
Cooking time: 50 minutes

Serves 4

- 2 tablespoons olive oil, plus extra
  for greasing
- 1 onion, finely sliced
- 2 cloves garlic, crushed and chopped
- 4 tomatoes, finely diced
- 2 red chilies, sliced
- salt and freshly ground black pepper
- 4 cups (480 g) shiitake mushrooms,
  trimmed and quartered
- 3 cups (450 g) baby spinach
- 3 cups (710 ml/24 fl oz) full-fat
  coconut milk
- cooked long-grain or wild rice, to serve

Preheat the oven to 400°F/200°C/Gas Mark 6. Grease a 9½ x 7-inch (24 x 18 cm) ovenproof dish with olive oil.

Put the onion, garlic, tomatoes, and chilies into a bowl, mix well, and season to taste with salt and freshly ground black pepper. Set aside.

Heat the olive oil in a saucepan. Add the mushrooms and stir fry for 10 minutes, until golden brown. Mix the mushrooms with the tomatoes.

Arrange one-third of the baby spinach across the bottom of the prepared ovenproof dish. Pour half the tomato–mushroom mixture over the spinach layer. Cover with one-third of the coconut milk. Create another spinach layer using another third of the spinach. Cover with the remaining tomato–mushroom mixture. Pour over another third of the coconut milk. Make a final spinach layer with the remaining spinach and cover with the remaining coconut milk. Cover the dish with aluminum foil and bake for 30 minutes, then remove the foil and bake for another 10 minutes, until the top is golden. Serve with rice.

SPINACH WITH SESAME

Preparation time: 20 minutes
Cooking time: 15 minutes

Serves 4

- 2¼ lb (1 kg) spinach, chopped
- 2 tablespoons dashi
- 1 teaspoon granulated or superfine (caster)
  sugar
- tamari or soy sauce
- 2 tablespoons sesame seeds
- cooked basmati or jasmine rice, to serve

Bring a very large saucepan of water to a boil; in a large bowl prepare an ice bath. Add the spinach to the pan and cook over medium heat for 3 minutes, until the spinach leaves are nicely wilted. Drain the spinach, transfer to the ice bath for 10 minutes, and let cool. Drain the spinach in a colander, then press with your hands to squeeze out as much water as you can. Remove the hard ribs from the spinach leaves, then transfer the spinach to a large bowl.

Whisk the dashi and sugar together in a small bowl until the sugar is completely dissolved. Pour this mixture over the spinach and toss to coat the cooked leaves. Add the tamari or soy sauce to taste.

Heat a dry skillet (frying pan), then add the sesame seeds and toast for 2 minutes, stirring constantly, until fragrant. Using a blender, process the toasted seeds to a powder and sprinkle over the spinach leaves. Toss to coat and serve immediately with rice.

TEMPEH AND TOFU IN MUSHROOM STEW

Heat the oil in a saucepan. Add the tempeh and tofu and stir fry for about 8 minutes over medium heat, until golden brown. Add the mushrooms and stir fry for 5 minutes, until they start to turn slightly golden. Transfer the tempeh, tofu, and mushrooms to a bowl, leaving behind the oil.

Put the onion and garlic into the same pan and sauté for 2 minutes, until fragrant. Add the tomatoes and fry for 6–7 minutes, until the tomatoes are tender. Stir in the tomato purée and red wine. Add the sweet paprika and season to taste with salt and freshly ground black pepper. Return the fried tempeh, tofu, and mushrooms to the pan, add the sambal sauce or chili-garlic sauce, stir, and simmer for 5 minutes.

Transfer the mixture to a serving plate, garnish with the cilantro, and serve with polenta or couscous.

Preparation time: 35 minutes
Cooking time: 25 minutes

Serves 4

- 4 tablespoons coconut oil
- 1 lb 2 oz (500 g) tempeh, diced
- 9 oz (250 g) firm tofu, diced
- 225 g (8 oz) shiitake mushrooms, trimmed and sliced
- 1 onion, chopped
- 2 cloves garlic, crushed
- ½ cup (100 g) diced tomatoes
- 4 tablespoons tomato purée (passata)
- ½ cup (120 ml/4 fl oz) red wine
- 1 tablespoon sweet paprika
- salt and freshly ground black pepper
- 2 tablespoons sambal paste or chili-garlic paste
- 2 tablespoons chopped cilantro (coriander), to garnish
- cooked polenta or couscous, to serve

TOFU PICANTE

Heat the oil in a saucepan. Add the tofu and stir fry over medium heat for about 8 minutes, until the tofu is golden on all sides. Add the onion and garlic and gently stir fry for 5–6 minutes, until slightly golden. Add the cumin, mint, paprika, crushed red chili flakes, and nutritional yeast. Stir well until the tofu is well coated, then add the stock and cook over very low heat for 4–5 minutes, until the liquid is reduced by a third.

Garnish with the parsley and serve with rice.

Preparation time: 30 minutes
Cooking time: 20 minutes

Serves 4

- 2 tablespoons olive oil
- 1 lb 10½ oz (750 g) firm tofu, diced
- 1 onion, sliced
- 3 cloves garlic, finely chopped
- 1 teaspoon ground cumin
- 1 teaspoon dried mint
- 1 teaspoon hot paprika
- 1 teaspoon crushed red chili flakes
- 2 tablespoons nutritional yeast
- 4 tablespoons vegetable stock (broth)
- 2 tablespoons chopped parsley, to garnish
- cooked basmati or wild rice, to serve

SQUASH WITH PRUNES

Preparation time: 30 minutes
Cooking time: 30 minutes

Serves 4

- 3 tablespoons olive oil
- 1 teaspoon ground cardamom
- 1 teaspoon ground cloves
- 2 onions, sliced
- 2¼ lb (1 kg) butternut squash, peeled and cut into 2-inch (5 cm) dice
- 3 cloves garlic, finely chopped
- 2 tablespoons fresh lime juice
- 2 cups (480 g) pitted (stoned) and chopped prunes,
- 1½ cups (350 ml/12 fl oz) vegetable stock (broth)
- 2 tablespoons ground toasted almonds, to garnish
- cooked wild rice or warm naan, to serve

Heat the olive oil in a saucepan. Add the cardamom and ground cloves and cook over medium-high heat for about 1 minute, until fragrant, then add the onion and squash. Cook for about 15 minutes, until the onion is golden. Add the garlic, lime juice, prunes, and stock, bring to a boil, then reduce the heat to low and simmer for 15 minutes, until the butternut squash is tender.

Transfer to a serving plate, garnish with the ground almonds, and serve with rice or naan.

SQUASH WITH PRUNES

SWEET AND SOUR TOFU WITH PINEAPPLE

Preparation time: 30 minutes, plus 1 hour draining
Cooking time: 25 minutes

Serves 4

- 1 lb 2 oz (500 g) firm tofu
- 1 cup (240 ml/8 fl oz) vegetable stock (broth)
- 4 tablespoons apple cider vinegar
- 4 tablespoons agave syrup
- 1½ cups (255 g) peeled, cored, and diced pineapple
- 2 cups (200 g) diced red bell pepper
- 1 tablespoon tamari or soy sauce
- 1 teaspoon sriracha
- 2 cloves garlic, finely chopped
- 1 tablespoon cornstarch (cornflour)
- 2 tablespoons vegetable oil
- ¼ cup (60 g) toasted cashews, coarsely chopped
- salt and freshly ground black pepper
- 2 scallions (spring onions), chopped, to garnish

Place the tofu in a clean sink, place a weight, such as a cast-iron saucepan, over it, and leave to sit for 1–2 hours to squeeze out the water and compress the tofu. Then cut it into ½-inch (1 cm) dice.

Put the stock, cider vinegar, agave syrup, pineapple, bell pepper, tamari or soy sauce, sriracha, and garlic into a saucepan set over medium heat and bring to a simmer. Cook for 15 minutes, stirring occasionally.

Whisk 2 tablespoons cold water with the cornstarch in a large bowl. Add the pineapple sauce mixture, stir to mix, and set aside.

Heat the vegetable oil in a skillet (frying pan). Add the tofu and cashews and stir fry gently for 10 minutes over medium heat, until the tofu is golden brown on all sides. Pour the pineapple sauce over the tofu and season to taste with salt and freshly ground black pepper. Stir to coat and remove from the heat. Serve immediately, garnished with the chopped scallions.

TEMPEH AND SPINACH STEW

Preparation time: 40 minutes
Cooking time: 20 minutes

Serves 4

- ½ cup (120 ml/4 fl oz) vegetable oil
- 1 lb 2 oz (500 g) baby spinach
- 3 green chilies, seeded and finely chopped
- 2 tomatoes, sliced
- 2 tablespoons chopped cilantro (coriander)
- 2 onions, chopped
- 1 tablespoon grated fresh ginger
- 3 cloves garlic, finely chopped
- 1 tablespoon chili powder
- 1 tablespoon ground turmeric
- 2 teaspoons ground coriander
- 1 lb 2 oz (500 g) smoked tempeh, diced
- 1 cup (240 g) unsweetened vegan Greek yogurt
- ½ cup (120 ml/4 fl oz) soy cream
- salt and freshly ground black pepper
- cooked basmati rice or fried potatoes, to serve

Heat 2 tablespoons of the oil in a saucepan. Add the baby spinach, chilies, tomatoes, and chopped cilantro and stir fry gently for 3–4 minutes over medium heat. Set aside.

Heat the remaining oil in a large saucepan. Add the onion, ginger, garlic, chili powder, turmeric, ground cilantro, and tempeh and stir fry over low heat for 10 minutes, until the tempeh and onion are golden brown. Add the yogurt, mix well, and simmer over low heat for 5 minutes. Stir in the baby spinach mixture, then cover the skillet and simmer for 4–5 minutes, until the spinach is completely wilted. Add the soy cream and season to taste with salt and freshly ground black pepper, then serve immediately, with rice or potatoes.

TURNIP AND SAUERKRAUT CASSEROLE

Preheat the oven to 350°F/180°C/Gas Mark 4. Grease an ovenproof dish with the margarine.

Bring water to a boil in a steamer pan. Place the turnips in the steamer basket and steam for 20 minutes, until tender-crisp.

Heat the oil in a large skillet (frying pan). Add the onion and sauté for 5–6 minutes over medium heat, until golden brown. Set aside.

Put half of the sauerkraut into the prepared ovenproof dish, sprinkle over the caraway seeds, then arrange the turnips on top and brush with the mustard. Cover with a layer of the remaining sauerkraut and top with the fried onions. Bake for 40 minutes, until golden brown. Stir and serve with potatoes.

Preparation time: 25 minutes
Cooking time: 1 hour 5 minutes

Serves 4

- 1 tablespoon vegetable margarine, for greasing
- 6 turnips, peeled and sliced
- 2 tablespoons vegetable oil
- 1 onion, chopped
- 1 lb 2 oz (500 g) sauerkraut
- 1 teaspoon caraway seeds
- ¼ cup (60 g) Dijon mustard
- boiled or baked potatoes, to serve

VEGETABLE HOT POT

To make the garlic oil, use a mortar and pestle or a high-speed blender to crush the garlic with a pinch of salt, then slowly drizzle in the olive oil while continuing to blend, until all the oil has been incorporated. Add the lemon juice and mix well. Refrigerate until serving.

To make the hot pot, put the stock into a large saucepan and bring to a boil. Add the carrots, potatoes, paprika, and turnip and cook over medium heat for 20 minutes. Add the green beans and cabbage and cook for another 20 minutes, until the potatoes and turnip are tender. Season to taste with salt and freshly ground black pepper. Drain the vegetables, reserving the stock in a large bowl.

Transfer the vegetables to a serving plate and garnish with the cilantro. Serve with the stock and garlic oil on the side.

Preparation time: 25 minutes
Cooking time: 40 minutes

Serves 4

For the garlic oil:
- 4 cloves garlic, finely chopped
- a pinch of salt
- 4 tablespoons olive oil
- 1 tablespoon fresh lemon juice

For the hot pot:
- 4 cups (950 ml/32 fl oz) vegetable stock (broth)
- 1 lb 2 oz (500 g) carrots, sliced
- 1 lb 2 oz (500 g) potatoes, sliced
- 1 tablespoon sweet paprika
- 1 lb 2 oz (500 g) small turnips, peeled and diced
- 2½ cups (250 g) green beans, trimmed
- 1 small white cabbage, cored and cut into 8 pieces
- salt and freshly ground black pepper
- 1 bunch cilantro (coriander), chopped, to garnish

TOMATO SAUCE WITH BREADS

Preparation time: 1 hour, plus rising
Cooking time: 50 minutes

Serves 4

For the breads:
- 2 cups (480 g) white semolina flour
  or type 00 flour
- ¼ cup (30 g) all-purpose (plain) flour
- 1 teaspoon onion powder
- 1 clove garlic, finely chopped
- 1 teaspoon active dry yeast
- salt
- oil, for greasing

For the tomato sauce:
- 2 tablespoons olive oil
- 1 onion, chopped
- about 1 lb 5 oz (600 g) cherry tomatoes
- 1 jalapeño pepper, seeded and chopped
- 4 okra pods, washed and sliced
- 2 cloves garlic, finely chopped
- 1 tablespoon fresh lemon juice
- 5 basil leaves
- salt and freshly ground black pepper

To make the breads, combine the semolina, all-purpose flour, onion powder, garlic, and yeast in a large bowl and season to taste with salt. Mix well, then add 1¼ cups (300 ml/10 fl oz) lukewarm water and knead to form dough. Cover the bowl tightly and leave to proof in a warm place for several hours, until the dough doubles in volume. Work the dough gently with your hands for few minutes, then cover and leave to rise by about a third of its volume.

Preheat the oven to 400°F/200°C/Gas Mark 6. Grease three baking sheets with oil.

After the second proofing, wet your hands and pick up roughly half a handful of the dough. Shape into a ball and flatten one side into a conventional bread form; place this on the prepared tray. Repeat with the remaining dough, placing the pieces 2 inches (5 cm) apart. Cover the baking sheets with aluminum foil and position on the lower rack of the oven. Bake for about 15 minutes, until the underside of each bread is golden, but the top remains pale. (If you want the tops to be golden, flip the bread over and bake for another 3–4 minutes.) Remove from the oven and keep warm for serving.

While the breads are baking, make the tomato sauce. Heat the oil in a saucepan over medium heat. Add the onion and sauté for 5–6 minutes, until golden brown. Add the whole cherry tomatoes, jalapeño, and okra and cook for 20 minutes, stirring frequently, until the tomato skins start to crack. Stir in the garlic and fresh lemon juice, then mash the contents of the pan with a wooden spoon. Add the basil, cover the pan, and cook for about 5 minutes.

Season to taste with salt and freshly ground black pepper. Ladle into bowls and serve with the breads on the side.

VEGETABLES IN PEANUT SAUCE

To make the sauce, heat the oil in a saucepan, add the onion, and sauté over medium heat for 5–6 minutes, until golden. Add the garlic and sauté for 2–3 minutes, until slightly golden Add the tomato purée and stock, mix until well blended, and cook for 2–3 minutes over medium heat. Remove the pan from the stove and stir in the peanut butter until completely blended. Add the bay leaves, season to taste with salt and freshly ground black pepper and set aside.

To make the vegetables, heat the margarine in a saucepan. Add the zucchini, carrot, eggplant, and peppers and sauté over medium heat for 4–5 minutes, until tender.

Transfer the vegetables to a serving bowl, top with the sauce, and serve with white rice or pasta on the side.

Preparation time: 25 minutes
Cooking time: 10 minutes

Serves 4

For the sauce:
- 2 tablespoons vegetable oil
- 1 red onion, finely chopped
- 5 cloves garlic, finely chopped
- 2 tablespoons tomato purée (passata)
- 2½ cups (600 ml/20 fl oz) vegetable stock (broth)
- 1 cup (240 g) smooth or chunky peanut butter
- 2 bay leaves
- salt and freshly ground black pepper

For the vegetables:
- 2 tablespoons vegetable margarine
- 1 zucchini (courgette), sliced
- 1 carrot, peeled and chopped
- 1 large eggplant (aubergine), diced
- 1 cup (240 g) diced mixed red, yellow, and green bell peppers
- cooked white rice or pasta, to serve

CABBAGE GRATIN

Preheat the oven to 350°F/180°C/Gas Mark 4. Grease an ovenproof 9½ x 7-inch (24 cm x 18 cm) dish with oil.

Bring a saucepan of salted water to a boil, then carefully add the cabbage and boil for about 10 minutes, until tender. Drain and set aside.

Melt the margarine in a saucepan over medium heat. Stir in the flour and cook for 3–4 minutes, until lightly browned. Reduce the heat to low, add the soy cream, and bring to a simmer, stirring constantly. Simmer for about 2–3 minutes, until the flour is completely incorporated and the sauce has thickened.

Put the white cabbage into the prepared dish, then pour over the soy cream mixture and sprinkle over the breadcrumbs. Mix to blend. Season to taste with salt and freshly ground black pepper. Sprinkle over the cheese and bake for 10–12 minutes, until golden brown. Serve with bread.

Preparation time: 30 minutes
Cooking time: 30 minutes

Serves 4

- vegetable oil, for greasing
- salt and freshly ground black pepper
- 2¼ lb (1 kg) white cabbage, trimmed and shredded
- 3 tablespoons vegetable margarine
- 1 tablespoon all-purpose (plain) flour
- 1 cup (240 ml/8 fl oz) soy cream
- 1 cup (120 g) breadcrumbs
- 1½ cups (150 g) grated vegan cheddar cheese
- bread, to serve

BAKED POTATOES WITH MIXED VEGETABLES

Preparation time: 25 minutes
Cooking time: 1 hour 20 minutes

Serves 4

- Cooking spray, for greasing
- 4 medium to large starchy potatoes (preferably russets)
- 1 red bell pepper, chopped
- 1 cup (200 g) canned black beans, drained
- 1 cup (240 g) canned corn
- 1 cup (125 g) shredded vegan cheese
- 4 tablespoons vegan sour cream
- 1 tablespoon finely chopped chives
- 1 red chili, minced, plus extra as needed
- salt and freshly ground black pepper

Preheat the oven to 400°F/200°C/Gas Mark 6. Coat a rimmed baking sheet with cooking spray.

Wrap each potato in aluminum foil. Arrange on another rimmed baking sheet and bake for 1 hour, until soft but still firm. Set aside until cool enough to handle, then halve the potatoes lengthwise and scoop out most of the flesh, leaving about ½ inch (1 cm) of potato flesh on the skin. Place the scooped potato in a large bowl. Reserve the potato skins.

Put the bell pepper, beans, corn, cheese, sour cream, chives, and chili into the bowl with the potato flesh and season to taste with salt and freshly ground black pepper. Mix carefully until well combined. Spoon the mixture into the reserved potato skins. Arrange the potato skins on the prepared baking sheet. Bake for 20 minutes, or until the filling is lightly browned.

Serve immediately.

BAKED BUTTERNUT SQUASH WITH ORANGE

Preparation time: 30 minutes
Cooking time: 45 minutes

Serves 4

- finely grated zest and juice of 2 oranges
- 3 tablespoons fresh parsley
- 2 garlic cloves, crushed
- One (1-inch/2 cm) piece of ginger, peeled and finely grated, plus extra as needed
- 1 large butternut squash, cut into slices ¾ inch (1.5 cm) thick
- 1 tablespoon olive oil
- salt and freshly ground black pepper

Preheat the oven to 400°F/200°C/Gas Mark 6.

Using a high-speed blender, process the orange zest and juice, parsley, garlic, and ginger on a high-speed setting until smooth. Set aside.

Arrange the squash in an ovenproof dish and brush with the olive oil. Season to taste with salt and freshly ground black pepper, then spoon over the orange mixture. Cover the dish with aluminum foil and bake for 40–45 minutes, until the squash is tender. Serve immediately.

CHICKPEA AND VEGETABLE TAGINE

Heat the oil in a large saucepan or wok over medium-low heat. Add the onions and carrots, cover the pan with a lid, and sauté gently for 10 minutes, stirring occasionally. Stir in the cinnamon, coriander, cumin, turmeric, paprika, and garlic and cook for 2 minutes, stirring frequently. Add the sliced vegetables, chickpeas, chopped tomatoes along with their juice, pulp and peel of the preserved lemon, and stock. Bring to a boil, then reduce the heat to low, cover the pan, and simmer very gently for about 45 minutes. Remove from the heat, let cool for 5 minutes, then season to taste with salt and freshly ground white pepper.

Arrange the couscous on a serving platter and garnish with mint. Serve with the stew and a small bowl of harissa. Roll the couscous with a small mound of stew in a lettuce leaf to eat.

Preparation time: 30 minutes
Cooking time: 1 hour

Serves 4

- 1 tablespoon olive oil
- 2 red onions, chopped
- 2 carrots, sliced
- 2 teaspoons ground cinnamon
- 2 teaspoons ground coriander
- 2 teaspoons ground cumin
- 1 teaspoon ground turmeric
- 1 teaspoon smoked paprika
- 3 cloves garlic, finely chopped
- 1 lb 10 oz (750 g) sliced vegetables such as zucchini (courgettes), carrots, sweet potato, fennel, parsnips, rutabaga (swede), turnip, and corn
- 2 cups (200 g) canned chickpeas, drained
- 1 cup (200 g) canned tomatoes with their juice
- 1 preserved lemon, peel chopped and pulp blended
- scant ½ cup (100 ml/3½ fl oz) vegetable stock (broth)
- salt and freshly ground white pepper
- chopped mint, to garnish
- cooked couscous, to serve
- harissa, to serve
- large romaine (cos) lettuce leaves, to serve

SPICED VEGETABLE AND MUSHROOM STEW

Preparation time: 20 minutes
Cooking time: 1 hour 5 minutes, plus
  5 minutes standing

Serves 4

- 3 tablespoons vegetable oil
- 1 onion, roughly chopped
- 2 cloves garlic, crushed and roughly
  chopped
- 2 green chilies, seeded and chopped
- 9 oz (250 g) potatoes, sliced ¼ inch
  (5 mm) thick
- 4½ oz (130 g) carrots, sliced
- 4½ oz (130 g) fresh shiitake mushrooms,
  trimmed and quartered
- 1 cup (240 ml/8 fl oz) vegetable stock
  (broth)
- 4 small zucchini (courgettes), sliced
- 6 baby corn
- 1 cup (100 g) snow peas (mangetout)
- 1 cup (150 g) fresh or frozen green peas
- 2 tablespoons chopped thyme, plus extra
  to garnish
- 1 tablespoon light brown sugar
- 2 tablespoons yellow curry powder
- 1 teaspoon ground turmeric
- ½ cup (120 ml/4 fl oz) canned coconut milk,
  plus extra as needed
- salt and freshly ground white pepper
- steamed rice or cooked polenta or naan,
  to serve

Heat the vegetable oil in a large saucepan. Add the onion and garlic and sauté over medium-high heat for 5–6 minutes, until fragrant. Add the chili and sauté for 2 minutes, until softened. Stir in the potatoes, carrots, and mushrooms and cook for 4 minutes, stirring frequently, until lightly browned. Add the stock, cover the skillet with a lid, and simmer gently over low heat for 30 minutes, until vegetables are just tender.

Add the zucchini and baby corn to the pan and continue to simmer the mixture over low heat for 15 minutes, until tender. Keep the pan covered to help the zucchini and corn steam as there is little cooking liquid. Add the snow peas and green peas and cook until they are just warmed through and still vibrant green, 2–3 minutes.

In a bowl, mix the thyme, sugar, curry powder, turmeric, and coconut milk and stir it into the vegetables. Season to taste with salt and freshly ground white pepper. Bring to a boil and simmer for 5–10 minutes at low heat. If the stew becomes too dry, add extra coconut milk.

Remove the skillet from the stove and let stand for 5 minutes before serving. Garnish with thyme and serve with rice, polenta or naan.

BAKED KIBBEH

To make the kibbeh, put the bulgur into a large bowl and add enough water to cover it completely. Set aside for 1 hour.

Preheat the oven to 440°F/230°C/Gas Mark 7½. Grease the sides and bottom of an ovenproof 9½ x 4¾-inch (24 x 12 cm) baking dish with half of the oil.

Thoroughly drain the bulgur in a strainer (sieve), pressing it with your hands to squeeze out excess water. Using a food processor, blend the bulgur with the chickpeas, onion, bell pepper, cinnamon, cayenne pepper, and cumin and season to taste with salt. Pulse until the ingredients are well combined, and the onions and peppers are the size of rice granules. Transfer the mixture into a large bowl, add the pine nuts, raisins, and parsley, and mix well with your hands.

Spread the bulgur mixture in the prepared baking dish and press with your hands to form an even, compact layer. Spread the remaining oil on top and bake in the oven for 30 minutes, or until the top of bulgur turns golden brown. Set aside to cool.

While the kibbeh bakes, make the dip. Combine the tahini, olives, lime or lemon juice, olive oil, parsley, and garlic and blend until completely smooth. Season to taste with salt.

When cool, cut the kibbeh into 2-inch (5 cm) squares. Arrange in a single layer on a serving tray and drizzle half of the dip on the top. Serve with the remaining dip on the side.

Preparation time: 35 minutes, plus
  1 hour soaking
Cooking time: 40 minutes

Serves 4

For the kibbeh:
- 6 tablespoons olive oil
- 2 cups (280 g) bulgur
- 1½ cups (350 g) cooked chickpeas
- 1 red onion, coarsely chopped
- 1 red bell pepper, chopped
- ½ teaspoon ground cinnamon
- ½ teaspoon cayenne pepper
- ¼ teaspoon cumin seeds
- salt
- 1 cup (140 g) toasted pine nuts
- ½ cup (80 g) golden raisins (sultanas)
- 1 bunch parsley, chopped

For the dip:
- ¼ cup (60 g) tahini
- ½ cup (70 g) kalamata olives, pitted (stoned)and chopped
- 3 tablespoons fresh lime or lemon juice
- 2 tablespoons olive oil
- 2 tablespoons chopped parsley
- 1 clove garlic, mashed to a paste
- salt

GREEN BELL PEPPERS STUFFED WITH LENTILS

Preparation time: 20 minutes, plus
  1 hour soaking
Cooking time: 50 minutes

Serves 4

- 4 tablespoons vegetable oil
- 4 green bell peppers, tops sliced off and reserved, seeded
- 1 teaspoon cumin seeds
- 2 onions, chopped
- 2 green chilies, seeded and chopped
- 1 tablespoon grated fresh ginger
- 1 cup (200 g) red lentils, soaked in water for 1 hour
- 1¼ cups (300 ml/10 fl oz) vegetable stock (broth)
- salt and freshly ground black pepper
- 1 teaspoon ground coriander
- 2 tablespoons chopped cilantro (coriander)
- cooked long-grain white rice, to serve

Heat half of the oil in a large skillet (frying pan). Add the bell peppers and fry over medium heat for 5 minutes, until golden brown. Set aside.

Add the remaining oil to the skillet and heat it over medium heat. Add the cumin seeds and cook for 2 minutes, until they begin to pop. Add the onion and chilies and fry for 8 minutes, stirring frequently. Stir in the ginger. Drain the lentils and add them to the pan along with the stock. Stir well, bring the stock to a low simmer, and cover the skillet with a lid. Cook over medium heat for 15–20 minutes, until the liquid has evaporated. Season to taste with salt and freshly ground black pepper and stir in the ground coriander and chopped cilantro.

Meanwhile, preheat the oven to 350°F/180°C/Gas Mark 4.

Stuff the peppers with the lentil mixture and close with the lids. Transfer the stuffed peppers to an ovenproof dish, ensuring they are standing upright, and bake for 15–20 minutes or until golden brown. Serve with long-grain white rice.

PLANTAIN BOATS WITH EGGPLANT

Preparation time: 20 minutes
Cooking time: 55 minutes, plus
  20 minutes cooling

Serves 4

For the plantain boats:
- 2 tablespoons vegetable oil, for greasing
- salt
- 6 very ripe plantains, peeled

For the filling:
- 2 tablespoons olive oil
- 2 onions, finely diced
- 3 cloves garlic, finely chopped
- 1 red bell pepper, diced
- 4 large tomatoes, diced
- 2 large eggplants (aubergines), diced
- salt and freshly ground black pepper
- 1 teaspoon cayenne pepper
- 1 teaspoon dried oregano
- 1 cup (125 g) grated vegan cheddar cheese
- 1 tablespoon chopped chives, to garnish

Preheat the oven to 350°F/180°C/Gas Mark 4. Grease a rimmed baking sheet with the vegetable oil.

Fill a large saucepan with salted water and bring to a boil, then carefully add the plantains and boil for 4–5 minutes. Remove the plantains from the water and set aside to cool for 20 minutes. Halve the plantains lengthwise and place on the greased baking sheet, leaving 1 inch (2.5 cm) between them.

To make the filling, heat the olive oil in a saucepan over medium heat. Add the onion and cook, stirring, for 5–6 minutes, until transparent. Add the garlic, bell pepper, tomatoes, and eggplant and mix. Cover the pan with the lid, bring the mixture to a simmer and simmer for about 20 minutes, until the vegetables are cooked through and the liquid has evaporated. Season to taste with salt and freshly ground black pepper and stir in the cayenne pepper and oregano.

Spoon the filling evenly on top of the plantains. Top with cheese and bake for about 20 minutes, until the cheese is bubbly and starts to turn golden brown. Garnish with chives and serve.

GREEN ENCHILADAS

To make the enchiladas, preheat the oven to 350°F/180°C/Gas Mark 4. Grease an ovenproof 9½ x 7-inch (24 cm x 18 cm) dish with the oil. Set the dish aside while you make the sauce.

To make the sauce, heat the oil in a saucepan over medium heat. Add the garlic and sauté for 4–5 minutes, until slightly golden. Add the oregano and cayenne pepper and cook over medium heat for 2 minutes. Stir in the flour until it is fully combined with the oil. Slowly add the tomato purée and stock, stirring constantly. Simmer over low heat, stirring, for about 10 minutes, until the sauce has thickened. Season to taste with salt and add the vinegar. Set aside.

To make the filling, heat the oil in a saucepan, then add the onion and garlic and sauté over medium heat for about 5 minutes, until soft. Add the cumin, green chiles, and pinto beans and cook, stirring, for 5 minutes. Mash the beans with a potato masher until they have the consistency of thick paste. Set aside.

Spoon 2 tablespoons of the filling on a tortilla, roll it up, and place into the prepared dish. Repeat with the remaining tortillas and filling. Pour 1 cup (240 ml/8 fl oz) of the sauce over the enchiladas and bake for 15–20 minutes, until bubbling.

Garnish the enchiladas with chopped green and red chilies and serve with the remaining sauce on the side.

Preparation time: 25 minutes
Cooking time: 40 minutes

Serves 4

For the enchiladas:
- 2 tablespoons vegetable oil, plus extra, for greasing
- 1 red onion, diced
- 3 cloves garlic, finely chopped
- 1 teaspoon ground cumin
- 2 cups (200 g) mild green chilles, seeded and chopped
- 2½ cups (625 g) canned pinto beans
- 12 fresh tortillas
- chopped green and red chilies, to garnish

For the sauce:
- 2 tablespoons vegetable oil
- 3 cloves garlic, crushed
- 1 tablespoon dried oregano
- 2 tablespoons cayenne pepper
- 2 tablespoons all-purpose (plain)flour
- ¾ cup (180 g) tomato purée (passata)
- 3 cups (750 ml/25 fl oz) vegetable stock (broth)
- salt
- 1 tablespoon apple cider vinegar

LEEK CROUSTADE

Preparation time: 30 minutes
Cooking time: 50 minutes

Serves 4

- 3 tablespoons olive oil, plus extra for greasing
- 1 cup (120 g) fresh breadcrumbs
- 1 cup (135 g) ground almond meal
- ½ cup (45 g) finely chopped walnuts
- ½ cup (120 g) vegetable margarine
- 2 large leeks, sliced
- 1 tablespoon all-purpose (plain) flour
- 1¼ cups (300 ml/10 fl oz) soy cream
- 1 tablespoon nutritional yeast
- 3 cups (300 g) grated vegan Cheddar cheese
- salt and freshly ground black pepper
- chopped parsley or cilantro (coriander), to garnish

Preheat the oven to 350°F/180°C/Gas Mark 4. Grease a medium-size ovenproof dish with oil.

Combine the breadcrumbs, almond meal, walnuts, and margarine in a bowl and mix by hand until nicely blended. Transfer to the prepared baking dish, tamp evenly onto the bottom of the dish, and bake for 10 minutes, until the top becomes golden brown.

Meanwhile, heat 2 tablespoons of the olive oil in a skillet (frying pan) over medium heat. Add the leeks and cook for 10 minutes, until tender. Transfer the cooked leek to the dish, placing it on top of the cooked breadcrumb mixture. Set aside.

Heat the remaining olive oil in a saucepan over medium heat, stir in the flour, mix well, and gradually add the soy cream. Add the nutritional yeast and keep stirring as the sauce thickens. Season to taste with salt and freshly ground black pepper. Pour the sauce over the leeks. Sprinkle the grated vegan cheese on top, then return the dish to the oven and bake for 30 minutes, until the top is golden brown. Garnish with parsley or cilantro and serve.

OYSTER MUSHROOM GRATIN

Preparation time: 30 minutes
Cooking time: 1 hour 35 minutes

Serves 4

- 4 tablespoons vegetable margarine, plus extra for greasing
- 2 cloves garlic, finely chopped
- 1 lb 2 oz (500 g) oyster mushrooms, halved
- 4 large leeks, white and pale green parts only, sliced
- 1 tablespoon finely chopped thyme
- 1¾ cups (420 ml/14½ fl oz) vegetable stock (broth)
- 1½ cups (350 ml/12 fl oz) soy cream
- 4 tablespoons dry white wine
- salt and freshly ground black pepper
- 3¼ lb (1.5 kg) russet potatoes, sliced into thin rounds
- 2 cups (250 g) grated vegan cheese
- green salad, to serve
- French or Italian dressing, to serve

Preheat the oven to 400°F/200°C/Gas Mark 6. Grease an ovenproof dish with vegetable margarine.

Melt 2 tablespoons of the margarine in a large, heavy skillet (frying pan) over medium heat. Add the garlic and mushrooms and sauté for 8–10 minutes, until the mushrooms are tender and golden. Transfer to a large bowl and set aside.

Melt the remaining margarine in same skillet over medium heat. Add the leeks and thyme and sauté for about 8–10 minutes, until the leeks are tender and beginning to brown. Transfer to the same bowl as the mushrooms and mix well.

Pour the stock, soy cream, and white wine into a jar, season to taste with salt and freshly ground black pepper and whisk well to combine.

Layer one-third of the potatoes on the bottom of the prepared dish. Top with half of the mushroom–leek mixture, then half of the cheese. Follow with another layer of potatoes and pour over half of the cream mixture. Top with remaining mushroom-leek mixture and cover with the remaining potatoes. Pour over the remaining cream mixture and sprinkle over the remaining cheese. Bake for 1¼ hours, until the potatoes are tender and the top is golden brown. Remove the dish from the oven and let stand for 20 minutes. Serve with a lightly dressed salad.

MIDDLE EASTERN VEGETABLE BAKE

Preheat the oven to 375°F/190°C/Gas Mark 5. Use 1 tablespoon of the olive oil to grease an ovenproof 9½ x 7-inch (24 cm x 18 cm) dish.

To make the tomato sauce, heat the oil in a large cast-iron skillet (frying pan). Add the scallions and fry for 3–4 minutes, until slightly golden. Stir in the garlic and fry, stirring, for 3–4 minutes, until slightly golden. Add the bell pepper and tomato purée, and cook for 2 minutes over medium heat. Stir in the texturized vegetable protein and stir fry for 2–3 minutes, until slightly golden. Add the remaining ingredients, bring to a boil, then immediately reduce the heat to low and simmer gently for 20 minutes, until the sauce thickens. Season to taste with salt and freshly ground black pepper.

To make the cheese sauce, put all the ingredients into a medium saucepan set over medium heat and whisk. Bring the sauce to a boil, stirring constantly, then reduce the heat to medium-low and simmer for about 8 minutes, until the sauce thickens. Reduce the heat to low and cook for another 2 minutes. Set aside.

To make the bake, arrange half the eggplant, overlapping, across the base and up the sides of the prepared dish. Pour over half of the tomato sauce. Over it layer half of the zucchini, then add half the cheese sauce. Repeat the layering until all the ingredients are used up. Sprinkle over the cheese and paprika, and drizzle with the remaining olive oil. Bake for 35 minutes, until golden brown. Allow to cool for 20 minutes before serving.

Preparation time: 45 minutes
Cooking time: 1 hour 20 minutes

Serves 4

For the tomato sauce:
- 2 tablespoons olive oil
- 3 scallions (spring onions), chopped
- 3 cloves garlic, chopped
- 1 red bell pepper, chopped
- 2 tablespoons tomato purée (passata)
- 2 cups (440 g) texturized vegetable protein
- 2 cups (480 g) canned tomato sauce
- 8 sun-dried tomatoes, rehydrated in water for 2 hours, chopped
- 1 teaspoon smoked paprika
- 2 tablespoons coconut oil
- 1 teaspoon dried mint
- 1 teaspoon ground cumin
- ½ cup (120 ml/4 fl oz) vegetable stock (broth)
- salt and freshly ground black pepper

For the cheese sauce:
- 2 cups (200 g) grated vegan cheese, plus extra for sprinkling
- 2 cups (475 ml/16 fl oz) soy cream
- 1 tablespoon all-purpose (plain) flour
- 3 tablespoons nutritional yeast
- 2 tablespoons olive oil
- 1 teaspoon garlic granules
- 2 tablespoons vegetable margarine
- 1 teaspoon turmeric
- 4 tablespoons vegetable stock (broth)
- salt and freshly ground black pepper

For the bake:
- 3 tablespoons olive oil
- 1 large eggplant (aubergine), cut lengthwise into thin slices and fried on a grill (griddle) pan
- 2 medium zucchini (courgettes), cut lengthwise into thin slices and cooked on a grill (griddle) pan
- 1 tablespoon ground sweet paprika

CABBAGE ROLLS

Preparation time: 45 minutes
Cooking time: 1 hour

Serves 4

For the filling:
- 2 tablespoons vegetable oil
- 3 small white onions, chopped
- 1 carrot, grated
- 9 oz (250 g) white basmati or other long-grain rice
- 1 cup (240 ml/8 fl oz) tomato purée (passata)
- 4½ oz (125 g) walnuts, crushed
- 2 tablespoons tamari or soy sauce
- salt and freshly ground black pepper

For the cabbage rolls:
- 2 large heads of white cabbage
- 6¼ cups (1.5 liters/50 fl oz) vegetable stock (broth)
- 3 tablespoons fresh lemon juice, plus extra to serve
  salt and freshly ground black pepper

For the sauce:
- 3 tablespoons vegetable oil
- 3 small white onions, chopped
- 1 carrot, chopped
- reserved cabbage leaves (see method), chopped
- ½ cup (120 ml/4 fl oz) tomato sauce
- 3 bay leaves

To make the filling, heat the oil in a saucepan. Add the onion and carrot and sauté over medium heat for 10 minutes, until the onion is transparent and the carrots slightly golden. Add the rice and stir-fry for 10 minutes, stirring constantly, adding a little water to the pan to prevent the rice from sticking to the bottom. Stir in the tomato purée, walnuts, and tamari or soy sauce and season to taste with salt and freshly ground black pepper. Heat for 1–2 minutes, stirring frequently until well blended, then remove the pan from the stove and leave to cool.

To prepare the cabbage leaves for the rolls, core each cabbage. Fill a large heatproof bowl with hot water and sprinkle in 2 teaspoons salt. Put the cabbage into the salty hot water and leave to marinate for 10 minutes, until the leaves can be removed easily. Then drain and set aside until cool.

Separate the individual cabbage leaves and remove any hard spines. Reserve 20 leaves that are the size of the palm of your hand. The remaining leaves will be chopped and added to the sauce.

To make the sauce, heat the vegetable oil in a large saucepan. Add the onion, carrot, and cabbage and sauté over medium heat for 10–12 minutes. Add the tomato sauce, bring to a simmer, remove the pan from the heat, and mix well. Arrange the bay leaves over the sauce, then remove the pan from the stove and set aside.

To prepare the cabbage rolls, put 1 tablespoon of the filling on the center of a reserved cabbage leaf. Fold one side of the leaf over the filling, then roll the length of it to close up the leaf around the filling. Using your finger, press the mass in the roll on the open side and close the roll. Repeat with the remaining leaves and filling.

Arrange the cabbage rolls snugly on the bottom of a large saucepan. Arrange another layer over that one, and continue layering until all the rolls are in the pan. Pour in the stock. Drizzle the lemon juice and season to taste with salt and freshly ground black pepper. Bring to a boil, then reduce the heat to medium-low, cover, and simmer gently for 20 minutes, without stirring, until well cooked.

To serve, remove the cabbage rolls from the stock, transfer to deep bowls, covered with the sauce, and top with a squeeze of lemon juice. Serve the remaining stock on the side in small bowls.

POLENTA WITH EGGPLANT SAUCE

ITALY

Heat 1 tablespoon of the olive oil in a large, deep skillet (frying pan) over medium heat. Add the shallot, garlic, and onion and stir-fry for 3–5 minutes, until softened. Add the mushrooms and cook for 4–5 minutes, until golden brown. Transfer to a large bowl and set aside.

Heat the remaining oil in the same skillet. Add the eggplant and cook over medium-high heat for 5 minutes, until golden and starting to soften. Add the bell pepper and cook for 3–4 minutes over medium heat, until lightly browned. Add the tomatoes and the onion–mushroom mixture, bring to a boil, then reduce the heat to low and simmer for 45 minutes, until the sauce thickens, stirring occasionally.

Meanwhile, bring 6¼ cups (1.5 liters/50 fl oz) water to a boil and slowly whisk in the polenta, then reduce the heat to low and cook for 30 minutes, whisking frequently, until thick and creamy. Season to taste with salt and freshly ground black pepper. (If using instant polenta, cook according to packet instructions.)

Transfer the polenta to a deep serving plate, spoon over the eggplant sauce, garnish with parsley, and serve immediately.

Preparation time: 20 minutes
Cooking time: 1 hour

Serves 4 to 6

- 3 tablespoons olive oil
- 1 shallot, finely chopped
- 2 cloves garlic, finely chopped
- 1 medium onion, chopped
- 1 cup (75 g) shiitake mushrooms, trimmed and quartered
- 2 medium eggplants (aubergines), diced
- 1 red bell pepper, seeded and chopped
- 2½ cups (590 g) canned tomatoes, crushed
- 1⅔ cups (250 g) polenta
- salt and freshly ground black pepper
- 2 tablespoons chopped parsley, to garnish

POTATO CAKE

FRANCE

Preheat the oven to 350°F/180°C/Gas Mark 4.

Combine the potatoes, onion, garlic, bay leaves, and olive oil in an ovenproof dish. Mix well. Cover the dish with aluminum foil and bake for 20 minutes. Remove the foil and bake for another 15 minutes, until the potatoes and onions are well cooked.

Grease a 9½ x 7-inch (24 cm x 18 cm) ovenproof dish with oil. Arrange half of the potato mixture in the dish and sprinkle with half of the cheese. Layer the remaining potato mixture on top, top with herbes de Provence and basil, then cover with the remaining cheese. Season to taste with salt and freshly ground black pepper. Cover the dish with aluminum foil and bake for 15 minutes, until the cheese is completely melted.

Serve with a lightly dressed salad.

Preparation time: 35 minutes
Cooking time: 50 minutes

Serves 4

- 8 large potatoes, thinly sliced
- 1 large onion, thinly sliced
- 2 cloves garlic, finely chopped
- 2 bay leaves
- 4 tablespoons olive oil, plus extra for greasing
- 9 oz (250 g) grated vegan cheddar cheese
- 2 tablespoons hèrbes de Provence
- ½ cup (30 g) finely chopped basil
- salt and freshly ground black pepper
- green salad, to serve
- Italian or French dressing, to serve

SWEET POTATO AND SHIITAKE BAKE

Preparation time: 30 minutes
Cooking time: 50 minutes

Serves 4

- 1 tablespoon vegetable margarine, plus extra for greasing
- 6 medium sweet potatoes, sliced
- 2 onions, sliced
- 1 lb 2 oz (500 g) fresh shiitake mushrooms
- 2 teaspoons ground thyme
- salt and freshly ground black pepper
- 1 cup (240 ml/8 fl oz) soy cream
- 1 tablespoon nutritional yeast
- 3 tablespoons chopped parsley

Preheat the oven to 400°F/200°C/Gas Mark 6. Grease a baking pan with vegetable margarine.

Layer the sweet potatoes, onions, and shiitake mushrooms in the prepared pan. Sprinkle over the thyme and season to taste with salt and freshly ground black pepper.

Mix the soy cream with the nutritional yeast and pour the mixture over the vegetables. Cover the pan with aluminum foil and bake for 30 minutes. Remove the foil and bake for another 20 minutes, until the potatoes are tender and the sauce has thickened and is creamy and smooth.

Sprinkle with parsley and serve.

ZUCCHINI AND PEACH ROAST

Preparation time: 30 minutes
Cooking time: 40 minutes

Serves 4

For the yogurt sauce:
- 9 oz (250 g) unsweetened vegan Greek yogurt
- 4 cloves garlic, finely chopped
- 4 tablespoons fresh lemon juice
- salt

For the roast:
- 2 red or yellow bell peppers, sliced
- 3 zucchini (courgettes), sliced
- 4 tablespoons olive oil
- 8 plum tomatoes, chopped
- 3¼ lb (1.5 kg) peaches, pitted (stoned) and diced
- ½ cup (30 g) chopped mint, to garnish

Preheat the oven to 400°F/200°C/Gas Mark 6.

To make the yogurt sauce, whisk together the yogurt, garlic, and lemon juice in a bowl and season to taste with salt. Refrigerate until ready to serve.

To make the roast, mix the bell peppers and zucchini in a 10 x 70-inch (26 x 18 cm) ovenproof dish, drizzle with half of the olive oil, and bake, uncovered, for 20 minutes. Add the tomatoes and peaches, cover the dish with aluminum foil, and cook for another 20 minutes, until the peaches are well cooked.

Remove the dish from the oven, transfer the roast to a serving plate, garnish with the mint, and serve with the yogurt sauce on the side.

BUCKWHEAT DUMPLINGS

To make the filling, bring a saucepan of water to a boil. Add the bok choy and cook over medium heat for 5 minutes, until wilted. Drain, let cool enough to handle, and squeeze dry. Set aside

Using a food processoror high-speed blender, grind the poppy seeds and peppercorns to a powder. Add the garlic and ginger and pulse until well blended. Add the onion and pulse again. Add the bok choy cottage cheese or tofu, and chili powder, season to taste with salt, and process for about 10 seconds, until well combined. Set aside.

Heat the vegetable margarine in a skillet (frying pan) over medium heat until completely melted and simmering. Add the filling and mix until well combined with the vegetable margarine. Season to taste with salt and freshly ground black pepper.

To make the dough, combine the flours in the bowl of a food processor fitted with an S-blade. With the motor running, pour 1 cup (240 ml/ 8 fl oz) water through the feed tube and process until the dough forms a ball.

Transfer the dough to a flour-dusted work surface and dust the ball with flour. Cut the dough into 8 pieces and dust each of these with flour. Using either a rolling pin or a pasta machine, roll out each piece to a thickness of 2 mm, dusting with flour occasionally to prevent sticking.

Cut the sheets into 4 x 2-inch (10 x 5 cm) rectangles. Place 1 teaspoon of the filling mixture on the center of one side of a rectangle, then repeat with each rectangle. Brush the edges lightly with water and fold the rectangles over to make squares, pressing the edges with your fingers or the tines of a fork to seal them well.

Bring a large saucepan of water to a simmer. Cook the dumplings, in batches, in the simmering water for about 7 minutes, until tender. Transfer to a paper towel–lined plate to drain.

To finish, heat the vegetable oil in a pan or wok. Add the dumplings and stir-fry over medium heat for 8–10 minutes, until golden brown on each side. Transfer to a paper towel–lined plate to absorb the excess oil. Serve immediately, with soy sauce and sriracha on the side.

Preparation time: 30 minutes
Cooking time: 20 minutes

Serves 4

- 3 tablespoons vegetable oil
- soy sauce, to serve
- sriracha, to serve

For the filling:
- 1 lb 5 oz (600 g) bok choy, trimmed and quartered
- 3 tablespoons poppy seeds
- 1 teaspoon Szechuan peppercorns
- 2 cloves garlic, finely chopped
- one (1-inch /2.5 cm) piece fresh ginger, peeled and sliced
- 1 red onion, quartered
- ½ cup (120 g) vegan cottage cheese or silken tofu
- 1 teaspoon chili powder
- salt and freshly ground black pepper
- ½ cup (120 g) vegetable margarine

For the dough:
- 2 cups (250 g) all-purpose (plain) flour, plus extra for dusting
- 1 cup (125 g) buckwheat flour

CHEESE PIE

Preparation time: 30 minutes
Cooking time: 45 minutes

Serves 4

- 1 tablespoon vegetable oil, for greasing
- ½ cup (120 g) silken tofu (smoked if available)
- 1 cup (240 ml/8 fl oz) soy milk
- ¼ cup (65 g) raw cashews, lightly toasted and coarsely ground
- ¼ cup (30 g) raw sunflower seeds, lightly toasted and ground
- 1 tablespoon sesame seeds, lightly toasted and ground
- 3 tablespoons chickpea flour
- 3 tablespoons nutritional yeast
- ¼ teaspoon ground turmeric
- 2 tablespoons fresh lemon juice
- 2 tablespoons vegetable margarine
- 1 lb 5 oz (600 g) vegan puff pastry dough
- unsweetened soy yogurt or vegan sour cream, to serve

Preheat the oven to 375°F/190°C/Gas Mark 5. Lightly grease a 6 x 9-inch (15 x 23 cm) ovenproof dish.

Using a food processor or high-speed blender, process the silken tofu and soy milk together until smooth.

Transfer the mixture to a large bowl. Add the cashews, sunflower and sesame seeds, chickpea flour, nutritional yeast, turmeric, and lemon juice and season to taste with salt and freshly ground black pepper. Mix until well blended and set aside.

Melt the vegetable margarine in a small saucepan over low heat.

Roll out and cut the pastry dough as needed to line the prepared dish. Brush the dough with the melted vegetable margarine.

Pour one-third of the filling mixture into the dish over the pastry lining and spread it evenly across the pastry. Carefully top with another layer of pastry, then brush again with melted vegetable margarine. Assemble another 2–3 layers until the filling is used up, ending with a layer of pastry on top. Brush the top with margarine. Bake for 45 minutes, until the pastry is puffy and golden brown.

Let the pie cool for 20 minutes before cutting. Serve with soy yogurt or sour cream on the side.

BAKED SAUERKRAUT

Preparation time: 35 minutes
Cooking time: 1 hour 30 minutes

Serves 4

- 2 tablespoons olive oil or vegetable oil, plus extra for greasing
- 1 onion, sliced
- 2 cloves garlic, crushed
- 1 teaspoon salt, plus more to season
- 5 cups (750 g) sauerkraut
- 1 lb 5 oz (600 g) russet potatoes, peeled and diced
- 1 tablespoon crushed red chili flakes
- 1 tablespoon sweet paprika
- 4 bay leaves
- freshly ground black pepper

Preheat the oven to 400°F/200°C/Gas Mark 6. Grease a 9½ x 7-inch (24 cm x 18 cm) ovenproof dish with oil.

Put half of the onion, the garlic, and 1 teaspoon salt into the bottom of a medium-size Dutch oven (casserole). Add the first layer of sauerkraut (a third), followed by a layer of potatoes. Season with the chili flakes, paprika, some freshly ground black pepper, and 1 bay leaf. Repeat with the remaining onion, a third of the sauerkraut, and the remaining potatoes and seasoning, then add the last third of sauerkraut. Drizzle over the oil, cover the dish with aluminum foil, and bake for 1 hour, or until well cooked. Remove the foil, reduce the heat to 350°F/170°C/Gas Mark 5, and bake the sauerkraut for another 30 minutes. Serve immediately in individual bowls.

CABBAGE STUFFED WITH CHEESE

To make the filling, combine all the ingredients in a large bowl, season to taste with salt, and mix well. Cover the bowl with plastic wrap (clingfilm) and refrigerate for 2 hours.

To make the cabbage, bring a saucepan of salted water to a boil; in a large bowl prepare an ice bath. Cook the cabbage in the salted water for about 10 minutes, until soft. Separate into individual leaves, discarding any hard spines, and place in the ice bath.

Spread out a cabbage leaf on a cutting board. Put 2 tablespoons of the filling in the center of the leaf, fold one side over the filling, and roll up. Pin down the loose end of the leaf with a small bamboo skewer. Repeat with the remaining leaves and filling.

Bring a steamer pan of water to a boil. Using your finger, spread melted vegetable margarine on the stuffed leaves, then stack in the steamer basket. Steam for about 10 minutes, until the stuffing is cooked. Transfer the steamed rolls to a large plate. Cover with a clean kitchen towel to keep the rolls warm until the sauce is ready.

To make the sauce, melt the vegetable margarine in a saucepan. Add the mustard seeds and onion and sauté over medium heat for 5–6 minutes, until the onion is golden brown. Add the garlic, ginger, and chili powder and stir-fry over low heat for 2 minutes, until lightly golden. Add the tomatoes and stock and season to taste with salt and freshly ground black pepper. Bring to a simmer, then cook over medium-low heat for 10–12 minutes, until the sauce thickens.

Carefully transfer the stuffed cabbage rolls to the pan with the sauce and cook over low heat for 8–10 minutes, until the sauce continues to thicken.

Transfer to the cabbage rolls and sauce to a serving plate and garnish with the scallions. Serve with roti or naan and vegan yogurt on the side.

Preparation time: 1 hour, plus 2 hours chilling
Cooking time: 50 minutes

Serves 4

For the filling:
- 1 lb 2 oz (500 g) vegan feta cheese or similar, in crumbles
- 1 cup (140 g) finely chopped onions
- ½ scallion (spring onion), finely chopped
- 1 cup (200 g) cooked white long-grain rice
- 2 teaspoons finely chopped dill
- 2 cloves garlic, finely chopped
- 1 teaspoon finely chopped fresh ginger
- 3 red chilies, seeded and finely chopped
- 1 teaspoon ground turmeric
- 1 teaspoon ground cumin
- 1 teaspoon freshly ground black pepper
- 1 teaspoon cornstarch (cornflour)
- 2 tablespoons egg replacer (diluted in 1¾ oz/50 ml warm water)
- salt

For the cabbage:
- salt
- 1 head of white cabbage, cored
- 2 tablespoons vegetable margarine, melted
- 2 scallions (spring onions), finely chopped, to garnish
- roti or naan, to serve

For the sauce:
- 2 tablespoons vegetable margarine
- 1 teaspoon mustard seeds
- 2 cups (280 g) chopped onions
- 2 cloves garlic, finely chopped
- 1 teaspoon grated fresh ginger
- 1 teaspoon chili powder
- 1 cup (200 g) chopped tomatoes
- 1 cup (240 ml/8 fl oz) vegetable stock (broth)
- salt and freshly ground black pepper
- 1 cup (240 g) unsweetened vegan Greek yogurt or vegan sour cream, to serve

CHICKPEA CURRY BURRITOS WITH MINT AND CHILI SAUCE

Preparation time: 35 minutes
Cooking time: 50 minutes

Serves 4

For the mint and chili sauce:
- 2 teaspoons granulated sugar
- 1 teaspoon salt
- 1 tablespoon chopped fresh ginger
- 1 small serrano or jalapeño pepper, seeded and chopped
- 1 clove garlic, finely chopped
- 3 cups (75 g) mint, chopped
- 2 tablespoons rice vinegar or apple cider vinegar

For the burritos:
- 3 large cloves garlic, finely chopped
- 1 tablespoon finely chopped fresh ginger,
- 1 jalapeño pepper, trimmed, seeded, and chopped
- 1 large onion, chopped
- 1 tablespoon canola (rapeseed) oil
- 1½ tablespoons curry powder
- 1 tablespoon ground cumin
- 1 lb 2 oz (500 g) potatoes, diced
- ½ cup (80 g) currants or raisins
- salt
- 2 cups (280 g) canned chickpeas, drained
- 1 cup (240 g) frozen peas, defrosted
- ½ cup (60 g) cilantro (coriander), chopped
- 8 flour tortillas

To make the mint and chili sauce, first put the sugar and salt into the bowl of a high-speed blender or mini food processor. With the motor running, drop in the ginger, chili pepper, and garlic and process until finely chopped. Add the mint and vinegar. Pulse until everything is finely chopped, scraping down the sides of the bowl if needed. Transfer to a small serving bowl and refrigerate until ready to serve.

To make the burritos, use a food processor or high-speed blender to process the garlic, ginger, and jalapeño, pulsing until the mixture is reduced to a paste. Add the onion and pulse until it is coarsely chopped.

Heat the oil in a large nonstick skillet (frying pan). Add the onion mixture and stir-fry over medium heat, stirring constantly, for 5–6 minutes, until light golden. Add the curry powder and cumin and cook, stirring constantly, for about 2 minutes, until fragrant. Add the potatoes, 1½ cups (350 ml/12 fl oz) water, and the currants or raisins and season to taste with salt. Bring to a simmer, then reduce the heat to low, cover the skillet with a lid, and simmer for about 30 minutes, until the potatoes are tender. Stir in the chickpeas, peas, and cilantro. Cook for about 3–4 minutes over medium heat and adjust the seasoning as necessary.

Meanwhile, gently heat the tortillas in a hot skillet. Wrap them in aluminum foil to keep them warm.

To serve, set out the warm tortillas on a plate, with the curry filling and the mint and chili sauce in separate bowls.

CHICKPEA CURRY BURRITOS WITH MINT AND CHILI SAUCE

DALAI LAMA DUMPLINGS

Preparation time: 35 minutes
Cooking time: 1 hour 10 minutes

Serves 4

For the dumplings:
- 1 lb 2 oz (500 g) russet potatoes or similar
- 3 tablespoons olive oil
- 6 onions, chopped
- 9 oz (250 g) shiitake mushroom caps, chopped
- 9 oz (250 g) grated vegan cheese
- 1 bunch cilantro (coriander), chopped
- 2 tablespoons nutritional yeast
- salt and freshly ground black pepper
- 40 round or square vegan wanton wrappers

For the soup:
- 2 tablespoons olive oil
- 1 onion, chopped
- 2 tomatoes, chopped
- 1 tablespoon chopped cilantro (coriander)
- 2 cups (480 ml/16 fl oz) vegetable stock (broth)

- chopped scallions (spring onions), to serve
- soy sauce, to serve

To make the dumplings, put the potatoes into a saucepan and cover them with water. Bring to a boil and cook for 35–40 minutes, until the potatoes are fork-tender. Drain the potatoes, then using a food processor or high-speed blender, mash them until smooth. Set aside to cool.

Heat the olive oil in a saucepan. Add the onion and cook over medium heat for 5–6 minutes, until soft. Add the mushrooms, cover the pan, and cook for about 5 minutes, until the mushrooms are soft. Transfer the mixture to a bowl and leave to cool. Once cool, mix in the cooled potatoes, grated vegan cheese, chopped cilantro, and nutritional yeast and season to taste with salt and freshly ground black pepper.

Lay a wonton wrapper on a work surface. Place 1 tablespoon of the filling mixture on the wrapper, then fold the wrapper over the filling and press the edges together to seal. (Use the tines of a fork to press the edges to seal them effectively.) Set aside on a tray and repeat with the remaining wrappers and filling, but do not pile up the dumplings on the tray—keep them separate.

Fill a large steamer pan with water. Bring the water to a boil. Steam the dumplings in batches, arranging them in the steamer basket so that they are placed well apart—they will expand during cooking, so if they are too closely placed, they will stick together. Steam each batch for about 15 minutes, until dumplings are firm.

To make the soup, heat the olive oil in a saucepan. Add the onion and cook over medium heat for 5–6 minutes, until soft. Add the tomatoes and chopped cilantro and cook for 5 minutes, then add the stock, bring to a simmer over medium heat, and cook for 4–5 minutes.

Ladle the soup and evenly divide the dumplings into bowls. Serve with chopped scallions and soy sauce on the side.

DALAI LAMA DUMPLINGS

KARACHI DUMPLINGS

Preparation time: 30 minutes
Cooking time: 30 minutes

Serves 4

For the dumplings:
- 2 cups (200 g) yellow lentil flour
- 1½ teaspoons baking soda (bicarbonate of soda)
- vegetable oil, for deep-frying
- salt

For the yogurt sauce:
- 1 lb 10½ oz (750 g) unsweetened vegan yogurt
- 2 teaspoons superfine (caster) sugar
- 1 teaspoon salt
- 2 tablespoons garam masala

To make the dumplings, combine the lentil flour, baking soda, and ½ cup (120 ml/4 fl oz) water in a large bowl and mix well until smooth. Set aside for 20 minutes.

Heat enough oil in a wok, deep saucepan, or deep-fat fryer over medium heat to deep-fry the dumplings. Line a tray with paper towels. Carefully drop 1 tablespoon of the batter into the hot oil and repeat to fry the first batch, reducing the heat to medium-low to avoid burning the dumplings. As soon they become golden brown, 8–9 minutes, remove them from the oil with a slotted spoon and transfer to the paper-lined tray to absorb the excess oil. Repeat with the remaining batter. Leave the cooked dumplings to cool.

To make the yogurt sauce, use a food processor or blender to combine the yogurt with the sugar, salt and garam masala.

Serve the dumplings at room temperature with the yogurt sauce on the side.

KARACHI DUMPLINGS

HAZELNUT AND BEAN BURGER

Preparation time: 40 minutes
Cooking time: 35 minutes

Serves 4

- 1½ cups (120 g) hazelnuts or almonds, crushed
- 1 cup (200 g) canned tomatoes
- 1½ cups (360 g) cooked kidney or pinto beans
- 2 cups (240 g) breadcrumbs, plus extra as needed
- 1 tablespoon tahini
- 1 teaspoon ground cumin
- 2 tablespoons nutritional yeast
- salt and freshly ground black pepper

To serve:
- 4 burger buns
- lettuce leaves, to garnish
- tomatoes slices, to garnish
- sliced onion, to garnsh
- dill pickles, to garnish
- your favorite burger sauces

Preheat the oven to 375°F/190°C/Gas Mark 5.

Using a food processor or high-speed blender, process all ingredients to a smooth purée.

Divide the mixture into 4 equal portions and form each into a patty. If the mixture is too wet, add more breadcrumbs. Transfer the patties to a baking sheet and bake for 35 minutes, until well cooked.

Split the burger buns. Make a bed of salad leaves and tomato slices on the bottom half of each bun, then place a burger on top. Top the burger with your favorite sauces and cover with the top of the bun.

HAZELNUT AND BEAN BURGER

CORN CAKE

Preparation time: 45 minutes, plus
1 hour chilling
Cooking time: 1 hour 50 minutes

Serves 4

For the corn cake:
- 4 cups (960 g) yellow cornmeal
- 2½ cups (600 ml/20 fl oz) fresh orange juice
- salt
- ½ cup (120 ml/4 fl oz) coconut oil
- 1 cup (240 ml/8 fl oz) olive oil, plus extra for greasing
- 1–3 banana leaves

For the filling:
- 2 tablespoons olive oil
- 2 onions, chopped
- 2 cloves garlic, finely chopped
- 1 red bell pepper, chopped
- 4 tomatoes, diced
- 2 potatoes or sweet potatoes, peeled, boiled, and diced
- 1 cup (120 g) corn kernels, fresh or frozen
- 1 teaspoon ground cumin
- 1 teaspoon sweet paprika
- 1 teaspoon cayenne pepper
- 1 tablespoon nutritional yeast
- 1 bunch mint, finely chopped
- 2 teaspoons raisins
- 1 cup (140 g) kalamata olives, pitted (stoned) and sliced
- 3 tablespoons fresh lemon juice
- salt and freshly ground black pepper

- green salad, to serve
- French dressing, to serve
- sriracha sauce, to serve

To make the corn cake dough, put the cornmeal and orange juice into the bowl of a food processor and season to taste with salt. Process to combine, then keep the motor running while you slowly add the oils. Process until the dough is smooth but firm.

Grease a large ovenproof dish with olive oil. Cover the bottom and sides with a banana leaf. Use two if necessary to cover the dish, overlapping each other—do not cut the leaves as you need will the overhanging parts to cover the dough.

To make the filling, heat the olive oil in a saucepan. Add the onion, garlic, and bell pepper and stir-fry for 5–6 minutes over medium heat, until the onion and garlic are golden brown. Transfer to a large bowl, mix in the remaining filling ingredients, and season to taste with salt and freshly ground black pepper.

Divide the dough into 4 portions. Spread out 1 portion of dough in a layer on the bottom of the prepared dish. Top this with one-third of the filling mixture. Add another layer of dough, then add a second layer of the filling, using half of the remaining mixture. Top this with another layer of dough, then add a final layer of the filling mixture. Top with the final portion of dough. Cover the dish with the overhanging banana leaves, adding 1 more leaf if necessary to cover the dough completely. Refrigerate for 1 hour.

Preheat the oven to 375°F/190°C/Gas Mark 5.

Transfer the dish to the oven and bake for 1 hour, then reduce the heat to 275°F/140°C/Gas Mark 1 and cook for another 30 minutes, until cooked through and browned on top. Let cool for 15 minutes.

Serve with a lightly dressed salad and sriracha sauce on the side.

CORN CAKE

PIZZA WITH LEMONS AND BRUSSELS SPROUTS

Preparation time: 1 hour
Cooking time: 20 minutes

Serves 4

For the dough:
- 1 packet (15 g/½ oz) dry active yeast
- 2 tablespoons agave syrup
- 3 tablespoons olive oil, plus extra for brushing, greasing, and drizzling
- 1 teaspoon salt
- 1 cup (125 g) bread flour, plus extra for dusting
- 1 cup (125 g) unbleached all-purpose (plain) flour

For the topping:
- 9 oz (250 g) Brussels sprouts, halved
- 1 shallot, finely chopped
- 1 Meyer lemon
- 9 oz (250 g) vegan mozzarella cheese
- 4 teaspoons olive oil
- salt and freshly ground black pepper

To make the dough using a stand mixer with a dough hook attachment, combine ¾ cup (175 ml/6 fl oz) warm water with the yeast and agave syrup until the yeast is dissolved. Set aside for 20 minutes to allow the yeast to become active. Add the oil, salt, and bread flour to the mixer bowl, then set the mixer to a low-speed setting and mix the ingredients for 7–8 minutes, scraping down the sides if needed, until the dough is smooth. With the motor running, add 2 tablespoons of the all-purpose flour at a time, in 2–3-minute intervals, allowing the flour to be fully incorporated into the dough before making the next addition. After the final addition, when the dough starts to come together, mix for another 2–3 minutes, then transfer the dough to a large bowl, brush with olive oil, and cover with a clean kitchen towel. Set aside in a warm place for 1 hour and let rise.

To make the topping, using a food processor fitted with an S-blade, pulse the Brussels sprouts and shallot until nicely shredded. Set aside.

Thinly slice the Meyer lemon, then cut each slice in two, removing the seeds as needed. Set aside.

Preheat the broiler (grill) of your oven and arrange a rack in the upper-third section of the oven. Grease a baking sheet with olive oil.

Divide the dough into 4 equal portions and roll each portion into a ball in your hands. Roll out 1 portion into a circle roughly 10 inches (25 cm) in diameter. Transfer the dough to the prepared baking sheet. Sprinkle over a quarter of the Brussels sprout–shallot mix, then arrange a quarter of the Meyer lemon slices on the top. Finish with a quarter of the vegan mozzarella cheese. Bake for 3–4 minutes, watching closely to prevent the crust from burning. Repeat with the remaining pizza dough and ingredients. Drizzle 1 teaspoon of olive oil over each cooked pizza, season to taste with salt and freshly ground black pepper, and serve.

PIZZA WITH LEMONS AND BRUSSELS SPROUTS

PORTOBELLO BRUSCHETTA

Preparation time: 40 minutes
Cooking time: 10 minutes,
  plus 1 hour 30 minutes chilling

Serves 4

- For the marinated mushrooms:
- ½ cup (120 ml/4 fl oz) olive oil
- 4 tablespoons balsamic vinegar
- 2 cloves garlic, finely chopped
- 1 tablespoon dried basil
- 1 tablespoon tamari or soy sauce
- 4 large portobello mushrooms, trimmed

  For the bruschetta topping:
- 2 tablespoons olive oil
- 2 tablespoons balsamic vinegar
- 1 tablespoon Dijon mustard
- 1 tablespoon vegannaise (page 52)
  or store-bought
- salt and freshly ground black pepper
- 4½ oz (125 g) cherry tomatoes, diced
- ¼ red bell pepper, diced
- 2 cloves garlic, finely chopped
- 1 small onion, diced
- 1 tablespoon chopped basil
- 1 baguette, halved crosswise
- olive oil, for brushing

To make the mushrooms, put all the ingredients, except the mushrooms, into a large bowl and whisk together until well combined. Add the mushrooms into the marinade and toss to coat. Refrigerate for 1 hour.

Preheat the broiler (grill). Line a broiler pan with aluminum foil and arrange the mushrooms on top. Grill the mushrooms for 2–3 minutes on each side, until light golden brown. Let cool.

To make the bruschetta, put the olive oil, vinegar, mustard, and vegannaise into a large bowl, season to taste with salt and freshly ground black pepper, and whisk until smooth. Add the tomatoes, bell pepper, garlic, onion, and basil, toss the vegetables in the dressing, and refrigerate for 30 minutes.

Split each baguette half lengthwise. Brush the insides of the bread with a little olive oil.

Dice the mushrooms. To serve, divide the mushrooms among the baguette pieces. Spoon the vegetables on top and serve.

PORTOBELLO BRUSCHETTA

POTATO PATTIES

Preparation time: 35 minutes, plus
  2 hours chilling
Cooking time: 20 minutes

Serves 4

- 9 oz (250 g) mashed potatoes
- 9 oz (250 g) silken tofu
- ½ cup (70 g) chopped onion
- ½ cup (70 g) chopped scallions (spring onions)
- 2 tablespoons cilantro (coriander), chopped
- 1 teaspoon cayenne pepper
- 4 green chilies, seeded and finely chopped
- 1 teaspoon garam masala
- 4 slices white bread, soaked 10 minutes in soy milk or almond milk and drained
- 2 tablespoons egg replacer, mixed with 4 tablespoons warm water
- salt and freshly ground black pepper
- breadcrumbs, for coating
- ¼ cup (60 ml) vegetable oil
- green salad, to serve
- salad dressing, to serve

Put the potato, tofu, onion, scallions, cilantro, cayenne pepper, chilies, garam masala, bread, and egg replacer into a large bowl and mix well with a wooden spoon until well blended. Season to taste with salt and freshly ground black pepper.

Spread out the breadcrumbs on a plate. Divide the mixture into 4 equal portions and shape each into a patty. Carefully, coat the patties in breadcrumbs and refrigerate for 2 hours.

Heat the oil in a large skillet (frying pan). Add the patties and cook over medium-low heat for 6–8 minutes on each side until golden.

Serve the patties with a lightly dressed salad.

SPINACH SQUARES WITH SWEET POTATOES

Preparation time: 25 minutes, plus
  15 minutes chilling
Cooking time: 50 minutes, plus 10 minutes
  cooling

Serves 4

- 1 tablespoon canola (rapeseed) oil, plus extra for greasing
- salt
- 1 lb 10½ oz (750 g) fresh spinach, trimmed
- 1 leek (white and pale green parts only), sliced
- 2 cloves garlic, finely chopped
- 225 g (8 oz) sweet potatoes, peeled and grated
- ½ cup (120 g) silken tofu
- 2 tablespoons fresh lemon juice
- 1 teaspoon dried oregano
- salt and freshly ground black pepper
- green salad, to serve
- Italian dressing, to serve

Preheat the oven to 350°F/180°C/Gas Mark 4. Grease an 8 x 8-inch (20 x 20 cm) baking dish.

Bring a large saucepan of salted water to a boil. Add the spinach, cover the pan, and cook over medium heat for 5 minutes, until the spinach has wilted. Drain and let cool for 15 minutes, then squeeze and chop the spinach and transfer it to a large bowl.

Heat the canola oil in a saucepan. Add the leek and garlic and stir-fry over medium heat for 5–6 minutes, until golden brown. Add the sweet potato and cook for 3–4 minutes. Transfer the mixture to the bowl with the spinach.

Blend the silken tofu with the fresh lemon juice in a small bowl until smooth, add the oregano, and stir well. Add the mixture to the bowl with the spinach and sweet potato and mix to blend. Season to taste with salt and freshly ground black pepper.

Transfer the mixture in the prepared dish and bake for 35 minutes, until firm and golden brown on top. Let cool for 10 minutes, then cut into 4 squares and serve with a lightly dressed salad.

RED BEAN, BEET, AND HUITLACOCHE BURGERS

Heat 2 tablespoons of the olive oil in a saucepan over a medium heat. Add the onion and stir-fry for 5–6 minutes, until golden. Add the huitlacoche and garlic, raise the heat to high, and stir-fry for 3–4 minutes, until golden brown. Transfer to a paper towel–lined plate to remove excess of oil.

Mix the grated beet, carrots, corn, jalapeños, paprika, thyme, and kidney beans in a bowl. Season to taste with salt and freshly ground black pepper. Add the huitlacoche mixture along with the breadcrumbs and combine.

Divide the mixture into 4 equal portions and shape each into a patty. Refrigerate for 20 minutes.

Heat the remaining olive oil in a large skillet (frying pan). Add the patties and fry over medium-low heat for 3–4 minutes on each side until golden-brown.

To serve, split the burger buns, then spoon the vegannaise onto both sides of each bun. Arrange 1 lettuce leaf on the bottom half of each bun. Cover with a cooked patty. Add tomatoes, pickles, your favorite burger sauce and cover with the top half of the bun.

Serve the burger with fries or potato wedges.

Preparation time: 45 minutes
Cooking time: 10 minutes, plus 20 minutes chilling

Serves 4

- 4 tablespoons olive oil
- 1 onion, thinly sliced
- 9 oz (250 g) huitlacoche (corn mushrooms), chopped if large (or use portobello mushrooms)
- 1 clove garlic, crushed
- ½ beet (beetroot), cooked, peeled, and grated
- 1 carrot, grated
- 2 tablespoons corn kernels
- 1 tablespoon chopped seeded jalapeño pepper
- 1 teaspoon smoked paprika
- 1 teaspoon chopped thyme
- 2 tablespoons chopped canned red kidney beans,
- salt and freshly ground black pepper
- 4 tablespoons breadcrumbs
- 4 burger buns
- 6 tablespoons vegannaise (page 52) or store-bought
- 4 large romaine (cos) lettuce leaves
- 2 tomatoes, sliced
- 2 pickles, sliced
- burger sauce, to serve
- fries or potato wedges, to serve

CRISPY FRIED TEMPEH

Preparation time: 30 minutes
Cooking time: 30 minutes

Serves 4

- ¼ cup (60 g) raw cashews
- 1 clove garlic, finely chopped
- 1 teaspoon coriander seeds
- 1 tablespoon grated galangal
- 1 tablespoon fresh lime juice
- 1 cup (125 g) rice flour
- 2 tablespoons cornstarch (cornflour)
- 3 cups (570 g) tempeh or smoked tempeh, diced
- vegetable oil, for deep-frying
- sriracha, to serve

First make the spice batter. Put the cashews, garlic, coriander seeds, and galangal into a food processor or high-speed blender and blend to a paste. Add the lime juice and 1 cup (240 ml/8 fl oz) water and whisk to combine. Add the rice flour and cornstarch and whisk until smooth.

Begin to heat enough oil to deep-fry the tempeh in a wok, deep saucepan, or deep-fat fryer over medium-high heat. Line a plate with paper towels. Dip the tempeh into the batter individually and carefully slide them into the hot oil. Deep-fry for 3–4 minutes over medium heat, until golden brown and crisp. Drain the tempeh and transfer to the paper towel–lined plate to absorb excess oil.

Serve the tempeh with sriracha on the side.

To make the pie, put the potatoes into a saucepan and cover them with water. Bring to a boil, then reduce the heat to medium and simmer for 35–40 minutes, until the potatoes are tender enough to mash. Drain the potatoes, then use a food processor or high-speed blender to mash them until smooth. Transfer to a bowl, mix in the margarine, season to taste with salt and freshly ground black pepper, and set aside.

Preheat the oven to 400°F/200°C/Gas Mark 6. Grease a large ovenproof dish.

Heat the oil in a saucepan. Add the onion and sauté over medium heat for 5–6 minutes, until light golden brown. Add the tomatoes, mixed vegetables, and stock, season to taste with salt and freshly ground black pepper, and bring to a boil. Cook over medium-low heat, stirring often, for 12–14 minutes, until the liquids have reduced by half. Set aside.

To make the sauce, heat the oil in a saucepan. Add the onion and cook over medium heat for 5–6 minutes, until golden brown. Add the cream and bring to a simmer. Slowly sprinkle in the cornstarch, whisking constantly, until it has all been blended in and the mixture is smooth. Season to taste with salt and freshly ground black pepper, then mix in the vegan cheese.

Spread half of the mashed potatoes in a single layer on the bottom of the prepared dish. Pour over the vegetable mixture, then cover it with the remaining mashed potatoes. Pour the sauce over the top, and bake for about 10 minutes, until the top is golden brown.

Garnish the pie with parsley and serve immediately.

Preparation time: 45 minutes
Cooking time: 1 hour 10 minutes

Serves 4

For the pie:
- 3¼ lb (1.5 kg) potatoes, quartered
- 4½ oz (125 g) vegetable margarine
- salt and freshly ground black pepper
- 4 tablespoons vegetable oil, plus extra for greasing
- 1 onion, finely chopped
- 2 cups (400 g) canned chopped tomatoes with their juice
- 2¼ lb (1 kg) frozen mixed vegetables, defrosted
- 1 cup (240 ml/8 fl oz) vegetable stock (broth)
- 2 tablespoons finely chopped parsley

For the sauce:
- 1 tablespoon vegetable oil
- 1 onion, sliced
- 2 cups (480 ml/16 fl oz) soy cream
- 3 tablespoons cornstarch (cornflour)
- salt and freshly ground black pepper
- 2 cups (200 g) grated vegan cheddar cheese

SPINACH PIE

Preparation time: 30 minutes, plus
  1 hour chilling
Cooking time: 45 minutes, plus
  15 minutes cooling

Serves 4

For the dough:
- 2 cups (250 g) all-purpose (plain) flour,
  plus extra for dusting
- 2 tablespoons vegetable oil, plus extra
  for greasing
- 1 teaspoon dried oregano
- a pinch of salt

For the filling:
- 2 tablespoons vegetable oil
- 2 cloves garlic, finely chopped
- 3 scallions (spring onions), sliced
- 2 shallots, finely chopped
- salt and freshly ground black pepper
- 9 oz (250 g) silken tofu
- 4 tablespoons soy cream
- 1 tablespoon nutritional yeast
- 1 lb 10½ oz (750 g) baby spinach
- green salad, to serve
- Italian or French dressing, to serve

To make the dough, combine half of the flour, 1 cup (240 ml/8 fl oz) warm water, and the remaining ingredients in a large bowl. Knead for 4 minutes, slowly adding the remaining flour as you knead, until the dough no longer sticks to your hands. Place the dough in a large bowl and set aside in the refrigerator until chilled, about 30 minutes.

Grease a 10- or 11-inch (24 or 28 cm) pie dish. Dust a work surface with flour. Roll out the dough to a circle that measures 2 inches (5 cm) more than the diameter of the pie dish. Line the greased dish with the dough, pressing it into the bottom and up the sides of the dish. Set aside in the refrigerator for 30 minutes.

Preheat the oven to 375°F/190°C/Gas Mark 5.

To make the filling, heat the oil in a saucepan over medium heat, add the garlic, and fry for 2–3 minutes, until golden. Add the scallions and shallots and stir-fry gently for another 2–3 minutes. Season to taste with salt and freshly ground black pepper and set aside.

In a large bowl, whisk the silken tofu, soy cream, and nutritional yeast until smooth. Add the baby spinach, and the fried garlic and scallion, and stir well. Transfer to the pie dish, and bake for 40 minutes, until nicely golden on the top.

Let cool for 15 minutes before serving. Serve with a lightly dressed green salad.

SAVORY PUMPKIN PIE

To make the piecrust, put the diced pumpkin into the bowl of a food processor, pulse a couple of times to break it down a little, then add a scant ½ cup (100 ml/3½ fl oz) water and pulse again to form a paste. Set aside in a large bowl.

Put another scant ½ cup (100 ml/3½ fl oz) water into the bowl of the food processor, add the drained pumpkin seeds, and blend to form a very firm paste. Mix this with the pumpkin purée until well blended. Put the rice flour and xanthan gum into a small bowl and whisk together. Add this to the pumpkin mixture and, using your hands, knead the mixture to form a moist, sticky dough. If the dough is too dry, add a little water. When smooth, put the dough into a bowl, cover the bowl with a slightly damp kitchen towel, and refrigerate for 1 hour.

Grease a 10-inches (22–24 cm) pie dish with oil or vegetable margarine. Lay out a large sheet of wax (greaseproof) paper on a work surface and dust it with flour. Put the dough on the paper and dust with flour. Roll out the dough to a circle that measures 2 inches (5 cm) more than the diameter of the pie dish. Line the prepared pie dish with the dough and trim away excess dough with a spatula or large knife. Refrigerate for 2 hours.

Preheat the oven to 375°F/190°C/Gas Mark 5.

To make the filling, heat the olive oil in a large skillet (frying pan) or wok over medium heat. Add the onion and sauté for 5–6 minutes, until transparent and lightly brown. Transfer the onion to the bowl of a food processor. Add the tomato, tofu, pumpkin, and drained cashews and pulse to break down the mixture, then increase the speed to a high setting and process until filling is smooth. Season to taste with salt and freshly ground black pepper and mix in the sage, onion paper, and garlic powder.

Transfer the filling to the lined pie dish, garnish with the pumpkin seeds, and bake for 45 minutes, until the filling is firm and golden brown. If the pie begins to brown earlier, cover it with aluminum foil for the remaining baking time.

Serve the pie with a lightly dressed salad mixed with cherry tomatoes.

Preparation time: 35 minutes, plus overnight soaking and 3 hours chilling
Cooking time: 50 minutes

Serves 4

For the piecrust:
- 1 cup (190 g) Hokkaido pumpkin, diced
- 1½ cups (225 g) pumpkin seeds, soaked in water overnight and drained
- 2 cups (250 g) brown rice flour, plus extra for dusting
- 1 teaspoon xanthan gum
- oil or vegetable margarine, for greasing

For the filling:
- 2 tablespoons olive oil
- 1 onion, chopped
- 1 cup (200 g) diced tomatoes
- 1 cup (240 g) silken tofu
- 1 cup (190 g) canned pumpkin (or baked pumpkin)
- ½ cup (65 g) raw cashews, soaked in water overnight and drained
- salt and freshly ground black pepper
- 1 teaspoon dried sage
- 1 teaspoon onion powder
- 1 teaspoon garlic powder
- 1 tablespoon pumpkin seeds, to garnish
- 2 tablespoons nutritional yeast
- green salad, to serve
- cherry tomatoes, to serve
- Italian or French dressing, to serve

VEGGIE BURGERS

Preparation time: 25 minutes
Cooking time: 15 minutes, plus
  1 hour chilling

Serves 4

For the burgers:
- 1 cup (240 g) white short-grain rice
- 1 cup (200 g) Puy lentils
- ½ cup (120 g) pecans
- 1 red onion, finely chopped
- 1 portobello mushroom, finely chopped
- 1 cup (200 g) cornstarch (cornflour)
- 2 slices sandwich bread
- ½ cup (75 g) raw sunflower seeds, processed into paste
- 1 handful of parsley, chopped
- 1 teaspoon baking powder
- 1 teaspoon chili powder
- 1 teaspoon curry powder
- ½ cup (120 g) silken tofu
- salt and freshly ground black pepper
  2 tablespoons vegetable oil

To assemble:
- 2 tablespoons vegetable oil
- 1 portobello mushroom, finely chopped
- ½ onion, sliced into rings
- 4 burger buns, split
- Iceberg lettuce leaves, roughly chopped
- ¼ cucumber, sliced
- 2 dill pickles, sliced
- 2 tablespoons vegannaise (page 52) or store-bought
- 2 tablespoons ketchup
- 2 tablespoons Dijon mustard
- 4 slices vegan cheese

To make the burgers, cook the rice and lentils according to the packet instructions. Drain and set aside.

Grease a baking sheet with oil.

Using a food processor or high-speed blender, pulse the pecans to chop coarsely. Put them into a large bowl along with the red onion and mushroom and mix well. Add the cooked rice and lentils and the remaining ingredients, except the silken tofu, and mix well. Using a fork, mash the silken tofu to a purée and add to the mixture. Season to taste with salt and black pepper and stir until well combined. Divide the mixture into 4 equal portions and, with slightly wet hands, shape each portion into a tight round patty. Arrange the patties on the prepared baking sheet and freeze for 1 hour.

Heat 2 tablespoons vegetable oil in a large skillet (frying pan) over medium heat. Add the patties and fry gently for 6–7 minutes on each side, until golden brown on both sides.

Meanwhile, heat the remaining oil in another large skillet (frying pan). Add the mushrooms and onion rings and stir-fry for 7–8 minutes, until golden brown. Transfer to a bowl and set aside.

Put the burger buns in the same skillet, cut sides down, and toast for 2 minutes over medium-low heat.

Arrange the lettuce, cucumber, and pickles on the bottom half of each bun. Evenly divide half of the sauce and spread on each bottom bun, then carefully place a patty on top. Divide the cheese, the rest of the sauce, and the mushrooms and onion rings among the burgers. Place the top half of the buns over the sauce and serve immediately.

VEGGIE BURGERS

ZUCCHINI BURGERS

Preparation time: 35 minutes, plus 1 hour
   draining and chilling
Cooking time: 10 minutes

Serves 4

- 3 cups (390 g) grated zucchini (courgette)
- salt and freshly ground black pepper
- 2 cups (240 g) breadcrumbs
- 3 bay leaves
- 1 teaspoon celery seeds
- 1 teaspoon freshly ground white pepper
- 1 teaspoon ground nutmeg
- ½ teaspoon ground cloves
- 1 teaspoon ground allspice
- 1 teaspoon sweet paprika
- ½ teaspoon crushed red chili flakes
- ¼ cup (60 g) silken tofu
- 2 tablespoons vegannaise (page 52)
   or store-bought
- 1½ tablespoons fresh lemon juice
- 1 tablespoon Dijon mustard
- 1 teaspoon grated fresh ginger
- 1 teaspoon potato starch
- ¼ cup (30 g) parsley, chopped
- 2 tablespoons vegetable oil, for frying
- lemon wedges, to serve
- sriracha, to serve
- burger sauce, to serve

Put the zucchini into a colander set over a bowl and generously sprinkle the zucchini with salt. Set aside to drain for 1 hour.

Put the breadcrumbs into a large bowl along with the bay leaves, celery seeds, white pepper, nutmeg, cloves, allspice, paprika, and crushed red chili flakes, mix well, and set aside.

In a separate bowl, whisk together the tofu, vegannaise, lemon juice, mustard, ginger, potato starch, and parsley until smooth. Set side.

Using your hands, squeeze as much excess liquid as you can from the zucchini. Combine the zucchini and tofu-vegannaise mixture with the breadcrumb mixtureuntil well blended. Season to taste with salt and freshly ground black pepper. Refrigerate for 1 hour.

Divide the chilled mixture into 8 equal parts and shape these into balls. Flatten them slightly with your hand to form thick disks.

Heat the oil in a skillet (frying pan) over medium-high heat. Add the zucchini cakes in batches of 4 and fry for 3 minutes on each side, until golden brown.

Serve hot, with lemon wedges, sriracha, and your favorite burger sauce on the side.

CASHEW AND PINEAPPLE STIR-FRY

Cook the brown rice according to the packet instructions. Set aside.

Meanwhile, heat the oil in a large wok. Add the garlic and mixed vegetables and cook over medium heat, stirring regularly, for 15 minutes, until the vegetables are just tender.

While the vegetables are cooking, combine the pineapple pulp, tamari or soy sauce, rice vinegar, and agave syrup in a bowl and stir well to combine.

When the vegetables are just tender, add the pineapple chunks, cashews, and black beans (if using), along with the pineapple sauce. Continue to cook for 2 minutes, until hot. Add the brown rice, stir, and garnish with cilantro.

Preparation time: 20 minutes
Cooking time: 40 minutes

Serves 4

- 1 cup (200 g) brown rice
- 2 tablespoons vegetable oil
- 2 cloves garlic, finely chopped
- 2 cups (480 g) mixed chopped vegetables (carrot, broccoli, bok choy, mung sprouts)
- ½ cup (120 ml/4 fl oz) blended pineapple pulp
- 2 tablespoons tamari or soy sauce
- 1 tablespoon rice vinegar
- 2 tablespoons agave syrup
- 1½ cups (270 g) diced pineapple
- ½ cup (75 g) raw cashews
- ½ cup (30 g) cooked black beans (optional)
- 2 tablespoons chopped cilantro (coriander), to garnish

VEGETABLE TORTILLA

Put the onion, bell pepper, carrot, and garlic in a large saucepan with the stock. Bring to a boil, then reduce the heat to medium and simmer, stirring occasionally, for about 8 minutes. Add the scallions, Napa cabbage, tamari or soy sauce, chili powder, and oregano and cook, stirring occasionally, for 10 minutes. Add the tomatoes, spinach, and beans and season to taste with salt and freshly ground black pepper. Cook for another 5 minutes. Remove the saucepan from the heat and stir in the cilantro and hot sauce to taste.

Transfer to a large bowl and serve with tortillas.

Preparation time: 25 minutes
Cooking time: 25 minutes

Serves 4

- 1 onion, chopped
- 1 green bell pepper, chopped
- 1 carrot, halved lengthwise and sliced
- 1 teaspoon finely chopped garlic
- ½ cup (120 ml/4 fl oz) vegetable stock (broth)
- 4½ oz (125 g) scallions (spring onions), cut into 1-inch (2.5 cm) pieces.
- 1½ cups (360 g) shredded Napa cabbage
- 1 tablespoon tamari or soy sauce
- 1 teaspoon chili powder
- 1 teaspoon dried oregano
- 2 cups (400 g) plum tomatoes, chopped
- 2 cups (300 g) baby spinach
- 4½ oz (125 g) canned black beans, drained
- salt and freshly ground black pepper
- 2 tablespoons chopped cilantro (coriander)
- your favorite hot sauce
- warm tortillas, to serve

CRISPY ORANGE-GINGER TOFU WITH BROCCOLI

Preparation time: 35 minutes,
  plus 1–2 hours draining
Cooking time: 45 minutes

Serves 4

- 1 lb 10½ oz (750 g) extra-firm tofu
- 1 cup (240 ml/8 fl oz) fresh orange juice
- ⅓ cup (80 g) plus 1½ tablespoons cornstarch (cornflour)
- 2 tablespoons light brown sugar
- 1 tablespoon tamari or soy sauce
- 1 tablespoon grated fresh ginger
- 2 cloves garlic, finely chopped
- 1 tablespoon finely grated orange zest
- 2 tablespoons vegetable oil
- 1 large head of broccoli, broken into florets
- cooked basmati or other long-grain rice, to serve
- 2 scallions (spring onions), finely chopped, to garnish
- 1 tablespoon sesame seeds, to garnish
- 1 tablespoon crushed red chili flakes, to garnish

Place the tofu in a clean sink and weigh it down with something heavy, such as a cast-iron saucepan, for 1–2 hours to squeeze out the water and compress the tofu.

Pour half of the orange juice into a bowl and stir in 1½ tablespoons of cornstarch until dissolved. Set aside.

Put the remaining orange juice into a small saucepan along with the brown sugar, tamari or soy sauce, ginger, garlic, and orange zest. Bring to a low simmer and cook over medium-low heat for about 15 minutes, until reduced by half.

Stir in the cornstarch mixture until completely blended. Remove the pan from the stove and set aside.

Cut the tofu into cubes and roll in the remaining cornstarch to coat.

Coat the bottom of a large skillet (frying pan) with the vegetable oil and set over medium-high heat. Add the tofu cubes and cook over medium heat for 5–6 minutes on each side, until browned and crispy. Transfer to a plate lined with paper towels to absorb excess oil.

Bring water to a boil in a steamer pan. Place the broccoli in the steamer basket and steam for about 20 minutes, or to your desired tenderness.

Return the tofu to the skillet along with the broccoli and sauce. Toss everything to coat.

Serve over rice, garnished with scallions, sesame seeds, and crushed red chili flakes.

CRISPY ORANGE-GINGER TOFU WITH BROCCOLI

CRUSTED SEITAN WITH OYSTER MUSHROOMS

Preparation time: 30 minutes
Cooking time: 20 minutes

Serves 4

- juice of 1 lemon
- 1 tablespoon tamari or soy sauce
- 1 tablespoon cornstarch (cornflour)
- 2 tablespoons vegetable oil
- 1 tablespoon sesame oil
- 2 cups (480 g) diced seitan
- 1 teaspoon grated fresh ginger
- 2 cloves garlic, finely chopped
- 2 cups (240 g) sliced oyster mushrooms
- 1 green bell pepper, julienned
- cooked basmati or other long-grain white rice, to serve
- 1 tablespoon sesame seeds, to garnish
- 2 scallions (spring onions), chopped, to garnish

Put the lemon juice, tamari or soy sauce, and cornstarch into a small bowl and whisk to blend. Set aside.

Heat 1 tablespoon of the vegetable oil and the sesame oil in large skillet (frying pan) over medium-high heat. Add the seitan and stir-fry for 6–7 minutes over medium heat, until golden brown. Transfer the seitan to a paper towel–lined plate.

Add the remaining vegetable oil to the skillet along with the ginger, garlic, oyster mushrooms, and peppers and stir-fry over medium heat for 3–4 minutes. Return the seitan to the skillet, add the lemon-soy mixture, and toss to coat in the sauce. Stir-fry another 2–3 minutes, until the seitan and vegetables are well coated and the liquid has reduced by half.

Serve over rice, garnished with the sesame seeds and scallions.

FRIED TURNIPS AND ONIONS WITH FRIED POTATOES

Preparation time: 30 minutes
Cooking time: 35 minutes

Serves 4

For the fried potatoes:
- 4 tablespoons vegetable margarine
- 2 tablespoons extra-virgin olive oil, plus more as needed
- 4 large russet potatoes, peeled and sliced ⅛-inch (3 mm) thick
- 1 large onion, sliced thin
- ½ teaspoon garlic powder
- ½ teaspoon dried dill
- salt and freshly ground black pepper

For the turnips and onions:
- 2 tablespoons vegetable margarine
- 4 tablespoons olive oil
- 2 onions, finely chopped
- 8 turnips, finely diced
- 4 tablespoons dried rosemary
- salt and freshly ground black pepper

To make the fried potatoes, melt the vegetable margarine in a large skillet (frying pan) over medium-high heat, add the olive oil, and heat until shimmering.

Add the sliced potatoes and onion, cover, and cook for 10 minutes, until browned on the bottom. Using a spatula, carefully turn the potatoes and onion so they do not break apart. If the potatoes appear too dry, add some more olive oil.

Sprinkle the potato mixture with garlic powder and dried dill, season to taste with salt and freshly ground black pepper, and continue to cook, uncovered, for another 5 minutes, until the potatoes begin to turn slightly brown, turning occasionally. Set aside and cover with a lid to keep warm.

To make the turnips and onions, melt the vegetable margarine in a large skillet (frying pan) over medium heat and add the olive oil. Add the onions and sauté over medium heat for 5–6 minutes, until golden brown. Stir in the turnips and rosemary. Increase the heat to medium-high and cook for 6–7 minutes, until the turnips are tender and golden brown.

Serve the turnips and onions hot, with the fried potatoes on the side.

FRIED KOMBU DASHI TOFU

Sprinkle all sides of the tofu with the salt. Place the tofu cubes in a strainer (sieve) and let drain for 1–2 hours.

Put the dashi, tamari or soy sauce, and sugar into a small saucepan and season to taste with salt. Heat until the sugar and salt dissolve. Stir well and cover to prevent evaporation, then keep warm over very low heat.

Grate the daikon and transfer to paper towels to dry as much as possible.

Heat the oil in a large, heavy skillet (frying pan) over medium heat until it shimmers.

Meanwhile, put the potato starch into a small bowl. Carefully roll each block of tofu in the starch, ensuring the blocks are evenly coated; brush off any excess starch. Gently add the tofu to the hot oil and fry the tofu for 6–7 minutes, using chopsticks or tongs to roll each piece in the oil, until all sides are medium brown and crisp and the tofu looks slightly puffy. Transfer to a paper towel–lined plate to absorb excess oil. To serve, place tofu in bowls, sprinkle the dashi mixture on top, and garnish with the grated daikon and scallions. Serve with rice and tamari on the side.

Preparation time: 35 minutes, plus 1–2 hours draining
Cooking time: 10 minutes

Serves 4

- 1 lb 2 oz (500 g) silken tofu, cut into 4 cubes
- 1 teaspoon salt, plus extra to season
- 1 cup (240 ml/8 fl oz) dashi
- 2 teaspoons tamari or soy sauce, plus extra to serve
- 1 teaspoon superfine (caster) sugar
- 3½ oz (100 g) peeled daikon radish, to garnish
- 5 tablespoons vegetable oil
- 1 cup (125 g) potato starch
- 1 scallion (spring onion), finely chopped, to garnish
- cooked long-grain rice, to serve

FRIED EGGPLANT WITH ORANGE JUICE

Fill a large saucepan with water and bring to a boil. Add the eggplant and cook over medium-low heat for 7 minutes. Drain in a colander and transfer to a paper towel–lined plate to absorb any remaining water. Set aside.

Spread the flour across a plate. Line another plate with paper towels.

Heat the oil in a skillet (frying pan). Dip the eggplant slices in the flour, then transfer to the skillet and fry them in batches over medium heat for 3–4 minutes on each side, until nicely golden. Transfer to the paper towel–lined plate to absorb excess oil.

Pour the orange juice into a jar (jug). Season to taste with salt and freshly ground black pepper and whisk until well blended. Transfer the eggplant to a large serving bowl, drizzle over the seasoned orange juice, and serve immediately, with lemon wedges.

Preparation time: 30 minutes
Cooking time: 40 minutes

Serves 4

- 4 eggplants (aubergines), cut into large slices
- 1 cup (125 g) all-purpose (plain) flour
- 1 cup (240 ml/8 fl oz) olive oil
- 1 cup (240 ml/8 fl oz) fresh orange juice
- salt and freshly ground black pepper
- lemon wedges, to serve

JACKFRUIT GYROS

Preparation time: 20 minutes
Cooking time: 30 minutes

Serves 4

- 1 tablespoon vegetable margarine
- 1 large onion, halved and thinly sliced
- 1 lb (about 500 g) canned jackfruit in brine, rinsed, drained, and shredded
- ¾ cup (175 ml/6 fl oz) vegetable stock (broth)
- 4 tablespoons fresh lemon juice
- 2 teaspoon dried oregano
- 2 teaspoons tamari or soy sauce
- 1 teaspoon ground coriander
- salt and freshly ground black pepper
- naan or cooked basmati or wild rice, to serve

Heat the vegetable margarine in a large skillet (frying pan) over medium heat until completely melted. Add the onion and sauté for 5–6 minutes, until lightly golden. Add the jackfruit and cook for 10 minutes, until golden brown and caramelized. Stir in the stock, 2 tablespoons of the lemon juice, the oregano, tamari or soy sauce, and cilantro. Season to taste with salt and freshly ground black pepper. Bring the mixture to a simmer over medium-low heat and cook for 10–15 minutes, until the liquid has almost completely evaporated. Stir in the remaining lemon juice.

Serve immediately, with naan or rice.

POTATO AND TOASTED CASHEW SAUCE

Preparation time: 30 minutes
Cooking time: 35 minutes

Serves 4

- 4 potatoes, peeled and diced
- 1 tablespoon vegetable oil
- 3 tablespoons vegetable margarine
- 2 cloves garlic, finely chopped
- 1 green chili, seeded and chopped
- 225 g (8 oz) toasted cashews
- 1 tablespoon tamari or soy sauce
- 2 tablespoons pomegranate seeds
- salt and freshly ground black pepper
- 1 tablespoon toasted sesame oil, to garnish
- green salad, to serve
- your favorite salad dressing, to serve

Rinse the potatoes under cold running water. Drain and set asideon paper towels to dry completely.

Heat the oil and vegetable margarine in a large saucepan over medium heat. Add the garlic and green chili and stir-fry gently over medium heat for 3–4 minutes, until slightly golden. Add the potato dice and stir-fry for about 10 minutes, until they begin to turn golden. Add ½ cup (120 ml/4 fl oz) water, the cashews, and tamari or soy sauce, stir, and bring to a simmer. Cook over medium heat for 20 minutes, until the potatoes are tender.

Add the pomegranate seeds and stir well. Season to taste with salt and freshly ground black pepper and transfer to a serving dish. Drizzle over the sesame oil and serve with a lightly dressed salad.

HOISIN TOFU WITH MUSHROOMS

To make the cauliflower rice, put the cauliflower pieces into the bowl of a food processor and pulse until chopped into rice grain–size pieces. Set aside.

Heat the vegetable oil in a large skillet (frying pan) over medium heat. Add the cauliflower and sauté for 2–3 minutes. Divide among 4 large serving bowls and set aside.

To make the sauce, put all the ingredients in a bowl along with 4 tablespoons water and whisk to combine. Set aside.

To make the hoisin tofu and mushrooms, heat 1 tablespoon of the oil in a large saucepan over medium heat. Arrange the mushroom pieces in the pan in a single layer. Cook for about 5 minutes, then flip and cook for another 5 minutes, until golden brown on both sides. Distribute these evenly among the 4 bowls, over the cauliflower rice.

Heat the remaining oil in the same saucepan and add the tofu cubes. Cook for 6–7 minutes over medium heat, until golden brown on all sides. Pour half of the sauce on top and cook for another 2 minutes over medium heat, stirring gently to coat the cubes evenly with the sauce.

Arrange the tofu over the cauliflower rice and shiitake mushrooms, top with the remaining sauce, and garnish with the sesame seeds and scallions.

Preparation time: 25 minutes, plus
  30 minutes draining
Cooking time: 20 minutes

Serves 4

For the cauliflower rice:
- 1 medium cauliflower, cut into large pieces
- 2 tablespoons vegetable oil

For the sauce:
- ½ cup (120 ml/4 fl oz) hoisin sauce
- 2 tablespoons rice vinegar
- 2 tablespoons tamari or soy sauce
- 1 teaspoon toasted sesame oil
- 2 cloves garlic, finely chopped

For the hoisin tofu and mushrooms:
- 2 tablespoons vegetable oil
- 2¼ lb (1 kg) shiitake mushrooms, trimmed and quartered
- 1 lb 2 oz (500 g) firm tofu, drained and pressed for ½ hour, diced
- 2 teaspoons sesame seeds, to garnish
- 2 scallions (spring onions), chopped, to garnish

STIR-FRIED BOK CHOY WITH TOFU

Preparation time: 20 minutes
Cooking time: 20 minutes

Serves 4

- 3 tablespoons vegetable oil
- 1 onion, chopped
- 3 cloves garlic, finely chopped
- 1 cup (240 g) diced tofu
- 3 cups (270 g) baby bok choy, chopped
- 1 cup (240 g) diced summer squash
- 2 cups (260 g) diced zucchini (courgette)
- 1 cup (180 g) cherry tomatoes, halved
- 2 tablespoons grated fresh ginger
- 1 tablespoon tamari or soy sauce
- ½ cup (120 ml/4 fl oz) vegetable stock (broth)
- 1 tablespoon fresh lime juice
- salt and freshly ground black pepper
- chopped cilantro (coriander), to garnish
- cooked white rice, to serve

Heat 2 tablespoons of the oil in a wok. Add the onion and garlic and stir-fry over medium heat for 5–6 minutes, until golden. Add the tofu and stir-fry gently for 3–4 minutes over medium heat, until lightly browned. Add the bok choy, squash, zucchini, and tomatoes. Stir-fry gently for 4–5 minutes. Remove the vegetables and tofu from the wok and set aside.

Heat the remaining oil in the same wok over medium heat. Add the ginger and tamari or soy sauce. Cook for 1–2 minutes, until the tamari starts to simmer. Add the stock, bring to a boil, then reduce the heat to medium-low and simmer for about 10 minutes, until the liquid has reduced by half. Add the lime juice and season to taste with salt and freshly ground black pepper. Return the vegetables and tofu to the wok. Cook for 2 minutes, until fork-tender.

Garnish with cilantro and serve immediately, with rice.

STIR-FRIED BOK CHOY WITH TOFU

STIR-FRIED TOFU WITH GREEN MANGO SLAW

Preparation time: 25 minutes
Cooking time: 5 minutes

Serves 4

For the dressing:
- 2 tablespoons vegannaise (page 52) or store-bought
- 1 tablespoon Dijon mustard
- 2 tablespoons mirin or rice vinegar
- 1 tablespoon toasted sesame oil
- 2 tablespoons fresh lemon juice
- 3 tablespoons fresh orange juice
- salt and freshly ground black pepper

For the stir-fry:
- 2 tablespoons tamari or soy sauce
- 1 lb 5 oz (600 g) smoked tofu, sliced into ½-inch (1 cm) thick steaks
- freshly ground black pepper
- 2 tablespoons vegetable oil
- 2 large green mangos, shredded
- 1 cucumber, peeled, seeded, and diced
- cooked basmati or other long-grain white rice, to serve

To make the dressing, put all the ingredients into a large bowl, season to taste with salt and freshly ground black pepper, and whisk until smooth and creamy. Cover and refrigerate until needed.

To make the stir-fry, pour the tamari or soy sauce into a shallow dish. Add the tofu steaks one by one and rub the tamari into both sides of each steak. Season each side with freshly ground black pepper.

Heat the oil in a large skillet (frying pan). Add the tofu steaks and fry over medium heat for 5–6 minutes on each side, until golden brown.

Add the mango and cucumber to the bowl with the dressing and toss to coat.

Make a bed of green mango slaw on a serving plate and top with the tofu; serve with rice.

STIR-FRIED TEMPEH IN GINGER AND CHILI

Preparation time: 35 minutes
Cooking time: 40 minutes

Serves 4

- 3 cloves garlic, finely chopped
- ¼ cup (30 g) grated fresh ginger
- 6 scallions (spring onions), white and pale green parts only, finely chopped
- 1 green chili, seeded and finely chopped
- 1 teaspoon allspice
- 1 teaspoon dried thyme
- 1 teaspoon ground cinnamon
- 1 teaspoon ground nutmeg
- 2 tablespoons olive oil
- 1 tablespoon fresh lemon juice
- 1 cup (240 ml/8 fl oz) apricot juice
- 2 tablespoons maple syrup
- salt and freshly ground black pepper
- 1 cup (240 g) diced tempeh
- cooked long-grain rice or fried vegetables, to serve

To make the tempeh sauce, whisk together all the ingredients, except for the tempeh and the rice, in a medium bowl and season to taste with salt and freshly ground black pepper.

Dip the tempeh in the sauce, flip over, and then dip again. Repeat until all of the tempeh is completely coated.

Preheat the oven to 350°F/180°C/Gas Mark 4.

Put the tempeh into a baking pan. Cover with aluminum foil and bake for 35 minutes, until well done. Let cool for 5 minutes, then serve with rice or vegetables.

STIR-FRIED VEGETABLES AND COCONUT FLAKES

Wash the bean sprouts and remove any brown tails. Drain and set aside.

Bring a saucepan of water to a boil. Place the bean sprouts in a colander in a clean sink. Pour the hot water over the bean sprouts, then immediately rinse the sprouts under cold running water. Drain well and set aside.

Bring a saucepan of water to a boil. Carefully add the green beans and carrots and boil for about 4 minutes, until al dente. Drain and set aside.

Bring a pan of salted water to a boil. Add the white cabbage and blanch for 3 minutes, until tender. Drain and set aside.

Put the coconut in a small bowl. Add the onion, sriracha, lime juice, and tamari or soy sauce and season to taste with salt. Mix together until well blended.

Cut the bamboo shoots into strips the same size as the beans.

Heat the oil in a large saucepan over medium heat. Add all the vegetables, stir to mix, and cook for 8–9 minutes. Pour in the coconut mixture, stir well, and cook for another 2–3 minutes, until well blended. Season to taste with salt and freshly ground black pepper. Serve immediately with rice and sriracha on the side.

Preparation time: 30 minutes
Cooking time: 35 minutes

Serves 4

- 9 oz (250 g) bean sprouts
- 9 oz (250 g) green beans, stringed and halved
- 4 carrots, sliced
- salt and freshly ground black pepper
- ½ small head of white cabbage, trimmed and shredded
- 1 cup (220 g) shredded fresh coconut
- 1 onion, finely chopped
- 1 teaspoon sriracha, plus extra to serve
- 2 tablespoons fresh lime juice
- 2 tablespoons tamari or soy sauce
- 9 oz (250 g) canned bamboo shoots, drained
- 2 tablespoons vegetable oil
- cooked white rice, to serve

GRAINS
&
BEANS

ALMOND AND PISTACHIO RICE

Preparation time: 20 minutes
Cooking time: 30 minutes

Serves 4

- 1 lb 2 oz (500 g) basmati or other long-grain rice
- ½ cup (120 ml/4 fl oz) olive oil
- 1 oz (25 g) raw almonds, crushed
- 1 oz (25 g) raw pistachios, crushed
- ½ cup (90 g) dates, pitted (stoned) and chopped
- ½ cup (85 g) dried apricots, chopped
- 1½ cups (120 g) coconut powder
- 1 cup (240 ml/8 fl oz) coconut milk
- salt

Bring a saucepan of water to a boil. Add the rice, reduce the heat to low, cover the pan, and cook the rice for 16–18 minutes, until all liquid is absorbed but the rice is still al dente. Remove the pan from the heat, drain the rice, and set aside.

Warm the oil in a large skillet (frying pan) over medium heat. Add the almonds, pistachios, dates, and apricots and cook, stirring, for about 2 minutes. Add the reserved rice, mix well, and cook, stirring, for about 2 minutes. Add the coconut powder, stir well, and then stir in the coconut milk. Cook over medium heat, tasting frequently, for 5–6 minutes.

Season to taste with salt, then ladle into bowls and serve immediately.

BAJA BEANS

Preparation time: 25 minutes
Cooking time: 1 hour

Serves 4

- 2 tablespoons olive oil
- 1 onion, chopped
- 2 green chilies, seeded and chopped
- 1 tablespoon yellow curry powder
- 1 cup (200 g) brown rice
- 1½ cups (360 g) canned tomatoes, chopped
- 3 zucchini (courgettes), chopped
- 1 red bell pepper, chopped
- 1 green bell pepper, chopped
- 1 cup (250 g) canned cannellini beans or other small beans, drained
- 2 cups (280 g) canned corn
- ¼ cup (30 g) cilantro (coriander), chopped, to garnish

Heat the olive oil in a saucepan set over medium heat until shimmering. Add the onion, chilies, and curry powder and cook, stirring, for 5–6 minutes, until the onion is softened. Add the rice and tomatoes along with 2 cups (475 ml/16 fl oz) water, stir well, and bring to a boil. Reduce the heat to bring the mixture to a simmer, cover the pan, and cook, stirring occasionally, for about 20 minutes, until the rice is cooked al dente.

Add the zucchini and bell peppers to the saucepan and cook for about 30 minutes, stirring 2 or 3 times, until the vegetables are cooked through. Add the beans and corn and heat through gently for about 5 minutes.

Transfer to a serving bowl, garnish with the cilantro, and serve.

BLACK BEANS AND RICE

Using a food processor or high-speed blender, combine the onions, tomatoes, garlic, coconut oil, and cumin, then season to taste with salt and freshly ground black pepper. Pulse the ingredients until combined, then transfer the mixture to a saucepan and cook for 5 minutes over medium heat, stirring occasionally. Add the black beans and bring to a boil. Reduce the heat to medium-low to bring the mixture to a simmer, cover the pan, and simmer for 5 minutes. Add the brown rice, stir to combine, reduce the heat to low, and cook for 10 minutes, stirring frequently, until well blended.

Season to taste with salt and freshly ground black/white pepper and let cool for 4–5 minutes before serving.

Preparation time: 20 minutes
Cooking time: 25 minutes

Serves 4

- 1 onion, chopped
- 2 large tomatoes, chopped
- 2 cloves garlic, finely chopped
- 2 tablespoons coconut oil
- 1 teaspoon ground cumin
- salt and freshly ground black/white pepper
- 1½ cups (375 g) canned black beans, drained
- 2 cups (380 g) cooked brown rice

PEPPERS STUFFED WITH QUINOA AND ZUCCHINI

SPAIN

Preheat the broiler (grill).

Arrange the peppers in a broiling (grill) pan and broil for about 20 minutes, until they are soft and the skins just beginning to become dark brown. Turn the peppers over and roast the other side until golden brown. Let cool for 15 minutes, then halve peppers lengthwise, remove the seeds, and transfer to a baking pan.

Preheat the oven to 400°F/200°C/Gas Mark 6.

Combine the quinoa, zucchini or squash, basil, tomato sauce, garlic, and half of the cheese in a large bowl and season to taste with salt and freshly ground black/white pepper. Divide the quinoa mixture equally among the pepper halves; top with the remaining cheese. Bake for 15 minutes, until the cheese has melted and is golden brown. Serve immediately.

Preparation time: 20 minutes
Cooking time: 50 minutes,
  plus 15 minutes cooling

Serves 4

- 2 red bell peppers
- 2 cups (340 g) quinoa, cooked according to the packet instructions
- 2 cups (340 g) shredded zucchini (courgette) or summer squash
- 1 tablespoon chopped basil
- ½ cup (120 g) tomato sauce or crushed tomatoes
- 1 clove garlic, finely chopped
- ½ cup (120 g) grated vegan mozzarella cheese
- salt and freshly ground black/white pepper

BUTTERNUT SQUASH AND SAGE RISOTTO

Preparation time: 30 minutes
Cooking time: 1 hour 15 minutes, plus
  20 minutes cooling

Serves 4

- 3 tablespoons olive oil, plus extra for
  greasing
- 2 butternut squash, halved lengthwise,
  seeds and fibers removed
- 1 shallot, finely chopped
- 1½ cups (360 g) Arborio or Carnaroli rice
- 2 cups (475 ml/16 fl oz) vegetable stock
  (broth)
- 1 orange
- salt and freshly ground black/white pepper
- 2 tablespoons all-purpose (plain) flour
- 1 handful of sage leaves
- 1 tablespoon vegetable margarine
- grated vegan parmesan cheese, to garnish
- ¼ cup (30 g) pine nuts, to garnish

Preheat the oven to 400°F/200°C/Gas Mark 6. Grease a baking pan with olive oil.

Arrange the butternut squash halves on the prepared baking pan with the cut sides facing down. Cover the pan with aluminum foil and bake for about 45 minutes, until fork-tender. Let cool for 20 minutes.

Heat the oil in a large skillet (frying pan) over medium heat. Add the shallot and stir-fry for 2 minutes, until golden. Add the rice and stir well to coat in the oil. Stir in 1 ladle of stock, then cook over very low heat until the stock has been absorbed. Immediately, add another ladle of stock, repeating until the rice is cooked but still al dente.

Meanwhile, cut the orange in half, juice the halves, and remove the white pith from the peel before cutting half of the peel into fine strips. Set aside.

Peel the cooked butternut squash, then finely dice it, and add the squash to the risotto along with the orange juice. Stir carefully until everything is nicely blended. Cook over very low heat for 3–4 minutes. Season to taste with salt and freshly ground black pepper.

Spread the flour on a plate and fill a small bowl with warm water. Dip the sage leaves, one at a time into the warm water, then dip them into the flour to coat.

Melt the vegetable margarine in a saucepan. Add the flour-coated leaves and fry for few seconds, until fragrant. Set aside.

Ladle the risotto into bowls and garnish with vegan cheese, strips of orange zest, the pine nuts, and the fried sage leaves.

BUTTERNUT SQUASH AND SAGE RISOTTO

COUSCOUS STEW WITH MUSHROOMS

Preparation time: 20 minutes
Cooking time: 20 minutes

Serves 4

- 2 cups (475 ml/16 fl oz) vegetable stock (broth)
- 2 tablespoons olive oil
- 1 lb 2 oz (500 g) shiitake or portobello mushrooms, sliced
- 1 green chili, seeded and finely chopped
- 2 shallots, finely chopped
- 2 carrots, diced
- 1 lb 2 oz (500 g) medium-grain couscous
- 9 oz (250 g) green peas
- salt and freshly ground black/white pepper
- 3 tablespoons chopped chives
- 2 tablespoons chopped parsley
- sriracha or harissa, to serve

Bring the stock to a boil in a large saucepan. Reduce the heat to low and keep the stock simmering.

Heat 1 tablespoon of the olive oil in a large saucepan. Add the mushrooms and chili and sauté over medium heat for 5 minutes, until the mushrooms have released their juices. Drain with a slotted spoon and transfer to a bowl. Set aside.

Heat the remaining olive oil in the same saucepan over medium heat. Add the shallots and sauté for 2 minutes, until soft. Add the carrot and sauté for 4–5 minutes, then add the couscous and cook for 3 minutes, stirring constantly, until lightly browned. Stir ¼ cup (60 ml) of the stock into the mixture. Reduce the heat to low and add another ¼ cup (60 ml) of the stock. Repeat the process until all the stock has been absorbed by the couscous.

Stir the peas and the mushroom mixture into the saucepan and cook over medium heat for another 2 minutes, until the peas are hot. Season to taste with salt and freshly ground black pepper.

Transfer to a serving plate, sprinkle over the chives and parsley. Serve immediately, with sriracha or harissa on the side.

COUSCOUS STEW WITH MUSHROOMS

COUSCOUS WITH GREEN LENTILS

Preparation time: 10 minutes
Cooking time: 15 minutes

Serves 4

- 2 tablespoons vegetable oil
- 1 onion, chopped
- 3 cloves garlic, finely chopped
- ⅓ cup (80 g) tomato purée (passata)
- 1 teaspoon superfine (caster) sugar
- 2 cups (475 ml/16 fl oz) vegetable stock (broth)
- 2 tablespoons dried herbes de Provence
- 2 cups (400 g) cooked green or brown lentils
- 2 cups (320 g) medium-grain couscous
- salt and freshly ground black pepper
- sriracha or harissa, to serve

Heat the vegetable oil in a saucepan over medium heat. Add the onion and garlic and stir-fry for 5–6 minutes, until golden brown. Stir in the tomato purée and sugar, then add the stock and herbes de Provence, stir well, and bring the mixture to a simmer over low heat. Simmer for 5 minutes, then add the drained lentils, followed by the couscous. Bring the mixture to a simmer and cook over medium heat for about 5 minutes, until the couscous is tender.

Season to taste with salt and feshly ground black/white pepper. Serve with sriracha or harissa.

COUSCOUS WITH PISTACHIO AND APRICOT

Preparation time: 20 minutes
Cooking time: 25 minutes

Serves 4

- 1 tablespoon vegetable oil
- 3 cloves garlic, finely chopped
- 2 cups (400 g) medium-grain couscous
- 2½ cups (600 ml/20 fl oz) vegetable stock (broth)
- 1 cinnamon stick
- 1 teaspoon ground cumin
- 1 teaspoon ground cardamom
- finely grated zest and juice of 1 lime
- salt and freshly ground black/white pepper
- ¼ cup (7 g) chopped mint
- ½ cup (100 g) dried apricots, diced
- ½ cup (60 g) pistachio nuts, shelled

Heat the vegetable oil in a saucepan. Add the garlic and stir-fry over medium heat for 3–4 minutes, until golden brown. Add the couscous and stir-fry for 4–5 minutes, stirring constantly, until the couscous grains are lightly toasted. Add the stock, cinnamon stick, cumin, cardamom, and lime zest and season to taste with salt and freshly ground black/white pepper. Bring the mixture to a boil, then immediately reduce the heat to produce a low simmer. Cover the pan and cook over medium-low heat for 10 minutes, until most of the stock has been absorbed by the couscous.

Add half of the mint to the saucepan along with the apricots, pistachios, and lime juice. Stir well, cover the pan, and cook over very low heat for another 5 minutes. Discard the cinnamon stick, fluff the couscous with a fork, and season to taste with salt and freshly ground black/white pepper.

Transfer the mixture to a serving plate, garnish with the remaining mint, and serve.

RED BELL PEPPER AND RICE STEW

Heat the oil in a large saucepan over medium heat. Add the onion and sauté for 3 minutes. Add the carrots, bell peppers, rice, and stock and stir to combine. Stir in the paprika, bring the mixture to a simmer, and cook over low heat for 18–20 minutes. Remove the saucepan from the heat, cover with a lid, and set aside for about 10 minutes, until the rice has absorbed all the stock.

Season to taste with salt and freshly ground black/white pepper, garnish with chopped cilantro, and serve.

Preparation time: 20 minutes
Cooking time: 25 minutes
  plus 10 minutes chilling

Serves 4

- 2 tablespoons vegetable oil
- 1 large onion, diced
- 2 carrots, grated
- 1 red bell pepper, diced
- 1 cup (200 g) basmati or jasmine rice
- 3 cups (710 ml/24 fl oz) vegetable stock (broth)
- 1 teaspoon sweet paprika
- salt and freshly ground black/white pepper
- chopped cilantro (coriander), to garnish

RED RICE PILAF

Melt the vegetable margarine in a medium sauté pan over medium heat. Add the onion and shallot and sauté for 5–6 minutes, until tender and golden brown. Stir in the chilies, ginger, garlic, orange or Mandarin juice and zest, Szechuan pepper, perilla leaves, and tamari or soy sauce. Season to taste with salt, stir well, and cook for 2 minutes, until fragrant. Add the stock and rice. Bring the mixture to a boil, then reduce the heat to low and simmer for 30 minutes, until the rice is tender but still al dent and the stock has been absorbed. If the mixture becomes too dry during cooking, add a little water and stir only occasionally (every 10 minutes). Once the rice is cooked, cover the pan and set aside for 10 minutes.

To serve, transfer the rice to a large bowl and garnish with the sesame seeds. Serve with finely chopped red chili on the side.

Preparation time: 20 minutes
Cooking time: 40 minutes

Serves 4

- 2 tablespoons vegetable margarine
- 1 red onion, finely chopped
- 1 shallot, finely chopped
- 2 small red chilies, seeded and finely chopped, plus extra to serve
- 1 tablespoon fresh grated ginger
- 2 teaspoons minced garlic
- finely grated zest and juice of 1 orange or Mandarin orange
- 1 teaspoon ground Szechuan pepper
- ¼ cup (7 g) perilla leaves
- 2 tablespoons tamari or soy sauce
- salt
- 3 cups (710 ml/24 fl oz) vegetable stock (broth)
- 1 cup (200 g) Bhutanese red rice or Chinese black Emperor rice
- 1 teaspoon white sesame seeds, to garnish
- 1 teaspoon black sesame seeds, to garnish

QUINOA MATHROOBA

Preparation time: 20 minutes
Cooking time: 45 minutes

Serves 4

- 2½ cups (600 ml/20 fl oz) vegetable stock (broth)
- 2 cups (340 g) quinoa, rinsed
- 1 tablespoon coconut oil
- 3 large onions, roughly chopped
- 3 cloves garlic, finely chopped
- 1 green chili, plus more to taste, seeded and finely chopped
- 4 large tomatoes, roughly chopped
- 2 tablespoons tomato purée (passata)
- 1 tablespoon curry powder
- 1 teaspoon ground turmeric
- 1 teaspoon ground cinnamon
- 1 teaspoon ground cardamom
- 1 teaspoon ground cumin
- ½ cup (120 g) canned red lentils, drained
- salt and freshly ground black/white pepper
- cooked long-grain white rice, to serve
- sprig of cilantro (coriander), to serve

Bring 2 cups (475 ml/16 fl oz) of the stock to a boil in a large saucepan. Add the quinoa, then bring the mixture to a simmer over low heat and cook for 14–15 minutes, until the quinoa is cooked. Use a fork to fluff the grains. Set aside.

Heat the coconut oil in a large skillet (frying pan) or wok. Add the onions, garlic, and chili and sauté for 5–6 minutes over medium heat, until lightly golden. Add the tomatoes, tomato purée, curry powder, turmeric, cinnamon, cardamom, and cumin and cook over medium heat, stirring frequently, for 7–8 minutes, until the tomatoes are nicely cooked. If the mixture becomes too dry, add a little water to the pan.

Add the quinoa and lentils to the skillet, along with enough of the remaining stock or water to roughly cover, and simmer over low heat for 20 minutes, until all the ingredients are cooked through.

Season to taste with salt and freshly ground black/white pepper. Serve with rice.

QUINOA MATHROOBA

RICE WITH COCONUT
AND PAPAYA

Preparation time: 20 minutes
Cooking time: 20 minutes

Serves 4

- 2 cups (400 g) short-grain white rice, such
  as Arborio or Carnaroli
- 2 cups (475 ml/16 fl oz) coconut milk
- 1 teaspoon ground cinnamon
- salt
- 1 small papaya, finely diced
- 2 cups (340 g) diced pineapple, to serve

Mix the rice, coconut milk, ⅓ cup (80 ml/2⅔ fl oz) water, and cinnamon in a large saucepan and season to taste with salt. Bring the mixture to a boil. Reduce the heat to produce a low simmer. Cover the pan and cook over low heat for 20 minutes, until the rice is al dente. If it becomes too dry during cooking, add a little water. Once the rice is cooked, fluff it with a fork, then cover the pan and set aside.

Put half of the papaya in a bowl and mash it with a fork. Add the mashed papaya to the rice and stir to blend, then add the remaining papaya and mix carefully to avoid mashing the dice. Serve warm, with the diced pineapple on top.

RICE WITH COCONUT AND PAPAYA

VEGETABLE PAELLA

Preparation time: 20 minutes
Cooking time: 35 minutes

Serves 4

- 2 tablespoons olive oil
- 1 onion, chopped
- 1 green bell pepper, diced
- 2 cloves garlic, finely chopped
- 2 cups (480 g) paella rice
- 4 cups (950 ml/32 fl oz) vegetable stock (broth)
- 1 cup (200 g) plum tomatoes, diced
- 2 green chilies, seeded and chopped
- 1 teaspoon ground turmeric
- 1 teaspoon sweet paprika
- 1 cup (190 g) canned kidney beans, drained
- 1 cup (140 g) canned or frozen corn kernels
- salt and freshly ground black/white pepper
- lemon wedges, to serve
- crushed red chili flakes, to serve

Heat the olive oil in a large skillet (frying pan). Add the onion and stir fry for 5–6 minutes, until golden brown. Add the green pepper and garlic and stir-fry over medium heat for 4–5 minutes, until golden. Add the rice, stock, tomatoes, green chilies, turmeric, and sweet paprika. Bring the mixture to a boil, then reduce the heat to low, cover, and simmer at low heat for 20 minutes.

Stir the kidney beans and corn into the rice mixture, then cover the pan and cook for 5 minutes, until well cooked. Season to taste with salt and freshly ground black/white pepper. Serve with lemon wedges and crushed red chili flakes on the side.

SOUTH AMERICAN COUSCOUS

Preparation time: 25 minutes
Cooking time: 20 minutes

Serves 4

- 2 cups (360 g) couscous
- 1 teaspoon ground cumin
- 2 cups (475 ml/16 fl oz) vegetable stock (broth)
- 2 cups (500 g) canned black beans or kidney beans, drained
- 1 cup (140 g) canned corn
- 1 cup (140 g) chopped red onion
- ¼ cup (15 g) chopped cilantro (coriander)
- 1 jalapeño pepper, seeded and finely chopped
- salt and freshly ground black/white pepper
- 2 tablespoons roasted garlic olive oil
- 2 tablespoons fresh lime juice
- sriracha, to serve

Mix the couscous and ground cumin in a large heatproof bowl. Bring the stock to a boil and pour it over the couscous. Cover the bowl with a clean kitchen towel or lid and set aside for 10 minutes, until all the liquid has been absorbed. Fluff the couscous with a fork. If the grains are not tender enough, add ½ cup (120 ml/4 fl oz) boiling water, cover the bowl, and let sit for another 10 minutes.

Add the beans, corn, onion, cilantro, and jalapeño to the couscous. Season to taste with salt and freshly ground black/white pepper. Drizzle the roasted garlic oil and lime juice on top and serve warm or at room temperature, with sriracha on the side.

VEGETABLE PAELLA

VEGETABLE SAFFRON PAELLA

Preparation time: 25 minutes
Cooking time: 25 minutes,
  plus 10 minutes cooling

Serves 4

- 6¼ cups (1.5 liters/50 fl oz) vegetable stock (broth)
- 1 teaspoon ground saffron
- ¼ cup (60 ml/2 fl oz) olive oil
- 1 cup (140 g) yellow onion, chopped
- 3 cloves garlic, finely chopped
- 1 sweet Romano red pepper, chopped finely
- 1 yellow bell pepper, cut into strips
- 8 green asparagus spears, trimmed and cut into small pieces
- 1 tomato, diced
- 1 cup (140 g) fresh or frozen green peas
- 8 button mushrooms, sliced
- 2 artichoke hearts preserved in brine, diced
- 3 cups (720 g) paella rice
- salt and freshly ground black/white pepper

Bring the stock to a boil in a large saucepan, then remove the pan from the stove and add the saffron. Set aside for 2 minutes, stirring a couple of times.

Preheat the oven to 400°F/200°C/Gas Mark 6.

Select a 14-inch (36 cm) paella pan or Dutch oven (casserole) that is 2–2½ inches (5–6 cm) deep. Put the oil into the pan and set over medium heat. Add the onion, garlic, Romano and bell peppers, asparagus, tomato, peas, mushrooms, and artichoke hearts and cook for 2 minutes, stirring frequently. Add the paella rice, mix well with the vegetables, and add the saffron-infused stock. Season to taste with salt and freshly ground black/white pepper. Transfer the paella pan to the oven, positioning it as low in the oven as possible. Bake for 20 minutes, until all of the stock has been absorbed. Let cool for 10 minutes before serving.

WILD MUSHROOM RAGU

Preparation time: 15 minutes
Cooking time: 20 minutes

Serves 4

- 2 tablespoons olive oil
- 3 cups (360 g) trimmed and sliced assorted wild mushrooms
- 1 cup (100 g) sliced scallions (spring onions), white and pale green parts only
- 1 cup (200 g) peeled, seeded, and chopped tomatoes,
- 4 bay leaves
- 1 shallot, finely chopped
- 3 cloves garlic, finely chopped
- 2 cups (475 ml/16 fl oz) vegetable stock (broth)
- 2 tablespoons vegetable margarine
- salt and freshly ground black/white pepper
- 1 lb (500 g) cooked flat noodles or gnocchi, to serve

Heat the olive oil in a large saucepan. Add the mushrooms and sauté for 4–5 minutes over medium heat, until golden and starting to soften. Stir in the scallions, tomatoes, bay leaves, shallots, and garlic and stir-fry for 2–3 minutes, until softened. Pour in the stock, bring to a boil, then reduce the heat to low and simmer for 4–5 minutes, until the mushrooms are cooked. Add the vegetable margarine and simmer gently for 2–3 minutes, until the margarine has melted. Season to taste with salt and freshly ground black pepper.

Add the cooked noodles or gnocchi to the ragu, cover the pan, and simmer very gently over low heat until the noodles or gnocchi are warmed through (according to packet instructions). Serve immediately.

ZUCCHINI AND GRAPE STEW

ITALY

Heat the oil in a large skillet (frying pan). Add the onion and stir-fry over medium heat for 4 minutes, until slightly golden. Add the zucchini and cook for 3–4 minutes, stirring frequently. Stir in the stock, bring to a boil, then immediately reduce the heat to bring the mixture to a simmer and add the cinnamon and saffron. Cook for about 5 minutes over medium-low heat, until the zucchini is very tender.

Add the grapes to the saucepan and cook for about 10 minutes, until the stock is reduced by half. Season to taste with salt and freshly ground black/white pepper. Transfer to a serving bowl, garnish with the chopped sage, and serve with rice.

Preparation time: 20 minutes
Cooking time: 25 minutes

Serves 4

- 4 tablespoons olive oil
- 2 onions, diced
- 6 zucchini (courgettes), diced
- 2 cups (475 ml/16 fl oz) vegetable stock (broth)
- 1 tablespoon ground cinnamon
- 1 teaspoon ground saffron
- 1 cup (100 g) seedless green grapes, halved
- 1 bunch sage, chopped, to garnish
- salt and freshly ground black/white pepper
- cooked white rice, to serve

WILD RICE WITH PEARS AND CRANBERRIES

ENGLAND

Put the stock and rice into a large saucepan set over medium heat and bring to a boil. Reduce the heat to produce a low simmer, cover the pan, and cook over medium-low heat for about 10 minutes, until the rice is tender but al dente and almost all the stock has been absorbed. If the rice becomes too dry during cooking, add a little water.

Heat the oil in a saucepan or wok. Add the onion and stir-fry for 5–6 minutes, until golden brown. Stir in the sugar and cook over very low heat for 20 minutes, until the sugar is completely dissolved. Stir in the cranberries, cover the pan, and cook over low heat for 10 minutes, stirring occasionally. Add the pear and cinnamon, mix well, and cook for 4–5 minutes, until the pear is fork-tender. Season to taste with freshly ground black/white pepper and set aside until the rice is cooked.

Transfer the rice to a large serving bowl and stir in the cranberry-pear mixture. Garnish with orange zest and walnuts and serve.

Preparation time: 25 minutes
Cooking time: 50 minutes

Serves 4

- 2 cups (475 ml/16 fl oz) vegetable stock (broth)
- 2 cups (400 g) wild rice
- 2 tablespoons vegetable oil
- 3 onions, chopped
- 1 teaspoon light brown sugar
- 1 cup (180 g) dried cranberries, soaked in water overnight and drained
- 1 cup (200 g) finely diced firm pears
- 1 teaspoon ground cinnamon
- freshly ground black/white pepper
- finely grated zest of 1 orange, to garnish
- 1 tablespoon crushed walnuts, to garnish

PASTA & NOODLES

AVOCADO PASTA

Preparation time: 30 minutes
Cooking time: 10 minutes

Serves 4

- salt, plus extra to season
- 1 lb 2 oz (500 g) spaghetti
- 2 ripe avocados, halved, pitted (stoned), and peeled
- ½ cup (30 g) basil
- 2 cloves garlic, finely chopped
- 2 tablespoons fresh lemon juice
- freshly ground black/white pepper
- 5 tablespoons olive oil
- 1 cup (200 g) cherry tomatoes
- 1½ cups (120 g) fresh or canned corn kernels
- grated vegan parmesan cheese, to serve
- ¼ cup (15 g) chopped cilantro (coriander) leaves, to garnish

Bring a large saucepan of water to a boil and add enough salt to make the water taste like the sea. Add the pasta and cook according to the packet instructions, until al dente. Drain well and transfer to a large bowl.

While the pasta is cooking, combine the avocados, basil, garlic, and lemon juice in the bowl of a food processor and season to taste with salt and freshly ground black/white pepper. Process until smooth. With the motor still running, add the olive oil in a slow and steady stream and continue processing until the sauce is emulsified.

Transfer the sauce to the bowl with the spaghetti, add the tomatoes and corn, and toss to combine. Top with the vegan grated cheese, garnish with the chopped cilantro, and serve immediately.

FETTUCCINE WITH ASPARAGUS, MORELS, AND TARRAGON

Preparation time: 20 minutes
Cooking time: 30 minutes

Serves 4

- 2 tablespoons vegetable margarine
- 1½ cups (240 g) sliced shallots
- 2 cups (240 g) fresh morel mushrooms, larger mushrooms halved
- 1 lb 2 oz (500 g) asparagus, trimmed and cut into 1½-inch (4 cm) pieces
- 1¼ cups (300 ml/10 fl oz) vegetable stock (broth)
- ⅔ cup (150 ml/5 fl oz) soy cream
- 2½ tablespoons chopped tarragon
- salt and freshly ground black/white pepper
- 1 lb 2 oz (500 g) fettuccine
- 1 tablespoon olive oil
- 2 cups (250 g) grated vegan parmesan cheese

Melt the vegetable margarine in a large, heavy skillet (frying pan) over medium heat. Add the shallots and morels and sauté for about 6 minutes, until the shallots are tender. Add the asparagus and stock. Bring to a boil, then reduce the heat to bring the mixture to a simmer, cover the skillet with a lid, and cook over medium heat for 3–4 minutes, until the stock is reduced. Stir in the soy cream and 2 tablespoons of the chopped tarragon. Simmer, uncovered, for about 4 minutes, until the sauce thickens slightly. Season to taste with salt and freshly ground black/white pepper. Cover the skillet and set aside.

Cook the pasta according to the packet instructions until al dente. Drain the fettuccine and set aside. Add the olive oil and stir to coat evenly. Transfer the fettuccine to a large serving bowl, add the mushrooms and half of the vegan cheese, and toss to combine. Sprinkle over the remaining tarragon and the cheese and serve immediately.

COLD SESAME NOODLES
WITH MUNG BEANS

Cook the rice noodles or fettuccine according to the packet instructions until ad dente. Drain and rinse under cold water. Drain again, then transfer to a large bowl. Mix in the sesame paste or peanute butter, carrot, cucumber, and bean sprouts and toss to combine.

Put the soy sauce, brown sugar, vinegar, and sriracha into a small bowl along with 3 tablespoons water, the Szechuan pepper, and the garlic. Whisk to combine. Pour the sauce over the noodle mixture and toss to coat.

Divide the noodles among 4 bowls, garnish with the scallions, and serve.

Preparation time: 30 minutes
Cooking time: 15 minutes

Serves 4

- 1 lb 2 oz (500 g) rice noodles or fettuccine
- 1 tablespoon toasted sesame paste or peanut butter
- 2 cups (260 g) grated carrots
- 2 cups (280 g) diced seeded cucumber
- 1 cup (200 g) mung bean sprouts
- 1 tablespoon tamari or soy sauce
- 2 teaspoons brown sugar
- 2 teaspoons rice vinegar or apple cider vinegar
- 1 teaspoon sriracha
- 1 teaspoon ground Szechuan pepper
- 1 clove garlic, finely chopped
- 2 scallions (spring onions), trimmed and thinly sliced, to garnish

CREAMY MUSHROOM
AND CORN PENNE

Cook the penne according to the packet instructions until al dente and set aside.

Using a food-processor or high-speed blender, combine the cauliflower, soy cream, basil, garlic, and cashews and purée until smooth and creamy.

Heat the vegetable oil in a saucepan. Add the mushrooms, rosemary, oregano, and paprika and sauté for 6–7 minutes, until the mushrooms are tender. Add the cauliflower sauce and simmer over medium-low heat for 3–4 minutes. Remove the pan from the stove and add the penne and nutritional yeast.

Season to taste with salt and freshly ground black/white pepper and stir well. Serve immediately.

Preparation time: 20 minutes
Cooking time: 15 minutes

Serves 4

- 1 lb 2 oz (500 g) corn penne
- 4 cups (560 g) cauliflower florets, steamed
- 1 cup (240 ml/8 fl oz) soy cream
- 1 large handful of basil, chopped
- 3 cloves garlic, crushed
- ½ cup (125 g) raw cashews, soaked in water overnight and drained
- 2 tablespoons vegetable oil
- 3 cups (360 g) sliced mushrooms, such as shiitake or portobello
- 1 teaspoon dried rosemary
- 1 teaspoon dried oregano
- 1 teaspoon sweet paprika
- 1 tablespoon nutritional yeast
- salt and freshly ground black/white pepper

FETTUCCINE WITH SAFFRON, TOMATO, AND COCONUT

Preparation time: 20 minutes
Cooking time: 25 minutes

Serves 4

For the sauce:
- 2 tablespoons vegetable oil
- 9 oz (250 g) canned tomatoes with their juice
- 1 clove garlic, finely chopped
- 1 teaspoon ground saffron
- 1 cup (240 ml/8 fl oz) coconut milk
- 1 tablespoon finely grated lemon zest
- salt and freshly ground black/white pepper

For the pasta:
- 1 lb 2 oz (500 g) fettuccine or penne
- salt and freshly ground black/white pepper
- grated vegan parmesan cheese, to serve
- chopped basil, to garnish

To make the sauce, heat the vegetable oil in a heavy skillet (frying pan) or saucepan over medium heat. Add the tomatoes, garlic, and saffron, bring to a simmer, and cook over medium-low heat for 15 minutes, until most of the liquid has evaporated and the sauce is reduced by about half. Stir in the coconut milk and lemon zest, and season to taste with salt and pepper. Simmer gently for a couple of minutes, stirring frequently, until hot and combined. Set aside.

Cook the pasta according to the packet instructions until al dente. Drain and transfer to a deep bowl. Add the sauce, toss to combine, and season to taste with salt and freshly ground black/white pepper. Top with grated cheese and chopped basil and serve immediately.

FETTUCCINE WITH PINE NUTS AND CASHEWS

Preparation time: 25 minutes
Cooking time: 20 minutes

Serves 4

- 2 tablespoons olive oil
- 3 dried chilies, crushed and finely chopped
- 4 cloves garlic, crushed
- 4 oz (120 g) pine nuts
- 4 oz (120 g) raw cashews
- 1 lb 2 oz (500 g) fettuccine
- 2 tablespoons vegetable margarine
- 9 oz (250 g) baby spinach
- 2 tablespoons nutritional yeast
- 3 tablespoons chopped basil, to garnish

Heat the olive oil in a saucepan over medium heat, add the dried chilies, and allow the chilies to gently infuse for 5 minutes. Take the pan off the heat and let cool, then strain and reserve the oil and discard the chilies.

Put the garlic into the same pan and cook for 3–4 minutes over medium heat until golden. Set aside.

Toast the pine nuts in a nonstick skillet (frying pan) for 2–3 minutes over medium-low heat, until golden brown. Set aside. Repeat with the cashews. Let cool.

Cook the fettuccine according to the packet instructions until al dente. Drain and transfer to a large bowl. Add the margarine and stir to coat the fettuccine. Add the baby spinach and pine nuts and mix well.

Using a food processor or high-speed blender, pulse the cashews until broken down. Transfer the cashews to a small bowl and combine with the nutritional yeast and garlic. Sprinkle the mixture over the pasta, drizzle with the chili oil, and toss to combine. Garnish with the basil and serve immediately.

LEMON FETTUCCINE

Cook the fettuccine in a large saucepan according to the packet instructions until al dente. Drain, reserving 3–4 tablespoons of the cooking water in a bowl.

Meanwhile, to make the lemon sauce, whisk the silken tofu, lemon zest and juice, soy cream, and cheese in a bowl, transfer to a saucepan, and heat gently over medium-low heat.

Return the pasta to the large saucepan it was cooked in, add the vegetable margarine and stir gently over medium-high heat. Season to taste with salt and freshly ground black/white pepper, and add enough of the reserved cooking water to slightly moisten the pasta. When the fettuccine is hot, add the lemon sauce and toss to combine. Divide the pasta among 4 bowls, garnish each with a lemon wedge, and serve.

Preparation time: 20 minutes
Cooking time: 20 minutes

Serves 4

For the pasta:
- 1 lb 2 oz (500 g) fettuccine
- 2 tablespoons vegetable margarine
- salt and freshly ground black/white pepper
4 lemon wedges, to serve

For the lemon sauce:
- 1 cup (240 g) silken tofu
- finely grated zest of 1 lemon
- 2 lemons, juiced
- 1 cup (240 ml/8 fl oz) soy cream
- 1 cup (120 g) grated vegan parmesan cheese

LINGUINE WITH TRUFFLES

Cook the linguine according to the packet instructions until al dente. Drain and return the pasta to the pan. Add 1 tablespoon of the truffle oil and half of the cheese, toss to combine, and set aside.

Put the soy cream into a saucepan with the remaining truffle oil and bring to a simmer over medium-low heat. Add the nutritional yeast, mix well, and pour the sauce over the linguine. Toss to combine.

Transfer the pasta to a serving platter and season to taste with salt and freshly ground black/white pepper. Garnish with the scallions, then shave the truffle on top. Serve with the remaining cheese on the side.

Preparation time: 20 minutes
Cooking time: 15 minutes

Serves 4

- 1 lb 2 oz (500 g) linguine
- 2 tablespoons truffle oil
- 4½ oz (125 g) grated vegan parmesan cheese,
- 4 tablespoons soy cream
- 2 tablespoons nutritional yeast
- salt and freshly ground black/white pepper
- ¼ cup (50 g) chopped scallions (spring onions)
- black or white truffle, shaved, to garnish

FIVE-SPICE STIR-FRIED SOBA NOODLES

Preparation time: 20 minutes
Cooking time: 15 minutes

Serves 4

For the soba noodles:
- 1 lb 2 oz (500 g) soba noodles
- 1 tablespoon vegetable oil

For the sauce:
- ½ cup (120 ml/4 fl oz) fresh orange juice
- 1 tablespoon cornstarch (cornflour)
- 1 teaspoon five-spice powder
- 1 teaspoon crushed red chili flakes
- 2 tablespoons soy sauce
- 2 teaspoons agave syrup

For the stir-fry:
- 2 tablespoons olive oil
- 1 lb 2 oz (500 g) trimmed and sliced mushrooms
- 2 cups (280 g) baby carrots, sliced
- 1 onion, sliced
- 2 cloves garlic, finely chopped
- 3 cups (520 g) broccoli florets

Cook the soba noodles according to the packet instructions. Drain and return to the pan. Stir in the vegetable oil, toss to coat the noodles, then cover the pan and set aside.

To make the sauce, combine the ingredients in a large bowl and whisk until well blended. Set aside.

To make the stir-fry, heat the olive oil in a saucepan over medium heat. Add the mushrooms, carrots, onion, and garlic and stir fry for 5 minutes, until onion and garlic are golden. Add the broccoli florets, cover the pan, and cook for 5–6 minutes, stirring occasionally, until the vegetables are crisp-tender. Add the sauce and stir for 3 minutes or until the sauce has thickened.

Transfer the soba noodles to a serving bowl. Pour the vegetable-sauce mixture over the noodles, toss to combine, and serve immediately.

FIVE-SPICE STIR-FRIED SOBA NOODLES

LASAGNA WITH WILD MUSHROOM SAUCE

Preparation time: 30 minutes
Cooking time: 1 hour 10 minutes

Serves 4

For the mushroom sauce:
- 1 tablespoon extra-virgin olive oil
- 1 cup (140 g) chopped yellow onion
- 1 lb 2 oz (500 g) button mushrooms, trimmed and sliced
- ¼ cup (30 g) chopped parsley
- 2 teaspoons ground rosemary
- 1 cup (200 g) canned plum tomatoes

For the filling:
- ½ cup (30 g) chopped parsley
- ¼ cup (15 g) basil
- 2 cups (60 g) packed baby spinach
- 1 lb (480 g) firm tofu
- 2 cups (250 g) grated vegan cheddar cheese
- 4 tablespoons rice or almond milk
- 1 teaspoon ground nutmeg
- salt and freshly ground black/white pepper
- 2 lb (1 kg) vegetables such as broccoli, artichoke hearts, zucchini, green beans, asparagus, and yellow and red bell peppers

For the lasagna:
- 10 whole-wheat lasagna sheets
- olive oil, for greasing
- salt and freshly ground black/white pepper
- 2 cups (250 g) grated vegan cheddar cheese

To make the mushroom sauce, heat the oil in a large skillet (frying pan). Add the onion and stir-fry over medium heat for 4–5 minutes, until transparent and golden brown. Stir in the mushrooms, parsley, rosemary, and tomatoes. Simmer over medium-low heat for 20 minutes, until well cooked and soft. Set aside.

To make the filling, combine the parsley, basil, and spinach leaves in a food processor and pulse until minced. Add the tofu, cheese, and rice or almond milk. Add the nutmeg and season with salt and freshly ground black/white pepper to taste. Mix well and set aside.

Chop the mixed vegetables, combine them in a large bowl, and set aside.

Cook the lasagna sheets according to the instructions on the packet, drain, and pat them dry. Using your fingers or a brush, add a little bit of olive oil on the top of each lasagna sheet and set aside.

To make the lasagna, preheat the oven to 400°F/190°C/Gas Mark 6. Grease a 10 x 13-inch (28 x 14-cm) ovenproof dish with olive oil. Spoon a fine layer of mushroom sauce on the bottom, cover it with a layer of lasagna sheet. Add a third of the vegetables and cover with a third of the mushroom sauce, sprinkle a third of the vegan cheddar cheese, cover with another layer of lasagna sheet and so on, until the lasagna is complete, finishing with the remaining a third of cheese. Cover the dish with aluminum foil and bake for 30 minutes. Remove the aluminum foil and bake another 5 minutes, until the sauce starts to bubble. Let the lasagna cool for 10 minutes before serving.

LASAGNA WITH WILD MUSHROOM SAUCE

LASAGNA WITH CREAM SAUCE

Preparation time: 30 minutes
Cooking time: 50 minutes

Serves 4

- 2 tablespoons vegetable oil, plus extra for greasing
- 2 tablespoons vegetable margarine
- 3 cloves garlic, finely chopped
- 1 cup (200 g) sliced carrots
- 1 cup (100 g) finely diced red bell pepper
- 2 cups (280 g) canned corn
- 1 cup (200 g) plum tomatoes, chopped
- 1 teaspoon dried oregano
- 1 teaspoon crushed red chili flakes
- 1 cup (240 ml/8 fl oz) vegetable stock (broth)
- ½ cup (120 ml/4 fl oz) tomato sauce
- 2 tablespoons fresh lemon juice
- salt and freshly ground black/white pepper
- 8 lasagna sheets
- ½ cup (120 ml/4 fl oz) soy cream
- 1 cup (125 g) grated vegan cheddar cheese
- 1 cup (125 g) grated vegan mozzarella cheese
- 6 basil leaves, to garnish
- green salad, to serve

Preheat the oven to 400°F/200°C/Gas Mark 6. Grease a square ovenproof dish or lasagna pan.

Heat the oil and vegetable margarine in a saucepan. Add the chopped garlic and sauté over medium heat for 3–4 minutes, until golden. Add the carrots, bell pepper, corn, tomatoes, oregano, chili flakes, and stock. Cover the pan and simmer over low heat for about 14 minutes, until the vegetables are fork-tender. Stir in the tomato sauce and lemon juice, mix well, and remove the pan from the heat. Season to taste with salt and freshly ground black/white pepper.

To assemble the lasagna, start with the first layer—arrange 2 pasta sheets across the bottom of the prepared dish. Spread one-third of the vegetables over the pasta, pour over one-third of the cream, and scatter over one-third of the cheese. Repeat the process two more times, and top with the remaining lasagna sheets. Bake for 25 minutes, until the lasagna is golden brown. Let cool for 8–10 minutes, garnish with basil and serve with a salad on side.

LINGUINE WITH CHANTERELLES AND LEEKS

Preparation time: 20 minutes
Cooking time: 30 minutes

Serves 4

- 1 lb 2 oz (500 g) chanterelles
- 1 lb 2 oz (500 g) fresh linguine
- 2 tablespoons vegetable margarine
- 1 large leek, halved lengthwise and thinly sliced
- salt and freshly ground black/white pepper
- 3 cloves garlic, finely chopped
- 5 tablespoons dry white wine
- 2 teaspoon chopped thyme
- 1 bunch parsley, chopped, to garnish
- ⅓ cup (40 g) grated vegan Parmesan cheese, to serve

Clean and trim the mushrooms and remove hard stems from the largest ones. Cut the mushrooms into thick slices.

Cook the linguine according to the packet instructions until al dente.

Meanwhile, melt the vegetable margarine in large sauté pan. Add the leeks and season to taste with salt and a few pinches of freshly ground black/white pepper. Cook over medium heat for 3 minutes. Add the garlic, cover the pan, and cook for 6–7 minutes, until the leeks are tender. Add the mushrooms and wine and simmer over medium-low heat for about 10 minutes.

Drain the cooked pasta, add it to the sauté pan along with the thyme, and toss well to coat the linguine in the mushroom-leek mixture. Garnish with parsley and serve with the cheese on the side.

LINGUINE WITH CAULIFLOWER, LEMON, AND CAPERS

Cook the linguine according to the packet instructions until al dente. Drain the pasta, reserving 1 cup (240 ml/8 fl oz) of the cooking water.

Meanwhile, heat 1 tablespoon of the olive oil in a large saucepan over medium heat. Add the garlic, breadcrumbs, and walnuts and cook, stirring often, for 2–4 minutes, until the breadcrumbs are golden brown and toasted. Transfer the mixture to a small bowl.

Put the remaining oil into the same saucepan and set the pan over medium heat. Add the onion and sauté 5–6 minutes, stirring occasionally, until golden brown. Add the cauliflower and crushed red chili flakes and season to taste with salt. Cook, stirring occasionally, for 5–6 minutes.

Add three-quarters of the reserved pasta cooking water and cook for about 10 minutes, until the cauliflower is fork-tender, adding more cooking water as needed. Add the pasta to the saucepan and stir in the capers, parsley, cheese, the toasted breadcrumb mixture, and the lemon juice.

Season to taste with salt and pepper. Divide the pasta among 4 bowls, top with additional cheese, parsley, and the kalamata olives, and serve immediately.

Preparation time: 20 minutes
Cooking time: 25 minutes

Serves 4

- 1 lb 2 oz (500 g) linguine
- 2 tablespoons olive oil
- 3 cloves garlic, finely chopped
- 1 cup (120 g) breadcrumbs
- 1 cup (90 g) chopped walnuts
- 1 yellow onion, diced
- 1 lb 10 oz (750 g) cauliflower florets
- 1 teaspoon crushed red chili flakes
- salt and freshly ground black/white pepper
- 3 tablespoons capers, drained
- 2 tablespoons chopped parsley, plus extra to garnish
- 1 cup (125 g) grated vegan parmesan cheese, plus extra to garnish
- 4 tablespoons fresh lemon juice
- 2 tablespoons chopped kalamata olives, to garnish

PEANUT BUTTER PASTA

Cook the pasta according to the packet instructions until al dente. Rinse under cold running water to stop the cooking, drain completely, and set aside in a large bowl.

Put the stock into a large saucepan set over medium heat and bring to a simmer. Then stir in the peanut butter and mix until smooth. Add tamari or soy sauce, wine or vinegar, agave or maple syrup, ginger, chili powder, and peas and bring to a simmer. Cook over low heat for 2–3 minutes, until combined. Add the pasta, season to taste with salt and freshly ground black/white pepper, and toss to combine. Divide the pasta among 4 bowls and serve.

Preparation time: 15 minutes
Cooking time: 15 minutes

Serves 4

- 1 lb 2 oz (500 g) fusilli or rotini
- 1 cup (240 ml/8 fl oz) vegetable stock (broth)
- ½ cup (130 g) crunchy peanut butter
- 3 tablespoons tamari or soy sauce
- 2 tablespoons white wine or rice vinegar
- 1 tablespoon agave or maple syrup
- 1 teaspoon grated fresh ginger
- 1 teaspoon chili powder
- 2 cups (280 g) frozen green peas, defrosted
- salt and freshly ground black/white pepper

MACARONI AND ROASTED CAULIFLOWER BOWL

Preparation time: 25 minutes
Cooking time: 40 minutes

Serves 4

For the lemon dressing:
- 5 tablespoons fresh lemon juice
- 4 tablespoons olive oil
- 2 tablespoons agave syrup
- 1 tablespoon finely chopped or grated fresh ginger
- 2 cloves garlic, finely chopped
- 1 tablespoon ground cumin
- 1 teaspoon ground cinnamon
- ½ teaspoon salt
- ½ teaspoon freshly ground black/white pepper

For the cauliflower:
- 2 lb (1 kg) cauliflower florets
- 1 lb 2 oz (500 g) macaroni
- 1 cup (220 g) slivered dried apricots
- ½ cup (75 g) sliced green olives
- 1 cup (240 g) crumbled vegan feta cheese
- ¼ cup (30 g) chopped mint

Preheat the oven to 400°F/200°C/Gas Mark 6. Line a large baking sheet with parchment paper or aluminum foil.

To make the lemon dressing, combine the ingredients in a bowl and whisk until well combined.

To make the cauliflower, put it into a large bowl and add 3 tablespoons of the dressing; toss to combine. Reserve the remaining dressing.

Arrange the cauliflower in an even layer on the prepared baking sheet. Roast for 30 minutes or until golden brown, tossing halfway through.

Meanwhile, cook the pasta according to the instructions on the packet. Drain the pasta, reserving ½ cup (120 ml/4 fl oz) of the cooking water. Return the pasta to the pan, add the roasted cauliflower, apricots, olives, feta, mint, the reserved pasta water, and the remaining dressing. Toss to combine and serve.

MACARONI AND ROASTED CAULIFLOWER BOWL

PASTA DE PROVENCE

Preparation time: 20 minutes
Cooking time: 15 minutes

Serves 4

- 1 lb 2 oz (500 g) penne
- 2 tablespoons olive oil
- 2 cloves garlic, finely chopped
- 1 onion, chopped
- 1½ lb (750 g) zucchini (courgettes), sliced
- 1 green bell pepper, chopped
- 2 cups (240 g) button mushrooms, sliced
- 1½ cups (300 g) tomato purée (passata)
- 1 tablespoon chopped basil
- 1 tablespoon herbes de Provence
- 1 teaspoon dried oregano
- salt and freshly ground black/white pepper
- grated vegan parmesan cheese, to serve

Cook the penne according to the packet instructions until al dente. Rinse under cold running water to stop the cooking, drain completely, and set aside in a large bowl.

Heat the olive oil in a Dutch oven (casserole) or large saucepan over medium heat. Add the garlic, onion, zucchini, peppers, and mushrooms and stir fry over medium heat for 7–8 minutes, stirring frequently, until the onion and garlic turn golden brown. Add the tomato purée, basil, herbes de Provence, and oregano and cook for 3–4 minutes. Remove the Dutch oven from the stove, add the penne, and season to taste with salt and freshly ground black/white pepper. Toss gently to combine and serve with cheese on the side.

PASTA WITH CREAMED BROCCOLI

Preparation time: 15 minutes
Cooking time: 25 minutes

Serves 4

- 1 lb 2 oz (500 g) penne
- 2 cups (475 ml/16 fl oz) soy cream
- 1½ cups (120 g) nutritional yeast
- 1 tablespoon chopped fresh basil
- 1 teaspoon onion powder
- 1 tablespoon vegetable margarine
- 2 heads of broccoli, trimmed and cut into florets
- salt and freshly ground black/white pepper
- 1 cup (125 g) grated vegan cheddar cheese

Cook the penne according to the packet instructions until al dente. Rinse under cold running water to stop the cooking, drain completely, and set aside in a large bowl.

Put the soy cream, nutritional yeast, basil, onion powder, and vegetable margarine into a saucepan and heat over medium heat for 4–5 minutes, stirring frequently, until the mixture starts to simmer. Add the broccoli and cook for 5–6 minutes, until the broccoli is tender but al dente. Season to taste with salt and freshly ground black/white pepper. Stir in the pasta and cook for 2 more minutes, then serve immediately with the cheese on the side.

PENNE IN RED CURRY AND ALMOND SAUCE

Preheat the oven to 400°F/200°C/Gas Mark 6.

To make the sauce, arrange the pumpkin slices on a baking sheet, cover with aluminum foil, and bake for about 30 minutes, until tender. Let cool for 30 minutes.

To make the pasta, bring a large stockpot of salted water to a boil over high heat. Add the spaghetti and cook for 3 minutes less than the suggested cooking time. Add the baby broccoli to the spaghetti and cook for about 3 minutes, until the pasta and broccoli are both al dente.

Place the baby spinach, kale, or Swiss chard leaves in a colander and drain the spaghetti and broccoli over the leaves so the boiling spaghetti water rapidly blanches the greens. Transfer the pasta and vegetables to a large bowl and set aside.

Using a food processor or high-speed blender, purée the cooked pumpkin, then transfer to a bowl. Stir in the almond butter, vinegar, red curry paste, garlic, and agave syrup or maple syrup. Add enough hot water to dilute the mixture into a smooth sauce. Season with salt to taste and set aside.

Heat the oil in a large nonstick saucepan. Add the smoked tempeh and stir fry over medium heat for 6–7 minutes, until golden brown on all sides. Reduce the heat to low and stir in the sauce, then cook for 3–4 minutes, until it thickens. Add the spaghetti-broccoli-greens mixture and toss to combine. Transfer to a large serving bowl, garnish with the almonds, and serve immediately.

Preparation time: 20 minutes, plus
    30 minutes cooling
Cooking time: 45 minutes

Serves 4

For the sauce:
- 2 cups (240 g) pumpkin, peeled and sliced
- ⅓ cup (80 g) almond butter
- 4 tablespoons white wine vinegar
- 2 tablespoons red curry paste
- 4 cloves garlic, grated
- 1 tablespoon agave or maple syrup
- salt

For the pasta:
- salt
- 1 lb 2 oz (500 g) spaghetti
- 1 lb 2 oz (500 g) baby broccoli, trimmed and cut into florets
- 9 oz (250 g) baby spinach, kale, or Swiss chard
- 2 tablespoons olive oil
- 1½ cups (360 g) smoked tempeh, cut into medium dice
- ½ cup (55 g) toasted slivered almonds, to garnish

PENNE PRIMAVERA

Preparation time: 20 minutes
Cooking time: 40 minutes

Serves 4

- 3 tablespoons olive oil
- 1 onion, finely chopped
- 3 cloves garlic, chopped
- 1 teaspoon coriander seeds
- 2 cups (400 g) canned Puy lentils, drained
- ¾ cup (175 ml/6 fl oz) dry white wine, plus more as needed
- 1 teaspoon mixed dried Italian herbs
- 1 teaspoon mild curry powder
- 1 teaspoon grated nutmeg
- 1 cup (140 g) frozen green peas, defrosted
- salt and freshly ground black/white pepper
- 2 cups (475 ml/16 fl oz) soy cream
- finely grated zest of 1 lemon
- 1 lb 2 oz (500 g) penne
- 1 tablespoon chopped parsley, to garnish
- 1 teaspoon crushed pink peppercorns, to garnish

Heat the oil in a saucepan over medium heat. Add the onion and stir fry for 5–6 minutes, until golden brown. Add the garlic and coriander seeds and cook for 2 minutes, stirring constantly. Add the lentils and cook for 3–4 minutes. Add the wine, mixed herbs, curry powder, nutmeg, and peas. Reduce the heat to low, cover the pan, and cook for about 10 minutes. Season to taste with salt and freshly ground black/white pepper.

Add the cream to the saucepan 3–4 tablespoons at a time, stirring well between each addition. Leave the pan set on low heat and cook for another 3–4 minutes. If the sauce becomes too thick, add a little wine to loosen it. Stir in half of the zest.

Meanwhile, cook the penne according to the packet instructions until al dente. Rinse under cold running water to stop the cooking, drain completely, and set aside in a large bowl.

When the sauce is ready, mix in the pasta. Transfer to a large serving bowl, garnish with the parsley, the remaining zest, and the pink peppercorns, and serve.

PENNE PRIMAVERA

SWEET POTATO GNOCCHI

Preparation time: 30 minutes
Cooking time: 35 minutes

Serves 4

For the gnocchi:
- salt
- 4 sweet potatoes, peeled and chopped
- 2 tablespoons vegetable margarine
- 2 tablespoons egg replacer, diluted in 4 tablespoons warm water
- a pinch of ground nutmeg
- 1 tablespoon nutritional yeast
- 3 cups (375 g) all-purpose (plain) flour, plus extra for dusting

For the peanut and cinnamon sauce:
- 2 tablespoons vegetable margarine
- 1 onion, sliced
- ½ cup (120 ml/4 fl oz) soy cream
- 2 tablespoons smooth peanut butter
- a pinch of ground cinnamon
- salt and freshly ground black/white pepper

To make the gnocchi, bring a saucepan of salted water to a boil. Add the sweet potato and simmer for 15 minutes, until the potatoes are tender enough to mash. Rinse under cold running water and drain well, then transfer to a bowl. Add the vegetable margarine, egg replacer, nutmeg, and nutritional yeast and mash with a fork, mixing well. Slowly add the flour, 1–2 tablespoons at a time, and mix until it is well blended with the potatoes. Set aside to cool.

Dust your hands and a work surface with flour. Divide the potato mixture into 4 equal portions and roll each into a long rope that is about 1 inch (2.5 cm) thick. Slice each rope into ½-inch (1 cm) pieces.

Bring a large saucepan of water to a gentle simmer. Cook the gnocchi in batches in the boiling water until they come up and float on the surface. Remove them carefully with a slotted spoon. Set aside on a serving plate.

To make the peanut and cinnamon sauce, melt the margarine in a saucepan over medium heat. Add the onion and stir-fry gently for 5–6 minutes, until golden brown. Add the soy cream and peanut butter and bring to a simmer, then add the cinnamon and season to taste with salt and freshly ground black pepper. Pour the sauce over the gnocchi and serve immediately.

SUN-DRIED TOMATO-GARLIC-CHILI PASTA

Preparation time: 15 minutes
Cooking time: 30 minutes

Serves 4

- 1 tablespoon vegetable margarine
- 2 tablespoons olive oil
- 3 cloves garlic, finely chopped
- 2 shallots, finely chopped
- ½ cup (90 g) sun-dried tomatoes, rehydrated in water and finely chopped
- 2 small red chilies, seeded and finely chopped
- salt
- 1 lb 2 oz (500 g) lasagna sheets, broken into bite-size pieces
- 2 tablespoons pine nuts
- 3 tablespoons grated vegan parmesan cheese, to serve
- 2 tablespoons finely chopped parsley, to garnish

Melt the vegetable margarine in the olive oil in a large skillet (frying pan). Add the garlic and shallots and stir fry gently over medium heat for 5–6 minutes, until golden brown. Add the sun-dried tomatoes and chilies and season to taste with salt. Cook over very low heat for 15 minutes. Remove the skillet from the stove and set aside.

Bring a large stockpot of salted water to a boil over high heat. Cook the broken lasagna sheets according to packet instructions until al dente. Drain and mix with the sun-dried tomato mixture. Add the pine nuts and stir well. Transfer to a serving plate, top with the cheese and garnish with the chopped parsley.

PENNE IN SAFFRON CREAM

Bring the soy cream to a simmer in a small saucepan over medium heat. Remove the pan from the heat, add the saffron, and set aside.

Bring a large stockpot of salted water to a boil over high heat. Cook the penne according to the packet instructions until al dente. Rinse under cold running water to stop the cooking, drain completely, and set aside in a large bowl.

Heat 1 tablespoon of the oil in a large skillet (frying pan) over medium-high heat. Add the leeks, season to taste with salt and freshly ground black pepper, and cook, stirring occasionally, for 6–7 minutes, until golden brown. Add the remaining oil, stir in the mushrooms, and cook for 6-7 minutes, until the mushrooms are golden brown. Add the asparagus and snap peas, season to taste with salt and freshly ground black/white pepper, and cook, stirring occasionally, for about 4 minutes, until tender. Stir the saffron-infused cream, then add it to the skillet and cook for 2–3 minutes, until the asparagus is knife-tender.

Add the penne to the saucepan and toss with tongs to coat the pasta in the sauce. Add 1 tablespoon tarragon, stir well, then transfer the mixture to a serving plate and garnish with the remaining tarragon. Serve immediately.

Preparation time: 20 minutes
Cooking time: 20 minutes

Serves 4

- 1 cup (240 ml/8 fl oz) soy cream
- 1 teaspoon saffron threads
- 1 lb 2 oz (500 g) penne
- 2 tablespoons olive oil
- 3 leeks, white and light green parts only, halved lengthwise and thinly sliced
- salt and freshly ground black/white pepper
- 1 cup (240 g) mixed mushrooms, such as shiitake, button, and oyster, trimmed and sliced
- 1 lb 2 oz (500 g) thin asparagus, trimmed and cut into ½-inch (1 cm) pieces
- 9 oz (250 g) sugar snap peas, cut into ½-inch (1 cm) pieces
- 2 tablespoons chopped tarragon

PENNE WITH BRUSSELS
SPROUTS AND LEEKS

Preparation time: 15 minutes
Cooking time: 20 minutes

Serves 4

- 1 lemon, plus 4 lemon wedges, to serve
- 1 lb 2 oz (500 g) Brussels sprouts
- 1 large leek, white and pale green
  parts only
- 4 tablespoons olive oil, plus 4 teaspoons,
  to serve
- salt and freshly ground black/white pepper
- 4 cloves garlic, finely chopped
- ½ cup (120 ml/4 fl oz) dry white wine
- 1 lb 2 oz (500 g) rigatoni
- ½ cup (50 g) grated vegan parmesan
  cheese, plus extra to serve
- 2 tablespoons nutritional yeast

Remove the peel from the lemon using a vegetable peeler and reserve the lemon for another use. Cut the peel into very thin strips. Set aside in a bowl.

Trim the Brussels sprouts with a paring knife, then snap off and discard several dark outer leaves from each sprout. Halve the sprouts and set aside. Cut half the leek into ½-inch (1 cm) rings. Slice finely the remaining leek.

Heat 2 tablespoons of the olive oil in a large skillet (frying pan) over medium heat. Add the Brussels sprouts and leek rings. Season to taste with salt and freshly ground black/white pepper and cook for 6–7 minutes, until golden brown. Transfer to a large bowl. Add half of the lemon peel strips, stir well, and set aside.

Pour the remaining oil into the same skillet set over medium heat. When the oil is hot, add the sliced leek and garlic, season to taste with salt and freshly ground black/white pepper, and cook, stirring frequently, for 7–8 minutes, until golden. Add the white wine, bring to a boil, reduce the heat to medium, and simmer for 3–4 minutes, until the skillet is almost dry. Remove the skillet from the stove and set aside.

Bring a large stockpot of salted water to a boil over high heat. Cook the rigatoni according to the packet instructions until al dente. Drain the pasta, reserving 1 cup (240 ml/8 fl oz) of the pasta water in a bowl. Add the rigatoni to the skillet with the chopped leek, then add the Brussels sprouts–leek ring mixture and the reserved pasta cooking water and toss to combine. Bring the mixture to a simmer over medium heat, then reduce the heat to low, add the cheese and nutritional yeast, and season to taste with salt and freshly ground black/white pepper.

Divide the pasta among 4 bowls and garnish with the remaining lemon peel strips into. Top with vegan cheese, then drizzle 1 teaspoon olive oil into each bowl. Serve with lemon wedges.

PINE NUT PASTA

Mix the zucchini, snow peas, bell peppers, broccoli, and mushrooms in a large bowl. Set aside.

Bring a large stockpot of salted water to a boil over high heat. Cook the pasta according to the packet instructions until al dente. Rinse under cold running water to stop the cooking, drain completely, and set aside in a large bowl.

Heat the oil in a large saucepan. Add the pine nuts and stir-fry gently over medium-low heat for 2–3 minutes until golden brown. Add the vegetables and cook over medium heat for 4–5 minutes, until fork-tender. Add the tomatoes and cook for 3–4 minutes.

Transfer the pasta to a large serving bowl and top with the vegetables. Top with vegan cheese and basil leaves and serve.

Preparation time: 15 minutes
Cooking time: 20 minutes

Serves 4

- 2 zucchini (courgettes), finely sliced
- 1 yellow zucchini, finely sliced
- 1 cup (140 g) snow peas
- 1 green bell pepper, chopped
- 1 yellow bell pepper, chopped
- 1 cup (100 g) broccoli florets
- 1 cup (120 g) button mushrooms, sliced
- salt
- 1 lb 2 oz (500 g) spaghetti or penne
- 5 tablespoons olive oil
- ½ cup (70 g) pine nuts
- 2 tomatoes, finely diced
- grated vegan parmesan cheese, to serve
- basil leaves, to garnish

SPAGHETTI WITH WALNUTS AND TOMATOES

Heat 2 tablespoons of the olive oil in a saucepan. Add the walnuts and stir fry over medium heat for 3–4 minutes, until golden brown. Set aside.

Cook the spagetti according to the packet instructions until al dente. Drain the pasta, reserving 1 cup (240 ml/8 fl oz) of the cooking water. Set aside.

Heat the remaining oil in a large heavy-bottomed skillet (frying pan). Add the shallots and garlic and stir-fry over medium heat for 3–4 minutes, until golden brown. Add the tomatoes, bring to a simmer, and cook over medium heat for 5 minutes. Add ½ cup (120 ml/4 fl oz) of the pasta cooking water and the pomegranate molasses, stir to incorporate, bring the sauce to a low simmer, and cook for about 10 minutes, until it thickens and reduces by a third. Add the vegetable margarine and sugar and stir well to blend. Cook for 4 minutes over low heat, until the shallots and tomatoes are fork-tender.

Remove the skillet from the stove, add the spaghetti, and stir well to coat with the sauce. Season to taste with salt and freshly ground black/white pepper. Transfer the mixture to a serving plate and garnish with the walnuts and basil. Serve with grated vegan cheese on the side.

Preparation time: 15 minutes
Cooking time: 25 minutes

Serves 4

- 4 tablespoons olive oil
- 9 oz (250 g) walnuts
- 1 lb 2 oz (500 g) spaghetti
- 4 shallots, finely chopped
- 6 cloves garlic, finely chopped
- 2¼ lb (1 kg) plum tomatoes, chopped
- 2 tablespoons pomegranate molasses
- 2 tablespoons vegetable margarine
- 1 teaspoon superfine (caster) sugar
- ¼ cup (30 g) basil leaves, thinly sliced, to garnish
- grated vegan parmesan cheese, to serve

TOFU STEAKS WITH
SOBA NOODLES

Preparation time: 15 minutes,
plus 2 hours for draining the tofu
Cooking time: 15 minutes

Serves 4

- 1 lb 2 oz (500 g) extra-firm tofu
- 4 tablespoons mirin or sweet rice wine
- 2 tablespoons sake
- 1 tablespoon grated fresh ginger
- 2 tablespoons rice vinegar
- 2 tablespoons agave syrup
- 1 tablespoon toasted sesame oil
- 1 teaspoon sweet paprika
- 1 clove garlic, finely chopped
- 2 tablespoons olive oil
- 1 cup (240 ml/8 fl oz) vegetable stock (broth)
- 4 heads of baby bok choy, halved lengthwise
- 2 cups (450 g) cooked soba noodles
- 1 cup (100 g) sliced scallions (spring onions), to garnish
- 2 tablespoons toasted sesame seeds, to garnish

Place the tofu block into a clean sink, then place a weight, such as a cast-iron saucepan, over it and leave for 1–2 hours to squeeze out the water and compress the tofu. Cut the tofu block in 4 steaks. Set aside.

Put the mirin or rice wine, sake, ginger, rice vinegar, agave syrup, sesame oil, sweet paprika, and garlic into a bowl and whisk to combine.

Heat the olive oil in a saucepan. Add the tofu steaks, then pour the marinade over the tofu and cook over medium-low heat for 4 minutes on each side, until the steaks start to turn golden. Remove the pan from the heat, cover with a lid, and set aside.

Bring the stock to a boil in a large skillet (frying pan). Add the bok choy, cover the skillet with a lid, and cook over medium heat for 2 minutes, until bok choy is wilted. Remove the bok choy from the stock and set aside. Add the tofu steaks to the skillet, bring the broth to a simmer, and cook for 3–4 minutes.

Divide the soba noodles equally among 4 bowls. Top each with a tofu steak and garnish with the scallions and sesame seeds. Finish with 2 bok choy halves in each bowl.

CARUSO PENNE

Cook the penne according to the packet instructions until al dente. Drain the penne and set aside.

Heat the olive oil in a skillet (frying pan). Add the onion and sauté over medium heat for about 5 minutes, until soft and fragrant. Add the mushrooms and sauté for 6–7 minutes, until tender. Set aside.

Heat the vegetable margarine in a large saucepan over medium heat. Whisk in the flour and cook, stirring constantly, for 3–4 minutes, until the color changes to golden. Then slowly pour in the soy cream, stirring constantly. Stir in the stock and cook over medium heat for about 12 minutes, until the sauce thickens. Season to taste with salt and freshly ground black pepper.

Remove the pan from the stove and add the shredded vegan mozzarella and grated vegan parmesan cheese. Add the penne and mushrooms to the sauce, then return the pan to the stove and cook over medium heat for 2 minutes, until hot. Serve immediately in a large serving bowl, garnished with parsley and red chilies.

Preparation time: 20 minutes
Cooking time: 30 minutes

Serves 4

- 1 lb 2 oz (500 g) penne
- 2 tablespoons olive oil
- 1 onion, chopped
- 2 cups (200 g) button mushroom, sliced
- 2 tablespoons vegetable margarine
- 2 tablespoons all-purpose (plain) flour
- 2 cups (475 ml/16 fl oz) vegan soy cream
- 1 cup (240 ml/8 fl oz) vegetable stock (broth)
- salt and freshly ground black/white pepper
- 1 cup (125 g) shredded vegan mozzarella cheese
- ½ cup (65 g) grated vegan Parmesan cheese
- 1 bunch parsley, chopped
- 2 red chilies, seeded and finely chopped

VEGETABLE NOODLE STEW

Peel and dice the carrots and sweet potatoes. Trim and cut the cauliflower into florets. Set the vegetables aside in a bowl.

Cook the noodles 2 minutes shy of the packet instructions. Drain and transfer to a large bowl. Toss with the vegetable oil and set aside.

Heat the mustard oil in a large saucepan. Add the onions and stir-fry over medium heat for 5–6 minutes, until light brown. Add the turmeric, garlic, ginger, cumin, and chilies and stir fry for 2 minutes over medium heat. Add the mixed vegetables and stir fry over medium heat for 5 minutes.

Add the tomatoes, tamari or soy sauce, stock, bay leaves, and lovage seeds to the saucepan. Bring to a simmer, cover with a lid, and cook for 6–7 minutes. Add the vegan yogurt, baby spinach, and rice noodles, reduce the heat to very low, and cook for 2–3 minutes, until well blended.

Season to taste with salt and freshly ground black/white pepper. Transfer to a serving bowl, garnish with the chopped cilantro, and serve with roti or naan.

Preparation time: 20 minutes
Cooking time: 35 minutes

Serves 4

- 3 cups (720 g) mixed vegetables, such as carrots, sweet potatoes, and cauliflower
- 1 lb 2 oz (500 g) rice noodles
- 1 tablespoon vegetable oil
- 2 tablespoons mustard oil
- 2 cups (280 g) chopped yellow onion
- 1 tablespoon fresh turmeric, peeled and finely chopped
- 3 cloves garlic, finely chopped
- 1 tablespoon finely chopped fresh ginger
- 1 teaspoon ground cumin
- 3 red chilies, seeded and finely chopped
- 1 cup (200 g) chopped tomatoes
- 2 tablespoons tamari or soy sauce
- 2 cups (475 ml/16 fl oz) vegetable stock (broth)
- 2 bay leaves
- 1 teaspoon lovage seeds
- ½ cup (120 g) unsweetened vegan yogurt
- 9 oz (250 g) baby spinach
- salt and freshly ground black/white pepper
- 1 tablespoon chopped cilantro (coriander), to garnish
- roti or naan, to serve

DESSERTS

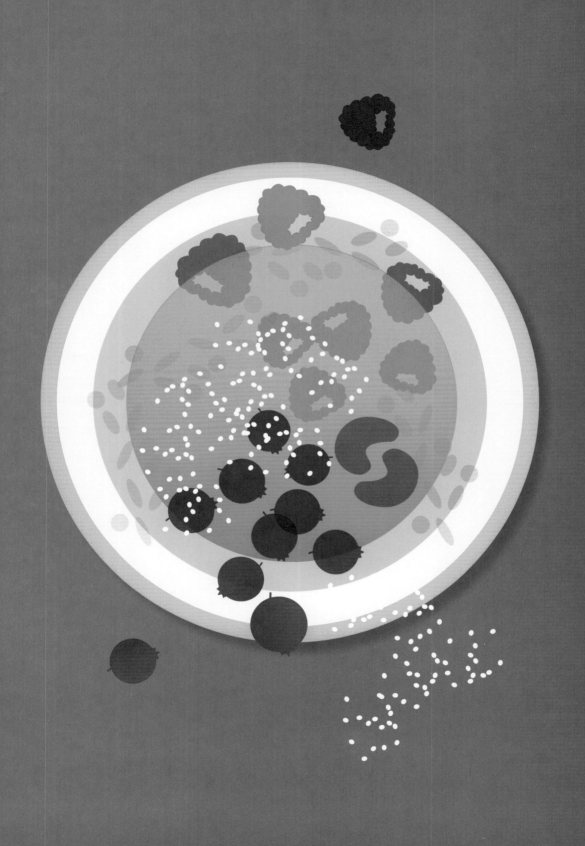

ALMOND AND CINNAMON CAKE

Preparation time: 30 minutes, plus overnight
  chilling and 20 minutes soaking
Cooking time: 30 minutes

Makes 1 (10-inch/25 cm) cake

For the dough:
- ¾ cup (175 ml/6 fl oz) coconut oil
- 3 cups (375 g) all-purpose (plain) flour,
  plus extra for dusting
- 2 teaspoons ground cinnamon
- 1 teaspoon ground nutmeg
- 1 teaspoon ground cloves
- 1 teaspoon ground ginger
- 1 teaspoon ground white pepper
- 1 teaspoon ground cardamom
- ½ teaspoon salt
- ½ teaspoon baking powder
- 1 teaspoon vanilla powder
- 1 cup (225 g) light brown sugar
- ¾ cup (175 ml/6 fl oz) almond milk
- vegetable margarine, to grease

For the filling:
- 1 cup (240 g) blanched almonds
- ½ cup (120 g) confectioners' (icing) sugar
- a pinch of ground cinnamon

To make the dough, refrigerate the coconut oil until cold, about
45 minutes.

Combine the flour, cinnamon, nutmeg, cloves, ginger, white pepper,
cardamom, salt, baking powder, and vanilla powder in a bowl and whisk
until combined. Set aside.

Using a food processor fitted with a blade, process the sugar and cold
coconut oil for about 3 minutes, until smooth and creamed together.
With the food processor set on low speed, pour half of the flour mixture
into the coconut oil mixture, then pour in half of the almond milk.
Repeat the process until all the flour and almond milk are incorporated
and the mixture forms a dough. Wrap the dough in plastic wrap
(clingfilm) and refrigerate overnight.

Preheat the oven to 375°F/190°C/Gas Mark 5.

To make the filling, put the blanched almonds into a bowl, and cover
with hot water and let soak for 20 minutes. Drain the almonds, transfer
to a food processor or high-speed blender, and pulse a few times until
coarsely chopped. Put the chopped almonds into a bowl and stir in the
sugar, cinnamon, and 4–5 tablespoons water.

Dust the work surface with flour. Cut the chilled dough in half and place
it on the floured work surface. Grease a 10-inch (25 cm) tart pan with
the vegetable margarine, dust the rolling pin with flour, and roll out half
the dough to a 12-inch (30 cm) circle. Line the tart pan with the rolled-
out dough. Press the dough into the bottom and sides of the pan, then
cut away any excess overhanging the sides of the pan by passing the
rolling pin over the rim. Spread the almond filling across the dough (the
dough won't fill the pan completely, but it will rise slightly to encase it).
Roll out the remaining dough and position it over the filling. Press the
dough down to seal so the filling will not escape from the edges, then
cut a few small slits in the top to let steam escape. Trim the excess
dough by passing a rolling pin over it. Bake for 30 minutes, until golden
brown. Let cool for 20 minutes, then transfer from the pan to a serving
plate. Cut into pieces and serve.

CHOCOLATE AND PRUNE CAKE

Preheat the oven to 350°F/180°C/Gas Mark 4. Grease a 9-inch (23 cm) square cake pan with vegetable margarine.

Using a food processor or high-speed blender, pulse the prunes a few times, then, with the motor still running, add ½ cup (120 ml/4 fl oz) water and process for 3–4 minutes until the mixture is smooth. Leave the mixture in the food processor or blender.

Combine the egg replacer with 2 tablespoons warm water in a bowl, then add the mixture to the food processor or blender and process until creamy. Add the sugar and blend until smooth.

Whisk together the flour, cocoa, baking soda, baking powder, and salt in a bowl. Stir in the almond milk and vinegar, then set aside for 10 minutes. Combine the prune mixture with the cocoa-flour mixture, whisking constantly until the batter is smooth and fluffy.

Spoon the batter into the prepared cake pan and bake for 35–40 minutes, until well baked. Let cool for 30 minutes, then remove from the pan.

Preparation time: 20 minutes
Cooking time: 1 hour 40 minutes, plus
   30 minutes cooling

Makes 1 (9-inch/23 cm) cake

- vegetable margarine, for greasing
- 1 cup (240 g) pitted (stoned) prunes (pruneaux d'Agen)
- 2 tablespoons egg replacer
- 2 cups (400 g) superfine (caster) sugar
- 2 cups (250 g) all-purpose (plain) flour
- 1 cup (100 g) unsweetened cocoa powder
- 2 teaspoons baking soda (bicarbonate of soda)
- 1 teaspoon baking powder
- a pinch of salt
- 1 cup (240 ml/8 fl oz) almond milk
- 2 teaspoons white vinegar

LEMON CHEESECAKE
WITH APRICOT CREAM

Preheat the oven to 350°F/180°C/Gas Mark 4. Grease an 8- or 9-inch (20 or 23 cm) round cake pan with vegetable margarine.

To make the cheesecake, whip the cream cheese with the almond milk in a bowl. Mix in half of the sugar, the egg replacer, cornstarch, and lemon juice.

Using a food processor or high-speed blender, process the mixture on a high speed for 3–4 minutes while gradually adding the remaining sugar.

Spoon the mixture into the prepared cake pan and put the pan into a large, deep ovenproof dish. Fill the dish with boiling water so that the water reaches halfway up the sides of the cake pan. Bake for 40 minutes. Remove from the water bath and let cool for 20 minutes.

To make the apricot cream, stir together the whipped soy cream and apricot jam in a bowl, or pureé until combined. Set aside.

Slice the cooled cake, serve on individual serving plates, and top with the apricot cream.

Preparation time: 25 minutes
Cooking time: 40 minutes, plus 20 minutes
   cooling

Makes 1 (8 or 9-inch/20 or 23 cm) cake

For the cheesecake:
- vegetable margarine, for greasing
- 1 cup (240 g) Vegan Cream Cheese (page 30), at room temperature
- 4 tablespoons almond milk
- ½ cup (100 g) superfine (caster) sugar
- 3 tablespoons egg replacer, mixed with 6 tablespoons warm water
- ¼ cup (60 g) cornstarch (corn flour)
- 2 tablespoons fresh lemon juice

For the apricot cream:
- 4 tablespoons whipped soy cream
- 2 tablespoons apricot jam or apricot purée

LEMON MOUSSE

Preparation time: 15 minutes

Cooking time: 15 minutes, plus 2 hours
   30 minutes chilling

Serves 4

- 2 cups (480 ml/16 fl oz) water
- 2 cups (480 ml/16 fl oz) coconut cream
- 3 tablespoons agar-agar
- 2 tablespoons maple syrup
- 4 tablespoons fresh lemon juice
- 3 tablespoons apple sauce, plus extra
  as needed
- 2 tablespoons finely grated lemon zest
- 1 teaspoon vanilla extract
- 2 tablespoons tahini
- a pinch of salt

Bring the water to a boil in a saucepan. Add all the ingredients and reduce the heat to low, then whisk and simmer for 12 minutes, until well blended. Remove the pan from the heat and let cool for 2 hours.

Using a food processor or high-speed blender, process the mixture to the consistency of a smooth and creamy custard. If the mixture is too thick, add more apple sauce. Refrigerate for 30 minutes before serving.

LEMON MOUSSE

APPLE STRUDEL

Preparation time: 30 minutes

Cooking time: 35 minutes

Serves 8

- 1 lb 2 oz (500 g) Honey Crisp or Pink Lady apples, cored and sliced
- 1 tablespoon balsamic vinegar
- 1 vanilla bean, seeds scraped
- ½ cup (120 ml/4 fl oz) brown rice syrup
- 2 tablespoons, plus ¼ cup (50 g) superfine (caster) sugar
- 1 teaspoon grated fresh ginger
- ½ cup (120 g) silken tofu
- 2 cups (200 g) pecans, crushed, plus ½ cup (50 g) pecans, finely ground
- 6 sheets phyllo (filo) pastry
- 4 tablespoons vegetable oil
- ½ cup (80 g) raisins
- vanilla custard or vegan vanilla ice cream, to serve

Preheat the oven to 350°F/180°C/Gas Mark 4.

Put the apple slices, vinegar, vanilla, half of the brown rice syrup, 2 tablespoons of the superfine sugar, ginger, 1 cup (240 ml/8 fl oz) water, and the silken tofu into a skillet (frying pan). Mix well and bring to a low simmer over medium heat. Simmer gently for 10 minutes. Remove the skillet from the stove and let cool.

Mix the pecans, the remaining brown rice syrup, and 2 tablespoons water in a saucepan. Set the pan over medium heat and heat the mixture for 10 minutes, until the pecans darken. Remove the pan from the stove and let cool.

Dust your work surface with flour and lay out 1 sheet of phyllo on the floured surface, the longer edges parallel to the edge of the work surface, and brush with a little vegetable oil. Sprinkle with roughly one-fifth each of the ground pecans and remaining ¼ cup superfine sugar. Top with a second sheet of pastry, and continue the steps until all of the 6 sheets are used.

Mix the raisins into the apple mixture, then spread it across the top of the phyllo stack, leaving roughly a 1-inch (2.5 cm) border around the edges. Starting at the edge closest to you, roll up the phyllo stack into a tube. Carefully transfer the roll to a baking sheet, top with the crushed pecan-syrup mixture, and bake for 15 minutes, until golden brown. Let cool for 15 minutes, then remove from the pan. Serve lukewarm, with vanilla custard or vegan vanilla ice cream.

BANANA AND PEANUT CREAM CAKE

Preheat the oven to 325°F/160°C/Gas Mark 3. Grease a 10-inch (25 cm) round cake pan with vegetable oil. Using a food processor or high-speed blender, process the bananas with the lemon juice, cinnamon, vanilla seeds, and peanut butter until combined. Set aside.

In a bowl, mix together the silken tofu, sugar, baking powder, and flour until combined. Add it to the banana mixture and pulse until the mixture is smooth and lump-free. Add the rum and pulse again a couple of times. Pour the cake batter into the prepared pan and bake for 1 hour, until lightly golden. Let cool completely, then remove from the pan and transfer to a large serving platter. Cut into wedges and serve.

Preparation time: 30 minutes
Cooking time: 1 hour

Makes 1 (10-inch/25 cm) cake

- vegetable oil, for greasing
- 2 ripe bananas
- 1 tablespoon fresh lemon juice
- 1 teaspoon ground cinnamon
- 1 vanilla bean, seeds scraped
- ¼ cup (65 g) crunchy peanut butter
- ½ cup (120 g) silken tofu
- ¼ cup (50 g) superfine (caster) sugar
- 1 teaspoon baking powder
- 1 cup (125 g) all-purpose (plain) flour
- 2 tablespoons dark rum

CHOCOLATE NUT CAKE

Preheat the oven to 350°F/180°C/Gas Mark 4. Grease a 7-inch (18 cm) square cake pan.

To make the cake batter, melt the vegetable margarine in a heatproof bowl set over a saucepan of simmering water until liquid.

Using a food processor or high-speed blender, grind the walnuts and almonds into a thick powder. Transfer the powder to a bowl and mix in the flour, sugar, cocoa powder, cinnamon, cloves, salt, and baking powder. Add the melted vegetable margarine and vanilla extract, mix well, then slowly stir in 1 cup (240 ml/8 fl oz) cold water. Mix until a smooth batter forms. Add the vinegar, stir well to combine, then pour the batter into the prepared cake pan. Bake for 1 hour, or until a skewer inserted into the center of the cake comes out clean. Let cool for 30 minutes, then remove from the pan before frosting.

To make the icing, combine the sugar, cocoa powder, cornstarch, vegetable margarine, and 4 tablespoons water in a saucepan. Bring to a low simmer and cook over medium-low heat for 2 minutes. Let cool.

When the cake and icing are cool, use an offset spatula (palette knife) to cover the top surface of the cake with the icing. Serve at room temperature.

Preparation time: 30 minutes
Cooking time: 1 hour, plus 30 minutes cooling

Makes 1 (7-inch/18 cm) square cake

For the cake:
- ⅓ cup (80 g) vegetable margarine, plus extra for greasing
- 1 lb (500 g) walnuts
- 1 cup (135 g) almonds
- 1¼ cups (155 g) whole-wheat (wholemeal) flour
- ⅔ cup (135 g) superfine (caster) sugar
- ¾ cup (75 g) unsweetened cocoa powder
- 1 teaspoon ground cinnamon
- 1 teaspoon ground cloves
- a pinch of salt
- 1 teaspoon baking powder
- 1 tablespoon vanilla extract
- 1 tablespoon white wine vinegar

For the icing:
- ⅓ cup (65 g) superfine (caster) sugar
- ¼ cup (25 g) unsweetened cocoa powder
- 2 tablespoons cornstarch (cornflour)
- 1 tablespoon vegetable margarine

CHOCOBANANAS

Preparation time: 20 minutes
Cooking time: 10 minutes, plus
  2 hours freezing

Serves 4

- 6 ripe bananas
- 12½ oz (360 g) dark chocolate chips
- 2 tablespoons crushed mixed nuts
  (peanuts, pistachio nuts, and almonds)
- 2 tablespoons grated coconut

Line an airtight container with parchment baking paper.

Peel the bananas and halve them crosswise. Insert a popsicle stick or a large skewer into the flat end of each banana half, pushing it into the banana about halfway through. Place the bananas in the prepared container and freeze for 2 hours.

Melt the chocolate in a heatproof bowl set over a pan of simmering water, then remove the bowl from the heat.

Place a plastic lidded container in the freezer, but without the lid.

Place the crushed nuts on a plate and the grated coconut on another plate. Dip 1 frozen banana into the melted chocolate and, using a spoon, cover any gaps that remain uncoated. Using a spoon, immediately coat the chocobanana with the crushed nuts and set aside in the freezer. Dip again into the chocolate, this time coating the chocolate-coated banana with grated coconut. Repeat the process, alternating between the 2 coatings, until all the bananas are coated. Act swiftly, as the melted chocolate becomes hard quickly. When done, place lid on the container of the chocobananas and freeze until ready to serve.

CHOCOBANANAS

BANANA CREAM IN ORANGE SAUCE

Preparation time: 20 minutes
Cooking time: 5 minutes

Serves 4

- ¼ cup (60 g) vegetable margarine
- 3 tablespoons grated coconut meat
- ¼ cup (50 g) superfine (caster) sugar
- 1 tablespoon finely grated fresh ginger
- 4 tablespoons fresh lime juice
- 1 tablespoon finely grated orange zest
- 4 bananas
- 4 tablespoons orange liqueur, such as Cointreau or triple sec
- 2 tablespoons black sesame seeds, to decorate
- 1 orange, sliced, to decorate

Melt 1 tablespoon of the vegetable margarine in a small nonstick skillet (frying pan) over medium heat. Add the grated coconut meat and cook, stirring constantly, for about 1 minute, until lightly colored. Transfer to a bowl and let cool.

Heat the remaining vegetable margarine in a large skillet over medium heat. Add the sugar, ginger, lime juice, and orange zest and mix well. Peel the bananas and slice lengthwise. Place them, with the cut sides facing down, in the skillet and cook over medium heat for 3–4 minutes, until the sauce mixture starts to become sticky. Flip over the bananas to coat them in the sauce. Transfer the bananas to dessert plates. Top with the coconut meat.

Return the large skillet to the heat and add the orange liqueur. Ignite the alcohol, allow the flames to die down, then pour the liquid over the bananas. Sprinkle over the black sesame seeds and serve decorated with orange slices.

GOJI CREAM

Preparation time: 20 minutes
Cooking time: none, plus 1 hour chilling

Serves 4

- ½ cup (120 g) dried goji berries
- 1 cup (240 ml/8 fl oz) mixed juice of pineapple, mango, and coconut
- ½ lb (250 g) honeydew melon
- ½ lb (250 g) cantaloupe melon
- 2 tablespoons chopped mint leaves
- ½ cup (120 g) chopped frozen pineapple, thawed

Soak the goji berries in the fruit juice for 1 hour.

Using a food processor or high-speed blender, process all the ingredients into a smooth and creamy mixture. Refrigerate for 1 hour before serving.

Serve in individual bowls, garnished with the chopped mint and pineapple.

BREAD PUDDING

Preheat the oven to 350°F/180°C/Gas Mark 4.

Place the sugar in a skillet (frying pan) over medium heat. As soon as the sugar starts to melt, reduce the heat to low and stir constantly with a wooden spoon until the sugar is liquid and golden brown. Add the almond milk and stir until the sugar is completely dissolved in the milk. Add the maple syrup, reduce the heat to low, and simmer for 3 minutes. Add the vegetable margarine and cook for another 2 minutes, stirring constantly, until all well blended.

Put the bread pieces into an ovenproof dish. Sprinkle over the raisins. Cover with the hot almond milk–maple syrup mixture, then sprinkle over the cheese. Cover the dish with aluminum foil and bake for 25 minutes. Let cool for 20 minutes before serving.

Preparation time: 15 minutes
Cooking time: 30 minutes, plus
  20 minutes cooling

Serves 4

- ¾ cup (150 g) superfine (caster) sugar
- 2 cups (480 ml/16 fl oz) almond milk
- ½ cup (120 ml/4 fl oz) maple syrup
- 2 tablespoons vegetable margarine, melted
- 6 slices of white bread, toasted and cut into
  1-inch (2.5 cm) pieces
- 1 cup (160 g) raisins
- 1 cup (240 g) grated vegan cheddar cheese

COCONUT AND
ORANGE CUSTARD

Preheat the oven to 250°F/130°C/Gas Mark ½.

Put the coconut cream into a saucepan along with the sugar, orange blossom water, and salt and stir constantly over low heat until the sugar has dissolved. Add the egg replacer and mix well.

Divide the custard across 4 (4 oz/120 ml) ramekins. Bake for about 20 minutes until the custard is just set. Remove from the oven and let cool for 20 minutes before serving.

Preparation time: 10 minutes
Cooking time: 20 minutes, plus
  20 minutes cooling

Serves 4

- 1 cup (240 ml/8 fl oz) coconut cream
- 1 cup (200 g) superfine (caster) sugar
- 1 teaspoon orange blossom water
- a pinch of salt
- 3 tablespoons egg replacer, mixed with
  6 tablespoons warm water

POMEGRANATE
AND SEMOLINA CAKES

Preparation time: 20 minutes
Cooking time: 20 minutes, plus
  35 minutes cooling

Serves 4

- 1 cup (240 ml/8 fl oz) pomegranate juice
- 1 cup (200 g) superfine (caster) sugar
- 2 cups (280 g) semolina flour
- 2 tablespoons rosewater
- 1 cup (135 g) ground almonds
- 2 tablespoons confectioners' (icing) sugar

Combine the pomegranate juice and sugar in a saucepan set over medium-low heat. Stir until the sugar has dissolved, then bring to a boil. Immediately remove the pan from the heat and let cool for 15 minutes.

Return the pan to the stove and bring the mixture to a low simmer. Stir in the semolina, then the rosewater, and simmer gently over medium-low heat for 10 minutes. Add the ground almonds, mix well, and let cool for 20 minutes.

When cool enough to handle with your hands, roll the mixture into small, walnut-size balls and set aside.

Put the confectioners' sugar into a bowl. Roll the semolina balls in the sugar to coat completely before serving.

POMEGRANATE AND SEMOLINA CAKES

CHOCOLATE MUFFINS

Preparation time: 20 minutes
Cooking time: 25 minutes, plus 20 minutes
  cooling

Makes 24 muffins

- 2¼ cups (300 g) all-purpose (plain) flour
- 1 cup (100 g) unsweetened cocoa powder
- 2 teaspoons baking soda (bicarbonate
  of soda)
- 1½ cups (300 g) superfine (caster) sugar
- 2 cups (200 g) grated coconut
- ¾ cup (175 ml/6 fl oz) vegetable oil
- ½ cup (120 ml/4 fl oz) cold coffee
- 3 tablespoons white vinegar

Preheat the oven to 400°F/200°C/Gas Mark 6. Line 2 (12-cup) muffin pans with paper cupcake liners.

Sift the flour, cocoa powder, baking soda, and sugar in a large bowl, then stir in the grated coconut.

Put the remaining ingredients in another bowl, whisk to combine, and add this mixture slowly to the dry ingredients, stirring constantly to create a smooth, lump-free batter. Divide the batter equally among the muffin cups and bake for 25 minutes. Let cool on a metal rack for 20 minutes before serving.

BEET AND CHOCOLATE CAKE

Preparation time: 35 minutes
Cooking time: 1 hour 30 minutes

Makes 1 (9-inch/23 cm) cake

For the cake:
- 1 tablespoon vegetable margarine
  or vegetable oil, for greasing
- 3 medium beets (beetroot)
- 1 cup (240 g) dairy-free dark Belgian
  chocolate chips
- 5 tablespoons canola (rapeseed) oil
- ½ cup (100 g) raw superfine (caster) sugar
- 1 teaspoon vanilla extract
- 1½ cups (360 ml/12 fl oz) almond milk
- 2 cups (250 g) all-purpose (plain) flour
- ½ cup (50 g) unsweetened cocoa powder
- ⅓ cup (70 g) ground flax seeds
- 2 cups (160 g) ground almonds
- 2 teaspoons baking powder
- 1 teaspoon baking soda (bicarbonate
  of soda)

For the frosting (icing):
- 1 cup (240 g) dairy-free dark Belgian
  chocolate chips
- 9 oz (250 g) vegan cream cheese (page 30)
  or store-bought
- 1 cup (120 g) confectioners' (icing) sugar
- shaved dark chocolate, to decorate

Preheat the oven to 400°F/200°C/Gas Mark 6. Grease a 9-inch (23 cm) round springform cake pan.

To make the cake batter, bring a large saucepan of water to a boil. Add the beets and cook over medium heat for 35 minutes, until soft. Remove the beets from the pan and rinse under cold running water, then peel off and discard the skins. Using a food processor or high-speed blender, purée the beets until smooth Set aside.

Melt the chocolate in a heatproof bowl set over a saucepan of simmering water. Reduce the heat to low, then add the beet purée and stir well. Add the oil, sugar, vanilla, and almond milk and stir well until completely blended.

In a separate bowl, combine the flour, cocoa, flax seeds, ground almonds, baking powder, and baking soda. Gradually stir the beet-chocolate mixture into the dry ingredients until incorporated. Transfer the cake batter to the prepared pan and bake for 1 hour to 1 hour and 10 minutes, or until a skewer inserted into the center of the cake comes out clean. Let cool for 30 minutes, then remove from the pan.

To make the frosting, melt the chocolate in a heatproof bowl set over a saucepan of simmering water. Remove the bowl from the heat and whisk in the vegan cream cheese and sugar until combined. Spread the frosting over the top surface of the cooled cake, then sprinkle over the shaved chocolate.

CHOCOLATE NUT BROWNIES

Preheat the oven to 350°F/180°C/Gas Mark 4. Lightly grease a 5 x 10-inch (13 x 25 cm) loaf pan with vegetable margarine.

Combine the flaxseeds and 3 tablespoons water in a bowl and set aside.

Using a food processor or high-speed blender, grind the pecans. Whisk together the ground pecans and almonds, cocoa powder, arrowroot flour, baking soda, and salt in a bowl.

Melt ½ cup (120 g) of the chocolate chips and the vegetable margarine together in a medium saucepan over very low heat until two-thirds of the chocolate melts, then remove the pan from the heat and stir until the chocolate is completely melted and the mixture is smooth. Stir in the flaxseeds, sugar, all-purpose flour, almond milk, and vanilla until combined. Pour the chocolate mixture over the ground pecan and almond mixture and stir well to combine. Add the walnuts and remaining chocolate chips.

Transfer the batter to the prepared cake pan and place a piece of parchment (baking) paper equal to the perimeter of the loaf pan on top. Press down on the parchment with your hands to spread out the batter. Discard the parchment. Bake for 30 minutes. Let cool, then remove the brownies from pan and cut into squares.

Preparation time: 25 minutes
Cooking time: 30 minutes

Makes 50 (1-inch/2.5 cm) square brownies

- ½ cup (120 g) vegetable margarine, plus extra for greasing
- 4 teaspoons ground flaxseeds
- 2 cups (240 g) pecans
- 1 cup (80 g) ground almonds
- 1 cup (100 g) unsweetened cocoa powder
- 2 tablespoons arrowroot flour
- 1 tablespoon baking soda (bicarbonate of soda)
- a pinch of salt
- ½ cup (120 g) dark chocolate chips, plus extra as needed
- 1 cup (200 g) superfine (caster) sugar
- ¾ cup (95 g) all-purpose (plain) flour
- 4 tablespoons almond milk
- 1 teaspoon vanilla extract
- 1 cup (90 g) walnuts, finely chopped

RASPBERRY PIE

Preparation time: 35 minutes, plus
  1 hour chilling
Cooking time: none

Serves 4

For the crust:
- 1 tablespoon coconut oil
- 8 Medjool dates, pitted (stoned)
- 1½ cups (135 g) walnuts
- 1 tablespoon agave or maple syrup
- a pinch of salt

For the filling:
- ½ cup (120 g) raw cashews, soaked
  in water overnight and drained
- 1 tablespoon agave syrup
- 1 teaspoon vanilla extract
- 1 tablespoon fresh lemon juice
- 1 cup (125 g) raspberries, divided
- 1 tablespoon confectioners' (icing) sugar,
  for dusting

To make the crust, using a food processor, pulse the ingredients until they form sticky crumbs. Spoon the crumbs into a 9-inch (23 cm) round tart pan and press them into bottom and sides. Set aside in the freezer.

To make the filling, using a food processor or high-speed blender, process the drained cashews, agave, vanilla extract, lemon juice, and ¼ cup (30 g) raspberries until smooth and creamy. Pour the filling onto the base and spread it evenly across the surface. Top with the remaining raspberries, pressing them carefully into the cashew cream. Refrigerate for 1 hour, then dust with confectioners' sugar over the raspberries and serve.

RASPBERRY PIE

COCOA AND RASPBERRY CAKE

Preparation time: 35 minutes
Cooking time: 1 hour, plus
  30 minutes cooling

Makes 1 (8-inch/20 cm) cake

For the filling:
- 1 cup (240 g) frozen raspberries
- 3 tablespoons superfine (caster) sugar
- 3 tablespoons brandy or cognac
- 1 teaspoon all-purpose (plain) flour

For the topping:
- 4 tablespoons vegetable margarine
- 1 tablespoon unsweetened cocoa powder
- ¼ cup (60 g) all-purpose (plain) flour
- 1 tablespoon confectioners' (icing) sugar,
  to decorate

For the cake:
- vegetable margarine, for greasing
- 2 tablespoons egg replacer, mixed with
  4 tablespoons warm water
- 1 cup (200 g) superfine (caster) sugar
- 1 teaspoon vanilla extract
- 1½ cups (190 g) all-purpose (plain) flour
- 1 teaspoon baking powder
- 1 tablespoon unsweetened cocoa powder
- 4 tablespoons almond milk
- 2 teaspoons baking soda (bicarbonate
  of soda)
- ¾ cup (175 ml/6 fl oz) soy sour cream

To make the filling, put the frozen raspberries in a saucepan with the sugar and brandy or cognac and defrost on low heat. When defrosted, cook gently for 10 minutes, until the raspberries become a purée. Strain the purée, pressing on solids, and set the solids aside. Continue to cook the strained raspberry liquid until it thickens. Return it to raspberry solids, stir well, stir in the flour, and whisk until well blended. Set aside.

To make the topping, cut the vegetable margarine in small pieces and put them into a bowl. Add the cocoa powder and flour and, using your hands, combine until a crumbly dough forms. Set aside.

Preheat the oven to 350°F/180°C/Gas Mark 4. Grease an 8-inch (20 cm) round cake pan that is 3 inches (7½ cm) deep with vegetable margarine.

To make the cake batter, mix the egg replacer, sugar, and vanilla extract in a large bowl and set aside.

Sift the flour, baking powder, and cocoa into a large bowl. Mix the dry ingredients into the egg replacer mixture, and slowly add the almond milk. Mix thoroughly to combine until the batter is thick.

Whisk the baking soda into the soy sour cream in a medium bowl and gently fold into the batter with a wooden spoon until completely incorporated.

Spoon half of the batter into the prepared cake pan. Spread the raspberry filling over the batter, then cover with the remaining batter. Scatter the topping over the batter and bake for 45 minutes, until baked through. Sprinkle the confectioners' sugar over the topping and let cool for 30 minutes before removing from the pan.

PECAN PIE

Preheat the oven to 375°F/190°C/Gas Mark 5.

To first make the crust, use a food processor to blend together the flour, salt, cinnamon, and cloves, then add the oil and pulse a couple of times to make crumbs. Add 4 tablespoons water and process for 10 seconds, until smooth but sticky.

Spoon the mixture into an 8-inch (20 cm) round tart pan and press the crumbs firmly onto the bottom and sides of the pan. Set aside in the freezer.

To make the filling, mix the dates with the maple or agave syrup, 3 tablespoons water, the cinnamon, and pecans in a bowl. Mix well and spread the filling evenly over the crust. Using the back of a tablespoon, spread the filling and smooth the top. Bake for 25 minutes or until the filling is golden brown. Let cool on a wire rack for 20 minutes before serving.

Preparation time: 20 minutes
Cooking time: 25 minutes, plus
  20 minutes cooling

Makes 1 (8-inch/20 cm) pie

For the crust:
- 1½ cups (190 g) all-purpose (plain) flour
- a pinch of salt
- 1 teaspoon ground cinnamon
- ½ teaspoon ground cloves
- 5 tablespoons vegetable oil

For the filling:
- 1 cup (175 g) Medjool dates, pitted (stoned) and finely chopped
- 3 tablespoons maple or agave syrup
- 1 teaspoon ground cinnamon
- 1 cup (125 g) pecans, crushed

GINGER COOKIES

Preheat the oven to 350°F/180°C/Gas Mark 4. Grease a large baking sheet with vegetable margarine.

Combine all the ingredients in a large bowl using a wooden spoon, then use your hands to blend the mixture into a smooth dough. Knead until the dough is elastic. Add 1 tablespoon of almond milk if the dough seems too firm.

Using your hands, roll the dough into a 1½ inch (4 cm) wide log and cut ¼-inch (6 mm) long slices from the dough. Arrange the slices on the prepared baking sheet and bake for 12–14 minutes, until golden brown. Let cool completely before serving.

Preparation time: 20 minutes
Cooking time: 15 minutes

Serves 4

- ½ cup (120 g) vegetable margarine, plus extra for greasing
- ½ cup (100 g) superfine (caster) sugar
- 2 tablespoons maple syrup or agave syrup
- 2 cups (250 g) all-purpose (plain) flour
- 1 teaspoon baking soda (bicarbonate of soda)
- 1 tablespoon grated ginger
- 1 teaspoon baking powder
- 2 tablespoons almond milk, plus extra as needed
- a pinch of salt

ORANGE-CHOCOLATE CHEESECAKE

Preparation time: 40 minutes, plus
  1 hour freezing and 3 hours chilling
Cooking time: none

Makes 1 (5-inch/13 cm) cake

For the base:
- 1 tablespoon coconut oil, plus extra
  for greasing
- 1 cup (135 g) almonds
- ⅓ cup (80 g) pecans
- ⅓ cup (80 g) Medjool dates
- 1 tablespoon chia seeds
- 1 tablespoon unsweetened cocoa powder

For the filling:
- 1½ cups (360 g) raw cashews, soaked
  in water overnight and drained
- 1 tablespoon coconut oil
- juice of 1 orange
- 1 tablespoon finely grated orange zest
- 1 tablespoon coconut sugar
- ⅛ teaspoon ground turmeric

For the topping:
- 2 tablespoons coconut oil
- 1 tablespoon unsweetened cocoa powder
- 1 tablespoon coconut sugar

To make the base, line a 5-inch (13 cm) springform cake pan with plastic wrap (clingfilm). Grease the bottom and sides of the pan with coconut oil.

Using a food processor, blend the ingredients for the base together until sticky crumbs are formed. Press the mixture firmly into the bottom and sides of the prepared cake pan. Set aside in the freezer.

To make the filling, using a food processor or high-speed blender, blend the ingredients together until smooth and creamy. Spread the mixture across the base. Set aside while you make the topping.

To make the topping, using a food processor, combine the ingredients until well mixed. Pour the chocolate mixture on top of the cheesecake in the center. Then, using the back of a spoon, spread the mixture evenly in a circular motion to make a design of concentric circles. Freeze for 1 hour, then refrigerate for 3 hours before serving.

ORANGE-CHOCOLATE CHEESECAKE

FIG AND ALMOND TART

Preparation time: 30 minutes, plus
 30 minutes resting
Cooking time: 40 minutes, plus
 30 minutes cooling

Makes 1 (10-inch/25 cm) tart

For the crust:
- 1 cup (240 g) vegetable margarine, chilled
 and sliced, plus extra for greasing
- 3 cups (375 g) all-purpose (plain) flour,
 plus extra for dusting
- ⅓ cup (80 ml) soy sour cream or soy cream

For the filling:
- ½ cup (120 g) vegetable margarine, at room
 temperature
- ½ cup (100 g) superfine (caster) sugar
- 4 tablespoons egg replacer, mixed with
 8 tablespoons warm water
- 3 cups (410 g) ground almonds
- 3 tablespoons almond milk, plus more
 as needed
- 1 lb (500 g) fresh figs, quartered

Preheat the oven to 425°F/220°C/Gas Mark 7. Grease a 10-inch (25 cm) round tart pan with vegetable oil.

To make the crust, combine the vegetable margarine and flour in a large bowl and mix with your hands until the mixture forms fine crumbs. Stir in the soy sour cream or soy cream and mix well. Form dough into a ball and set aside.

Dust your work surface with flour. Roll out the dough to a circle roughly 11 inches (28 cm) in diameter. Line the prepared pan with the dough, pressing the dough gently into the bottom and sides of the pan. Trim the overhang and set aside.

To make the filling, using a food processor, combine the vegetable margarine with the sugar and egg replacer and pulse until the mixture is light and fluffy. Add the ground almonds and almond milk. Mix well until smooth, adding more almond milk if too dry.

Spread the almond mixture on the crust and top with the figs. Bake for about 40 minutes, or until golden brown. Let cool for 30 minutes, then remove the tart from the pan and serve.

GLAZED ORANGE CAKE

Preparation time: 25 minutes
Cooking time: 40 minutes, plus 30 minutes
 cooling and 30 minutes resting

Makes 1 (10-inch/25 cm) cake

For the cake:
- vegetable margarine, for greasing
- 2½ cups (310 g) all-purpose (plain) flour
- 1½ cups (300 g) superfine (caster) sugar
- 1 cup (90 g) finely grated coconut flakes
- a pinch of salt
- 2 teaspoons baking powder
- 2 teaspoons baking soda (bicarbonate
 of soda)
- 2 tablespoons egg replacer, mixed with
 4 tablespoons warm water
- 1 teaspoon vanilla extract
- 1 cup (240 ml/8 fl oz) coconut milk
- ½ cup (120 ml/4 fl oz) vegetable oil
- 1 cup (240 ml/8 fl oz) fresh orange juice
- 2 tablespoons finely grated orange zest

For the glaze:
- 3 cups (400 g) confectioners' (icing) sugar
- 4 tablespoons fresh orange juice
- 2 tablespoons toasted coconut chips

Preheat the oven to 350°F/180°C/Gas Mark 4. Grease a 10-inch (25 cm) round cake pan.

To make the cake, mix together the flour, sugar, coconut flakes, salt, baking powder, baking soda, egg replacer, and vanilla extract in a large bowl. Stir in the coconut milk, vegetable oil, and orange juice and blend with a wooden spoon until the batter is well combined. Mix in the orange zest. Transfer the batter to the prepared cake pan and bake for 40 minutes. Let cool for 30 minutes, then remove from the pan.

To make the glaze, combine the ingredients in a bowl. Brush the glaze over the cooled cake. Let the cake sit at room temperature for about 30 minutes before serving.

COCONUT AND BANANA
CREAM PIE

Preheat the oven to 400°F/200°C/Gas Mark 6. Grease a 10-inch (25 cm) round tart pan with vegetable margarine.

To make the crust, cut the vegetable margarine into pieces and put in a bowl. Using a fork, mix in the flour and sugar, then gradually sprinkle in just enough water as you continue to mix to bring the mixture together to form an elastic dough. Do not overmix to prevent the dough from becoming too dry. Let rest, uncovered, for 30 minutes.

Dust the work surface with flour. Roll out the dough into an 11-inch (28 cm) circle. Line the prepared tart pan with the dough, pressing it carefully into the bottom and sides of the pan. Cover the pan with aluminum foil and bake for 20 minutes. Remove the foil and pierce the dough with a fork across the surface. Bake for another 5–6 minutes, until golden brown.

To make the filling, whisk together the egg replacer, sugar, vanilla extract, and flour in a large bowl.

Put the almond milk and coconut into a large saucepan and bring to a simmer. Remove the saucepan from the stove and carefully whisk in the flour mixture until smooth. Set the pan over medium heat and simmer for about 15 minutes, until the mixture becomes a thick pudding. Pour the mixture into the crust.

To make the topping, slice the bananas and immediately place them on the top of the cooked pudding, pressing gently to position them firmly. Let cool for 15 minutes, then refrigerate until the filling is completely cold.

Whip the soy cream to firm peaks and spread this over the cooled pie. Sprinkle over the grated coconut or toasted coconut flakes, then refrigerate for another 20 minutes before serving.

Preparation time: 30 minutes, plus
   30 minutes resting
Cooking time: 40 minutes, plus
   1 hour chilling

Makes 1 (10-inch/25 cm) pie

For the crust:
- ½ cup (120 g) vegetable margarine, plus extra for greasing
- 1½ cups (180 g) all-purpose (plain) flour, plus extra for dusting
- 1 teaspoon superfine (caster) sugar

For the filling:
- 1 tablespoon egg replacer, mixed with 2 tablespoons warm water
- ½ cup (100 g) superfine (caster) sugar
- 1 teaspoon vanilla extract
- 3 tablespoons all-purpose (plain) flour
- 2 cups (475 ml/16 fl oz) almond milk
- 2 cups (200 g) grated coconut

For the topping:
- 2 ripe bananas
- 1 cup (240 ml/8 fl oz) whipping soy cream
- 1 tablespoon grated coconut or toasted coconut flakes

APPLE RICE PUDDING

Preparation time: 15 minutes
Cooking time: 15 minutes, plus
  20 minutes chilling

Serves 4

- 2 tablespoons vegetable margarine
- 5 tablespoons maple or agave syrup
- 1 teaspoon ground cinnamon
- 1 teaspoon ground nutmeg
- 2 apples, cored and chopped
- 2 cups (370 g) basmati or other long-grain rice, cooked
- ½ cup (80 g) raisins
- 2 cups (480 ml/16 fl oz) almond milk
- 1 cup (80 g) toasted coconut flakes

Heat the vegetable margarine, maple or agave syrup, cinnamon, nutmeg, and apples in a saucepan over medium heat until simmering. Add the rice, raisins, and almond milk. Bring to a simmer and cook over low heat for about 15 minutes, stirring frequently, until the apples are very tender.

Divide the pudding among 4 dessert cups, then let cool for 20 minutes. Decorate with the toasted coconut flakes and serve.

APPLE RICE PUDDING

LEMON-TOFU CHEESECAKE

Preparation time: 20 minutes
Cooking time: 35 minutes, plus 30 minutes
  cooling and 1½ hours chilling

Makes 1 (9-inch/23 cm) cake

For the base:
- 3 cups (375 g) vegan cracker crumbs
- 4 tablespoons maple syrup
- 1 teaspoon almond extract

For the topping:
- 1 lb 2 oz (500 g) silken tofu
- ⅓ cup (65 g) superfine (caster) sugar
- 1 tablespoon almond or peanut butter
- a pinch of salt
- 2 tablespoons fresh lemon juice
- 1 tablespoon finely grated lemon zest
- 1 teaspoon almond extract
- 2 tablespoons cornstarch (cornflour)
- 2 tablespoons almond milk, plus more as
  needed

Preheat the oven to 350°F/180°C/Gas Mark 4.

To make the base, using a food processor, pulse the crackers a couple of times to make crumbs.

Transfer the crumbs to a bowl, add the maple syrup and almond extract, and mix until well blended. Press the mixture into the bottom of a 9-inch (23 cm) round tart pan. Bake for 5 minutes, until firm. Set aside.

To make the topping, using a food processor, blend the silken tofu, superfine sugar, almond or peanut butter, salt, lemon juice, lemon zest, almond extract, cornstarch, and almond milk for about 1 minute, until smooth. If the mixture is too dry, add a little more almond milk to gain some elasticity.

Pour the mixture over the base and bake for 30 minutes, until well baked. Let cool at room temperature for 30 minutes, then refrigerate for 1½ hours before serving.

MACAROON AND CHOCOLATE CREAM PIE

Preparation time: 45 minutes, plus
  2 hours chilling
Cooking time: none

Serves 4

For the base:
- 1 lb (500 g) walnuts, cashews, almonds,
  or pecans
- a pinch of salt
- 1 cup (240 g) pitted dates

For the filling:
- 3 ripe bananas
- ½ cup (60 g) unsweetened cacao powder
- 1½ cups (135 g) grated coconut
- ⅓ cup (80 g) ground almonds
- 5 tablespoons maple syrup
- 1 teaspoon vanilla extract

To make the base, using a food processor fitted with a blade, pulse the nuts with the salt until coarsely ground. Add the dates and pulse until the mixture is sticky and the dates are well incorporated.

Divide the mixture across 4 (1 cup/240 ml) ramekins. Press the mixture into the bottom and up the sides of each dish to form a crust. Set aside in the freezer.

To make the filling, using a food processor, pulse the bananas, cocoa powder, grated coconut, ground almonds, maple syrup, and vanilla until well blended.

Spoon the filling into the ramekins and refrigerate for at least 2 hours before serving.

Preheat the oven to 350°F/180°C/Gas Mark 4.

To make the crust, mix the flour, sugar, salt, and baking powder in a large bowl, then gradually add the vegetable oil, stirring constantly with a fork, until the mixture is crumbly. Spoon the mixture into an 8-inch (20 cm) square ovenproof dish, pressing it with your fingers to cover the bottom and halfway up the sides of the dish with the base. Place the dish on the center rack of the oven and bake for 15 minutes. Set aside.

To make the topping, combine the tofu, agave or maple syrup, agar-agar, and turmeric in a small mixing bowl and stir until well blended.

To make the filling, arrange the peaches over the crust. Sprinkle with sugar and cinnamon. Spread the topping over the filling. Bake for 30 minutes until well baked. Serve lukewarm or chilled.

Preparation time: 20 minutes
Cooking time: 45 minutes

Makes 1 (8-inch/20 cm) pie

For the crust:
- 2 cups (320 g) all-purpose (plain) flour
- ¼ cup (50 g) superfine (caster) sugar
- a pinch of salt
- 1 teaspoon baking powder
- ½ cup (120 ml/4 fl oz) vegetable oil

For the topping:
- 1 cup (240 g) silken tofu
- 2 tablespoons agave or maple syrup
- 2 teaspoons agar-agar
- 1 teaspoon ground turmeric

For the filling:
- 9 peaches, peeled, pitted (stoned), and halved
- 2 tablespoons superfine (caster) sugar
- 1 teaspoon ground cinnamon

BANANA AND PASSIONFRUIT ICE CREAM

Preparation time: 20 minutes, plus
  overnight freezing
Cooking time: none

Serves 4

- 4 bananas
- 5 tablespoons fresh coconut water
- 2 passionfruits
- 1 tablespoon fresh lemon juice
- 1–2 tablespoons agave syrup, to taste
- 2 tablespoons coconut flakes, to decorate

Slice the bananas and place them in a sealed container in your freezer overnight (or longer). Also freeze the bowl or cups in which you will serve the ice cream.

Using a food processor, blend the frozen bananas with the coconut water until smooth. Cut the passionfruits in half, spoon out the pulp, and add it to the banana mixture along with the lemon juice and agave syrup. Pulse for few seconds until combined.

Transfer to the frozen bowl, garnish with coconut flakes, and serve immediately.

BANANA AND PASSIONFRUIT ICE CREAM

PLUM PIE

Preparation time: 1 hour 5 minutes
Cooking time: 50 minutes, plus 15 minutes
  resting and 20 minutes cooling

Makes 1 (9-inch/23 cm) pie

For the crust:
- 1 teaspoon dry active yeast
- 2 tablespoons raw sugar
- 3½ cups (435 g) whole-wheat (wholemeal) flour, plus extra for dusting
- a pinch of salt
- 2 tablespoons canola (rapeseed) oil

For the filling:
- 8 large ripe plums
- 4 tablespoons dark rum
- 2 teaspoons ground cinnamon
- juice of 1 lemon
- 3 tablespoons ground almonds
- 3 tablespoons superfine (caster) sugar

Preheat the oven to 350°F/180°C/Gas Mark 4.

To make the crust, mix the yeast, sugar, and ½ cup (120 ml/4 fl oz) warm water in a large bowl. Let sit for 10 minutes. Stir in the flour, salt, and oil with your hands to form a smooth, elastic dough. Knead with your hands for 3–4 minutes, until the dough is smooth and elastic, then form the dough into a ball, put it into a clean bowl, cover the bowl with a clean, damp kitchen towel, and leave in a warm place for 20 minutes.

To make the filling, halve and pit (stone) the plums, then cut each half into 3 wedges. Combine the wedges, rum, cinnamon, and lemon juice in a bowl and toss to coat the plums. Let sit for 15 minutes.

Dust your work surface with flour. Roll out the dough into a 10-inch (25 cm) circle. Line a 9-inch (23 cm) round tart pan with the dough, pressing the dough gently into the bottom and sides of the pan.

Using a spoon, sprinkle the ground almonds and superfine sugar over the crust, then arrange the spiced plums on top. Bake for 45 minutes, until the crust is golden brown. Let cool for 20 minutes on a wire rack. Serve lukewarm.

CHOCOLATE PUDDING CAKE

Preparation time: 30 minutes
Cooking time: 45 minutes

Makes 1 (8-inch/20 cm) cake

- vegetable margarine, for greasing
- 1 cup (125 g) all-purpose (plain) flour
- ⅔ cup (135 g) plus 6 tablespoons superfine (caster) sugar, divided
- ¼ cup (25 g) plus 2 tablespoons unsweetened cocoa powder, divided
- 2 teaspoons baking powder
- 2 tablespoons applesauce
- 1 teaspoon vanilla extract
- a pinch of salt

Preheat the oven to 350°F/180°C/Gas Mark 4. Grease an 8-inch (20 cm) square cake pan with the vegetable margarine.

Mix together the flour, ⅔ cup (135 g) sugar, ¼ cup (25 g) cocoa powder, baking powder, ½ cup (120 ml/4 fl oz) water, the applesauce, vanilla extract, and salt in a bowl until well blended. Pour the batter into the prepared cake pan.

Mix the remaining sugar with the remaining cocoa powder in a bowl and sprinkle it over the batter in the pan. Pour 1¾ cups (420 ml/14½ fl oz) hot water over the entire top surface, then bake for 45 minutes. Let cool on a wire rack and serve lukewarm.

COCONUT AND RICE CAKE
IN BANANA LEAF

To make the dough, put the rice flour into a large bowl, add the salt, and then slowly mix in ½ cup (120 ml/4 fl oz) water. Stir well, and in a slow stream add another ½ cup (120 ml/4 fl oz) water to form a smooth dough. Cover the bowl with a clean, damp kitchen towel and set aside.

To make the filling, put the sugar into a saucepan with 2 tablespoons water and warm over low heat until the sugar has completely dissolved. Add the coconut water and grated coconut, increase the heat to medium, and stir for 10 minutes, until the coconut has absorbed the liquid.

Bring a saucepan of water to a boil. Cut the banana leaves into 5-inch (13 cm) squares. Transfer the squares to a large steamer pan and set this over the pan of boiling water to steam for 2–3 minutes, to make the banana leaves easy to fold.

Coat your palm and fingers with oil. Take 2 teaspoons of the dough and flatten the dough on you palm until it is ¼ inch (5 mm) thick. Spoon 1 teaspoon of the coconut mixture onto the center of the dough and wrap the dough around the filling. Place the filled dough on the center of a banana leaf square, then fold each side of the banana leaf square toward the center. Place the parcel on a plate and repeat with the remaining dough and filling.

Bring a large saucepan of water to a boil. Arrange a batch of the banana-leaf parcels in a steamer basket and steam for 20 minutes, then repeat with subsequent batches. Let cool until warm and serve.

Preparation time: 30 minutes
Cooking time: 1 hour 10 minutes

Serves 4

For the filling:
- a generous 1 lb (500 g) glutinous or sticky rice flour
- a pinch of salt

For the filling:
- 1 cup (200 g) superfine (caster) sugar
- 1¼ cups (300 ml/10 fl oz) coconut water
- 1 lb 2 oz (500 g) grated coconut
- 2 banana leaves
- vegetable oil, to grease

SALTY CARAMEL CAKE

Preparation time: 20 minutes
Cooking time: 30 minutes, plus
  25 minutes cooling

Makes 1 (9-inch/23 cm) cake

- vegetable margarine, for greasing
- ½ cup (65 g) plus 1 tablespoon whole-wheat (wholemeal) flour
- 6 tablespoons unsweetened cocoa powder
- 2 teaspoons baking powder
- 3 tablespoons vegetable oil
- 3 tablespoons maple syrup
- 1 tablespoon vanilla sugar
- 6 tablespoons almond butter
- ¼ teaspoon salt
- 1 cup (240 ml/8 fl oz) almond milk
- 3 tablespoons dark chocolate chips

Preheat the oven to 350°F/180°C/Gas Mark 4. Grease a 9-inch (23 cm) round cake pan with vegetable margarine.

Mix the flour, cocoa powder, and baking powder in a bowl. Set aside. To make the caramel, combine the oil, maple syrup, vanilla extract, almond butter, and salt in a saucepan. Heat over medium heat, stirring constantly, for 6–7 minutes, until the caramel is bubbling and smooth. Set aside for 10 minutes.

Mix half the almond butter mixture with the flour mixture. Add the almond milk and chocolate and stir to combine. Pour the batter into the prepared cake pan. Drizzle the remaining almond butter mixture over the top. Bake for about 25 minutes or until a skewer inserted in the center of the cake comes out clean. Set aside to cool on a wire rack for 15 minutes before serving.

SALTY CARAMEL CAKE

COCONUT-CHOCOLATE CREAM PIE

Preparation time: 20 minutes
Cooking time: 10 minutes, plus 30 minutes
cooling and 30 minutes chilling

Makes 1 (9-inch/23 cm) pie

For the base:
- 1 lb (450 g) dairy-free chocolate wafer
- ½ cup (120 g) vegetable margarine

For the filling:
- ½ cup (120 g) finely chopped dark chocolate
- 2 cups (475 ml/16 fl oz) coconut milk
- ⅔ cup (135 g) superfine (caster) sugar
- 1 teaspoon vanilla extract
- a pinch of salt
- ⅓ cup (80 g) cornstarch (cornflour)

For the topping:
- 1 cup (240 ml/8 fl oz) whipping soy cream
- 2 tablespoons unrefined cane sugar
- 1 tablespoon cognac or brandy
- 1 teaspoon vanilla extract
- 2 cups (200 g) coconut flakes, toasted

Using a food processor, pulse the chocolate wafer in batches to form crumbs.

To make the base, melt the vegetable margarine in a saucepan, then mix with the cookie crumbs in a bowl until well combined. Transfer the mixture to a 9-inch (23 cm) round tart pan and press the crumbs into the bottom and sides of the pan. Freeze for 30 minutes.

To make the filling, melt the chocolate in a small saucepan over very low heat, stirring constantly, until smooth. Pour the chocolate over the frozen base and, using the back of a spoon, spread the chocolate across the base in a thin layer. Return the base to the freezer for 20 minutes.

Combine the coconut milk, sugar, vanilla, and salt in a medium saucepan and bring to a boil, then immediately reduce the heat to produce a low simmer. Mix the cornstarch with 2 tablespoons hot water until diluted, then stir this into the coconut milk mixture and cook over low heat for 9–10 minutes, until the cream starts to thicken to a pudding consistency. Spread the cream over the frozen base. Let cool for 30 minutes, then refrigerate for 30 minutes.

To make the topping, whip the soy cream until firm peaks form. Whisk in the sugar, cognac or brandy, and vanilla extract. Spread the topping over the filling and sprinkle over the toasted coconut flakes.

FRUIT CHEESECAKE

To make the base, mix the grated coconut, oatmeal, superfine sugar, cocoa powder, and agave or maple syrup in a bowl and mix with your hands until thick and sticky. Pat the mixture into the bottom of an 8-inch (20 cm) square cake pan.

To make the filling, using a food processor or high-speed blender, blend the drained cashews and pecans until smooth. Add the mango and process until very smooth, then add the passion fruit pulp and orange juice and blend until very creamy.

Heat the coconut oil in a saucepan over very low heat until completely melted. Add this to the filling mixture and mix well to blend. Spoon the mixture over the base. Top with the pineapple slices, pressing them gently into the filling to secure, but ensuring they stay on the surface. Freeze for 1 hour. Transfer to the refrigerator for 2 hours before serving.

Preparation time: 35 minutes, plus 1 hour freezing and 2 hours chilling
Cooking time: none

Makes 1 (8-inch/20 cm) cake

For the base:
- 1 cup (90 g) grated coconut
- ¾ cup (150 g) rolled oatmeal
- ½ cup (100 g) superfine (caster) sugar
- ¼ cup (40 g) cocoa powder
- ¼ cup (60 g) agave or maple syrup

For the filling:
- 1 cup (240 g) raw cashews, soaked in water overnight
- ½ cup (120 g) pecans, soaked in water overnight
- 2 sweet mangoes, sliced
- pulp from 2 passion fruits
- 4 tablespoons fresh orange juice
- 2 cups (480 g) coconut oil
- ½ sweet pineapple, sliced paper-thin

PEANUT BUTTER AND CHOCOLATE CREAM

Using a food processor, blend the tofu, chocolate, and peanut butter and process until very smooth. Add the agave or maple syrup and pulse to blend.

Slice the bananas and put them into a large bowl. Pour the tofu mixture over the bananas and flatten the surface with a rubber spatula or the back of a spoon. Refrigerate for 2 hours before serving.

Preparation time: 30 minutes, plus 2 hours chilling
Cooking time: none

Serves 4

- 1 lb (500 g) silken tofu
- 1 cup (240 g) dark chocolate chips, melted
- ¾ cup (170 g) smooth peanut butter, melted
- 2 tablespoons agave or maple syrup
- 2 ripe bananas

COCONUT PANNA COTTA WITH PINEAPPLE

Preparation time: 20 minutes
Cooking time: 30 minutes

Serves 4

For the coconut panna cotta:
- 2 cups (480 ml/16 fl oz) soy cream
- ⅔ cup (160 ml/5 fl oz) coconut milk
- 1 fresh vanilla pod, beans scraped
- ½ cup (100 g) superfine (caster) sugar
- 3 teaspoons agar-agar

For the pineapple:
- ½ cup (120 ml/4 fl oz) white wine
- ½ cup (50 g) superfine (caster) sugar
- 1 teaspoon vanilla extract
- finely grated zest and juice of 1 lemon
- 1 sweet pineapple, cored and sliced paper-thin
- 2 tablespoons grated coconut, to decorate

To make the panna cotta, heat the coconut milk, soy cream, vanilla seeds, and sugar in a saucepan. Bring the mixture to a boil, then immediately reduce the heat to low and simmer, stirring continuously, for 6–8 minutes, until the sugar has completely dissolved. Add the agar-agar and stir until it has melted. Pour the custard into 4 ramekins and let cool.

For the pineapple, combine the wine, 1½ cups (360 ml) water, sugar, vanilla extract, and lemon juice and zest in a large saucepan and bring the mixture to a boil. Reduce the heat to medium-low, bring the mixture to a simmer, and add the pineapple to the saucepan. Poach gently for 3–4 minutes. Drain the pineapple, reserving the liquid, and set aside to cool. Return the liquid to the saucepan and simmer over medium-low heat for about 15 minutes, until reduced by half and starting to thicken. Let cool.

Arrange equal portions of the pineapple slices on 4 dessert plates. Unmold the panna cottas and position each on top of the pineapple slices. Using a spoon, drizzle 1–2 spoons of the sauce on top. Decorate each panna cotta with ½ tablespoon of grated coconut and serve immediately.

COCONUT PANNA COTTA WITH PINEAPPLE

RAW LIME PIE

Preparation time: 30 minutes, plus
  1 hour freezing
Cooking time: none

Makes 1 (9-inch/23 cm) pie

For the base:
- 2 cups (480 g) raw cashews, crushed
- 1½ cups (120 g) grated coconut
- 1 cup (240 g) Medjool dates
- 1 teaspoon vanilla extract
- 2 tablespoons fresh lime juice
- a pinch of salt

For the filling:
- 2 ripe avocados
- 2 tablespoons finely grated lime zest
- 4 tablespoons fresh lime juice
- 4 tablespoons maple syrup, plus more
  as needed
- ½ teaspoon vanilla extract
- a pinch of salt

For the topping:
- finely grated lime zest
- 2 tablespoons maple syrup

To make the base, using a food processor, pulse the cashews and coconut to fine crumbs. Add the dates, vanilla extract, lime juice, and salt and pulse until a sticky mass forms. Spoon the mixture into a 9-inch (23 cm) round tart pan and press it gently onto the bottom and sides. Set aside in the freezer.

To make the filling, using a food processor or high-speed blender, process the ingredients until the mixture is smooth and creamy. Adjust the sweetness according to taste by adding extra maple syrup. Pour the filling over the base and spread it evenly across the surface. Smooth out the top with a rubber spatula. Freeze for 1 hour, then transfer to the refrigerator until ready to serve.

To make the topping, mix the maple syrup with the lime zest, then brush the mixture on the top of the cake and serve.

LEMON CAKE BARS

Preparation time: 20 minutes
Cooking time: 20 minutes

Makes about 16 (2-inch/5 cm) bars

For the crust:
- 1 cup (125 g) all-purpose (plain) flour
- ½ cup (60 g) whole-wheat (wholemeal)
  pastry flour
- 2 tablespoons superfine (caster) sugar
- ⅔ cup (80 g) vegetable margarine, cut
  into small pieces

For the topping:
- 3 tablespoons silken tofu
- ¾ cup (150 g) superfine (caster) sugar
- 5 tablespoons fresh orange juice
- 3 tablespoons fresh lemon juice
- 2 tablespoons all-purpose (plain) flour
- 2 tablespoons finely grated lemon zest
- 1 teaspoon baking powder

Preheat the oven to 325°F/160°C/Gas Mark 3.

To make the crust, combine the flours, sugar, and vegetable margarine in a large bowl and mix well until crumbly. Press the mixture into a 9-inch (23 cm) square cake pan. Bake for 15 minutes, until light golden. Set aside.

Meanwhile, to make the topping, use a food processor or high-speed blender, process the tofu, sugar, and orange and lemon juices until well blended. Add the flour, zest, and baking powder and pulse a couple of times. Pour the mixture over the baked crust, then bake for 2 minutes, until golden brown. Let cool, cut into bars, and serve.

NUT ROLLS
WITH ORANGE CREAM

To make the orange cream, whip the soy cream to firm peaks and set aside.

Put the orange juice, orange zest, and agave syrup into a saucepan, stir well, and bring to a simmer. Cook over medium heat for 3–4 minutes. Remove the pan from the stove and let cool for 15 minutes. Gradually fold the orange juice sauce into the whipping cream until well blended and refrigerate.

Preheat the oven to 400°F/190°C/Gas Mark 6.

To make the nut-syrup mixture, combine the walnuts, almonds, pistachios, sugar, cinnamon stick, and orange blossom water in a saucepan. Bring to a low simmer to dissolve the sugar slowly, then simmer for 6–7 minutes over medium-low heat, stirring frequently, and adding water as necessary to ensure the sauce remains liquid. Discard the cinnamon stick.

To make the phyllo rolls, place 1 sheet of phyllo on a dry work surface. Brush with melted vegetable margarine and sprinkle over 1 tablespoon of the nut-syrup mixture, reserving 2 tablespoons of the nut mixture for brushing and drizzling. Roll up the phyllo sheet around a chopstick, starting from a short end, to form a tube. Remove the chopstick and transfer the rolled pastry to a baking dish. Repeat with the remaining phyllo sheets, vegetable margarine, and nut–syrup mixture.

Bake the tubes for 20 minutes, until golden. Let cool. Brush the cooled tubes with reserved nut–syrup mixture. Refrigerate until ready to serve.

Cut the filo tubes in half. Place a quarter of the orange cream in the center of each crosswise 4 dessert plates. Place 1 filo tube on the top of the cream and drizzle over the reserved syrup. Garnish with the crushed pistachios and serve.

Preparation time: 30 minutes
Cooking time: 30 minutes

Serves 4

For the orange cream:
- 1 cup (240 ml/8 fl oz) whipping soy cream
- 2 tablespoons fresh orange juice
- 1 tablespoon finely grated orange zest
- 2 tablespoons agave syrup

For the nut-syrup mixture:
- ¼ cup (30 g) walnuts, crushed
- ¼ cup (35 g) almonds, crushed
- ¼ cup (25 g) pistachio nuts, crushed
- ½ cup (100 g) superfine (caster) sugar
- 1 cinnamon stick
- 2½ tablespoons orange blossom water

For the phyllo rolls:
- 1 cup (240 g) vegetable margarine, melted
- 16 sheets phyllo (filo) pastry
- 1 tablespoon crushed pistachio nuts, to decorate

MATCHA, CHOCOLATE, AND DATE CAKE

Preparation time: 40 minutes, plus
   3–4 hours chilling
Cooking time: none

Makes 1 (8-inch/20 cm) cake

- 1½ cups (135 g) walnuts
- ½ cup (90 g) Medjool dates
- 2 tablespoons ground almonds
- 3 tablespoons unsweetened cocoa
  powder, divided
- 2½ teaspoons matcha powder, divided
- 2 tablespoons maple syrup
- 1 teaspoon vanilla extract
- ½ cup (90 g) dark chocolate chips, melted
- 1 tablespoon ground ginger

Line an 8 x 4-inch (20 x 10-cm) cake pan with parchment (baking) paper.

Using a food processor, pulse the walnuts a couple of times, then add the dates and pulse until the mixture is broken down and sticky. Add the ground almonds, 2 tablespoons of the cocoa powder, 1½ teaspoons of the matcha, the maple syrup, vanilla, and melted chocolate. Pulse again until all the ingredients are well incorporated and the mixture is smooth. Transfer the mixture to a large bowl, add the ginger, and mix well to combine.

Spoon the mixture into the prepared cake pan and press it into the bottom in a thick layer. Use a rubber spatula to smooth out the top into a flat surface. Cover the pan with plastic wrap (clingfilm) and refrigerate for 3–4 hours.

To serve, cut the block into 1-inch (2.5 cm) squares. Dust the squares with the remaining cocoa and matcha powders just before serving.

MATCHA, CHOCOLATE, AND DATE CAKE

CARROT FUDGE

Preparation time: 30 minutes
  Cooking time: 1 hour 20 minutes, plus
  overnight chilling

Serves 4

- ½ cup (120 g) vegetable margarine, plus
  extra for greasing
- 3 cups (390 g) finely grated carrots
- 1 cup (240 ml/8 fl oz) almond milk
- 1 cup (240 ml/8 fl oz) soy cream
- 1 cup (200 g) granulated sugar
- 1 teaspoon ground cardamom
- 1 cup (110 g) slivered almonds, plus
  2 tablespoons toasted, slivered almonds,
  to decorate
- ½ cup (80 g) golden raisins
- ½ cup (120 g) raw cashews, crushed

Grease a 9-inch (20 cm) square cake pan with vegetable margarine.

Combine the grated carrots, almond milk, and soy cream in a saucepan. Bring the mixture to a boil and simmer over low heat for 1 hour, until the carrots are soft. Add the vegetable margarine, sugar, cardamom, almonds, raisins, and cashews and mix thoroughly. Bring to a simmer and cook, stirring frequently, for 20 minutes, until the mixture has thickened.

Remove the saucepan from the heat and transfer to the prepared pan. Spread the fudge into a layer that is about 2 inches (5 cm) thick. Refrigerate overnight.

Cut the block into 2-inch (5 cm) cubes. Serve chilled, topped with toasted, slivered almonds.

CHRISTMAS COOKIES

GERMANY

Mix the orange marmalade, ground almonds, ground hazelnuts, candied orange peel, and candied lemon peel in a large bowl. Add the soy flour, sugar, and ½ cup (120 ml/4 fl oz) water and mix well. Add the cinnamon, cardamom, cloves, pepper, nutmeg, cocoa powder, and salt and mix again until the mixture is well blended. Add a little more water if the dough is too dry. Refrigerate for 2 hours.

Preheat the oven to 375°F/180°C/Gas Mark 5. Line a baking sheet with parchment (baking) paper.

Make a 2-inch (5 cm) wide cylinder with the dough and cut it into ¼-inch (5 mm) slices. Place these on the prepared baking sheet, leaving enough space between them to allow the cookies to spread during baking. Bake for about 15 minutes. Set aside to chill.

Melt the dark chocolate in a heatproof bowl set over a pan of simmering water. Using a teaspoon, cover the cookies with the melted chocolate. Let cool for 15 minutes before serving.

Preparation time: 30 minutes
Cooking time: 15 minutes, plus 2 hours chilling and 15 minutes cooling

Makes about 16 (2-inch/5 cm) bars

- 3 tablespoons orange marmalade
- 1 cup (135 g) ground almonds
- 1 cup (135 g) ground hazelnuts
- 2 tablespoons chopped candied orange peel
- 2 tablespoons chopped candied lemon peel
- 3 tablespoons soy flour
- ⅔ cup (135 g) superfine (caster) sugar
- 1 teaspoon ground cinnamon
- 1 teaspoon ground cardamom
- ½ teaspoon ground cloves
- a pinch of freshly ground black/white pepper
- a pinch of ground nutmeg
- 2 tablespoons unsweetened cocoa powder
- a pinch of salt
- ¼ cup (60 g) dark chocolate chips, for glazing

FRIED BANANA AND PAPAYA WRAPS

PHILIPPINES

Spread the sugar on a plate. Cut the bananas in half lengthwise and immediately roll them in the sugar. Set aside.

Using a food processor, purée the mango. Set aside in the refrigerator.

Pour some water into a large bowl and soak 1 rice paper wrapper for 10 seconds. Transfer the wrapper to your work surface. Arrange a banana half in the middle of the wrapper, then add a quarter of the diced papaya on top. Fold the sides of the wrapper toward the center, over either end of the banana. Fold the top and bottom of the wrapper toward the center to wrap the banana tightly. Repeat with the remaining banana halves, diced papaya, and wrappers.

Heat the oil in a skillet (frying pan) over medium heat. Fry the wraps gently over medium-low heat until golden brown on all sides. Serve topped with the mango purée.

Preparation time: 20 minutes
Cooking time: 45 minutes

Serves 4

- 2 tablespoons packed light brown sugar
- 2 bananas
- ½ mango, peeled, pitted (stoned), and sliced
- 4 round spring-roll rice paper wrappers
- 1 small papaya, diced
- 3 tablespoons vegetable oil

ORANGE-GINGER CHEESECAKE

Preparation time: 30 minutes

Cooking time: 1 hour 30 minutes, plus
  50 minutes cooling and 3 hours chilling

Makes 1 (8-inch/20 cm) cake

For the base:
- 3 cups (375 g) vegan ginger snap crumbs
- ⅓ cup (80 ml) melted vegetable margarine

For the cheesecake filling:
- 3 cups (720 g) Vegan Cream Cheese (page 30), or store-bought, at room temperature
- 1 cup (240 g) vegan sour cream, at room temperature
- ½ cup (100 g) superfine (caster) sugar
- 4 tablespoons egg replacer, mixed with 8 tablespoons warm water
- grated zest and juice of 1 orange
- 1 cup (100 g) superfine (caster) sugar

For the topping:
- 1 cup (200 g) superfine (caster) sugar
- 2 tablespoons grated fresh ginger
- 4 oranges, peeled and membranes trimmed, segments divided

Preheat the oven to 250°F/130°C/Gas Mark ½.

To make the base, using a food processor fitted with a blade, pulse the ginger snaps to fine crumbs. Transfer to a bowl and mix in the melted vegetable margarine until combined. Press the mixture into the bottom of an 8-inch (20 cm) springform cake pan. Set aside in a freezer for 1 hour.

To make the cheesecake filling, whisk together the ingredients in a bowl until smooth. Taste and adjust the sweetness as needed. Pour the filling over the base. Bake for 1½ hours, until the filling is set. Let cool on a wire rack for 30 minutes.

To make the topping, put the sugar and ½ cup (120 ml/4 fl oz) water in a saucepan and heat gently over medium-low heat until the sugar has dissolved. Bring to a boil, then immediately reduce the heat to low and simmer for 3 minutes. Remove the pan from the heat, add the ginger and orange segments, and let cool for 20 minutes.

Arrange the orange segments over the cheesecake and brush with the ginger topping. Refrigerate for 2 hours before serving.

ORANGE-GINGER CHEESECAKE

MANGO CREAM

Preparation time: 20 minutes

Cooking time: 15 minutes, plus
  20 minutes chilling

Serves 4

- 2 tablespoons vegetable margarine
- 1 cup (125 g) vermicelli (seviyan)
- 4 cups (960 ml/32 fl oz) almond milk
- ½ cup (100 g) superfine (caster) sugar
- 1 cup (80 g) pistachios, crushed
- 2 tablespoons raisins
- 3 Ataulfo mangoes, diced

Melt the vegetable margarine in a skillet (frying pan). Add the vermicelli and fry gently over medium heat for 3–4 minutes. Set aside.

Put the almond milk into a saucepan and bring to a boil over medium heat, then and add the sugar and reduce immediately to medium-low and bring the mixture to a simmer. Add the vermicelli to the almond milk and simmer for 6 minutes, add pistachios and raisins and simmer for 3–4 minutes over low heat. Remove the pan from the stove and let cool for 20 minutes. Divide the mixture between 4 dessert cups, top with the mango, and serve.

PANNA COTTA
WITH CARAMEL SAUCE

Preparation time: 20 minutes

Cooking time: 30 minutes, plus
  30 minutes chilling

Serves 4

- 2 cups (480 ml/16 fl oz) almond milk
- 2 teaspoons agar-agar
- 2 tablespoons caster sugar
- 1 vanilla pod, seeds scraped
- 2 tablespoons agave or maple syrup, plus extra as needed
- ¼ cup (50 g) coconut sugar

Place the almond milk, agar-agar, and caster sugar in a saucepan and warm over medium heat. Add the vanilla seeds and bring to a low simmer. Add the agave or maple syrup, stir well, taste, and adjust the sweetness according to your taste.

Pour the mix into 4 (4-inch/10 cm) ramekins (10 cm) and let cool for 20 minutes, then refrigerate for 2 hours.

Put the coconut sugar in a small saucepan, over medium heat, with 2 tablespoons of water and warm until the sugar dissolves, stirring constantly. Remove the pan from the heat and let cool for 20 minutes. Cover the panna cotta in each ramekin with the liquid sugar and return to the refrigerator. Chill for 30 minutes before serving.

MANGO-CHOCOLATE MOUSSE

Using a food processor, purée the mangos until smooth. Leave the purée in the bowl of the food processor.

Heat the creamed coconut in a bain-marie until melted and add it to the mango purée. Blend for 2 minutes, until the mixture is smooth and creamy. Add the cocoa powder and blend until well incorporated. Leave the mixture in the bowl of the food processor.

With the motor of the food processor running on slow speed, gradually pour the melted chocolate into the mango-coconut mix and process until incorporated. Add the maple or agave syrup, increase the speed to high, and blend until the mixture is very creamy.

Spoon the mousse into 4 dessert cups and refrigerate for 2 hours before serving. Decorate with mint leaves to serve.

Preparation time: 30 minutes
Cooking time: 15 minutes, plus
  2 hours chilling

Serves 4

- 4 Ataulfo mangoes, sliced
- ½ cup (120 g) creamed coconut
- ½ cup (50 g) unsweetened cocoa powder
- 12½ oz (360 g) dark chocolate, melted
- 2 tablespoons maple or agave syrup
- mint leaves, to garnish

PAPAYA AND COCONUT PUDDING

Scoop out the papaya flesh. Transfer the papaya flesh to a bowl and mash it with a fork into a smooth purée.

Transfer the papaya purée to a saucepan, add the coconut cream, and bring to a simmer over medium-low heat, stirring frequently. Add the sugar and stir until it has completely melted, then add the cornstarch gradually, until fully incorporated. Simmer gently over low heat for 10 minutes until smooth. Pour the mixture into 4 dessert cups and refrigerate for 1 hour before serving.

Preparation time: 20 minutes
Cooking time: 15 minutes

Serves 4

- 12 oz (360 g) papaya, halved and seeded
- 1½ cups (360 ml/12 fl oz) coconut cream
- 1 cup (90 g) coconut sugar
- ½ cup (120 g) cornstarch (cornflour)

LIME CHEESECAKE (RAW)

Preparation time: 25 minutes, plus
   1 hour freezing and 2 hours chilling
Cooking time: none

Makes 1 (9-inch/23 cm) cake

   For the base:
- vegetable oil, for greasing
- 2 cups (240 g) raw cashews, soaked
  in water overnight and drained
- 1 cup (90 g) coconut flakes
- ½ cup (120 g) pitted (stoned) dates
- ½ cup (50 g) raw cacao nibs
- a pinch of salt

   For the filling:
- 1 large Hass avocado, peeled and pitted
  (stoned)
- 1½ cups (360 g) cashews, soaked in water
  for at least 2 hours and drained
- ½ cup (120 ml/4 fl oz) melted coconut oil
- ¼ cup (60 ml/2 fl oz) fresh lime juice
- ½ cup (120 ml/4 fl oz) maple syrup or
  agave syrup
- 1 teaspoon vanilla extract
- a pinch of sea salt
- 1 tablespoon finely grated lime zest
  (optional)

Grease a 9-inch (23 cm) springform cake pan with vegetable oil. To make the base, using a food processor, pulse the cashews, coconut flakes, pitted dates, cacao nibs, and salt a couple of times until they are mixed and broken down. Spoon the mixture evenly over the bottom of the prepared cake pan. Press with your fingers to make a firm base. Set aside in the refrigerator.

To make the filling, using a food processor or a high-speed blender, combine all the ingredients and process until smooth and creamy. Spread the filling over the base and, using a rubber spatula, create a smooth surface.

Chill the pie in the freezer for 1 hour, then transfer to the refrigerator for 2 hours before serving.

LIME CHEESECAKE (RAW)

APPLE AND CRANBERRY PURÉE

Preparation time: 20 minutes
Cooking time: 35 minutes, plus
   20 minutes chilling

Serves 4

- 2 cups (400 g) packed dark brown sugar
- 2 teaspoons ground cinnamon
- 1 teaspoon ground nutmeg
- 1 teaspoon ground cloves
- 1 cup (240 ml/8 fl oz) fresh orange juice
- 2 cups (360 g) fresh or frozen cranberries
- 10 Granny Smith apples, peeled, cored, and sliced

Put the sugar, cinnamon, nutmeg, and cloves in a saucepan and add the orange juice. Bring the mixture to a simmer and add the cranberries. Cook over medium heat for 20 minutes, until the cranberries begin to pop. Add the apples and cook over low heat, stirring frequently, for 12–14 minutes, until the apples are tender and falling apart. Using a food processor or high-speed blender, purée the mixture—or use a potato masher if you like more texture.

Refrigerate for 20 minutes before serving, or serve lukewarm.

COCONUT CREAM SQUARES

Preparation time: 20 minutes
Cooking time: 15 minutes

Serves 4

- 2 tablespoons vegetable margarine, plus extra for greasing
- 1 lb 2 oz (500 g) coconut meat, finely chopped
- 4½ oz (125 g) creamed coconut
- ¾ cup (180 g) silken tofu
- 1¼ cups (250 g) superfine (caster) sugar
- 1 teaspoon ground cardamom
- 2 teaspoons rose water
- 1 cup (110 g) slivered almonds

Preheat the broiler (grill). Grease a 9–10-inch (23–25 cm) square oven dish or cake pan with vegetable margarine.

Heat the vegetable margarine in a skillet (frying pan). Add the coconut meat and sauté over medium heat for 3–4 minutes, until golden. Reduce the heat to low, add the creamed coconut, silken tofu, superfine sugar, and ground cardamom, and stir to blend. Cook for 7–8 minutes, until the creamed coconut and sugar have completely melted. Mix in the rose water, then remove the pan from the stove. Transfer the coconut mixture to the prepared dish. Top with the slivered almonds.

Position the dish under the broiler at mid-height in the oven and broil (grill) for 3–4 minutes, until the almonds are turning golden. Remove immediately and let cool. Cut into squares before serving.

APPLE AND MANGO CASSEROLE

Preheat the oven to 400°F/200°C/Gas Mark 6. Grease a 9-inch (23 cm) square baking dish.

Melt the vegetable margarine in a saucepan over low heat, then add the breadcrumbs, mix well, and increase the heat to medium. Cook for 5 minutes, stirring frequently, until golden brown. Remove the pan from the stove.

Put the apple slices in a bowl with the superfine sugar, lemon juice, ground cinnamon, and nutmeg and toss to coat the apple in the spice mixture.

Spread half of the breadcrumb mixture in the prepared dish. Top with the apple–spice mixture and mango, then cover the fruit with remaining breadcrumb mixture. Spoon any remaining liquids from the apple bowl over the top. Cover the dish with aluminum foil and bake for 20 minutes, until the apples are well cooked and tender. Serve warm.

Preparation time: 15 minutes
Cooking time: 25 minutes

Serves 4

- ¼ cup (60 g) vegetable margarine, plus extra for greasing
- ½ cup (70 g) breadcrumbs
- 1 lb 2 oz (500 g) apples, cored and sliced
- ½ cup (115 g) superfine (caster) sugar
- juice of 1 lemon
- 2 teaspoons ground cinnamon
- 1 teaspoon ground nutmeg
- 1 lb 2 oz (500 g) Ataulfo mango, sliced

AVOCADO AND PINEAPPLE CREAM WITH RUM

Scoop the avocado flesh out of the shells. Using a food processor or high-speed blender, pulse the avocado, sugar, diced pineapple, and soy cream until combined. Add the rum and pulse 2–3 times to combine. Taste and adjust the sweetness by adding more sugar if needed.

Transfer the mixture to a serving bowl and refrigerate for 1 hour. Serve in dessert cups or ramekins, each garnished with a pineapple slice.

Preparation time: 20 minutes, plus 1 hour chilling
Cooking time: none

Serves 4

- 3 large avocados, halved and pitted (stoned)
- ½ cup (50 g) superfine (caster) sugar, plus more as needed
- ½ cup (120 g) diced pineapple, plus 4 thin pineapple slices, to garnish
- 1 cup (240 ml/8 fl oz) soy cream
- 2 tablespoons rum

CHOCOLATE-MINT MACARONS

Preparation time: 35 minutes, plus
  30 minutes resting
Cooking time: 20 minutes, plus
  45 minutes chilling

Serves 4

For the macarons:
- 2 cups (260 g) ground almonds
- 2 cups (240 g) confectioners' (icing) sugar
- 5 tablespoons liquid from canned chickpeas
- 1 teaspoon xanthan gum
- ⅓ cup (65 g) superfine (caster) sugar
- 1 teaspoon peppermint extract

For the chocolate cream:
- 1⅓ cups (300 g) dark chocolate chips
- 4 tablespoons coconut cream

To make the macarons, sift the ground almonds and confectioners' sugar into a bowl and set aside. Line a baking sheet with parchment (baking) paper.

Using a food processor or hand-held electric mixer, whisk the chickpea juice on a high-speed setting until it begins to thicken, then slowly sprinkle in the xanthan gum. Once soft peaks start to form, slowly whisk in the superfine sugar 1 teaspoon at a time. Add the peppermint extract and continue to whisk for 1 minute. Gradually whisk the ground almond mixture into the meringue until well combined and firm. Transfer the mixture to a pastry (piping) bag.

Pipe the meringue onto the parchment paper in 1-inch (2.5 cm) diameter circles. Flatten the little peaks on the tops of the macarons so that they are flat. Set aside for 30 minutes. Preheat the oven to 275°F/140°C/Gas Mark 1.

Bake the macarons for 15 minutes, then leave the oven door open for 2 minutes to let out the heat. Close the oven door and bake for another 5 minutes, until the macarons are firm. Let cool completely on the baking sheet.

To make the chocolate cream, melt the chocolate and coconut cream together in a saucepan over medium heat. Once the chocolate has melted, transfer to a container and refrigerate for 45 minutes.

To assemble the macarons, place 1½ teaspoons of chocolate cream on the flat surface of half of the macarons, and sandwich with the remaining macarons, pressing gently until the cream fills the space between the macarons completely. Repeat with the remaining macarons and chocolate sauce. Serve immediately.

CHOCOLATE-MINT MACARONS

SWEET CANNELLONI ROLLS

Preparation time: 20 minutes, plus
1 hour draining
Cooking time: 15 minutes

Serves 4

- 1 cup (200 g) superfine (caster) sugar
- 1 lb 2 oz (500 g) cannelloni
- 1 lb 2 oz (500 g) firm tofu
- ¼ cup (60 g) cashew cream
- 1 tablespoon fresh lemon juice
- 1 tablespoon finely grated orange zest
- ¼ cup (60 g) dark chocolate chips
- 1 tablespoon cognac or brandy
- 2 tablespoons maraschino cherries, halved, to decorate
- 1 tablespoon confectioners' (icing) sugar, for dusting

Put the sugar into a saucepan filled with water, bring to a boil, and add the cannelloni. Cook according to the packet instructions until al dente. Drain carefully under cold running water to stop the cooking, taking care not to break the shells. Set aside.

Drain the tofu and wrap it in a clean kitchen towel. Leave for 1 hour to remove as much excess water as possible.

Using a food processor, pulse the tofu to a thick cream. Put it into a large bowl with the sugar, cashew cream, lemon juice, orange zest, chocolate chips, and cognac or brandy and stir well to blend. Taste and adjust the sweetness by adding sugar if needed. Set aside in the refrigerator.

Fill a pastry (piping) bag with the sweetened tofu mixture. Pipe the mixture into each cannelloni shell and place on a tray. Decorate each end with half of a cherry and set the finished cannelloni on a plate. Repeat with the remaining shells, filling, and cherries. Dust the cannelloni with confectioners' sugar and serve.

APPLE AND CINNAMON COMPOTE

Preparation time: 20 minutes
Cooking time: 35 minutes, plus
20 minutes cooling

Serves 4

- 6 apples, cored and sliced
- 2 ripe bananas, mashed
- 2 tablespoons cornstarch (cornflour)
- ½ cup (80 g) raisins
- 1 teaspoon ground cinnamon
- 1 tablespoon crushed walnuts, to decorate

Preheat the oven to 350°F/180°C/Gas Mark 4. Mix the apples, bananas, cornstarch, raisins, and cinnamon in a baking dish. Bake for 35 minutes, until the apples are tender. Let cool for 20 minutes.

Spoon the mixture into dessert glasses or cups and sprinkle over the walnuts. Serve warm.

APPLE AND RAISIN PIE

To make the piecrust, mix the flours and salt in a large bowl. Add the olive oil and, using your hands, mix the oil into the flour evenly until the mixture forms a breadcrumb consistency. Add ½ cup (120 ml)/4 fl oz) water and mix until the dough is smooth. Form the dough into a ball, transfer to a bowl, cover with plastic wrap (clingfilm), and set aside at room temperature until ready to bake.

To make the filling, put half of the apple juice into a saucepan and bring to a boil, then add the raisins and cook over medium heat for about 15 minutes, until the apple juice is completely absorbed by the fruit.

Mix the remaining apple juice with the cornstarch in a skillet (frying pan) and bring to a boil, then immediately reduce the heat to a simmer and cook over medium-low heat for about 10 minutes, until the juice thickens. Add the thickened apple juice to the raisin mixture in the saucepan, stir well, and let cool.

Mix the sugar, flour, cinnamon, and salt in a small bowl. Set aside.

Preheat the oven to 425°F/220°C/Gas Mark 7. Grease a 10-inch (25 cm) round tart pan with the vegetable margarine.

Mix the lemon juice with 4½ cups (1 liter/34 fl oz) water in a large bowl. Add the apples and let soak for 10 minutes. Drain the apples and combine with the raisin–apple juice mixture. Sprinkle over the sugar-flour-cinnamon blend and stir well.

Dust your work surface with flour. Roll out the dough to a 11-inch (28 cm) circle. Line the pan with the rolled-out dough and press it into the bottom and sides. Cut away any overhang and, using a fork, pierce the dough a few times. Spread the apple-raisin mixture inside the piecrust. Bake for 10 minutes, then reduce the oven temperature to 350°F/180°C/Gas Mark 4 and bake for about 40 minutes, until golden brown. Let cool for 15 minutes. Serve lukewarm.

Preparation time: 30 minutes
Cooking time: 1 hour 25 minutes

Makes 1 (10-inch/25 cm) pie

For the piecrust:
- 1 cup (125 g) whole-wheat (wholemeal) flour
- ½ cup (65 g) all-purpose (plain) flour, plus extra for dusting
- a pinch of salt
- 4 tablespoons olive oil
- 1 tablespoon vegetable margarine, for greasing

For the filling:
- 1½ cups (350 ml/12 fl oz) apple juice
- 1½ cups (240 g) raisins
- 1 tablespoon cornstarch (cornflour)
- ½ cup (65 g) superfine (caster) sugar
- 1 tablespoon all-purpose (plain) flour
- 1 teaspoon ground cinnamon
- a pinch of salt
- 1 tablespoon fresh lemon juice
- 2 lb (1 kg) cored and sliced pie apples, such as Granny Smith

BAKED PAPAYA
WITH COCONUT CREAM

Preparation time: 20 minutes
Cooking time: 1 hour 30 minutes

Serves 4

- 2 small papayas (not too ripe), halved
  lengthwise, seeded
- ½ cup (100 g) granulated sugar
- 1 cup (240 ml/8 fl oz) coconut cream
- ⅓ cup (45 g) confectioners' (icing) sugar
- 1 teaspoon vanilla extract
- ½ cup (120 ml/4 fl oz) coconut milk

Preheat the oven to 375°F/190°C/Gas Mark 5.

Arrange the halved papayas, with the cut sides facing up, in a shallow baking dish. Sprinkle over the granulated sugar and add 4 tablespoons of water to the pan. Bake in the middle of the oven for 1½ hours, until the papayas are tender.

Meanwhile, make the coconut cream. Using a food processor or blender, process the coconut cream, confectioners' sugar, and vanilla extract for 2 minutes, until well blended. Transfer to a bowl and refrigerate until serving.

Using a spoon, collect the juice of the papaya every half hour. Reserve the juice to sprinkle over the coconut cream at serving time.

About 5 minutes before the end of cooking, raise the oven temperature to 400°F/200°C/Gas Mark 6. After 5 minutes, turn off the heat, transfer the papaya to plates, and pour the coconut milk into the cavities of the papayas. Serve on shallow plates, with the chilled thick coconut cream on side. Sprinkle the reserved papaya juice on top of the chilled thick coconut cream.

BAKED PAPAYA WITH COCONUT CREAM

MANGO CREAM CAKE

Preparation time: 30 minutes, plus
  3–4 hours chilling
Cooking time: none

Makes 1 (9-inch/23 cm) pie

- 4 Ataulfo mangoes, peeled and pitted
  (stoned)
- ¾ cup (180 g) coconut oil, melted
- ½ cup (100 g) superfine (caster) sugar
- ½ cup (120 ml/4 fl oz) almond milk
- 1 cup (240 ml/8 fl oz) soy whipping cream
- 24 vegan ladyfinger cookies (biscuits)

Roughly chop 3 of the mangoes, and using a food processor, blend the chopped mangoes, coconut oil, sugar, and almond milk for 3–4 minutes, until smooth. Set aside.

Whip the soy cream until firm peaks form. Set aside.

Arrange 12 ladyfingers across the bottom on a 9-inch (23 cm) square cake pan.

Fold the mango cream into the whipped cream, then pour half of the mixture over the ladyfingers. Arrange a second layer with the remaining ladyfingers on top, then cover with remaining cream. Slice the remaining mango into paper-thin slices and use them to decorate the cake. Refrigerate for 3–4 hours before serving.

PASSIONFRUIT AND LEMON PIE

Preparation time: 30 minutes, plus
  overnight and 2 hours freezing
Cooking time: none

Makes 1 (10-inch/25 cm) tart

For the filling:
- 1 cup (240 ml/8 fl oz) coconut cream
- ½ cup (120 g) vegan cream cheese
  (page 30) or store-bought, at room
  temperature
- 1 cup (120 g) confectioners' (icing) sugar
- ¾ cup (180 ml) passionfruit pulp, divided
- 3 tablespoons fresh lemon juice
- 1 teaspoon vanilla extract

For the base:
- ¾ cup (180 g) coarsely crumbled graham
  crackers (digestive biscuits)
- ⅓ cup (80 g) vegetable margarine, plus
  extra for greasing
- ¼ cup (50 g) superfine (caster) sugar

To start the filling, pour the coconut cream into a bowl and refrigerate overnight.

To make the base, using a food processor or a high-speed blender, pulse the graham crackers to crumbs, then add the vegetable margarine and sugar and pulse until well mixed.

Grease a 10-inch (25 cm) round tart pan with vegetable margarine and press the mixture into the bottom and sides. Set aside in the freezer.

Return to the filling: using a food processor, combine the chilled coconut cream with the cream cheese, sugar, ½ cup (120 ml/4 fl oz) of the passionfruit pulp, the lemon juice, and vanilla extract and process to a creamy and smooth mixture. Spread the mixture evenly across the base and freeze for 2 hours.

Transfer the pie from the freezer to the refrigerator 1 hour before serving. Top with the remaining passionfruit pulp and serve.

STRAWBERRY MOCHI

Preheat the oven to 350°F/180°C/Gas Mark 4.

Make 8 small balls with the red bean paste. Flatten each ball, so that they are large enough to wrap all around a strawberry. Wrap each strawberry in the flattened paste to seal it completely.

Put the rice flour into a bowl. Gradually mix in ½ cup (120 ml/4 fl oz) water, then stir in the sugar. Transfer the mixture to an ovenproof dish and bake for 10–12 minutes, until firm.

Spread the arrowroot powder on a plate. Roll each red bean–strawberry ball in the powder.

Wet your hands and make a ball with the rice flour dough. Separate the dough into 8 equal portions and roll each into a small ball. Flatten each ball into a thin circle. Wrap the rice flour circles around the red bean–strawberry balls. Sprinkle the confectioners' sugar over the strawberry mochi and refrigerate for 30 minutes before serving.

Preparation time: 30 minutes
Cooking time: 15 minutes

Serves 4

- ¾ cup (180 g) red bean paste
- 8 strawberries, hulled
- ⅔ cup (80 g) rice flour
- 2 tablespoons superfine (caster) sugar
- 2 tablespoons arrowroot powder
- 2 tablespoons confectioners' (icing) sugar, for dusting

CANTALOUPE
AND BANANA SORBET

Preparation time: 20 minutes, plus
  overnight and 2 hours freezing
Cooking time: none

Serves 4

- 2 lb (1 kg) sliced cantaloupe
- 2 bananas, sliced
- 1 tablespoon fresh lemon juice
- superfine (caster) sugar (optional)
- 1 tablespoon chopped mint leaves,
  to garnish

Put the cantaloupe and bananas into an airtight container and freeze overnight.

Using a food processor or high-speed blender, process the frozen fruits and lemon juice until smooth. Taste and adjust the sweetness by adding superfine sugar, if needed. Place the fruit purée in an airtight container and freeze for 2 hours.

Scoop the sorbet into bowls, decorate with chopped mint leaves, and serve.

CANTALOUPE AND BANANA SORBET

BANANA AKARAS

Preparation time: 20 minutes, plus
 30 minutes chilling
Cooking time: 30 minutes

Serves 4

- 4 ripe bananas
- 1 fresh vanilla bean, seeds scraped,
 or 1 teaspoon vanilla extract
- ½ cup (100 g) superfine (caster) sugar
- 1 cup (160 g) rice flour, plus more as
 needed
- vegetable oil, for deep-frying
- 2 tablespoons confectioners' (icing) sugar,
 for dusting

Using a food processor or high-speed blender, process the bananas with the vanilla and superfine sugar until very smooth. With the motor running at a slow-speed setting, gradually add the rice flour, then ½ cup (120 ml/4 fl oz) hot water until the mixture forms a dough. If the mixture becomes too liquid, add more rice flour as necessary. Transfer the mixture to a bowl and refrigerate for 30 minutes.

Heat 2 tablespoons of vegetable oil in a nonstick skillet (frying pan). Drop 3 or 4 tablespoonfuls of the batter into the oil, leaving enough space between each one to avoid sticking. Fry on both sides until golden brown. Transfer to a plate, dust with confectioners' sugar, and set aside. Repeat the process with additional oil and the remaining batter. Serve warm.

ALMOND-STUFFED MEDJOOL DATES

Preparation time: 30 minutes, plus 1 hour
 30 minutes chilling
Cooking time: none

Serves 4

- 1 cup (135 g) blanched almonds
- 1½ cups (190 g) confectioners' (icing) sugar
- 2 teaspoons almond extract
- 1 tablespoon rose water
- 1 tablespoon egg replacer, mixed with
 2 tablespoons warm water
- 1 lb 2 oz (500 g) Medjool dates
- 1 cup (100 g) coconut flakes
- 30 walnut halves, to garnish

Using a food processor, pulse the blanched almonds and confectioners' sugar until well combined. Add the almond extract and rose water and pulse to combine. Add the egg replacer and process to form a thick paste. Turn out the almond marzipan onto a clean, dry work surface and knead it a few times, then shape it into a ball, wrap it in plastic wrap (clingfilm), and refrigerate for 30 minutes.

Make a lengthwise cut in each date deep enough to remove and discard the pit, but not to cut the date in half. Discard the pits and insert enough of the marzipan mixture to fill each date, leaving a portion of the paste exposed.

Spread the coconut flakes on a plate. Roll the dates in the coconut flakes, and decorate each stuffed date by placing a walnut half on top of the marzipan paste. Refrigerate for 1 hour before serving.

BANANAS COOKED IN COCONUT MILK WITH TAPIOCA

Rinse the tapioca in a strainer (sieve) under cold running water.

Bring a saucepan of water to a boil. Add the tapioca and cook over medium heat for 10–12 minutes, stirring frequently, until translucent. Drain off excess liquid and set aside.

Peel each banana or plantain and cut into 3 or 4 pieces.

Bring the coconut milk to a simmer in a saucepan. Add the bananas and dates and cook gently over medium-low heat for 10–12 minutes, until the bananas are soft but not mushy. Remove the pan from the stove. Add the tapioca and stir well. Serve warm or with ice cubes.

Preparation time: 20 minutes
Cooking time: 25 minutes

Serves 4

- ½ cup (65 g) tapioca flour
- 8 bananas or very ripe plantains
- 2 cups (475 ml/16 fl oz) thick coconut milk
- 6 Medjool dates or other large dates, pitted (stoned) and finely chopped

FIG AND CREAM CHEESE VERRINE

Preheat the oven to 400°F/200°C/Gas Mark 6.

Arrange the figs in a baking dish, sprinkle with cinnamon, and drizzle with agave syrup. Bake for about 35 minutes or until the top is golden brown. Let cool for 20 minutes.

Whip the soy cream to stiff peaks, then gradually whisk in the cream cheese, confectioners' sugar, and vanilla extract and continue to whisk until the mixture is smooth.

Place 2 figs halves in a dessert cup, top with 1 tablespoon cream, add 1 tablespoon caramel popcorn, then cover the popcorn with cream. Continue adding figs and popcorn in alternating layers, with some cream between each layer, until all the ingredients except ¼ cup (25 g) of popcorn are used. Decorate the tops with popcorn and stick 1 cinnamon stick into the cream, like a straw.

Preparation time: 20 minutes
Cooking time: 35 minutes, plus 20 minutes chilling

Serves 4

- 16 fresh figs, halved vertically
- 2 teaspoons ground cinnamon
- 4 tablespoons agave syrup
- 1 cup (240 ml/8 fl oz) whipping soy cream
- ⅓ cup (80 g) Vegan Cream Cheese (page 30) or store-bought
- ½ cup (60 g) confectioners' (icing) sugar
- 1 teaspoon vanilla extract
- 1 cup (100 g) vegan caramel popcorn
- 4 cinnamon sticks, to decorate

BANANA-PINEAPPLE CAKE

Preparation time: 35 minutes
Cooking time: 40 minutes, plus
  30 minutes cooling and 50 minutes chilling

Makes 1 (10-inch/25 cm) cake

For the cake:
- vegetable margarine or oil, for greasing
- 2 cups (250 g) self-rising flour
- 2 teaspoons ground cinnamon
- 1½ cups (300 g) superfine (caster) sugar
- 4 ripe bananas
- 1 lb 2 oz (500 g) sweet pineapple pieces
- 1 cup (240 ml/8 fl oz) olive oil
- 2 tablespoons egg replacer, mixed with
  4 tablespoons warm water

For the frosting (icing):
- ½ cup (120 g) vegetable margarine
- 1½ cups (180 g) confectioners' (icing) sugar
- ½ cup (120 g) unsalted vegan cream
  cheese (page 30) or store-bought
- 3 tablespoons fresh lemon juice
- 1 tablespoon finely grated lemon zest

For the candied nuts:
- 1 tablespoon coconut oil
- 1 cup (120 g) walnuts or pecans, chopped
- 2 tablespoons superfine (caster) sugar

Preheat the oven to 400°F/200°C)/Gas Mark 6. Grease a 10-inch (25 cm) round can pan with vegetable margarine or oil.

To make the cake batter, in a bowl sift together the flour and cinnamon, then mix in the sugar.

Using a food processor, pulse together the bananas and pineapple, then add the oil and egg replacer and pulse until smooth.

Transfer the batter to a large bowl and slowly mix in the dry ingredients until well blended and lump-free. Pour the batter into the prepared cake pan and bake for 40 minutes, until golden brown. Let cool for 30 minutes, then remove from the pan.

To make the frosting, whisk together the vegetable margarine and confectioners' sugar in a bowl, then slowly whisk in the cream cheese, lemon juice, and half of the lemon zest until smooth and creamy. Using a rubber spatula, spread half of the frosting across the top of the cake, then refrigerate for 20 minutes.

To make the candied nuts, melt the coconut oil in a saucepan over medium heat, then add the crushed nuts and sugar and cook for 6–7 minutes, until the sugar has melted and the nuts are caramelized. Let cool for 10 minutes.

Dot the cooled candied nuts across the frosting on the cake, then cover with the remaining frosting. Sprinkle the remaining lemon zest on top and refrigerate the cake for 30 minutes before serving.

GRILLED BANANAS
WITH COCONUT CREAM

Preparation time: 20 minutes
Cooking time: 25 minutes

Serves 4

- ½ cup (120 g) applesauce
- ½ cup (100 g) superfine (caster) sugar
- ½ cup (120 ml/4 fl oz) coconut cream
- 1 cup (125 g) all-purpose (plain) flour
- ¼ cup (60 g) vegetable margarine
- 1 teaspoon vanilla extract
- ¼ teaspoon baking soda (bicarbonate
  of soda)
- 2 tablespoons coconut oil
- a pinch of salt
- 4 ripe bananas
- 4 banana leaves

Preheat the broiler (grill).

To make the coconut sauce, heat the applesauce, sugar, coconut cream, flour, vegetable margarine, vanilla extract, and baking soda in a saucepan over medium heat, stirring constantly, for 5 minutes, until blended. Add the coconut oil and salt, reduce the heat to low, and cook for 5 minutes. Set aside.

Peel the bananas, wrap each banana in a piece of banana leaf, and arrange them in a baking pan. Position the pan on a low rack in the oven and broil (grill) for 5–6 minutes, until golden brown on each side.

Unwrap the bananas and divide the bananas among 4 plates. Cover with the sauce and serve warm.

BANANAS IN ORANGE JUICE AND COCONUT

Preheat the oven to 400°F/200°C/Gas Mark 6.

Arrange the bananas in a 9-inch (23 cm) square baking dish. Pour over the melted vegetable margarine and drizzle with the orange and lemon juices. Sprinkle with the cinnamon, brown sugar, and coconut and bake for about 12 minutes, until lightly golden.

Sprinkle with the agave syrup, then return the dish to the oven in broil (grill) position and broil for 2 minutes, until golden brown. Serve immediately, with ice cream on the side, if using.

Preparation time: 15 minutes
Cooking time: 15 minutes

Serves 4

- 4 large bananas, sliced thick
- 3 tablespoons vegetable margarine, melted
- ½ cup (120 ml/4 fl oz) fresh orange juice
- juice of 2 lemons
- 1 teaspoon ground cinnamon
- ¼ cup (50 g) light brown sugar
- 2 cups (200 g) grated coconut
- 1 tablespoon agave syrup
- vegan vanilla ice cream, to serve (optional)

CHOCOLATE AND APPLE CAKE

Preheat the oven to 325°F/160°C/Gas Mark 3. Grease a 10-inch (25 cm) square cake pan with vegetable margarine.

Mix the dry ingredients together in a large bowl, then add the applesauce and stir until well mixed. Fold in the apples. Spoon the batter into the prepared cake pan and bake for 1 hour or until a skewer inserted into the center of the cake comes out clean. Let cool for 20 minutes, then remove from the pan.

Preparation time: 5 minutes
Cooking time: 1 hour, plus
  20 minutes cooling

Makes 1 (10-inch/25 cm) cake

- vegetable margarine, for greasing
- 2 cups (250 g) all-purpose (plain) flour
- 1 cup (200 g) superfine (caster) sugar
- 1 tablespoon cornstarch (cornflour)
- 2 teaspoons baking soda (bicarbonate of soda)
- a pinch of salt
- 1 teaspoon ground cinnamon
- ½ cup (50 g) unsweetened cocoa powder
- 1 lb 2 oz (500 g) unsweetened applesauce
- 2 ripe sweet apples, diced

LEMON-CINNAMON-RICE MILK

Preparation time: 30 minutes
Cooking time: 20 minutes

Serves 4

- 1¼ cups (260 g) long-grain white rice
- a pinch of salt
- 1 cinnamon stick
- finely grated zest of 1 lemon
- 4 cups (960 ml) coconut milk
- 1 cup (200 g) granulated sugar
- 1 teaspoon ground cinnamon, to garnish

Place the rice in a saucepot, and add the cinnamon, half of the zest, and salt. Cook the rice according to the packet instructions until cooked through. Add the coconut milk, sugar, and remaining lemon zest to the pan. Bring to a boil, then immediately reduce the heat to medium-low and simmer for about 15 minutes, until the mixture is very creamy. Remove the pan from the stove and transfer to serving bowls. Dust with cinnamon and serve warm.

LEMON-CINNAMON-RICE MILK

CANDIED KUMQUATS

Preparation time: 20 minutes
Cooking time: 35 minutes, plus 4 hours
   cooling

Serves 4

- 1½ cups (300 g) superfine (caster) sugar
- 1 lb 2 oz (500 g) kumquats, halved
- 1 teaspoon ground cinnamon
- 1 vanilla bean, seeds scraped
- vegan vanilla ice cream or sorbet, to serve

Combine the sugar and 1 cup (240 ml/8 fl oz) water in a medium saucepan and bring to a boil over medium heat. Add the kumquats, cinnamon, and vanilla bean and seeds. Reduce the heat to medium-low, and simmer gently for 20 minutes, until the kumquat skin is very tender. Remove the pan from the heat and let cool for 4 hours.

Strain the fruit from the syrup. Transfer the fruit to an airtight container. Pour the syrup into a saucepan and cook over medium heat for about 12 minutes, until thick.

Pour the syrup over the kumquats. Refrigerate until ready to serve.

Serve with 1 scoop of vegan vanilla ice cream or a sorbet.

CHERRY CLAFOUTIS

Preparation time: 15 minutes
Cooking time: 40 minutes, plus
   20 minutes cooling

Makes 1 (10-inch/25 cm) tart

- vegetable margarine, for greasing
- ½ cup (65 g) all-purpose (plain) flour
- 1 tablespoon cornstarch (cornflour)
- ⅔ cup (160 g) silken tofu
- 1 teaspoon vanilla extract
- 1 teaspoon almond extract
- 4 tablespoons almond milk
- ¼ cup (50 g) superfine (caster) sugar
- 1 cup (240 g) frozen black cherries,
   defrosted and drained
- 2 tablespoons confectioners' (icing) sugar,
   for dusting

Preheat the oven to 375°F/190°C/Gas Mark 5. Grease a 10-inch (25 cm) round tart pan with vegetable margarine.

Whisk the flour and cornstarch in a large bowl and set aside.

Using a food processor or blender, purée the silken tofu, vanilla and almond extracts, and 1 tablespoon of the almond milk until very smooth. Transfer the mixture to the bowl with the flour and mix well to blend. Add the sugar and cherries and stir until combined. Add the remaining almond milk and stir a few more times until the mixture is smooth.

Pour the mixture into the prepared tart pan and bake for about 40 minutes, until golden. Let cool for 20 minutes, then dust with confectioners' sugar. Serve at room temperature.

GREEK CUSTARD CREAM

To make the sauce, put all the ingredients into a saucepan over medium heat and add 1½ cups (360 ml/12 fl oz) of water. Bring to a boil, then immediately reduce the heat and bring the mixture to a gentle simmer. Cook over low heat for 10 minutes. Let cool.

Preheat the oven to 400°F/200°C/Gas Mark 6

Use some of the vegetable margarine to grease a 10 x 7 x 3½-inch (25 x 18 x 9 cm) ovenproof dish.

Put the almond milk, vanilla seeds, semolina, sugar, lemon zest, and cinnamon stick into a saucepan. Whisk well to combine, then bring the mixture to a simmer over medium heat and cook for 8–10 minutes, stirring frequently, until the mixture has thickened. Remove the pan from the stove and discard the cinnamon stick.

Place 1 sheet of phyllo inside the prepared baking dish with the edges of the sheet overhanging the sides of the dish. Brush it with the melted vegetable margarine. Add a second sheet of phyllo on top and repeat the process until all the phyllo sheets are used. Pour the cooled custard over the phyllo stack. Fold the filo sheets over the custard and brush with the remaining vegetable margarine. Bake for 45 minutes.

Pour the sauce over the baked phyllo and custard and let cool for 30 minutes, then refrigerate for 1 hour before serving.

Preparation time: 15 minutes
Cooking time: 55 minutes, plus
   30 minutes cooling and 1 hour chilling

Serves 4

For the pastry:
- ⅓ cup (80 g) vegetable margarine melted
- 3 cups (750 ml/25 fl oz) almond milk
- 1 fresh vanilla pod, seeds scraped
- ½ cup (80 g) fine semolina
- ½ cup (100 g) superfine (caster) sugar
- 1 tablespoon finely grated lemon zest
- 1 cinnamon stick
- 6 sheets of phyllo (filo) pastry

For the sauce:
- ¼ cup (50 g) superfine (caster) sugar
- 2 cinnamon sticks
- 1 teaspoon finely grated lemon zest
- 2 tablespoons fresh lemon juice

BLOOD ORANGE CRÈME BRÛLÉE

Preparation time: 15 minutes
Cooking time: 40 minutes, plus
  1 hour chilling

Serves 4

- 1 vanilla bean, seeds scraped
- 1 cup (240 ml/8 fl oz) soy cream
- ¼ cup (60 ml) almond milk
- 2 tablespoons egg replacer, mixed with
  4 tablespoons warm water
- ¼ cup (50 g) plus 2 tablespoons superfine
  (caster) sugar, divided
- 4 tablespoons fresh orange juice
- 1 tablespoon finely grated orange zest

Preheat the oven to 300°F/150°C/Gas Mark 2.

Combine the vanilla, soy cream, and almond milk in a saucepan and stir well. Bring the mixture to a boil over medium heat, then immediately reduce the heat to low and simmer for 6 minutes, whisking occasionally, until the mixture thickens.

Combine the egg replacer with the ¼ cup superfine sugar in a large bowl, then gradually pour in the thickened cream, whisking constantly. Mix in the orange juice and zest.

Pour the mixture into 4 ramekins and place them in a large baking pan. Pour boiling water into the baking pan so that it reaches halfway up the sides of the ramekins. Transfer to the oven and bake for 35 minutes. Remove the ramekins from the oven and the water bath and refrigerate for 1 hour before serving.

Just before serving, sprinkle ½ tablespoon sugar on top of each ramekin and, using a kitchen blowtorch, caramelize the sugar until golden brown.

BLOOD ORANGE CRÈME BRÛLÉE

ORANGE-GRAPEFRUIT AND MINT CREAM

Preparation time: 30 minutes
Cooking time: none

Serves 4

- ⅔ cup (160 ml/5 fl oz) fresh grapefruit juice
- ⅔ cup (160 ml/5 fl oz) fresh orange juice
- ½ cup (120 g) silken tofu
- 2 peaches, peeled, pitted (stoned), and sliced
- 2 bananas, sliced
- 1½ cups (250 g) strawberries, sliced
- 1 cup (240 g) vegan vanilla ice cream
- mint leaves, to decorate

Using a food processor or high-speed blender, process the fruit juices, tofu, peaches, bananas, strawberries, and vegan ice cream until smooth and creamy. Pour the mixture into tall dessert cups. Decorate with mint leaves to serve.

POACHED APPLES AND WALNUT FILLING

Preparation time: 15 minutes
Cooking time: 40 minutes

Serves 4

- 1 cup (200 g) superfine (caster) sugar
- juice of 1 lemon
- 4 green apples, peeled (peel reserved)
- 1½ cups (135 g) chopped walnuts
- 2 tablespoons raisins, chopped
- 1½ cups (360 ml/12 fl oz) coconut cream, refrigerated overnight
- 2 tablespoons confectioners' (icing) sugar

Heat 3 cups (720 ml/24 fl oz) water with the sugar and lemon juice in a saucepan set over medium heat, stirring frequently, until the sugar has dissolved. Set aside.

Core the apples and add to the saucepan. Bring the mixture to a gentle simmer and cook over medium-low heat for about 8 minutes, until the apples are fork-tender. Remove the apples from the saucepan with a slotted spoon, transfer them to rest upright in the cups of a muffin pan, and let cool.

Add the apple peelings to the saucepan and continue to simmer the sugar syrup, for 30 minutes. Discard the peel and set aside the syrup.

Mix the walnuts and raisins in a bowl. Fill the centers of the apples with the walnut-raisin mixture. (Do this while the apples sit in the muffin pan, so they do not make a mess on the serving plates.)

Whisk the cold coconut cream with the confectioners' sugar. Transfer the stuffed apples to plates, pour some cream over the walnut-raisin filling, and serve.

PEARS IN CRANBERRY JUICE

SCOTLAND

Combine the cranberry juice, sugar, orange zest, cinnamon, and cloves in a saucepan, bring to a boil, then immediately reduce the heat to bring the mixture to a simmer and add the pears. Cover the pan and cook for 15 minutes, until the pears are tender. Let cool for 20 minutes. Serve warm in dessert cups.

Preparation time: 15 minutes
Cooking time: 15 minutes, plus
  20 minutes cooling

Serves 4

- 2 cups (475 ml/16 fl oz) cranberry juice
- 2 tablespoons superfine (caster) sugar
- 1 tablespoon finely grated orange zest
- 2 teaspoons ground cinnamon
- 2 teaspoons ground cloves
- 4 ripe pears, peeled, halved lengthwise, and cored

PRUNES WITH ALMONDS AND RAISINS

ETHIOPIA

Put the prunes, raisins, cloves, red wine, cinnamon, and sugar into a saucepan over medium heat. Bring the mixture to a boil, stirring regularly, then immediately reduce the heat to bring the mixture to a simmer. Add the chopped almonds and simmer at medium-low heat for 3–4 minutes. Discard the cloves and pour the mixture into a large dessert bowl. Serve warm.

Preparation time: 15 minutes
Cooking time: 10 minutes

Serves 4

- 1 lb 2 oz (500 g) soft prunes (pruneaux d'Agen), pitted (stoned)
- ½ cup (80 g) raisins
- 3 whole cloves
- 2 cups (475 ml/16 fl oz) red wine
- 2 teaspoons ground cinnamon
- ½ cup (100 g) superfine (caster) sugar
- ½ cup (65 g) almonds, chopped

CRANBERRY PUDDING

Preparation time: 20 minutes
Cooking time: 30 minutes, plus
  1 hour chilling

Serves 4

- 2 cups (480 g) fresh cranberries
- 2 cinnamon sticks
- 4 whole cloves
- 1 cup (200 g) superfine (caster) sugar
- 1 cup (125 g) cornstarch (cornflour)

Put the cranberries in a saucepan. Pour in enough water to cover the berries, and add the cinnamon and cloves. Bring the water to a boil, then reduce the heat to medium-low and simmer for 10-12 minutes, until the cranberries begin to pop. Remove the pan from the heat and let cool for 20 minutes.

Using a food processor or a high-speed blender, process the mixture for 2–3 minutes until very smooth. Add the sugar and blend for 2–3 minutes, until the sugar has been completely incorporated.

Transfer the mixture to a saucepan. Add half of the cranberry mixture and the cornstarch, stirring constantly until everything is well blended. Stir in the remaining cranberry mixture, then bring everything to a simmer, stirring frequently. Cook over medium-low heat for about 10 minutes, until the mixture thickens.

Transfer the cranberry pudding to 4 individual dishes and let cool for 20 minutes. Refrigerate for 30 minutes before serving.

CRANBERRY PUDDING

APRICOT AND CHOCOLATE PUDDING

Preparation time: 20 minutes
Cooking time: 30 minutes

Serves 4

For the pudding:
- 1 cup (200 g) superfine (caster) sugar
- 2 tablespoons egg replacer mixed with 4 tablespoons warm water
- 3 tablespoons apricot jam
- 1 cup (125 g) all-purpose (plain) flour
- ¼ cup (30 g) unsweetened cocoa powder
- 1 teaspoon baking powder
- a pinch of salt
- 1 cup (240 ml/8 fl oz) almond milk
- 1 teaspoon baking soda (bicarbonate of soda)
- 1 teaspoon white vinegar

For the sauce:
- ¼ cup (60 g) vegetable margarine
- 1 cup (200 g) superfine (caster) sugar
- 1 cup (240 ml/8 fl oz) soy cream
- 1 teaspoon vanilla extract
- vegan vanilla custard or vanilla ice cream, to serve

Preheat the oven to 400°F/200°C/Gas Mark 6.

To make the pudding, put the sugar, egg replacer, and jam into a large bowl and mix well.

Put the flour, cocoa powder, baking powder, and salt into another large bowl and mix well.

Stir the flour mixture into the sugar mixture, then slowly add the almond milk and mix to form a smooth batter.

Mix together the baking soda and vinegar in a small bowl. Fold this mixture into the batter.

Pour the batter into a 10-inch (25 cm) round baking dish and bake for 30 minutes, until golden brown. Let cool.

To make the sauce, while the pudding is baking, mix the ingredients in a saucepan with ½ cup (120 ml/4 fl oz) boiling water. Bring the mixture to a boil, then immediately reduce the heat to low and simmer gently for 8–10 minutes, until the mixture thickens to custard consistency.

As soon as the pudding is out of the oven, pour the sauce over the top. Let cool a little, then serve with vegan custard or ice cream.

PUMPKIN PUDDING

Preparation time: 20 minutes
Cooking time: 1 hour, plus 30 minutes chilling

Serves 4

- ½ small Hokkaido pumpkin, peeled and chopped
- 2 cups (480 ml/16 fl oz) coconut water
- 1 cup (200 g) superfine (caster) sugar
- 1 cup (240 g) fresh coconut meat, finely chopped

Preheat the oven to 350°F/180°C/Gas Mark 4. Put the pumpkin pieces into a large oven dish.

Combine the coconut water with the superfine sugar. Arrange the coconut meat over the pumpkin, then cover with the sweet coconut water. Bake for about 60 minutes or until the pumpkin is very soft. Let cool for 30 minutes. Divide among 4 dessert cups to serve.

COCONUT RICE
AND MANGO PUDDING

Preheat the oven to 350°F/180°C/Gas Mark 4. Lightly grease a 9-inch (23 cm) round ovenproof dish with the vegetable margarine.

Mix the rice, coconut milk, almond milk, lime zest, and sugar in a large bowl. Pour the mixture into the prepared dish and bake for about 15 minutes, until it thickens. Stir well, then add the star anise and return the dish to the oven. Cook for another 10–12 minutes, until almost all the almond milk has been absorbed and a golden brown skin has baked on the top of the pudding. Cover the top of the pudding with aluminum foil if it starts to brown too much. Let cool for 15–20 minutes, then mix with the mango before serving.

Preparation time: 10 minutes
Cooking time: 25 minutes, plus
    15–20 minutes cooling

Serves 4

- 2 tablespoons vegetable margarine, plus extra for greasing
- ⅓ cup (80 g) short-grain rice, such as Arborio or Carnaroli
- 2½ cups (600 ml/20 fl oz) coconut milk
- 2½ cups (600 ml/20 fl oz) almond milk
- 1 tablespoon finely grated lime zest
- ¼ cup (50 g) superfine (caster) sugar
- a pinch of ground star anise
- 1 Ataulfo mango, diced

HOT CHOCOLATE CAKE

Preheat the oven to 350°F/180°C/Gas Mark 4.

To make the cake, sift together flour, sugar, cocoa powder and baking powder. Stir in the almond milk and melted vegetable margarine mix well. Spoon the mixture into an 8-inch (20 cm) round cake pan. Bake for about 45 minutes. Let cool for 15 minutes.

While the cake is cooling, make the chocolate sauce. Mix caster sugar and chocolate powder in a sauce pan, add 5 tablespoons of water and cook at medium heat stirring constantly until all well melted and smooth. Add water if the mix is too thick (depends on the quality and cooking property of your chocolate powder)

Cut the cooled cake into slices and serve on dessert plates covered with chocolate sauce and ice cream on the side.

Preparation time: 20 minutes
Cooking time: 45 minutes, plus
    15 minutes chilling

Serves 4

For the cake:
- 1 cup (125 g) all-purpose (plain) flour
- ¼ cup (50 g) superfine (caster) sugar
- 2 tablespoons unsweetened cocoa powder
- 2 teaspoons baking powder
- ½ cup (120 ml/4 fl oz) almond milk
- 2 tablespoons vegetable margarine, melted
- vegan vanilla ice cream, to serve

For the chocolate sauce:
- 1 cup (200 g) superfine (caster) sugar
- ¼ cup (30 g) unsweetened cocoa powder
- 5 tablespoons hot water

CHOCOLATE TRUFFLES

Preparation time: 25 minutes
Cooking time: 10 minutes, plus
  1 hour chilling

Makes: 24–30 truffles

- ½ cup (120 g) vegetable margarine
- 1 teaspoon vanilla extract
- ½ cup (100 g) superfine (caster) sugar
- 3 cups (270 g) quick-cooking oats
- ⅓ cup (180 g) dark chocolate chips
- 3 tablespoons cognac or brandy
- unsweetened cocoa powder, for rolling

Mix the vegetable margarine, vanilla, sugar, and oats in a bowl until well blended.

Melt the chocolate in a heatproof bowl set over a saucepan of simmering water. Mix the melted chocolate into the vegetable margarine–oat mixture. Add the cognac or brandy and stir to combine.

Spread the cocoa powder on a plate. Using your hands, take walnut-size pieces of the mixture and roll them into balls, then roll them in the cocoa powder. This mixture should yield 24–30 chocolate truffles. Refrigerate for 1 hour before serving.

CHOCOLATE TRUFFLES

PEANUT BUTTER SILK CAKE

Preparation time: 15 minutes, plus
  3 hours freezing and 30 minutes resting
Cooking time: none

Makes 1 (8-inch/20 cm) tart

For the base:
- 25 vanilla cookies (around 9 oz/250 g)
- 5 teaspoons vegetable margarine, melted

For the filling:
- 1 cup (240 g) vegan cream cheese
  (page 30) or store-bought, at room
  temperature
- 1 cup (240 g) creamy peanut butter
- 1 cup (200 g) superfine (caster) sugar
- 3 cups (750 g) whipped soy cream

To make the base, using a food processor, pulse the cookies to fine crumbs. Transfer the crumbs to a bowl and stir in the vegetable margarine. Press the mixture firmly to an 8-inch (20 cm) round tart pan. Set aside in the freezer for 1 hour until completely frozen.

To make the filling, whisk together the cream cheese, peanut butter, and sugar in a large bowl. Gradually add the whipped soy cream and mix well. Spread the filling over the base and freeze for 2 hours. Allow the pie to thaw at room temperature for 30 minutes before serving.

RASPBERRY AND CHOCOLATE PIE

Preparation time: 35 minutes, plus
  2 nights of overnight chilling
Cooking time: none

Makes 1 (9-inch/23 cm) tart

For the base:
- vegetable margarine, for greasing
- 1 packet (8 oz/220 g) graham crackers
  (digestive biscuits)
- ½ cup (50 g) unsweetened cocoa powder
- 2 tablespoons superfine (caster) sugar
- ⅔ cup (160 ml) melted vegetable margarine

For the filling:
- 2 cups (475 ml/16 fl oz) coconut cream
- ½ cup (60 g) confectioners' (icing) sugar,
  plus extra for dusting
- 1 teaspoon vanilla extract
- ½ cup (120 g) vegan cream cheese
  (page 30) or store-bought
- 9 oz (250 g) dark chocolate, melted
- 1 cup (125 g) raspberries

Place the coconut cream for the filling in a bowl and refrigerate overnight.

Grease a 9-inch (23 cm) round tart pan with vegetable margarine.

To make the base, using a food processor or high-speed blender, pulse the graham crackers, cocoa powder, and sugar, then gradually add the melted vegetable margarine and pulse to make crumbs. Press the mixture firmly into the bottom and sides of the prepared pan. Set aside in the freezer.

To make the filling, using a food processor or high-speed blender, pulse the chilled coconut cream with the sugar, vanilla extract, and cream cheese several times until smooth and creamy. Leave the mixture in the food processor.

Melt the chocolate in a heatproof bowl set over a pan of simmering water. Gradually add the melted chocolate to the mixture in the food processor with the motor running on a low-speed setting until well combined.

Pour the filling over the base and spread it evenly across the surface. Arrange the raspberries on top, pressing them gently into the chocolate filling until they are half submerged. Refrigerate overnight.

Remove the pie from the tart pan and dust with confectioners' sugar just before serving.

BLUEBERRY-STRAWBERRY CHEESECAKE

Line an 8-inch (20 cm) square tart pan with parchment (baking) paper, cutting the paper larger than the pan to make it easy to remove the cheesecake when ready.

To make the base, using a food processor, pulse the pecans and raisins to coarse crumbs. Transfer the mixture to a bowl and mix in 3 tablespoons water. Spoon the mixture into the prepared pan and press it onto the bottom to make a firm base for the cheesecake.

To make the filling, using a food processor, pulse the cashews coarsely, then add the melted coconut oil and maple syrup and process until smooth. Add the strawberries, blueberries, and lemon juice and process until smooth.

Pour the filling over the base and spread it evenly across the surface. Freeze for 1 hour, then transfer the cheesecake to the refrigerator and chill for 2 hours before serving.

Preparation time: 45 minutes, plus
1 hour freezing and 2 hours chilling
Cooking time: none

Makes 1 (8-inch/20 cm) cheesecake

For the base:
- 1 cup (240 g) pecans
- ¾ cup (180 g) raisins

For the filling
- 2 cups (480 g) raw cashews, soaked in water overnight and drained
- ½ cup (120 ml/4 fl oz) cup coconut oil, melted
- ½ cup (120 ml/4 fl oz) maple syrup
- 2 cups (340 g) strawberries, chopped
- 2 cups (200 g) blueberries
- 2 tablespoons fresh lemon juice

CHOCOLATE-CHERRY
AND PISTACHIO BISCOTTI

Preparation time: 30 minutes
Cooking time: 1 hour 15 minutes, plus
   15 minutes cooling

Serves 4

- 2 cups (250 g) all-purpose (plain) flour, plus extra for dusting
- 2 tablespoons canola (rapeseed) oil
- ½ cup (50 g) unsweetened cocoa powder
- ½ cup (60 g) confectioners' (icing) sugar
- 1 teaspoon baking powder
- a pinch of salt
- 2 tablespoons eggs replacer, mixed with 4 tablespoons warm water
- 1 vanilla bean, seeds scraped
- 1 tablespoon finely grated orange zest
- 1 cup (140 g) toasted pistachio nuts, crushed
- ½ cup (120 g) cherries, halved and pitted (stoned)
- ¼ cup (60 ml/2 fl oz) almond milk, plus more as needed

Preheat the oven to 350°F/180°C/Gas Mark 4. Dust a baking sheet with all-purpose flour.

Combine the flour, oil, cocoa powder, confectioners' sugar, baking powder, salt, and egg replacer in a bowl. Add the vanilla seeds and orange zest and stir until well combined. Add the nuts, cherries, and almond milk. Using your hands, knead together to form a soft biscuit dough. If the dough is too dry, add more almond milk.

Dust your hands with flour and dust your work surface, too. Using your hands, roll the dough into a log. Transfer it to the prepared baking sheet and bake for 30 minutes, until firm. Transfer the log to a cooling rack.

Reduce the oven heat to 275°F/140°C/Gas Mark 1.

Cut the log into slices. Place the slices flat on the same baking sheet and bake for about 45 minutes, until the biscotti are dry and crisped up. Let cool on a metal rack for 15 minutes before serving.

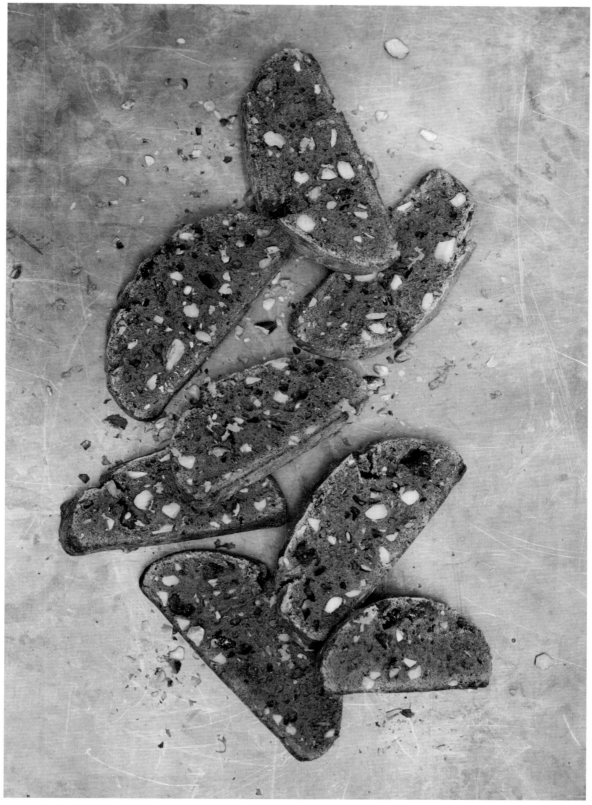

CHOCOLATE-CHERRY AND PISTACHIO BISCOTTI

CRANACHAN (SCOTTISH RASPBERRY OATMEAL)

Preparation time: 30 minutes
Cooking time: 5 minutes

Serves 4

- 2 cups (180 g) rolled oats
- 1 cup (125 g) raspberries
- 2 tablespoons maple syrup
- 1½ cups (360 ml/12 fl oz) vegan whipping cream
- 2 teaspoon vanilla extract
- 2 tablespoons malt whisky
- 1 tablespoon minced mint leaves

Preheat the broiler (grill). Put the oatmeal in a baking pan and position it under the broiler as low as possible in the oven. Broil for 5-6 minutes, until the oats become golden brown. Be extra careful during this process as the oats can easily burn if you keep them under the broiler for too long. Set aside.

Put the raspberries in a bowl and crush them with a fork. Mix in 1 tablespoon of the maple syrup and set aside.

Whip the cream in a bowl and, as you do, add the remaining maple syrup and vanilla extract, then gradually add the whisky. Whisk until the cream is stiff.

Reserve 2 tablespoons of the oats to decorate. Fold the remaining oats into the whipped cream.

Put 1 tablespoon of the cream into each of 4 desserts cups. Top with the raspberry mixture and finish off with a layer of the whipped cream. Sprinkle over the reserved oats, decorate with the minced mint leaves and serve immediately.

CREAM OF CHOCOLATE WITH CHIA SEEDS

Preparation time: 15 minutes
Cooking time: 20 minutes, plus 3-4 hours chilling

Serves 4

- 6 tablespoons chia seeds
- 2 tablespoons superfine (caster) sugar
- 2 tablespoons cocoa powder
- 1 teaspoon vanilla extract
- 2 tablespoons tahini
- 10 medjool dates, pitted (stoned)
- 2 cups (480 ml/16 fl oz) almond milk
- ¾ cup (170 g) cacao nibs or chocolate chips

Mix the chia seeds with ½ cup (120 ml/4 fl oz) water in a bowl and set aside for 20 minutes.

Using a food processor or a high-speed blender, process the sugar, cocoa powder, vanilla extract, tahini, dates, and almond milk for 3–4 minutes, until smooth and creamy. Add the chia seeds and its soaking liquid and process for 2 minutes, until smooth. Transfer the mixture to a large bowl and set aside.

Heat the chocolate nibs in a bain-marie or in a saucepan over very low heat until completely melted. Slowly pour the melted nibs into the chia mixture, stirring constantly, until well combined. Pour the mixture in 4 dessert cups and refrigerate for 3–4 hours before serving.

COCONUT-PECAN CREAM

Combine the almond milk, sugar, and vanilla in a saucepan. Cook over medium heat, stirring constantly, until the sugar dissolves and the mixture is hot.

Mix the cornstarch in 2–3 tablespoons hot water in a bowl until completely diluted. Add this mixture to the almond mix in the saucepan. Cook over low heat for 10-12 minutes, until the mixture thickens.

Remove the pan from heat and stir in coconut flakes and pecans. Stir well and let cool for 30 minutes. Serve warm.

Preparation time: 10 minutes
Cooking time: 15 minutes, plus
    20 minutes chilling

Serves 4

- 1½ cups (360 ml/12 fl oz) almond milk
- 1½ cups (300 g) superfine (caster) sugar
- 2 teaspoons vanilla extract
- 5 tablespoons cornstarch (cornflour)
- 1 lb (500 g) coconut flakes
- 1 cup (120 g) pecans, chopped

GRANADILLA PUDDING

Using a food processor, pulse the biscuits to make crumbs. Add the sugar and melted vegetable margarine and process until a firm dough forms. Divide the dough equally among 4 dessert glasses. Set aside.

Whip the soy cream to stiff peaks and refrigerate until ready to serve.

Put the sugar into a saucepan with 4 tablespoons water and warm over low heat until the sugar has dissolved. Add the halved kumquats and cook over low heat for 15 minutes. Add the almond milk, stir well, bring the mixture to a simmer, then add the agar-agar and stir well to combine, cook for another 5 minutes at low heat. Add reserved half kumquats in the 4 dessert glasses and pour the mixture on the top. Let cool for 20 minutes.

Top with the whipped cream, sprinkle over the confectioners' sugar and refrigerate for 1 hour before serving.

Preparation time: 20 minutes
Cooking time: 20 minutes, plus
    1 hour 20 chilling

Serves 4

- ½ cup (120 g) ground vegan toffee-flavored biscuits (like Nuttikrust)
- ⅓ cup (65 g) superfine (caster) sugar
- ¼ cup (60 g) vegetable margarine, melted
- 3 teaspoons agar-agar
- 1 cup (240 ml/8 fl oz) soy whipping cream
- 3 tablespoons granulated sugar
- 5½ oz (160 g) kumquats, halved
- ½ cup (120 ml/4 fl oz) almond milk
- 2 tablespoons confectioners' (icing) sugar

CARROT CAKE WITH
CREAM CHEESE FROSTING

Preparation time: 25 minutes
Cooking time: 1 hour, plus
  30 minutes chilling

Makes 1 (9-inch/23 cm) cake

For the cake:
- vegetable margarine, for greasing
- 1 cup (125 g) all-purpose (plain) flour
- 1 cup (200 g) superfine (caster) sugar
- 1 teaspoon ground cinnamon
- 1 teaspoon baking soda (bicarbonate of soda)
- a pinch of salt
- 2 tablespoons coconut flakes
- 2 cups (260 g) grated carrots
- 1½ cups (135 g) walnuts, chopped
- ½ cup (120 ml/4 fl oz) vegetable oil
- 2 tablespoons egg replacer, mixed in 4 tablespoons warm water
- 1 teaspoon vanilla extract
- 1 cup (170 g) chopped fresh sweet pineapple

For the frosting (icing):
- ½ cup (120 g) vegan cream cheese (page 30) or store bought
- ¼ cup (60 g) vegetable margarine
- ½ cup (60 g) confectioners' (icing) sugar

Preheat the oven to 350°F/180°C/Gas Mark 4. Grease a 9-inch (23 cm) round springform pan with vegetable margarine.

To make the cake batter, mix the flour, sugar, cinnamon, baking soda, and salt in a large bowl. Stir in the coconut flakes, carrots, and nuts, then the oil, egg replacer, vanilla, and pineapple and mix well to form a smooth, lump-free batter. Spread the batter in the prepared cake pan and bake for 45 minutes, until the cake is baked through but still spongy. Let cool, then remove from the pan.

To make the frosting, whisk the cream cheese and vegetable margarine with the sugar in a bowl until combined and fluffy. Using a silicone spatula, spread the frosting across the top surface of the cake. Refrigerate the cake for 30 minutes before serving.

CARROT CAKE WITH CREAM CHEESE FROSTING

CARROT AND PISTACHIO CREAM

Preparation time: 15 minutes
Cooking time: 20 minutes, plus
  50 minutes chilling

Serves 4

- 1 lb 2 oz (500 g) carrots, grated
- 2 cups (475 ml/16 fl oz) soy cream
- ¼ cup (50 g) superfine (caster) sugar
- 1 tablespoon rice flour
- 2 teaspoons ground cardamom
- 4 oz (120 g) silken tofu
- 2 tablespoons chopped almonds
- 2 tablespoons chopped pistachio nuts
- 1 tablespoon finely grated orange zest
- 2 tablespoons rose water or orange
  blossom water
- 1 orange, sliced, to decorate

Soak the grated carrots in cold water for 1 hour. Drain and set the carrots aside.

Put the soy cream into a saucepan and bring to a boil, then reduce the heat to low and add the sugar, drained carrots, and rice flour and cook for 5 minutes, stirring frequently. Add the cardamom and simmer for 15 minutes, until the carrots are fork tender. Add the tofu, almonds, pistachios, orange zest, and rose water or orange water and mix until combined.

Let cool for 20 minutes, then refrigerate for 30 minutes before serving in dessert cups, decorated with fresh orange slices.

BANANA-PEANUT-CREAM CAKE

Preparation time: 30 minutes
Cooking time: 1 hour

Makes 1 (10-inch/25 cm) cake

- vegetable oil, for greasing
- 2 ripe bananas
- 1 tablespoon fresh lemon juice
- 1 teaspoon ground cinnamon
- 1 vanilla pod, split lengthwise and seeds
  scrapped
- ¼ cup (65 g) crunchy peanut butter
- ½ cup (120 g) silken tofu
- ¼ cup (50 g) superfine (caster) sugar
- 1 teaspoon baking powder
- 1 cup (125 g) all-purpose (plain) flour
- 2 tablespoons dark rum

Preheat the oven to 325°F/160°C/Gas Mark 3. Grease a 10-inch (25 cm) round cake pan (cake tin) with the vegetable oil.

Using a food processor or blender, process the bananas with the lemon juice, cinnamon, vanilla, and peanut butter until combined. Set aside.

In a bowl, mix together the silken tofu, sugar, baking powder, and flour until combined. Add it to the banana mixture and pulse until the mixture is smooth and lump free. Add the rum and pulse again a couple of times. Pour the cake batter into the prepared form and bake for 1 hour, until lightly golden. Let cool completely on a wire rack, then remove from the pan and transfer to a large serving platter. Cut into wedges and serve.

COCONUT CREAM

Put the grated coconut into a large bowl and add 5 cups (1.2 liters/40 fl oz) hot water.

Cover the bowl with a clean kitchen towel and set aside for 3–4 hours. Once the soaking time has elapsed, strain the coconut mixture through a cheesecloth (muslin). Squeeze the remaining grated coconut in a cloth to extract as much liquid a possible—these quantities should yield 4 cups (960 ml/32 fl oz) coconut milk.

Mix the cornstarch with the sugar and salt in a large bowl. Add the coconut milk and cook over low heat, stirring constantly, for about 10 minutes, until the starch is cooked and the mixture begins to thicken. Add the vanilla extract and mix well. Remove the pan from the heat and divide the mixture amongh 4 ramekins. Sprinkle over the cinnamon and let cool for 20 minutes before serving.

Preparation time: 20 minutes, plus 3-4 hours soaking
Cooking time: 15 minutes, plus 20 minutes chilling

Serves 4

- 2 lb (1 kg) grated coconut
- ½ cup (120 g) cornstarch (cornflour)
- ½ cup (100 g) granulated sugar
- a pinch of salt
- 1 teaspoon vanilla extract
- 1 teaspoon ground cinnamon

BANANAS FOSTER WITH VANILLA CREAM

Peel and slice the bananas, put them in a bowl with the lemon juice, and toss to coat.

Melt the vegetable margarine in a saucepan, add the bananas and sauté over medium heat for 3–4 minutes. Sprinkle in the sugar and cook for 3–4 minutes, stirring constantly. Add the cinnamon, walnuts, and sauté for another 2 minutes. Reduce the heat to low and pour the rum into the pan all over the mixture. Ignite the alcohol carefully with a lighter, then flambé until the flames are dying. Garnish with the orange slices and serve immediately with ice cream or custard on the side.

Preparation time: 15 minutes
Cooking time: 10 minutes

Serves 4

- 4 bananas
- 4 tablespoons fresh lemon juice
- ¼ cup (60 g) vegetable margarine
- ½ cup (100 g) superfine (caster) sugar
- 1 teaspoon ground cinnamon
- ¼ cup (50 g) walnuts, crushed
- 4 tablespoons dark rum
- 1 orange, sliced, to garnish
- vegan vanilla ice cream or vegan vanilla custard, to serve

GUEST CHEFS

DAN BARBER

.

BLUE HILL

.

BLUE HILL AT STONE BARNS . 630 BEDFORD ROAD . POCANTICO HILLS, NY 10591 . UNITED STATES
BLUE HILL . 75 WASHINGTON PLACE . NEW YORK, NY 10014 . UNITED STATES

Dan Barber is the chef at Blue Hill, a restaurant in Manhattan's West Village, and Blue Hill at Stone Barns— located within the nonprofit farm and Stone Barns Center for Food & Agriculture, a working four-season farm and educational center thirty miles north of New York City that opened in 2004. He is author of *The Third Plate: Field Notes on the Future of Food*, and his opinions on food and agricultural policy have appeared in the *New York Times* and many other publications. Barber and his wife helped create the philosophical and practical framework for Stone Barns Center, and continue to help guide it in its mission to create a consciousness about the effect of everyday food choices. Sourcing from the surrounding fields, as well as other local farms, Blue Hill at Stone Barns highlights the abundant resources of the Hudson Valley in New York State. There are no menus at Blue Hill at Stone Barns. Instead, guests are offered the best seasonal produce from the fields and market.

V9 JUICE

Preparation time: 20 minutes, plus
  24 hours chilling
Cooking time: 10 minutes

Serves 4

For the tomato water:
- 15 lb (6.75 kg) tomatoes
- ¼ cup (2¼ fl oz/60 ml) vodka (optional)

For the juice:
- 6 lb (2.75 kg) tomatoes, preferably
  Purple Cherokee
- 2 cucumbers, peeled and seeded
- 2 parsnips
- 2 carrots
- 2 celery stalks
- 4 shallots
- 1 jalapeño pepper
- 1 head of fennel, chopped
- 5–6 tablespoons granulated sugar
- ½ cup (4 fl oz/120 ml) sherry vinegar
- 1½ tablespoons Worcestershire sauce
- 10 basil leaves
- ½ bunch tarragon
- 1 bunch parsley
- simple syrup (make your own using
  1 part sugar to 1 part water)
- hot sauce, such as Tabasco

To make the tomato water, in a blender, working in batches, purée the tomatoes and vodka, if using, until smooth.

Line a large colander with a several layers of cheesecloth (muslin) and place it over a deep bowl. Pour the blended tomatoes into the colander and refrigerate overnight. The resulting liquid in the bowl is the tomato water. You should have about 2 quarts (2 liters).

To make the juice, in a food processor, combine the tomatoes, cucumbers, parsnips, carrots, celery, shallots, jalapeño, fennel, sugar, vinegar, and Worcestershire sauce and pulse until the vegetables are chopped. Transfer to a bowl, cover, and refrigerate for 12 hours.

In a blender, combine the marinated vegetables, the tomato water, and herbs and blend until smooth. Season to taste with simple syrup and hot sauce, then strain through a chinois. Taste and adjust the seasonings as needed.

FALL FRUITS AND VEGETABLES

Layer the sliced fruits and vegetables in an overlapping pattern on a large serving plate until the plate is completely covered. Set the "carpaccio" aside.

In a sauté pan set over medium-high heat, warm the grapeseed oil. Add the celtuce leaves to the pan for 10–15 seconds, until warmed through and slightly softened.

Place the leaves on the carpaccio. Add a drizzle of lemon juice and white balsamic vinegar, then sprinkle with coarse sea salt and cracked white pepper for texture.

Preparation time: 15 minutes
Cooking time: 5 minutes

Serves 4

- 1 small Asian pear, thinly sliced
- 1 large Tokyo (white) turnip, thinly sliced
- 1 small avocado squash or zucchini (courgette), thinly sliced
- 1 small Cortland (Braeburn) apple, thinly sliced
- 1 tablespoon grapeseed oil
- celtuce (stem lettuce) leaves
- fresh lemon juice
- white balsamic vinegar
- coarse sea salt
- freshly cracked white pepper

ERIC RIPERT

•

LE BERNARDIN

•

155 WEST 51ST STREET . NEW YORK, NY 10019 . UNITED STATES

Eric Ripert is the chef and co-owner of the three-Michelin-starred New York restaurant Le Bernardin, which is on the World's 50 Best Restaurants list and received four stars from the *New York Times*. Born in Antibes, France, Eric attended culinary school in Perpignan and at seventeen moved to Paris to cook at the legendary Tour d'Argent. He then took a position as chef *poissonier* at the three-Michelin-starred restaurant Jamin, working under Joël Robuchon. In 1989 he worked for Jean-Louis Palladin as a sous-chef at Jean-Louis restaurant at the Watergate Hotel in Washington, D.C. In 1991 Ripert moved to New York to be David Bouley's sous-chef, before becoming chef at Le Bernardin. Ripert is the Vice Chairman of the board of City Harvest, which brings together New York's top chefs and restaurateurs to improve the quality and quantity of food donations to New York's neediest. The James Beard Foundation has named Ripert Outstanding Chef: New York City and Best Chef in America. He is the author of several books, including *Le Bernardin Cookbook* (1998), *On the Line* (2008), *Avec Eric* (2010), and *32 Yolks* (2016).

CAULIFLOWER "COUSCOUS" WITH MARKET VEGETABLES AND ARGAN OIL VINAIGRETTE

Preparation time: 1 hour
Cooking time: 30 minutes

Serves 4

For the market vegetables:
- salt
- mixed seasonal vegetables, such as halved baby carrots, halved baby turnips, asparagus tips, halved green beans, and baby bok choy

For the "couscous":
- 1 head of cauliflower, cut into florets
- juice of 1 lemon
- 3 tablespoons extra-virgin olive oil
- 4 tablespoons chopped mint
- 1 tablespoon chopped parsley

For the vinaigrette:
- 1 tablespoon Dijon mustard
- 4 tablespoons Champagne vinegar
- fine sea salt and freshly ground black pepper
- 6 tablespoons argan oil
- 4–6 tablespoons canola (rapeseed) oil

To serve:
- ½ cup (20 g) baby arugula (rocket)
- ½ cup (20 g) pea tendrils
- radishes, quartered
- cherry tomatoes, halved

To make the market vegetables, depending on how many types of seasonal vegetables are being used, bring several small pans of lightly salted water to a boil and prepare several bowls of ice water. Blanch the vegetables in separate pans, then drain and place immediately in ice water. Transfer to a tray or plate lined with paper towels and set aside.

To make the "couscous," place the cauliflower in a food processor and pulse until it resembles couscous. Pour just enough water into a sauté pan to cover the bottom, add the cauliflower, and set over low heat. Cook gently, stirring occasionally, until the cauliflower cooked through and most of the water has evaporated, about 5 minutes. Strain and transfer to a bowl to cool.

When cool, add the lemon juice, olive oil, mint, and parsley to the cooked cauliflower and set aside.

To make the vinaigrette, in a small bowl, combine the mustard and vinegar and season to taste with fine sea salt and freshly ground black pepper. Whisking constantly, drizzle in the argan oil and just enough canola oil to balance out the acidity; set aside.

To serve, place a 4-inch (10 cm) ring mold in the center of each of 4 plates and spoon in the "couscous," pressing gently to lightly pack down, then remove the mold. Toss the blanched vegetables, arugula, and pea tendrils in a bowl with just enough of the vinaigrette to coat them. Season to taste with salt and freshly ground black pepper. Arrange the dressed vegetables over the couscous and top with radishes and baby arugula. Drizzle more of the vinaigrette around the plates and serve immediately.

SPICY TOMATO CONSOMMÉ

Line a large strainer with at least 4 layers of cheesecloth (muslin) and set over a deep bowl.

Put the tomatoes into a blender, add 1 teaspoon fine sea salt, and pulse until almost puréed; you want just a few chunks remaining. Pour the blended tomato into the prepared strainer and refrigerate for at least 3 hours, or overnight if you wish. During that time, the purée will slowly drip clarified tomato water into the bowl.

Pour the tomato water into a medium pan set over medium heat. Save the remaining tomato purée for another use. Bring the tomato water to a boil, for 8–12 minutes, skimming off the foam that forms on the surface. Add the garlic, lemongrass, and bird's eye chili and season to taste with sea salt and and freshly ground white pepper. Immediately remove the consommé from the heat and let the aromatics steep for 8–10 minutes.

Using scissors, cut the cellophane noodles into bite-size pieces and place in a medium pan. Strain the boiling consommé over the noodles, bring back to a boil over medium heat, and fully cook the noodles, 4–6 minutes.

Using a slotted spoon, scoop equal amounts of the noodles into 4 serving bowls. Pour the consommé over the noodles and garnish with the scallions, grape tomatoes, and a few drops of extra-virgin olive oil. Serve immediately.

Preparation time: 30 minutes, plus
  3–12 hours straining
Cooking time: 40 minutes

Serves 4

- 8 lb (3.5 kg) ripe tomatoes, cored and coarsely chopped
- fine sea salt and freshly ground white pepper
- 4 cloves garlic, sliced
- 2 stalks lemongrass, sliced
- 3 bird's eye chilies, stemmed and thinly sliced
- 2 cups (10 oz/300 g) dried cellophane noodles
- 8 scallions (spring onions), thinly sliced, to garnish
- 8 grape tomatoes, sliced, to garnish
- extra-virgin olive oil, to garnish

KWANG UH

·

BAROO

·

5706 SANTA MONICA BOULEVARD . LOS ANGELES, CA 90038 . UNITED STATES

Kwang Uh is the chef and co-owner of Baroo. The restaurant's name references a bowl that Buddhist monks use to beg for food. Baroo's goal is to serve food with respect and love to nature and people, using local, sustainable, and organic ingredients. The menu at Baroo's free-style experimental kitchen changes often, depending on seasonality and inspiration.

CAROB-OOT

Preparation time: 20 minutes, plus
  1–2 weeks fermenting
Cooking time: 1 hour

Makes about 4 lb (1.75 kg)

- 1 lb 12 oz (800 g) carob
- 11 oz (300 g) lotus root, peeled and coarsely chopped
- 11 oz (300 g) burdock root, peeled and coarsely chopped
- 7 oz (200 g) dried shiitake mushrooms, rehydrated, stemmed, and coarsely chopped
- 3½ oz (100 g) dried kombu, rehydrated and coarsely chopped
- 3½ oz (100 g) kosher salt or sea salt
- 7 Thai bird chilies (optional)

In a saucepan set over high heat, cover the carob with cold water, and bring to a boil. Cook at a boil for 40 minutes, until softened. Remove from the heat, drain, and let cool completely. Halve the carob lengthwise, then seed and coarsely chop.

Combine the carob, lotus root, burdock root, shiitake, and kombu in a food processor or high-speed blender and process until a smooth paste forms. Add the salt and chilies, if using, and mix to combine. Transfer the paste to a 2-quart (2 liter) sterilized glass jar. Seal the jar, then let the mixture ferment at room temperature for at least 7 days and up to 2 weeks.

Use the finished carob-oot on its own as a condiment or combine one part of the paste with three parts dashi. You can also mix it with shredded, roasted seaweed and let it ferment again. Or you can purée it with other seasonings, such as sake, mirin, or tamari, and use the spread to season rice.

SHIMEJI MUSHROOM PICKLES WITH LEMON VERBENA

To make the mushrooms, in a large bowl, combine the shimeji mushrooms with the kosher salt and set aside for 60 minutes, until the mushrooms release some of their moisture.

To make the verbena tea, bring the filtered water to a boil, remove from the heat, and let cool to about 175°F/80°C. Meanwhile, place the verbena leaves in a square of cheesecloth (muslin) and tie the corners together to make a bag. Place in a large heatproof bowl, pour the hot water over it, and let steep for 1 hour. Strain and discard the bag.

To make the pickling liquid, in a pan, combine the vinegars, yuzu juice, and maple syrup and bring to a boil over high heat. Remove from the heat and add the orange blossom water. Season to taste with salt and set aside.

Strain and rinse the mushrooms, then place them in 2-quart (2 liter) sterilized glass jars. Top up with the pickling liquid and seal tightly. Set aside to pickle at room temperature for at least 2 days.

Serve the mushrooms on their own as a condiment or as a side dish. The pickling liquid can be used as a seasoning vinegar to make sauces and dips.

Preparation time: 1 hour 30 minutes, plus 4 days fermenting
Cooking time: 20 minutes

Makes about 1 lb 8 oz (700 g)

For the mushrooms:
- 2 lb 4 oz (1 kg) brown shimeji mushrooms, caps only
- 2 lb 4 oz (1 kg) white shimeji mushrooms, caps only
- ¼ cup (50 g) kosher salt

For the verbena tea:
- 8½ cups (2 liters/68 fl oz) filtered water
- 8 tablespoons lemon verbena leaves

For the pickling liquid:
- 2½ cups (600 ml/20 fl oz) rice vinegar
- a scant 1 cup (200 ml/7 fl oz) citrus champagne vinegar
- a scant ½ cup (100 g/3½ fl oz) yuzu juice
- a scant 2 cups (450 ml/15 fl oz maple syrup
- 2 teaspoons orange blossom water, plus extra as needed
- salt, preferably pink Himalayan salt

FERMENTED TOFU

Preparation time: 2 days, plus
  6 weeks fermenting
Cooking time: none

Makes about 1 lb 12 oz (800 g)

- 5 oz (150 g) shiso leaves
- 2 oz (50 g) perilla leaves or any seasonal
  wild plants
- 2 lb 4 oz (1 kg) firm tofu
- kosher salt
- 11 lb (5 kg) fermented soybean paste

Wash the shiso and perilla leaves and dry them in a salad spinner. Place in a dehydrator at 140°F/60°C until completely dried out, 2 hours. Then, using a spice grinder, grind into a powder.

Wrap the tofu in cheesecloth (muslin) and squeeze out the moisture (you might want to wear sanitized rubber gloves while doing this). Weigh the tofu and calculate 4 percent of the figure: this is the amount of kosher salt you will need. Thoroughly cover the drained tofu with salt. Put the tofu in clean cheesecloth and wrap tightly. Place on a rack set over a bowl, put a weight on top, and leave overnight for all the moisture to drip out.

Discard the tofu water, then open up the cheesecloth. Transfer the tofu to a bowl and add the dehydrated leaf powder to the tofu. Using sterilized kitchen gloves, mix the tofu with the leaf powder, then wrap again in the same cheesecloth.

Thoroughly sanitize a work surface and a rectangular container large enough to hold both the tofu and the soybean paste. Spread a 1-inch (2.5 cm) layer of soybean paste in the bottom of the container, then place the wrapped tofu on it. Spread the rest of the soybean paste over it to enclose completely. Cover with a lid and wrap in foil or paper towels to keep the light out. Let sit in a dark, ventilated space at room temperature (about 70°–80°F/20°–26°C) for at least 6 weeks. Check once a week for any filamentous fungus or a rotting odor. (It's unlikely to happen, since fermented soy bean paste already has enough salt to act as a proper preservative, and the tofu has already been generously salted.) Discard any excess water that collects.

When ready, the tofu should have a creamy texture, with a subtle fermented note, but rich and long-lasting umami tones.

It's great as a soup base or a dip, at room temperature. Or you can preheat the oven to 300°F/150°C/Gas Mark 2 and warm it through for 10 minutes and use it as a dip. You can also roast the tofu for 45 minutes, then dry it in a dehydrator and grind it to a fine powder, to use in place of salt.

KABOCHA SQUASH SOUP

Peel and seed 2 kabocha squash (save the seeds for another purpose). Cut the flesh into 1¼-inch (3 cm) chunks and put them into a heatproof bowl with the coconut milk and curry powder. Cover and place the bowl on top of a saucepan with simmering water, making sure the bottom of the bowl doesn't touch the water, and cook the pumpkin until soft, about 40 minutes. (You can also steam the pumpkin with a little bit of water in a bowl in a microwave.)

Meanwhile, bring a saucepan with salted water to a boil over high heat and prepare an ice bath in a large bowl. Thinly slice 2 strips of Buddha's hand, yuzo or citron, then blanch in boiling water for a few seconds. Using a spider, transfer immediately to the ice bath. Strain and set aside.

Strain the cooked kabocha through a chinois, and save the squash and liquid. Depending on how mature the kabocha is, you may need to use more or less liquid for the soup.

Purée the soup in two batches in a stand blender, with the cooked kabocha, strained coconut milk, dashi, and the reserved Buddha's hands. Season with the lemon oil, pecan butter (if using), and salt. If you like, add some hot sauce for an extra kick.

Strain the soup, then pour 1 cup (240 ml/8 fl oz) into each serving bowl. Top each bowl with 3 mochi and 3 pieces of kabocha and serve immediately.

Preparation time: 1 day
Cooking time: 2 hours

Serves 10

- 4 small to medium kabocha squash
- 5¾ cups (1.4 liters /46 fl oz) coconut milk
- 2 teaspoons mild curry powder, plus more as needed
- 2 small to medium Buddha's hands (fingered citrons), yuzu, or citron
- generous 2 cups (480 ml/16 fl oz) dashi
- a scant 3 cups (350 g) sweet rice flour
- a scant ½ cup (50 g) tapioca flour
- ¼ oz (10 g) baking powder
- ¼ cup (50 g) granulated sugar
- ½ fl oz (15 ml) lemon oil
- pecan butter (optional)
- salt, preferably pink Himalayan
- hot sauce, such as Tabasco (optional)
- 30 mochi (page 417), to serve

PRESERVED BUDDHA'S HAND WITH PASSIONFRUIT SYRUP

Preparation time: 1 day
Cooking time: 10 minutes

Makes about 1 lb 8 oz (700 g)

- kosher salt
- 1 Buddha's hand (fingered citron), finely sliced into strips
- 4½ cups (500 g) granulated sugar
- 3 tablespoons passionfruit syrup

Bring a saucepan with salted water to a boil and prepare an ice bath in a large bowl. Blanch the Buddha's hand for few seconds, then immediately transfer to the ice bath. Strain, then place in a sterilized 2-quart (2 liter) mason (clip-top) jar.

Combine the sugar with a generous 2 cups (480 ml/16 fl oz) water in a pan set over high heat and stir until the sugar dissolves to make a simple syrup. Add the passionfruit syrup, then pour the liquid into the mason jar and cover with a lid. Let sit at room temperature for at least 1 day. Refrigerate for up to 1 week. To use, mince and use as a garnish wherever you like.

QUICK-ROASTED KABOCHA KIMCHI

Preparation time: 25 minutes, plus 3 hours infusing
Cooking time: 40–50 minutes

Serves: 4

- ½ kabocha squash, seeded and cut into crescents ⅝-inch (1.5 cm) thick
- a scant 1 cup (7 fl oz/200 ml) dashi
- ¼ cup (2 fl oz/50 ml) yuzu juice
- 3½ oz (100 g) preserved Buddha's hand (see above)
- kosher salt
- 3 tablespoons lemon oil

Put a bowl on a zeroed set of scales, then add the kabocha, dashi, yuzu juice, and Buddha's hand. Note the weight, then calculate 7 percent of that figure: this is the amount of salt you now need to add. Mix well, vacuum seal, then set aside at room temperature for 3–4 hours to infuse.

Preheat the oven to 350°F/180°C/Gas Mark 4. Strain the kabocha mixture, saving the liquid for future use. Toss the mixture with the lemon oil and salt and place on a rimmed baking sheet. Roast for 40–50 minutes, until soft and evenly caramelized.

KABOCHA SQUASH MOCHI FRITTER STUFFED WITH SPICY CHOCOLATE

To make the kabocha mochi, peel and seed the kabocha. Cut the flesh into ½-inch (2 cm) chunks and put into a heatproof bowl with the dashi, 2 teaspoons lemon oil, and kosher salt. Place in a steamer over simmering water and cook until soft, about 40 minutes.

Strain, reserving the liquid for future use. Put the steamed kabocha into a pan with the honey and Buddha's hand, then mash with a spoon into a coarse purée.

In a bowl, combine the sweet rice flour and tapioca flour, along with the sugar, baking powder, and soybean powder. Add the mixture to the mashed kabocha and slowly drizzle in a scant ½ cup (3½ fl oz/100 ml) hot filtered water and add the remaining lemon oil. Mix and knead by hand, adjusting the consistency with more hot water or sweet rice flour as needed to make a medium-firm dough; it should be neither sticky nor dry. Set aside.

To make the filling, chop the chocolate, seeds and nuts. Put into a bowl with the pecan butter (if using), honey, and salt, and mix together.

In a deep-fryer or a cast-iron pan set over medium heat, warm the oil to 325°F/160°C.

Meanwhile, break the mochi mixture into ¾-oz (20 g) pieces and roll into golf-size balls. Push your thumb into the center of each one, add a bit of the filling, then re-cover with the mochi and roll again into a ball.

Deep-fry the mochi a few at a time for 4–5 minutes, then raise the heat so the temperature of the oil reaches 340°F/170°C. The balls are ready when they float to the surface. Drain on paper towels, garnish with powdered sugar or cocoa powder on top, and serve immediately.

Preparation time: 1 day
Cooking time: 1 hour

Makes about 1 lb 8 oz (700 g)

For the kabocha mochi:
- 12 oz (350 g) kabocha squash
- 2 tablespoons dashi
- 2 teaspoons, plus 1 tablesppon lemon oil
- 1 teaspoon kosher salt
- 4 teaspoons honey
- 2 tablespoons preserved Buddha's hand (fingered citron), chopped (see page 416)
- a scant 2¼ cups (350 g) sweet rice flour, plus more as needed
- a scant ½ cup (50 g) tapioca flour
- ¼ cup (50 g) granulated sugar
- 2 teaspoons baking powder
- ¾ oz (20 g) roasted soybean powder (optional)

For the filling:
- 1 oz (30 g) spicy dark chocolate, such as Valrhona
- 1¾ oz (50 g) pumpkin seeds
- ¾ oz (25 g) pistachio nuts
- ¾ oz (25 g) sunflower seeds
- 1 tablespoon pecan butter (optional)
- 1 tablespoon honey

- canola oil (rapeseed), for deep-frying
- confectioners' (icing) sugar, to garnish
- unsweetened cocoa powder, to garnish

TONY LU

·

FU HE HUI

·

1037 YUYUAN ROAD . CHANGNING DISTRICT . SHANGHAI . CHINA . 200050

Lu Yi Ming (Tony Lu) was born and raised in Shanghai, China. By the age of eighteen, he knew his future would take him down a culinary path. He became a restaurant chef in just three years. Renowned for his deep knowledge, chef Lu soon came to international prominence as the culinary mastermind behind Shanghai's finest independent Chinese restaurants, Fu1039, Fu1088, and Fu1015. In 2013, he began work on a vegan-concept restaurant—Fu He Hui. It strongly reflects his style, featuring traditional cuisine, with a touch of modernity as well as quality seasonal ingredients sourced from local farms. Fu He Hui attracted local patrons, ushering in a new era of vegan food in China. It is widely acclaimed for promoting a healthy lifestyle and a new attitude on life.

CHANTERELLES WITH ASPARAGUS AND CORN PURÉE

Preparation time: 10 minutes, plus
  10 hours chilling
Cooking time: 15 minutes

Serves 4

- 4 oz (100 g) high-protein bread
  (strong) flour
- salt
- sunflower oil, for brushing and deep-frying
- 5 oz (120 g) green asparagus
- olive oil, for shallow frying
- ½ oz (15 g) corn kernels
- ½ cup (120 ml) vegetable stock (broth)
- 1¼ oz (30 g) chanterelle mushrooms

In a bowl, combine the flour and a small pinch of salt with 3 tablespoons plus 1 teaspoon water and mix to form a dough. Knead well, then shape it into a rectangle and brush with sunflower oil. Cover and refrigerate for 10 hours.

Bring the dough to room temperature. In a saucepan set over medium-high heat, warm 2 inches (5 cm) of sunflower oil to 265°F/130°C. Divide the dough into 4 pieces, then shape it into 4 twists, and fry until golden, about 3 minutes. Set aside.

Bring a small pot of salted water to a boil over high heat. Reduce the heat to low, and cook the asparagus until just tender, about 2 minutes, then transfer to a blender and finely chop.

In a skillet (frying pan) set over medium heat, warm a little olive oil and add the chopped asparagus and the corn. Cook, stirring, until warmed through, about 4 minutes. Add the stock to warm through and season with a generous pinch of salt. Remove from the heat and set aside.

In another skillet set over medium heat, warm a little olive oil and cook the mushrooms, stirring, until browned, 5–7 minutes.

To serve, make a bed of chopped asparagus and sweet corn on 4 plates, top with the fried mushrooms, and decorate with a bread twist.

CHICKEN MUSHROOMS

Steam the pumpkin over simmering water until fork-tender, about 20 minutes. Transfer to a blender and purée until smooth.

Preheat the oven to 140°F/60°C/Gas Mark 0. In a ramekin, combine the egg replacer with a pinch of salt and bake for 30 minutes, until completely dried out. Using a mortar and pestle, finely crush the egg replacer.

Put half of the olive oil into a skillet (frying pan) set over medium heat and fry the crushed yolk until crispy, about 4 minutes. Add the pumpkin purée, reduce the heat to low, and bring to a simmer. Stir in the sugar and mushroom extract and keep warm.

Pour the remaining olive oil into another skillet set over medium heat and cook the mushrooms and cauliflower, stirring, until softened and browned, about 10 minutes. Season with the soy sauce and oyster sauce and remove from the heat.

Arrange the pumpkin purée on 4 plates and top with the mushrooms and cauliflower. Garnish with the pea shoots and serve.

Preparation time: 10 minutes
Cooking time: 15 minutes

Serves 4

- 3 oz (85 g) pumpkin, peeled
- 2 tablespoons egg replacer, diluted with 2 tablespoons water
- 4 tablespoons olive oil
- a scant 2 teaspoons granulated sugar
- 4 teaspoons mushroom extract
- 8 oz (350 g) chicken mushrooms (*Collybia albuminosa*)
- 5 oz (140 g) cauliflower
- 2 teaspoons light soy sauce
- 4 drops vegan oyster sauce
- salt
- ½ oz (15 g) pea shoots, to garnish

SPICY GANBA MUSHROOM WITH ORZO AND PEAS

Preparation time: 10 minutes
Cooking time: 25 minutes

Serves 4

- 3 oz (85 g) ganba mushrooms (*Thelephora ganbajun*)
- salt
- 2 oz (60 g) orzo pasta
- 1 oz (30 g) shelled green peas
- 4 teaspoons olive oil
- ½ teaspoon grated fresh ginger
- 1 scallion (spring onion), trimmed, finely chopped
- 1 dried red chili, crushed
- 4 drops light soy sauce
- a scant 2 teaspoons vegan oyster sauce

Wash the mushrooms in water to remove any grit, then tear it into pieces.

Bring a pot of salted water to a boil over high heat. Add the pasta and cook until al dente, about 8 minutes. Drain and set aside.

Bring another pot of salted water to a boil over high heat. Add the peas and cook until tender, about 5 minutes. Drain and set aside.

Pour the olive oil into a skillet (frying pan) set over medium heat and fry the ginger, scallions, and dried chili until fragrant, about 1 minute. Add the ganba mushrooms and cook until browned and cooked through, 10–15 minutes.

Combine the ganba mixture with the orzo, season with the soy sauce and oyster sauce, and top with the peas. Serve immediately.

MICHEL BRAS

·

LE SUQUET

·

ROUTE DE L'AUBRAC . 12210 LAGUIOLE . FRANCE

Michel Bras was born in Gabriac, in southern France, in 1946. His parents ran a hotel and restaurant called Lou Mazuc in nearby Laguiole, and it was there that he was initiated into the local cuisine. Eager to learn more, he studied culinary literature and explored many avenues until he finally found his own culinary path. Together with his wife, Ginette, he achieved a solid reputation for Lou Mazuc, but the couple wanted a restaurant in the middle of the natural world they loved. So it was that Le Suquet opened in 1992, in the remote setting of the Aubrac highlands. Its aim was to share the best that nature has to offer, and the restaurant has become famous for its foraged ingredients, particularly herbs and flowers. Today Michel and Ginette keep a low profile, but their son, Sébastien, and his wife, Véronique, continue to maintain the Michelin-starred restaurant's high standards.

GARGOUILLOU OF YOUNG VEGETABLES

Preparation time: 8 hours, plus 3–4 hours
  infusing, 10–24 hours soaking, and
  3–4 days sprouting
Cooking time: 8 hours

Serves: varies, depending on how many
  vegetables are prepared

For the perennial vegetables:
- green asparagus, ferns, hop shoots, black
  bryony, artichokes, cardoons
- salt
- vegan butter or olive oil, for sautéing
- vegetable stock (broth) flavored with
  coriander seeds, orange zest, and shallots,
  plus a drizzle of aromatic oil

For the leaf and flower vegetables:
- amaranth, giant orange amaranth, green
  and red orache, Malabar spinach, lamb's-
  quarter and bonbonnerie, comfrey, spinach,
  parsley, New Zealand spinach, cabbage,
  Chinese leaves (pe-tsai), bok choy, pointed
  cabbage, Brussels sprouts, mustard greens
- salt
- Swiss chard, white borage, celery
- buchu, broccoli rabe, cabbage shoots
- broccoli, cauliflower
- watercress, clover, geslu, crystalline ice
  plant, chickweed, lettuce leaves of all colors
- vegan gravy (optional)

For the bulb vegetables:
- garlic, wild garlic, sand leeks, shallots,
  grelot onions
- salt
- Welsh onions, scallions (spring onions),
  young onions, leeks, white onions
- fennel
- Cévennes onions, Lézignan onions

For the root vegetables:
- potato bean, carrots, chervil root, skirrets,
  turnips, parsnips, parsley root, radishes,
  kohlrabi, Jerusalem artichokes
- salt
- beets (beetroot), crapaudine beets
  (crapaudine beetroot)
- black radish, daikon radish
- celery root (celeriac), salsify, black salsify
- Chinese artichokes, pignuts
- great or common burdock, rampions
- vegan butter or oil, for sautéing (optional)

With the changing of the seasons, kitchen gardens, markets, and nature offer a multitude of vegetables, herbs, leaves, and seeds. Gargouillou, a classic dish reinvented by Bras, combines their colors and flavors with total freedom. Depending on supplies, make use of perennial, root, and fruiting vegetables—the list can never be too long. Let inspiration be your guide as you play with different accents and create a gargouillou to suit your taste.

To make the perennial vegetables, trim the asparagus, ferns, hop shoots, and black bryony, breaking off the woody part of the stalks, or simply scraping them, as necessary. Cook or blanch in boiling salted water. Refresh in an ice bath, then set aside.

Pick the leaves off the artichokes and trim the rest of the vegetable, leaving the heart. Remove the leaves from the cardoons and cut the stalks into small lengths. Place both the artichokes and the cardoons in the flavored stock, bring to a boil, then simmer until tender. Set aside.

To make the leaf and flower vegetables, for most of those listed, cut off the stems; for others, remove the tough central rib. The tender leaves can be lightly sautéed in oil for a few minutes. The tougher ones can be boiled in salted water until tender, then drained and refreshed in an ice bath. Set all the leaves aside.

Separate all the various cabbage leaves, then prepare and cook them as described in the previous step. Set aside.

Separate the Swiss chard, borage, and celery leaves and cut the fibrous strings from the stalks. Boil each type of leaf separately for 1 minute, until tender. Drain, refresh in an ice bath, and set aside. The leaves can also be cooked until soft in leftover gravy.

Tie the buchu, rabe, and cabbage shoots into thin bundles. Cook in plenty of boiling salted water until tender. Drain, refresh in an ice bath, and set aside.

Separate the broccoli and cauliflower florets from the stems. Select the tenderest stalks and peel off the woody outer layer to expose the core. Finely slice. Cook the florets and sliced core separately in boiling salted water for 3 minutes, until tender. Drain, refresh in an ice bath, and set aside.

Select the best leaves within the watercress group and remove their stems. While generally used raw, some may be lightly cooked, like the tender leaves above, if you wish.

To make the bulb vegetables, peel the garlic, wild garlic, sand leek, shallot, and grelot onion. Cook in boiling salted water until soft, or, even better, braise them in the flavored broth used for the perennial vegetables. Alternatively, simply roast the bulbs in their skins in the oven. Set aside.

Wash the Welsh onion, scallion (spring onion), young onion, leek, and white onion bulbs. Separate the white parts from the green. Boil or braise as described in the previous step, but for the best results, cook the white part first, and then the green part. Drain, refresh in an ice bath, and set aside.

Remove the fennel leaves. The bulb can be used raw, boiled, or braised, as in the garlic step above. Set aside.

Peel the Cévennes and Lézignan onions. A particularly good way to cook them is to wrap them in foil, then roast in the oven at 400°F/200C/Gas Mark 6, until tender. Set aside.

To make the root vegetables, peel the potato bean group of roots with a knife, leaving a short bunch of tops attached to the smaller ones. Slice these vegetables lengthwise with a mandoline to a thickness of ⅛ inch (3 mm). Boil in salted water, until tender. Drain, then set aside. Potato bean, chervil root, and parsley root can be puréed, if you wish.

While both types of beet listed are generally cooked in boiling water until tender, you can also use them raw, grated, or julienned. Set aside.

Rub the black and daikon radishes with sandpaper, then rinse and slice with a mandoline to a thickness of ⅛ inch (3 mm). If you wish, lightly sauté in oil until tender. Set aside.

Scrape the tough outer skin off the celery root, salsify, and black salsify, then chop. Cook in separate pans of salted boiling water, with a drizzle of oil to prevent oxidation, then drain and set aside.

Clean the Chinese artichokes and pignuts by rubbing them with coarse salt and against each other. Rinse. Lightly sauté the Chinese artichokes until tender. Set aside. The pignuts can be eaten as they are.

Scrape the great or common burdock and rampion roots and use them raw or cooked. Set aside.

To make the pulses, de-string the green beans, Saint Fiacre pole beans, and snow peas. Cook each pulse in a separate pan using plenty of salted boiling water until tender. Set aside.

Shell the fava beans and cook them in salted boiling water until tender. Refresh in an ice bath, then drain and peel the individual beans. Set aside.

Prepare the shelling beans, flageolet beans, lentils, chickpeas, grass peas, okra, and soybeans as necessary. These pulses require slow cooking at a low temperature with accompaniments and herbs. Set aside.

To make the fruiting vegetables, cut the chayote, pattypan squash, zucchini (courgette), and spaghetti squash into slices ⅛-inch (3 mm) thick. Cook in salted boiling water or lightly sauté in vegan butter or aromatic oil until tender. Set aside.

Clean and cut the fresh cucumbers and leave them in salt for a few hours to release their residual water. Rinse, pat dry with paper towels, then sauté in an aromatic oil until tender. Set aside. The pickled cucumbers can be served as they are.

Peel and seed the red and yellow tomatoes. Set aside.

Peel and seed the green tomatoes, then make them into preserves.

Lightly oil the bell peppers and roast in a very hot oven. Clean off the charred outer layer and submerge the flesh in the oil.

For the pulses:
- green beans, Saint Fiacre pole beans, snow peas (mange-tout), fava (broad) beans
- salt
- shelling beans, flageolet beans, lentils, chickpeas, grass peas, okra, soybeans (soya beans)

For the fruiting vegetables:
- chayote, pattypan squash, zucchini (courgettes), spaghetti squash
- salt
- fresh cucumber, gherkins (pickled cucumbers)
- red and yellow tomatoes
- green tomatoes
- red, green, or yellow bell peppers
- red kuri squash, pumpkin
- vegan butter or aromatic oil, for sautéing

For the porcini mushrooms:
- 7 oz (200 g) small porcini mushrooms
- a scant ½ cup (100 ml/3½ fl oz) oil
- 2 garlic cloves
- 10 coriander seeds
- 4 sprigs wild thyme
- 1 bay leaf
- parsley
- 5 peppercorns
- salt
- juice of 1 lemon

For the parsley oil:
- ½ cup (30 g) parsley
- a scant ¼ cup (50 ml/1¾ fl oz) grapeseed oil
- salt

For the wild herbs:
- salad burnet, yarrow, black bryony

For the sprouted seeds:
- alfalfa, fenugreek, wheat, chickpeas, lentils, soybeans (soya beans)

You can sprout the seeds of many varieties of plant: cereals, brassicas, vegetables, pulses, mucilaginous herbs, oleaginous plants, and those of the celery family.

For the glassy leaves:
- garden herbs
- vegetable leaves
- aromatic oil
- Guérande sea salt

To serve:
- vegan butter
- fine herbs (tarragon, parsley, chives, coriander, chervil), to garnish

Cut the thick skin off the red kuri squash and pumpkin, then chop the flesh and cook in boiling salted water until tender. Drain and purée, then set aside.

To make the porcini mushrooms, using a knife, scrape the mushroom stems. Wipe the heads and stems with a damp cloth. Plunge them into a pan of boiling water for 30 seconds. Drain, refresh in an ice bath, then pat dry with paper towels. Put the oil, a scant ¼ cup (50 ml/1¾ fl oz) water, garlic, seeds, herbs, and peppercorns into a pan. Season with salt, bring to a simmer, and cook for 5 minutes. Add the mushrooms and simmer for another 5 minutes. Season to taste with lemon juice. Adjust the seasoning and set aside. (You can adapt this method to any variety of small, firm mushrooms.)

To make the parsley oil, pick over and wash the parsley. Add to the oil along with a pinch of salt. Leave to infuse for 3–4 hours, then pour through a fine strainer (sieve). The oil can be stored for several days in the refrigerator. (It is easy to make a large batch of this oil for future use. A similar oil can be prepared with chives, Welsh onion, and wild celery.)

To make the wild herbs, pick over and wash the salad burnet, yarrow, and black bryony, along with any other plants, flowers, and roots you might be able to gather in the wild.

To make the sprouted seeds, first soak the seeds either in store-bought seed trays made for the purpose or in large jars. The soaking time depends on the variety of seed: alfalfa, fenugreek, and wheat need 10–12 hours; chickpeas, lentils, and soybeans need 12–24 hours.

Put the seeds in trays or jars and cover them with plenty of water. Place cheesecloth (muslin) over the top and fasten with a rubber band. Set aside for the required time.

When the seeds have germinated (pushed out tiny shoots), discard the water and rinse the seeds very well. Re-cover the tray or jar with cheesecloth and place at a 45-degree angle with the opening facing downward. Cover the whole tray or jar with a dark cloth and set aside, rinsing the seeds twice a day. For correct sprouting, it is important to keep the seeds moist, warm, dark, and aerated. The sprouts will be ready to use after a few days. You can keep them fresh by rinsing regularly. Certain varieties of seeds can be sprouted without the need for darkness.

To make the glassy leaves, preheat the oven 200°F/95°C/Gas Mark 0. Pick the leaves and wash well, taking care not to crease them. Vegetable leaves should be blanched after washing, then patted dry with a cloth. Brush the leaves with a drop of aromatic oil to add gloss. Sprinkle them with salt. Place them on a baking sheet lined with parchment (baking) paper and place in the oven until the leaves are shiny and brittle like glass, with their color intact. Set aside. (The method described here can be used on many garden herbs and vegetable leaves, such as parsley, tarragon, cabbage, and leek.)

When ready to serve, warm the vegan butter in a deep skillet (frying pan) and add the vegetable stock. Add another knob of the vegan butter to form an emulsion. Roll all the prepared vegetables in the emulsion to warm through. Arrange them on plates, giving them a sense of movement.

Decorate with the tips of fine herbs, the wild herbs, sprouted seeds, and glassy leaves, then add the porcini and parsley oil.

ALEXIS GAUTHIER

·

GAUTHIER SOHO

·

21 ROMILLY STREET . LONDON W1D 5AF . UNITED KINGDOM

Alexis Gauthier is from Avignon, France. He began his career under Chef Alain Ducasse in the grand hotels of Nice and Monaco, where he formed his fundamental cooking style: a light and uncomplicated celebration of the best seasonal produce, often led by fruits and vegetables. After cooking in California, Gauthier relocated to London as a head chef at Roussillon, where he offered London's first plant-focused "garden menu" and earned his first Michelin star. In 2010 he opened Gauthier Soho.

ROASTED PORCINI MUSHROOMS WITH BLACK GARLIC, SPELT, AND PARSLEY JUS

Preparation time: 1 hour
Cooking time: 35 minutes

Serves 4

For the spelt:
- a generous 1 cup (200 g) spelt
- 6 cloves garlic, coarsely chopped
- 1 large carrot, thinly sliced
- 1 bay leaf
- 4 sprigs thyme
- salt

For the garlic cream:
- olive oil
- 3 heads of black garlic, halved crosswise
- 2 large Bouchon porcini, cleaned and coarsely chopped
- 9 oz (250 g) button mushrooms, cleaned and coarsely chopped
- ½ shallot, sliced
- a scant ½ cup (100 ml/3½ fl oz) brandy

For the porcini:
- 8 large Bouchon porcini, cleaned
- olive oil
- 2 cloves garlic, thinly sliced

For the parsley jus:
- olive oil
- ⅔ cup (100 g) freshly shelled peas
- salt
- ½ bunch watercress
- 1 bunch flat-leaf parsley, leaves picked

To make the spelt, preheat the oven to 350°F/175°C/Gas Mark 4. Combine the spelt, garlic, carrot, bay leaf, thyme, 6 cups (1.5 liters) water and a pinch of salt in a heavy pan and bring slowly to a boil over low heat. Cover with a lid and place the pan in the oven for 30 minutes, until the spelt is cooked through. Remove from the oven and let the spelt cool to room temperature.

To make the garlic cream, in a sauté pan set over low heat, add a little olive oil and pan-fry the garlic, cut side down, for 5 minutes, until fully softened. Peel the garlic cloves, put them in a bowl, and set aside.

Put the sauté pan back over low heat, warm a little olive oil, and add the chopped porcini, button mushrooms, and shallot. Cook for 2 minutes, then add the brandy and cook for another 2 minutes, until the alcohol evaporates. Remove from the heat and add to the bowl of garlic. Using a fork, mash until the mixture is the consistency of thick cream.

To make the porcini. halve the porcini lengthwise, making sure the head is still attached to the stem. In a large pan set over low heat, warm a little olive oil and add the porcini and the garlic. Cook gently until the porchini are soft and light golden brown, about 4 minutes. It is very important not to overcook porcini, as they will become bitter. Remove from the heat and set aside.

To make the parlsey jus, warm 2 tablespoons of olive oil in a sauté pan set over low heat until it shimmers. Add the peas and lightly cook until bright green but not at all brown. Season to taste with a pinch of salt. Add the watercress and ¾ cup (200 ml/6 fl oz) water, cover, and cook for 3 minutes on very high heat. Remove from the heat, add the parsley leaves, and transfer everything to a blender. Blend immediately to a very thin jus.

When ready to serve, combine the spelt and garlic cream in a pan and gently warm, until heated through. Evenly divide the mixture among 4 large soup plates. Place a few roasted porcini on each serving and drizzle with the parsley jus. Serve immediately.

BAKED HERITAGE BEETS, CELERY ROOT WITH HORSERADISH PURÉE, AND TOASTED ALMONDS

To make the beets, preheat the oven to 325°F/160°C/Gas Mark 4. In a large bowl, using your hands, combine the flaky sea salt and flour with ¾ cup (175 ml/6 fl oz) water until the mixture has a texture similar to wet sand. Place the beets in a Dutch oven (casserole) and cover them with the salt mixture. Roast in the oven for 3 hours, until tender. Discard the salt mixture. When cool enough to handle, peel and quarter the beets.

To make the celery root purée, in a heavy pan set over low heat, warm 2 tablespoons of olive oil. Add the celery root, onion, and garlic and stir while they warm. Add a pinch of salt and ¾ cup (175 ml/ 6 fl oz) water. Cover the pan and let cook at a lively simmer for about 4 minutes. Transfer the contents of the pan to a blender and process the vegetables to a smooth purée. Stir in the mustard and horseradish and set aside.

To make the pickled beet garnish, in a pan set over high heat, bring the sugar and vinegar to a lively simmer. Remove the pan from the heat and add the sliced beets. Let them pickle until the liquid is cool, then lift out, pat dry, and dress with olive oil; reserve.

When ready to serve, preheat the oven to 350°F/180°C/Gas Mark 4. Put the quartered beets in a baking dish with a little olive oil and salt and reheat in the oven for about 10 minutes.

Place a large spoonful of celery root purée in the middle of 4 large plates. Add an equal number of quartered beets to each serving, and place the pickled beet slices in between. Sprinkle with the mustard and fennel seeds and top with the toasted almonds. Add a few drops of olive oil and some freshly ground black pepper. Serve immediately.

Preparation time: 3 hours
Cooking time: 45 minutes

Serves 4

For the beets:
- 2¼ lb (1 kg) flaky sea salt
- a generous ¾ cup (100 g) all-purpose (plain) flour
- 3 golden beets (beetroot), scrubbed
- 3 purple beets, scrubbed
- 3 Cylindra beets, scrubbed

For the celery root purée:
- extra-virgin olive oil
- 1 whole celery root (celeriac), cut into large chunks
- ¼ white onion, sliced thick
- 1 clove garlic, sliced
- salt
- 2 teaspoons English or Dijon mustard
- 1½ oz (40 g) freshly grated horseradish

For the pickled beet garnish:
- ½ cup (100 g) superfine (caster) sugar
- 1 cup (240 ml/8 fl oz) white wine vinegar
- 2 purple beets, thinly sliced
- extra-virgin olive oil

To serve:
- extra-virgin olive oil
- 2 teaspoons mustard seeds
- 2 teaspoons fennel seeds
- ⅓ cup (40 g) slivered (flaked) almonds, toasted
- a pinch of freshly ground black pepper

WHOLE ROASTED CARROTS WITH CITRUS CONFIT AND HERB SALAD

Preparation time: 1 hour 30 minutes,
  plus 6–24 hours chilling
Cooking time: 1 hour

Serves: 4

For the pastry:
- 1 lb 2 oz (500 g) all-purpose (plain) flour
- ¼ cup (90 g) coarse sea salt
- 2 sprigs rosemary, leaves picked and finely chopped
- finely grated zest of 2 oranges
- juice of 2 oranges

For the carrots:
- 4 large multicolored carrots
- extra-virgin olive oil
- flaky sea salt

For the garnishes:
- 1¼ cups (250 g) granulated sugar
- 1 large carrot,
- finely sliced
- 8 kumquats
- ½ orange, supremed
- ½ blood orange, supremed
- 1 lime
- ½ bunch lemon balm, leaves picked
- ½ bunch chervil, leaves picked
- 6 teaspoons canola (rapeseed) oil
- 2 teaspoons aged balsamic vinegar
- salt and freshly ground black pepper

To make the pastry, combine the flour, coarse sea salt, rosemary, orange zest, and juice with ¾ cup (6 fl oz/175 ml) water, then knead until a smooth and elastic dough forms. Wrap it in plastic wrap (clingfilm) and refrigerate for at least 6 hours, or preferably overnight.

To make the carrots, preheat the oven to 325°F/160°C/Gas Mark 3. In a large bowl, toss the carrots with some olive oil and salt. Set aside. Roll the chilled pastry into a rectangle about 38 inches (1 meter) long and 6 inches (15 cm) wide. Place the carrots on it end to end with equal space between them and at either end. Cut the pastry between each carrot, then wrap it around each one, ensuring both ends are tightly sealed. Sprinkle a bit of flour over the wrapped carrots, place on a baking sheet, and bake for 40 minutes, until the pastry is crisp and the carrot inside is tender.

To make the garnishes, while the carrots are baking, combine the sugar and 2¼ cups (500 ml/18 fl oz) water in a pan set over medium-high heat and bring to a boil. Remove from the heat and add the finely sliced carrot and the kumquats. Let cool, then remove the carrot slices and kumquats from the syrup and pat dry. Quarter the kumquats.

Transfer the carrots and kumquats to a large bowl and add the orange segments, along with the lemon balm and chervil. Dress with the canola oil and balsamic vinegar, and season to taste with salt and freshly ground black pepper.

To serve, halve each carrot parcel lengthwise and place in the middle of a serving plate. Top with the garnishes and serve immediately.

JONATHAN KARPATHIOS

•

VORK & MES

•

PAVILJOENLAAN 1 . 2131 LZ HOOFDDORP . THE NETHERLANDS

Jonathan Karpathios trained in London with Pierre Koffmann, and has since worked in many of the best kitchens in Holland, becoming one of the country's top chefs when he was only twenty-six years old. When his son was born, his perspective on life and work completely changed, and in 2007 he opened his restaurant Vork & Mes with the aim of practicing and teaching responsibility in the way we cook and eat. He grows much of the produce for his menu in his own greenhouse and gardens.

CELERY ROOT BAKED IN ITS SKIN WITH PEARS AND VEGAN BLUE CHEESE

Preparation time: 50 minutes
Cooking time: 2 hours

Serves 4

- 1 celery root (celeriac)
- 6 tablespoons olive oil, plus extra for drizzling
- salt and freshly ground black pepper
- 2 ripe dessert pears
- 1 cup (25 g) arugula (rocket)
- 1⅓ cups (200 g) crumbled vegan blue cheese

Wash but do not peel the celery root, then cut it into large pieces. Put into a pan with the olive oil and season lightly with salt and freshly ground black pepper. Place over high heat and cook until the celery root is browned on all sides. Remove from the heat and let cool. Meanwhile, peel and core the pears, then cut them into wedges.

Arrange the arugula on 4 plates. Top with the celery root and pears, then crumble the vegan cheese over them. Drizzle with a little extra virgin olive oil and sprinkle with freshly ground black pepper.

TARTE TATIN WITH PICKLED ONIONS, CURLY KALE, AND GARLIC

To make the pickling solution, in a small pot set over high heat, combine the sugar and vinegar with 1 cup (240 ml/8 fl oz) water and bring to a boil. Remove from the heat and let cool to room temperature.

To make the tart, preheat the oven to 350°F/180°C/Gas Mark 4.

Wrap the garlic in aluminum foil and roast in the oven until soft, about 30 minutes. Set aside. Reduce the oven temperature to 325°F/160°C/Gas Mark 3.

Bring a pan of salted water to a boil, add the onions, and cook until tender, about 15–20 minutes. Set aside.

Slice 1 onion into thin rings and place them in the pickling solution.

In another pan, combine the sugar with 3 tablespoons water, bring to a lively simmer, and heat without stirring until the mixture caramelizes to the color of a copper penny, about 3 minutes. Halve the remaining 2 cooked onions. Evenly divide the caramel among 4 ramekins. Divide the onion halves among the ramekins and cover each half with a puff pastry sheet, pressing down firmly to seal.

Bring a large pan of salted water to a boil over high heat and blanch the curly kale for about 2 minutes. Drain and cool the kale well in cold water, then pat dry with paper towels.

Crush the roasted garlic cloves and mix with the cream. Whisk the cream mixture until it is the consistency of yogurt. Set aside.

Place the ramekins on a rimmed baking sheet and bake the tarts in the oven for 20 minutes, or until the pastry is crisp and golden brown.

Mix the curly kale with the olive oil, and vinegar, season to taste with salt and freshly ground black pepper, and spoon over the tartlets. Top with the pickled onion rings and spoon the cream mixture over.

Preparation time: 1 hour 30 minutes
Cooking time: 1 hour

Serves 4

For the pickling solution:
- ½ cup (100 g) granulated sugar
- a scant ½ cup (100 ml/3½ fl oz) white vinegar

For the tarts:
- 3 garlic cloves
- salt and freshly ground black pepper
- 3 onions
- ½ cup (100 g) granulated sugar
- 4 (6-inch/15 cm) square sheets vegan puff pastry, thawed
- 1 lb 2 oz (500 g) curly kale, stemmed and chopped
- a scant ½ cup (100 ml/3½ fl oz) soy whipping cream
- a scant ½ cup (100 ml/3½ fl oz) olive oil
- 3½ tablespoons red wine vinegar

XAVIER PELLICER

•

CÉLERI

•

PASSATGE MARIMÓN 5 . 08021 BARCELONA . SPAIN

Xavier Pellicer is the chef of the highly acclaimed restaurant Céleri in Barcelona, Spain. Céleri offers diners small plates highlighting quality produce, and designed around eight in-season vegetables.

ROASTED CABBAGE, SERVED COLD WITH MUSTARD OIL, PICKLED RADISH, AND RED ONION

Preparation time: 35 minutes
Cooking time: 2 hours 45 minutes,
   plus 3–4 days marinating

Serves 4 people

- 1 head of cabbage
- extra-virgin olive oil
- sunflower oil
- ⅓ cup (75 ml/2½ fl oz) Sempio Jang Sauce
- a scant ½ cup (100 ml/3½ fl oz) mirin
- ⅓ cup (75 g) brown sugar
- a scant ½ cup (100 ml/3½ fl oz) apple cider vinegar
- 16 radishes
- 4 small or medium red onions
- mustard oil
- fresh flowers and shoots, to garnish (optional)
- sea salt and freshly ground black pepper

Preheat the oven to 350°F/180°C/Gas Mark 4. Wash the cabbage, insert a probe thermometer into the center, and roast in the oven until the core temperature reaches 170°F (75°C).

Peel off the well-roasted outer leaves and grind them to a powder.

Peel off a few more layers until you reach the whitest and most tender leaves in the center. Remove the leaves and put them in a vacuum bag with a half-and-half mixture of olive oil and sunflower oil, and cook sous vide for 2 hours at 160°F/70°C. Pour off and reserve the cabbage oil.

Wrap the center of the cabbage in plastic wrap (clingfilm) so the residual heat will finish cooking it. Once cool, vacuum-seal with the jang sauce for a maximum of 24 hours to marinate and compact the cabbage.

In a pan over medium-high heat, warm the mirin with the brown sugar, stirring, until the sugar has dissolved. Add the vinegar, bring to a boil, then immediately turn off the heat. Divide the pickling liquid equally between 2 medium bowls and let cool to 160°F/70°C.

Meanwhile, slice the radishes. Peel and halve the onions, then blanch them in boiling water. Add the radishes to one bowl of pickling liquid, and the onions to the other. Cover and refrigerate for a few days.

Cut the center of the cabbage into slices ½–1 inch (1–1.5 cm) thick. Cut these slices into triangles, retaining their thickness.

To serve, arrange the cabbage triangles on a plate, season with the cabbage oil, and add a drop of mustard oil to each piece. Place the pickled radishes and onions around them. Garnish with fresh flowers and shoots, if you wish, and scatter over the ground cabbage dust. Season to taste with sea salt and freshly ground black pepper, and finish by sprinkling a little toasted cabbage oil over the top.

BEET AND TOMATO GAZPACHO WITH GRAPES AND FLOWERS

Preheat the oven to 325°F/160°C/Gas Mark 3. Cut the leaves off the beets. Season with salt and pepper and wrap in wax (greaseproof) paper or parchment (baking) paper. Bake for 40-45 minutes, depending on size. Peel and set aside.

When the beets are cool enough to handle, chop them up and place in a bowl. Add the remaining ingredients, cover, and refrigerate for 2–3 days.

Purée the beet mixture in batches in a blender, then strain through a fine sieve. Season to taste with salt and freshly ground black pepper and refrigerate until thoroughly chilled.

Serve the gazpacho in bowls, garnishing each serving with the grapes, flowers, and a few slices of raw beet.

Preparation time: 30 minutes, plus 2–3 days chilling
Cooking time: 40–45 minutes

Serves 4

- 2 lb 4 oz (1 kg) organic beets (beetroot), (about 3 lb 4 oz/1.5 kg with leaves)
- salt and freshly ground black pepper
- 1 lb 10 oz (750 g) ripe organic tomatoes, chopped
- ½ Figueres onion, peeled and chopped
- a scant ¼ cup (50 ml/1¾ fl oz) sherry vinegar
- ½ cup (120 ml/4 fl oz) extra-virgin olive oil
- ¾ cup (75 g) rolled oats
- 16 grapes (4 per person), peeled and quartered, to garnish
- assorted flowers, to garnish
- 1 raw baby beet, sliced, to garnish

POTATO CAKES, RUNNER BEANS, AND CHANTERELLE MUSHROOMS

Preparation time: 40 minutes, plus
  2 hours chilling
Cooking time: 1 hour 30 minutes

Serves 4

- coarse salt, for baking
- 1 lb 2 oz (500 g) Agria potatoes
- 2 tablespoons egg replacer, mixed with
  2 tablespoons water
- finely grated zest of ½ lime
- finely grated zest of ½ lemon
- chives, 4 left whole, plus some finely
  chopped
- parsley, finely chopped
- extra-virgin olive oil
- salt and freshly ground black pepper
- 11 oz (300 g) Perona runner beans
- 7 oz (200 g) fresh chanterelle mushrooms

Preheat the oven to 325°F/160°C/Gas Mark 3.

Line a rimmed baking sheet with coarse salt and place the potatoes in it. Bake until tender, about 1 hour. Prick the potatoes with a knife from time to time until you are sure they are cooked: the blade should come out easily and be dry. Set the potatoes aside until they are cool enough to handle.

Halve the potatoes and scoop out the flesh with a spoon. Pass the flesh through a food mill and transfer to a bowl. Add the egg replacer, lemon and lime zests, chopped chives, and parsley. Add some olive oil and mix well. Season to taste with salt and freshly ground black pepper.

Line a baking sheet with parchment (baking) paper and spread the potato mixture over it to a thickness of ½ inch (1 cm). Cover with another piece of parchment and let rest for a couple of hours in the refrigerator.

Use a vegetable peeler to remove the strings from the runner beans and boil the beans in water until tender but still al dente.

Clean the mushrooms and sauté them in very little oil. Season with salt and freshly ground black pepper, then set aside.

Cut the chilled potato into 4 equal rectangles and add a little oil to a nonstick skillet (frying pan). Brown the potatoes on both sides.

Use the whole chives to tie the beans into 4 small bundles and add to the potatoes in the skillet. Heat until warmed through.

Place a potato cake on each plate and add a bundle of beans and some mushrooms. Drizzle with olive oil and serve.

INDEXES

INDEX – GENERAL

Page numbers in italics refer to illustrations

INDEX – RECIPES BY COUNTRY

Page numbers in italics refer to illustrations

Phaidon Press Limited
Regent's Wharf
All Saints Street
London N1 9PA

Phaidon Press Inc.
65 Bleecker Street
New York, NY 10012

phaidon.com

First published 2017
© 2017 Phaidon Press Limited

ISBN 978 07148 7391 6

A CIP catalogue record for this book is
available from the British Library and the
Library of Congress.

Commissioning Editor: Emily Takoudes
Project Editor: Olga Massov
Production Controller: Nerissa Vales
Photography: Sidney Bensimon
Design: Julia Hasting
Typesetting: Sean Yendrys

Printed in China

The publisher would like to thank the
following individuals for their help: Olivia Mac
Anderson, Vanessa Bird, Trish Burgess, Astrid
Chastka, Jane Ellis, Salima Hirani, Dorothy
Irwin, Lesley Malkin, João Mota, Tracey Smith,
and Ana Teodoro.

Illustrations by Julia Hasting with icons from
thenounproject.com: root by Botho Willer
(spine, p. 1, p. 3, p. 100, p. 446); raspberry by
Fiona Cardwell (back cover); blueberry by
walle_chan (back cover); jar 1 by Sbet (p. 8);
jar 2 by Blaise Sewell (p. 8); bottle by Nikita
Kozin (p. 8); bag by irene hoffman (p. 8);
green beans by Clockwise (p. 268); leaf 1
by Alessandro Sucaci (p. 76); leaf 2 by John
Fenton (p. 8, p. 76); carrot by Robert
Bjurshagen (p. 100); pasta by Andrew
Fortnum (p. 286).

Recipe Notes

- Vegan margarine should always be unsalted, unless otherwise specified.
- All herbs are fresh, unless otherwise specified.
- Individual vegetables and fruits, such as onions and apples, are assumed to be medium, unless otherwise specified.
- All salt is fine sea salt, unless otherwise specified.
- Breadcrumbs are always dried, unless otherwise specified.
- Cooking times are for guidance only, as individual ovens vary. If using a fan (convection) oven, follow the manufacturer's instructions concerning oven temperatures.
- Exercise a high level of caution when following recipes involving any potentially hazardous activity, including the use of high temperatures, open flames, slaked lime, and when deep-frying. In particular, when deep-frying, add food carefully to avoid splashing, wear long sleeves, and never leave the pan unattended.
- Exercise caution when making fermented products, ensuring all equipment is spotlessly clean, and seek expert advice if in any doubt.
- When no quantity is specified, for example of oils, salts, and herbs used for finishing dishes or for deep frying, quantities are discretionary and flexible.
- All herbs, shoots, flowers and leaves should be picked fresh from a clean source. Exercise caution when foraging for ingredients; any foraged ingredients should only be eaten if an expert has deemed them safe to eat.
- Both metric and imperial measures are used in this book. Follow one set of measurements throughout, not a mixture, as they are not interchangeable.
- All spoon and cup measurements are level, unless otherwise stated. 1 teaspoon = 5 ml; 1 tablespoon = 15 ml.
- Australian standard tablespoons are 20 ml, so Australian readers are advised to use 3 teaspoons in place of 1 tablespoon when measuring small quantities.

Author Biography

Jean-Christian Jury is a vegan and raw food chef from Toulouse, France. In 2008, he opened his vegan restaurant, La Mano Verde, in Berlin, Germany, and received praise from many international publications. He is based in Los Angeles, California, and travels frequently teaching vegan cooking classes across the globe.

Author Acknowlegements

This book was only possible because of the seven years of hard work and dedication of my La Mano Verde team in Berlin—for which I am eternally grateful. We set the bar high and showed the world that plant-based cooking can be both healthy and flavorful. A big-hearted thank-you to my dear guests and friends. I am grateful for your support and feedback during the beautiful years I spent in Berlin.

A very special thank-you to my daughter Naomi; and deep thanks to Christiane, Rose-Marie Donhauser, Stefan Elfenbein, Niko and Karin Rechenberg, Alexander Lobrano, Pino Bianco, Melly Klein, Nimi Ponnudurai and Anton Corbjin, Mimi Kirk, Anja Rose, Soren, and so many others.

I am deeply grateful to my agent, Deborah Ritchken.

To the great Phaidon team that made this publication possible: Emily Takoudes and Olga Massov—thank you for your patience and your motivation.